MORE PRAISE FOR

THE NEGRO'S CIVIL WAR

"Rewarding . . . McPherson has built his book effectively. A short explanatory text by Mr. McPherson connects the speeches, editorials, letters, petitions of Negro ministers, teachers, journalists, soldiers, escaped slaves. The picture becomes a firm outline, fascinating in detail."

The Christian Science Monitor

"Fill[s] the tremendous gap caused by the omissions of previous historians."

The Baltimore Evening Sun

"Tremendous research . . . Deserves a place on the shelves of readers interested in all phases of the 1861–65 struggle."

Houston Chronicle

"Impressive . . . This collection of material is a valuable contribution to history."

Charleston Evening Post

"A valuable background for consideration of today's continuing racial problems."

Providence Sunday Journal

"Richly documented."

The Baltimore Sun

"Fascinating."

Kansas City Star

Other Books by James M. McPherson

The Struggle for Equality: Abolitionists and the Negro in the Civil War and Reconstruction

Marching Toward Freedom: The Negro in the Civil War

Blacks in America: Bibliographical Essays (with others)

The Abolitionist Legacy: From Reconstruction to the NAACP

Region, Race, and Reconstruction: Essays in Honor of C. Vann Woodward (coeditor)

Ordeal by Fire: The Civil War and Reconstruction

Battle Cry of Freedom: The Civil War Era

Abraham Lincoln and the Second American Revolution

THE
NEGRO'S
CIVIL
WAR

HOW AMERICAN BLACKS FELT AND
ACTED DURING THE WAR FOR THE UNION

JAMES M. McPHERSON

Ballantine Books
New York

Library of Congress Catalog Card Number: 90-93518

ISBN: 0-345-37120-8

Cover design by William G. Geller

Cover art: lithograph for a recruiting poster published by the Supervisory Committee for Recruiting Colored Regiments, Camp William Penn (courtesy Bettmann Archive).

Manufactured in the United States of America

First Ballantine Books Edition: June 1991

10 9 8 7 6 5 4 3

FOR PAT

ACKNOWLEDGMENTS

The kind assistance of the staffs of the Princeton University Library, the Library of Congress, the Schomburg Collection of the New York Public Library, the Howard University Library, the University of California Library, the Duke University Library, and the University of Cincinnati Library made possible the location and use of the materials on Negro history contained in these repositories. A special vote of thanks must go to Mrs. Ruth B. Thornton of the Mother Bethel A.M.E. Church in Philadelphia, who graciously made available the Church's valuable file of the Christian Recorder. *Mr. Roger Des Forges has enriched the book with his excellent translations of articles and editorials from* L'Union *and* La Tribune de la Nouvelle Orléans. *A grant from the Princeton University Research Fund made possible part of the research for this book. And to my wife, Patricia, I owe a debt of gratitude beyond expression.*

JAMES M. MCPHERSON

CONTENTS

CONTENTS

ILLUSTRATIONS

Many of the illustrations in this book are reproductions of woodcuts which appeared in Harper's Weekly *and* Frank Leslie's Illustrated Newspaper *during the Civil War.* Harper's *and* Leslie's *employed the best journalistic artists of the day, and these artists visited every important battle front of the war to find material for their pictures. Their finest drawings captured the essential drama and action of the war much better than the stilted and posed photographs of one hundred years ago could do. Editorially,* Harper's Weekly *favored aggressive Northern action against slavery and supported the enrollment of Negro troops and the enactment of measures to make the Negro's freedom real and meaningful. As an illustrated weekly,* Leslie's *had no well-defined editorial policy, but the paper did give consistent and loyal support to Lincoln's war policy throughout the conflict.*

PREFACE TO THE 1991 EDITION

When this book was first published more than a quarter-century ago, Americans were commemorating the last months of the Civil War centennial, the civil rights movement was at a climactic moment of success celebrating the recent passage of the Civil Rights Act of 1964 and imminent enactment of the Voting Rights Bill of 1965, and United States troops were still only minimally involved in Vietnam. It was a time of optimism in race relations much like the heady days of 1865, exactly a century earlier, when African Americans who had experienced the extraordinary events of the past four years that had liberated four million slaves looked forward to a bright future. They could not foresee the dashed hopes of Reconstruction, the humiliations of statutory Jim Crow, the scandal of lynching, just as Americans both black and white in 1965 did not anticipate the trauma of urban race riots, the polarization of black power and white backlash, and the nightmare of Vietnam.

Despite change and turmoil in the world of which it becomes a part, a book has a life of its own. Although the preferred designation for people of African descent in the United States has changed from "Negro" at the time this book first appeared to "black" and "Afro-American" during the following two decades to "African American" today, the crucial part played by these people in the Civil War remained a constant historical reality. That reality was not very well known outside the circle of professional historians when the book was published in 1965. Several good monographs on African Americans in the war—especially on black soldiers in the Union army—had appeared during previous decades, but in the outpouring of books evoked by the Civil War centennial, the number that focused on blacks could be counted on the fingers of one hand—with a finger or two left over. And while many collections of letters and diaries and other types of documents written by whites during the Civil War were published at the time of the centennial, The Negro's

Civil War *was the first book to tell the story of African Americans during the war largely in their own words. It struck a responsive chord, for the book has remained continuously in print for the past twenty-six years, has been widely used in college and secondary school courses, and has been drawn upon and built upon by other historians who have expanded our knowledge and understanding of the subject.*

Yet the active role of African Americans in the Civil War did not become household knowledge, judged by a typical reaction of viewers to the film Glory *in 1990: "I never knew that black soldiers fought in the Civil War!" This lack of awareness did not result from a lack of scholarship. Indeed, one of the most prolific fields of activity among American historians during the past quarter-century has focused on the experiences of African Americans in slavery and in the transition to freedom in the Civil War era. These studies have confirmed the central thesis of* The Negro's Civil War: *that black people played a vital role in the Civil War and were active achievers rather than passive recipients of freedom.*

In one important respect, newer scholarship has expanded upon the material presented here. Most of the voices in the following pages are those of Northern blacks. They, of course, had more education and more access to the media of communication than did slaves. Yet the slaves were not without voices of their own. The work of Leon F. Litwack, Barbara J. Fields, Clarence L. Mohr, Ira Berlin and his colleagues in the Freedmen and Southern Society Project, and of numerous other scholars, as well as the painstaking efforts of George P. Rawick in gathering and publishing the W. P. A. and other interviews with ex-slaves in the 1930s, have uncovered those voices and generated new evidence on the actions of slaves and freedpeople that was not available when I put together the material in The Negro's Civil War. *If I were writing the book today, therefore, the words of Southern blacks would have a larger place. But the story would remain essentially the same. I have been gratified that the book has stood up so well all these years, and glad of the opportunity provided by Ballantine Books to bring out this new edition. I*

*hope that it will reach some of those whose interest in the part
played by African Americans in the Civil War was aroused by
Glory and who are seeking further knowledge and understanding. With minor changes in terminology, the text remains the
same as in the original edition, but to bring readers up to date
with the scholarship of the past quarter-century I have added
an afterword on bibliography.*

*James M. McPherson
Princeton, New Jersey
December 1990*

PREFACE TO THE FIRST EDITION

The Dred Scott decision of 1857 denied United States citizenship to the Negro. This decision was little more than a ratification of the status of black men in most parts of the American republic. In fifteen Southern states Negroes were denied not only the rights of citizenship, but many of the rights of humanity as well. In the eyes of the law, the slave was an article of property rather than a human being. He had almost no control over his own destiny or that of his family. The condition of Southern free Negroes was little better. Nor did most blacks in the North enjoy equal rights. In many Northern states blacks were educated in segregated schools when they were educated at all, subjected to the humiliations of Jim Crow in public transportation, denied the right to vote, and denied equal rights in the courts.

The Civil War wrought a revolution in the Negro's status, North as well as South. It brought freedom, citizenship, and eventually, equal civil and political rights (in theory at least) to all Negroes. It brought the rudiments of education to thousands of freedmen. The impetus of wartime change impelled the desegregation of schools and transporation facilities in many parts of the North. Time was to show that the revolution in the Negro's status was not so complete as it appeared, but in 1865 the black man could look back on four years of startling and rapid change, and could look forward hopefully to acceptance as an equal in American life.

In a biography of General Ulysses S. Grant published in 1928, Mr. W. E. Woodward stated that "the American negroes are the only people in the history of the world, so far as I know, that ever became free without any effort of their own. . . . [The Civil War] was not their business. They had not started the war nor ended it. They twanged banjos around the railroad stations, sang melodious sprirituals, and believed that some Yankee would soon come along and give each of them forty acres of land and a mule."[1] In spite of the large number of articles and books dealing with the Negro's active part in the Civil War that have been published since 1928, the belief still persists among many laymen and some historians that the slave was a passive, docile, uncomprehending recipient of freedom in 1865, and that the four and one-half million Negroes in the United States played no important or effective role in the tragic drama of civil war.

The "Negro Question" was one of the main issues of the war. The South went to war in 1861 to protect itself against the North's alleged threat to "Southern institutions." The chief Southern institution was slavery. In a speech at Savannah on March 21, 1861, Alexander Stephens, the newly elected vice president of the Confederacy, said that the slavery controversy was the "immediate cause" of Southern secession. "Our confederacy," continued Stephens, "is founded upon . . . the great truth that the negro is not equal to the white man. That slavery—subordination to the superior race, is his natural and normal condition. This, our new Government, is the first, in the history of the world, based upon this great physical and mortal truth."²

The South fought to protect and preserve slavery, but the North did not at first fight to destroy the "peculiar institution." The principal Northern war aim was restoration of the Union. Nevertheless, from the surrender of Fort Sumter to the surrender at Appomattox, the question of the Negro's status in the restored Union occupied much of the attention of the Northern people and their leaders. A writer in an antislavery newspaper declared in 1863 that the Negro was "the observed of all observers; the talked of by all talkers; the thought of by all thinkers; and questioned by all questioners."³ In April 1864, Senator James A. McDougall of California complained to the Senate that "from the time I took my place here until this day . . . hardly a quarter of an hour has passed that has not been occupied by discussing the status of the negroes in the southern confederacy. Our home policy, our finances, our legitimate business, our foreign relations, have all been ignored."⁴

Negroes, abolitionists, and antislavery Republicans in the North argued that the war could not be won nor the Union restored without the abolition of slavery. By 1863, President Lincoln had come to accept this argument. With his Emancipation Proclamation of January 1, 1863, the war took on a new dimension. The abolition of slavery became a Northen war aim inseparably linked with the restoration of the Union. The South had gone to war to preserve slavery. By 1863 the North was fighting to abolish slavery. From beginning to end, slavery was one of the central issues of the war.

Free Negroes and emancipated slaves played an active and vital part in the Northern war effort. Approximately 500,000 slaves came within Union lines during the war. Most of these freedmen went to work as laborers or soldiers for the North. More than 200,000 Negroes fought in the Union Army and Navy. Without their help, the North could not have won the war as soon as it did, and perhaps it could not have won at all. The Negro was crucial to the whole Union war effort.

Several books about the Negro in the Civil War have been written since 1928. Herbert Aptheker's brief account, The Negro in the Civil War, *and Bell Irvin Wiley's thorough study,* Southern Negroes, 1861–1865, *were published in 1938. In 1953 there appeared the very readable* The Negro in the Civil War, *by Benjamin Quarles, followed in 1956 by Dudley T. Cornish's scholarly and well-written* The Sable Arm: Negro Troops in the Union Army, 1861–1865. *In 1962 Benjamin Quarles published his informative* Lincoln and the Negro. *In addition, many articles dealing with various aspects of the Negro's contribution during the Civil War have appeared in* The Journal of Negro History *and other historical quarterlies.*

In recent years several collections of primary source materials touching upon the Negro in the Civil War have been published. Three separate editions, two of them in paperback, of Thomas Wentworth Higginson's famous Army Life in a Black Regiment *have appeared since 1960. Ray Allen Billingon's editon of* The Journal of Charlotte L. Forten *was published as a paperback in 1961. Between 1950 and 1955 the massive four-volume* Life and Writings of Frederick Douglass, *edited by Philip Foner, was published. Volume III of this collection includes most of Douglass' important writings and speeches during the Civil War. And finally, one section of Herbert Aptheker's* Documentary History of the Negro People in the United States *(1951; paperback edition, 1962) contains material on the history of the black man during the Civil War.*

These works have added immensely to our knowledge of the part played by Negroes in the sanguinary conflict. But there is still a need for a documentary collection that will present all aspects of the Negro's role in the war largely in the Negro's own words—his contributions and achievements, his hopes and aspirations, his opinions and frustrations. This book is designed to fill that need. Most of the material contained in these pages has been previously unavailable to the general reader. Some of the newspaper and manuscript sources have been heretofore untapped even by scholars and specialists. It is hoped that this material will fill many gaps in our understanding of the Negro's part in America's greatest crisis.

This collection is designed to be of value to the scholar, to the student seeking information about the history of American Negroes, and to the general reader. The book is arranged in narrative form, with considerable interpretive and factual information supplied by the editor to bridge and clarify the documents. It can be read as a narrative; and at the same time the scholar in search of specific source material can use the chapter titles and the index to find what he is looking for. Most of the items in this book are excerpts rather than entire documents. To have reproduced the documents in full would have reduced the scope and variety of the material that could be included, and would have bored the reader with much repetitive, irrelevant, and sometimes obscure discourse. Every effort has been made to avoid any distortion of the original meaning or intent of the documents in the process of excerption.

The Negro was not merely a passive recipient of the benefits conferred upon him by the war. Negro orators and writers provided leadership in the struggle for emancipation and equal rights. Blacks were active in the movements to bring education, suffrage, and land to Southern freedmen. And perhaps most important of all, the contribution of Negro soldiers helped the North win the war and convinced many Northern people that the Negro deserved to be treated as a man and an equal. The future status of the black man in America was one of the central issues of the Civil War. Then as today this issue divided the nation, and the demands of Negroes for freedom and equality in the 1860s are as fresh and relevant in our own time as they were one hundred years ago.

THE
NEGRO'S
CIVIL
WAR

CHAPTER I

THE ELECTION OF 1860

AND THE COMING OF WAR

The election of 1860 appeared to promise Negroes little hope for the future. In the first place, few black men could vote. The slaves and free Negroes of the South were disfranchised, of course, and in the North only the New England states (except Connecticut) allowed Negroes to vote on the same terms as whites. All the other Northern states except New York and Ohio denied the ballot to black men. In Ohio only those Negroes with a greater visible admixture of white than black blood were admitted to the polls. New York Negroes could vote only if they possessed property worth $250.[1]

In the second place, none of the four major parties contending for the presidency championed the cause of the Negro. The Constitutional Union party and the two factions of the Democratic party were pledged to preserve or even to strengthen the institution of slavery. The Republican party, nominally antislavery, was officially opposed only to the extension of slavery into the new territories. No major political party proposed to take action against slavery where it already existed. During the campaign, Democrats charged that if the Republicans won the election, they would abolish slavery and grant civil equality to Negroes. "That is not so," rejoined Horace Greeley, an influential Republican spokesman. "Never on earth did the Republican Party propose to abolish Slavery. . . . Its object with respect to Slavery is simply, nakedly, avowedly, its restriction to the

existing states." Most Republican orators echoed Greeley's state-
ment. Lincoln himself had repeatedly voiced his opposition to
equal rights for free Negroes. And although Lincoln had a deep-
rooted moral abhorrence of slavery, he favored no stronger
measures against the institution than its exclusion from the
territories.[2]

It is not surprising, therefore, that many black men had little
faith in either the Democratic or the Republican party. The
Anglo-African, *a weekly newspaper founded in 1859 by Thomas*
Hamilton as a spokesman for Negroes in New York City, de-
clared in March 1860 that

the two great political parties separate at an angle of two roads,
that they may meet eventually at the same goals. They both
entertain the same ideas, and both carry the same burdens. They
differ only in regard to the way they shall go, and the method
of procedure. . . . The Democratic party would make the white
man the master and the black man the slave, and have them
thus together occupy every foot of the American soil. . . . The
Republican party . . . though with larger professions for humanity, is by far its more dangerous enemy. Under the guise of humanity, they do and say many things—as, for example, they
oppose the re-opening of the slave-trade. . . . They oppose the
progress of slavery in the territories, and would cry humanity
to the world; but . . . their opposition to slavery means opposition to the black man—nothing else. Where it is clearly in their
power to do anything for the oppressed colored man, why then
they are too nice, too conservative, to do it. . . .

We have no hope from either [of the] political parties. We
must rely on ourselves, the righteousness of our cause, and the
advance of just sentiments among the great masses of the . . .
people.[3]

At a meeting of the Massachusetts Anti-Slavery Society on
January 27, 1860, Dr. John Rock of Boston chastised the Repub-
lican party for its antislavery shortcomings. Rock was one of
the best-educated Negroes of his day. Only thirty-five years old
in 1860, he had been a schoolteacher, a dentist, a physician,
and was now practicing law in Boston. He was a graduate of

the American Medical College in Philadelphia, a member of the Massachusetts Bar, and could read and speak both French and German. In the 1850s he had become known as an eloquent champion of equal rights for his race in the North. In his speech to the Massachusetts Anti-Slavery Society, Rock conceded that the Republicans were opposed to the expansion of slavery:

The Republicans are checkmating this power; and, in this respect, I think they are doing a good work. The idea of "no more slave States" is good. The fewer the better. (Applause.) But they do not carry it far enough. I would have them say, "No more slavery!" The Republicans, however, have no idea of abolishing slavery. They go against slavery only so far as slavery goes against their interests; and if they keep on lowering their standard, as they have been for the last few months, they will soon say in New England, what they have said already in the Middle States, that the Republican party is not only the white man's party, but that "it aims to place white men and white labor *against* black men and black labor." Such Republicanism is no better than [the] Democracy.[4]

H. Ford Douglass, a Negro leader from Illinois, made a lecture tour of the East in 1860 and spoke at the annual Fourth of July picnic of the abolitionists in Framingham, Massachusetts:

We have four parties in this country that have marshalled themselves on the highway of American politics, asking for the votes of the American people. . . . We have what is called the Union party, led by Mr. Bell, of Tennessee; we have what is called the Democratic party, led by Stephen A. Douglas, of Illinois; we have the party called the Seceders, or the Slave-Code Democrats, led by John C. Breckinridge, of Kentucky, and then we have the Republican party, led by Abraham Lincoln, of Illinois. . . . So far as the principles of freedom and the hopes of the black men are concerned, all these parties are barren and unfruitful; neither of them seeks to lift the negro out of his fetters, and rescue this day from odium and disgrace.

Take Abraham Lincoln. I want to know if any man can tell me the difference between the anti-slavery of Abraham Lincoln, and the anti-slavery of the old Whig party, or the anti-slavery of Henry Clay? Why, there is no difference between them. Abraham Lincoln is simply a Henry Clay Whig, and he believes just as Henry Clay believed in regard to this question. And Henry Clay was just as odious to the anti-slavery cause and anti-slavery men as ever was John C. Calhoun. . . .

I know the Republicans do not like this kind of talk, because, while they are willing to steal our thunder, they are unwilling to submit to the conditions imposed upon that party that assumes to be anti-slavery. They say that they cannot go as fast as you anti-slavery men go in this matter; that they cannot afford to be uncompromisingly honest, nor so radical as you Garrisonians; that they want to take time; that they want to do the work gradually. They say, "We must not be in too great a hurry to overthrow slavery; at least, we must take half a loaf, if we cannot get the whole." Now, my friends, I believe that the very best way to overthrow slavery in this country is to occupy the highest possible anti-slavery ground.

. . . I do not believe in the anti-slavery of Abraham Lincoln, because he is on the side of this Slave Power of which I am speaking, that has possession of the Federal Government. What does he propose to do? Simply to let the people and the Territories regulate their domestic institutions in their own way. . . . In regard to the repeal of the Fugitive Slave Law, Abraham Lincoln occupies the same position that the old Whig party occupied in 1852. . . . What did he say at Freeport? Why, that the South was entitled to a Fugitive Slave Law; and although he thought the law could be modified a little, yet, he said, if he was in Congress, he would have it done in such a way as *not to lessen its efficiency*! Here, then, is Abraham Lincoln in favor of carrying out that infamous Fugitive Slave Law. . . .

Then, there is another item which I want to bring out in this connection. I am a colored man; I am an American citizen; and I think that I am entitled to exercise the elective franchise. . . . No party, it seems to me, is entitled to the sympathy of anti-slavery men, unless that party is willing to extend to the black man all the rights of a citizen. I care nothing about that anti-slavery which wants to make the Territories free, while it is unwilling to extend to me, as a man, in the free States, all the rights of a man. (Applause.) In the State of Illinois . . . we have a code of black laws that would disgrace any Barbary State, or any uncivilized people in the far-off islands of the sea. Men of my complexion are not allowed to testify in a court of justice, where a white man is a party. If a white man happens to owe me anything, unless I can prove it by the testimony of a white man, I cannot collect the debt. Now, two years ago, I went through the State of Illinois for the purpose of getting signers to a petition, asking the Legislature to repeal the "Testimony Law," so as to permit colored men to testify against white men. I went to prominent Republicans, and among others, to Abraham Lincoln and Lyman Trumbull [senator from Illinois], and neither of them dared to sign that petition, to give me the right to testify in a court of justice! ("Hear, hear.") In the State of Illinois, they tax the colored people for every conceivable purpose. They tax the negro's property to support schools for the education of the white man's children, but the colored people are not permitted to enjoy any of the benefits resulting from that taxation. We are compelled to impose upon ourselves additional taxes, in order to educate our children. The State lays its iron hand upon the negro, holds him down, and puts the other hand into his pocket and steals his hard earnings, to educate the children of white men: and if we sent our children to school, Abraham Lincoln would kick them out, in the name of Republicanism and anti-slavery![5]

The nation's most prominent Negro was Frederick Douglass, the abolitionist orator, journalist, and tribune of his people. Douglass lived in Rochester, New York, where he published a newspaper (Douglass' Monthly), and he lectured all over the North in behalf of emancipation and equal rights. Douglass reached the minds and hearts of white people more effectively than any other man of his race. His monthly journal was read by many antislavery whites, and his lectures drew large numbers of white people. Douglass' first reaction to the nomination of Lincoln by the Republicans in May 1860 was favorable. He described the nominee as "a man of unblemished private character . . . one of the most frank, honest men in political life."

Douglass would have liked the Republicans to inscribe on their banners "Death to Slavery" instead of "No More Slave States." But the people will not have it so, and we are compelled to work and wait for a brighter day, when the masses shall be educated up to a higher standard of human rights and political morality. But as between the hosts of Slavery propagandism and the Republican party—incomplete as is its platform of principles—our preferences cannot hesitate. . . . We can but desire the success of the Republican candidates.[6]

Two months later Douglass said that the Republican party is now the great embodiment of whatever political opposition to the pretensions and demands of slavery is now in the field. . . . A victory by it in the coming contest must and will be hailed as an anti-slavery triumph. In view of this fact, we have no sympathy with those who regard all the parties alike, and especially those who go so far as to prefer the defeat of the Republican party at the coming election to its triumph.[7]

But as the campaign progressed and as Republican leaders repeatedly disavowed any intention to abolish slavery, to grant equal rights to Negroes, or even to repeal the Fugitive Slave Law, Douglass' attitude toward the party underwent a change. In September he wrote that the very best that can be said of that party is, that it is opposed to *forcing slavery into any Territory of the United States where the white people of that Territory do not want it.* That party . . . is simply opposed to allowing slavery to go where it is not at all likely to go. . . . Even the sentiments of the Republican party, as expressed by its leaders, have become visibly *thin* and *insipid* as the canvass has progressed. It promises to be about as good a Southern party as either wing of the old Democratic party.[8]

Douglass and several other Northern Negroes decided to support Gerrit Smith, the candidate of the Radical Abolitionist party, for president. The platform of the Radical Abolitionists proclaimed the constitutional right and duty of the federal government to abolish slavery in the states. The party held its national convention at Syracuse, New York, on August 29, 1860.

None of the delegates at Syracuse believed that Smith had any chance of winning the election; the purpose of the party was not to win a victory at the polls but to give voting abolitionists an opportunity to cast their ballots for a genuine abolitionist candidate. Frederick Douglass wrote that

to all those who believe that it is the first business of the American people, acting in their collective and national capacity through the forms of the National Government, to abolish and forever put away from among them the stupendous abomination of slavery; who believe . . . that he who stands by pure anti-slavery principle most firmly in this day of accommodation and truckling, bearing aloft the unsullied banner of pure Abolitionism, best serves the cause of the slave . . . will not ask us why we helped make these nominations, and why anti-slavery men, regardless of ridicule and protest, are asked to vote for them. For all such men as are herein described see plainly enough that to vote consistently, they must vote for just such men as have been nominated. Ten thousand votes for GERRIT SMITH at this juncture would do more, in our judgment, for the ultimate abolition of slavery in this country, than two million for ABRAHAM LINCOLN, or any other man who stands pledged before the world against all interference with slavery in the slave States, who is not pledged to the abolition of slavery in the District of Columbia, or anywhere else the system exists, and who is not opposed to making the free States a hunting ground for men under the Fugitive Slave Law. . . . Let Abolitionists, regardless of the outside pressure, regardless of smiles or frowns, mindful only of the true and right, vote in the coming election for the only men now in the field who believe in the complete manhood of the negro, the unconstitutionality and illegality of slavery, and are pledged to the immediate and unconditional abolition of slavery.[9]

Not all Northern Negroes shared Douglass' sentiments. Many of them supported the Republican candidates, despite the party's moderate stand on the slavery issue. As early as January 1860 a group of Philadelphia Negroes publicly debated the question: "Would the success of the Republican party in the present

*canvass be advantageous to our cause?" The negative side reit-
erated the standard criticisms of the Republican party; but the
affirmative pointed out that this party was the only major political organization that had taken any kind of a stand against
slavery, and that a Republican victory would represent a step
in the right direction. Negroes in several Northern cities formed
Republican clubs. The black Republican Club in Brooklyn raised
a "Lincoln Liberty Tree" in July 1860. The black "West Boston
Wide Awakes" marched in a massive Republican parade in
Boston.[10] Samuel Smothers, a Negro educator in Indiana, wrote
that*

the colored people are looking hopefully, and some of them are
laboring earnestly, for the general reform of the Republican
party. Yes, we are looking forward with bright anticipations to
the day when the Republican party in Indiana, Ohio, Illinois,
and throughout the entire North, shall be educated up to the
principles of their platform, and when we shall be recognized
as men, not only in New England, but all over the nation. Another thing that cheers our hopes and revives our drooping spirits is this: The best anti-slavery men in the nation are rallying
under the Republican banner. This causes us to look hopefully
to the Republican party for the ultimate abolition of slavery
throughout the entire nation, and the elevation of our race to
social and political equality.[11]

*Whatever their opinions of the Republican party had been,
most Northern Negroes rejoiced in the election of Lincoln in
November. Frederick Douglass wrote:*

What, then, has been gained to the anti-slavery cause by the
election of Mr. Lincoln? Not much, in itself considered, but very
much when viewed in the light of its relations and bearings. For
fifty years the country has taken the law from the lips of an
exacting, haughty and imperious slave oligarchy. The masters of
slaves have been masters of the Republic. Their authority was
almost undisputed, and their power irresistible. They were the
President makers of the Republic, and no aspirant dared to hope
for success against their frown. Lincoln's election has vitiated
their authority, and broken their power. It has taught the North

its strength, and shown the South its weakness. More important still, it has demonstrated the possibility of electing, if not an Abolitionist, at least an *anti-slavery reputation* to the Presidency.[12]

Southern leaders also concluded that Lincoln's election had broken their power, and they launched a movement that resulted in the secession of seven states and the formation of the Confederacy in February 1861. Many Northern Negroes welcomed the prospect of disunion. Less than two weeks after the election, H. Ford Douglass told the South: "Stand not upon the order of your going, but go at once. . . . There is no union of ideas and interests in this country, and there can be no union between freedom and slavery." A correspondent of the Anglo-African *wrote:*

The friends of universal emancipation are enabled to see by impending difficulties, that their labors have not been thrown away, for agitation has driven the South mad, and endangered this Union, which it should be the desire of every lover of freedom to see abolished. . . . He that is able to read this nation's destiny, can see and decipher the hand-writing upon the wall.[13]

Why did Northern Negroes welcome the advent of disunion in 1860-61? In the first place, many black men were members of the Garrisonian wing of the abolitionist-movement. The Garrisonians had been advocating the separation of the North and South for nearly twenty years. They argued that under the Constitution the national government was pledged to protect slavery. During the existence of the Union the number of slaves had increased from 700,000 to 4,000,000. The slave power had grown in strength and arrogance until in 1857 the Chief Justice of the Supreme Court had declared that Negroes were not citizens of the United States. The military power of the national government and the militias of the free states could be called upon to crush any slave uprising in the South. Garrisonians maintained that disunion would put an end to the protection of slavery by the power of the North and of the United States government. It would abolish the Fugitive Slave Law and thereby encourage a greater exodus of slaves from Dixie. The Declara-

*tion of Independence stated that any government which under-
mined natural and God-given rights should be destroyed and a
new one formed. Garrisonians believed that by attacking a
proslavery Constitution and Union they were fulfilling the revolutionary tradition of the founding fathers.*

*Robert Purvis was a distinguished, urbane, wealthy Negro
who lived in a fine home in a Philadelphia suburb. The son of
an English merchant father and a Jewish-Moorish mother,
Purvis could have passed as a white man and lived a life of
comfort and leisure. Instead he had thrown himself into the
movement for emancipation and equal rights, and had been one
of the founders of the American Anti-Slavery Society in 1833.
Purvis was a supporter of Garrison's disunion position, and in
1860 he expressed the attitude of many black men toward the
Union: "I say your government—it is not mine. Thank God, I
have no willing share in a government that deliberately, before
the world, and without a blush, declares one part of its people,
and that for no crime or pretext of crime, disfranchised and
outlawed. For such a government, I, as a man, can have no
feelings but of* contempt, loathing, *and* unutterable abhorrence!"[14]

*Frederick Douglass was not a Garrisonian, but he too favored
disunion in 1860-61. In a speech at Boston on December 3, 1860,
Douglass said:*

I am for a dissolution of the Union—decidedly for a dissolution of the Union! . . . I shall be glad of the news, come when
it will, that the slave States are an independent government,
and that you are no longer called upon to shoulder your arms
and guard with your swords those States. . . . In case of such a
dissolution, I believe that men could be found at least as brave
as a Walker,* and more skillful than any other filibusterer, who
would venture into those States and raise the standard of liberty
there. . . . I believe a Garibaldi would arise who would march

---

*William Walker, the "Grey-eyed Man of Destiny" who led a filibuster-
ing expedition into Nicaragua in 1855 and set himself up as dictator of that
country.

into those States with a thousand men, and summon to his standard sixty thousand, if necessary, to accomplish the freedom of the slave. (Cheers.)[15]

Douglass agreed with Republican leaders that secession was unconstitutional, but he opposed any compromise that would keep the South in the Union by giving additional guaranties to slavery. "If the Union," said Douglass,
can only be maintained by new concessions to the slaveholders; if it can only be stuck together and held together by a new drain on the negro's blood; if the North is to forswear the exercise of all rights incompatible with the safety and perpetuity of slavery, . . . then will every right minded man and woman in the land say, let the Union perish, and perish forever. As against compromises and national demoralization, welcome, ten thousand times over, the hardships consequent upon a dissolution of the Union.[16]

This opposition to compromise was a key issue. Even before South Carolina seceded on December 20, 1860, voices were heard in the North calling for concessions and conciliation to save the Union. Many compromise proposals were introduced into Congress. The most comprehensive of these measures was known as the Crittenden Compromise, named for its sponsor, Senator John Crittenden of Kentucky. As originally introduced, the Crittenden Compromise consisted of a series of constitutional amendments to protect slavery in the states and in the District of Columbia, to prohibit interference with the interstate slave trade, and to exclude slavery north of the line 36° 30' and guarantee it south of that line in all territories now held "or hereafter acquired." The Crittenden plan was later amended to include provisions for the disfranchisement and colonization abroad of free Negroes, North and South.[17]

Negroes condemned every part of the Crittenden Compromise, but they reserved their sharpest words for the section that would have disfranchised those few Northern Negroes who possessed the right to vote. The Virginia legislature issued an invitation to all the states for a Peace Convention to be held in Washington on February 4, 1861. The Crittenden Compromise

*formed the basis of the plan of conciliation discussed at this
conference. On February 6 a petition signed by 125 black citizens of Boston was presented to the Massachusetts legislature.
The petition stated:*

We, the undersigned, do respectfully memorialize your honorable body to the following effect:—

That as citizens of the Commonwealth of Massachusetts who
have heretofore felt perfectly secure in the enjoyment of the
rights pertaining to such citizenship, who have always looked to
your honorable body as the defender of the rights of the minority when they are threatened by the actions of the majority,—
would, in view of your determination to send commissioners to
Washington, to represent this State in the convention there assembled, . . . pray your honorable body to keep in view the
following facts:—

That Virginia, who invites Massachusetts to join her in convention with the above view, disfranchises her colored citizens.

That this is coupled with certain propositions, one of which
is as follows: That "the elective franchise and the right to hold
office, whether Federal, State, Territorial or Municipal, shall not
be exercised by persons who are in whole or in part of the African race."

That therefore your honorable body instruct the commissioners appointed in behalf of the State, to oppose and vote against
every proposition which may have in view or which may be
perverted to the disfranchisement of the colored citizens of this
Commonwealth.[18]

*On February 14, Massachusetts' Negro citizens held a mass
meeting in the Joy Street Baptist Church of Boston, and adopted
the following manifesto written by George T. Downing, a
wealthy Negro restaurateur:*

APPEAL TO THE WHITE CITIZENS OF THIS STATE

. . . In this hour of darkness and danger, we appeal to you,
fellow-citizens, to bear in mind the following facts:—

Virginia invites Massachusetts and other States to a convention, with a view, as alleged, of settling the present national difficulties.

The proposed basis of settlement is the "Crittenden compromise," the seventh clause of which, if adopted, deprives us of the right of voting in Massachusetts. The eighth looks to our expatriation; and it seems to be a studied design on the part of those who really understand this compromise to keep the people ignorant of the purpose to disfranchise and expatriate us. . . .

You, white fellow-citizens, constitute a very large majority of the voters. . . . Therefore we appeal to you to stand by us, and see that we are not unjustly punished. . . . We are weak—you are strong. We are few in numbers—you are numerous. O, men of Massachusetts! tell us not that there are two kinds of rights; rights of the rich, which you respect because you must; rights of the poor, on which you trample because you dare. . . .

Many of us are native-born citizens of the State; we appeal to you to protect us in the enjoyment of the little property which we have wrung, as it were, from adversity itself. . . .

Freedom has been your legacy from birth; by some of us it has been achieved. We know what oppression is; protect us from this political oppression. . . . Some of us have experienced the unutterable anguish of leaving our dear ones for the sake of freedom. We appeal to you to secure and protect us in the freedom which we have sought. Let us not be exiled from the State of our adoption. . . .

The injustice against which we protest is so self-evident that we have not deemed it necessary to argue. We have confined ourselves to an appeal to you as men and as Christians—in the name of social justice—in the name of American patriotism—in the name and by the sacred memory of the entombed fathers—in the name of the great God, before whom we must all appear, *hear us!* Speak out, Massachusetts! you are the acknowledged head of New England. The movers in this injustice will not disregard the voice of New England.[19]

The Massachusetts legislature instructed its commissioners to the Peace Convention to oppose the Crittenden Compromise,

*which was eventually rejected by both Houses of Congress. All
efforts to save the Union by compromise failed, and at Fort
Sumter on April 12, 1861, the nation reaped the harvest of three
decades of sectional controversy. William Howard Russell, correspondent of the London* Times, *was in Baltimore when the
news came of the firing on Fort Sumter. On the morning of
April 14 Russell entered the barbershop for his daily shave,
where the following conversation took place:*

At the black barber's I was meekly interrogated by my atten-
dant as to my belief in the story of the bombardment. He was
astonished to find a stranger could think the event was probable. "De gen'lmen of Baltimore will be quite glad ov it. But
maybe it'll come bad after all." I discovered my barber had
strong ideas that the days of slavery were drawing to an end.
"And what will take place then, do you think?" "Well, sar,
'spose coloured men will be good as white men."[20]

*All over the North, black men reacted to the news of Fort
Sumter in the same manner as the Baltimore barber. The North
was galvanized into a frenzy of patriotism by the event, and the
people responded enthusiastically to Lincoln's call for volunteers to crush the rebellion. Opposed to the pre-Sumter efforts to
save the Union by compromise, Northern Negroes applauded the
intention to restore the Union by war, for they saw in the war
fever of the North a force that would eventually compel the destruction of slavery. "What a change now greets us!" wrote
Frederick Douglass after the firing on Sumter.*

The Government is aroused, the dead North is alive, and its
divided people united. Never was a change so sudden, so universal, and so portentous. The whole North, East and West is in
arms. . . . The cry now is for war, vigorous war, war to the bitter end, and war till the traitors are effectually and permanently
put down. . . . The *Stars and Stripes* are now the symbols of
liberty. The Eagle that we left last month something like as good
as dead, has revived again, and screams terror in the ears of the
slaveholding rebels. . . . He who faithfully works to put down a
rebellion undertaken and carried on for the extension and perpetuity of slavery, performs an antislavery work. Even disunion

Abolitionists, . . . we have no doubt, [will] rejoice in the success
of the Government at Washington, in suppressing and putting
down this slave-holding rebellion.[21]

*Douglass declared that the Union could never be preserved
without the abolition of slavery:*

At last our proud Republic is overtaken. Our National Sin has
found us out. . . . Slavery has done it all. . . . We have sown the
wind, only to reap the whirlwind. . . . The power given to crush
the negro now overwhelms the white man. The Republic has
put one end of the chain upon the ankle of the bondman, and
the other end about its own neck. They have been planting ty-
rants, and are now getting a harvest of civil war and anarchy. . . . Could we write as with lightning, and speak as with
the voice of thunder, we should write and cry to the nation,
REPENT, BREAK EVERY YOKE, LET THE OPPRESSED GO FREE, FOR HEREIN
ALONE IS DELIVERANCE AND SAFETY! It is not too late. The moment
is propitious. . . . Now is the time to put an end to all our present national calamities. . . . Any attempt now to separate the
freedom of the slave from the victory of the Government, . . .
any attempt to secure peace to the whites while leaving the
blacks in chains . . . will be labor lost. The American people and
the Government at Washington may refuse to recognize it for a
time; but the "inexorable logic of events" will force it upon
them in the end; that the war now being waged in this land is a
war for and against slavery; and that it can never be effectually
put down till one or the other of these vital forces is completely
destroyed.[22]

In New York the Anglo-African *stated editorially that the outbreak of war*

is but another step in the drama of American Progress. We say
Progress, for we know that no matter what may be the desires
of the men of Expediency who rule, or seem to, the affairs of
the North,—the *tendencies* are for liberty.

God speed the conflict. May the cup be drained to its dregs,
for only thus can this nation of sluggards know the disease and
its remedy. . . .

The free colored Americans cannot be indifferent to the progress of this struggle. . . . Out of this strife will come freedom, though the methods are not yet clearly apparent. . . . Public opinion purified by the fiery ordeal through which the nation is about to pass, will rightly appreciate the cause of its political disquiet, and apply the remedy. . . . It must be that the key to the solution of the present difficulties, is the abolition of slavery; not as an act of retaliation on the master, but as a measure of justice to the slave—the sure and permanent basis of "a more perfect Union."[23]

CHAPTER II

THE NEGRO'S RESPONSE

TO THE WAR, 1861

In the first weeks after the fall *of Fort Sumter, Northern Negroes joined in the outburst of patriotism and offered their services to the government to help suppress the rebellion. On April 23 Jacob Dobson, a Washington Negro, sent a note to the Secretary of War:*

Sir: I desire to inform you that I know of some three hundred of reliable colored free citizens of this City, who desire to enter the service for the defence of the City.

I have been three times across the Rocky Mountains in the service of the Country with Fremont and others.

I can be found about the Senate Chambers, as I have been employed about the premises for some years.[1]

In Pittsburgh, a Negro organization called the "Hannibal Guards" sent a communication on April 17 to General James S. Negley, militia commander of Western Pennsylvania:

Sir: As we sympathize with our white fellow-citizens at the present crisis, and to show that we can and do feel interested in the present state of affairs; and as we consider ourselves American citizens and interested in the Commonwealth of all our white fellow-citizens, although deprived of all our political rights, we yet wish the government of the United States to be sustained against the tyranny of slavery, and are willing to assist in any honorable way or manner to sustain the present Administration. We therefore tender to the state the services of the Hannibal Guards.[2]

A meeting of Cleveland Negroes adopted the following resolutions:

Whereas, the affairs of our Government are approaching an important and serious crisis, regarding its future prosperity and perpetuity; and whereas, at this time, every man, without distinction of party, is called upon to show his hand and define his position in this important crisis of the Government,—

Resolved, That we, as colored citizens of Cleveland, desiring to prove our loyalty to the Government, feel that we should adopt measures to put ourselves in a position to defend the Government of which we claim protection.

Resolved, That to-day, as in the times of '76, and the days of 1812, we are ready to go forth and do battle in the common cause of the country.[3]

Despite the fact that Negro soldiers had fought for the United States in the Revolution and in the War of 1812, a federal law barred black men from serving in state militias, and there were no Negroes in the regular United States Army. A group of Boston Negroes met in the Twelfth Baptist Church on April 23 to call for the repeal of laws that kept black men out of the army. Robert Morris, a Negro lawyer in Boston, declared that "if the Government would only take away the disability, there was not a man who would not leap for his knapsack and musket, and they would make it intolerably hot for Old Virginia. (Great applause.)"[4] On April 29 a Negro drill company was organized in Boston, and in subsequent weeks the black men of Massachusetts sent several petitions to the legislature praying for the repeal of discriminatory militia laws. The following petition is representative:

Your petitioners, colored citizens of Massachusetts, respectfully represent—

. . . That they have never been wanting in patriotism, but have always exhibited the utmost loyalty to the country and to the Commonwealth, notwithstanding the great national injustice to which they are in many ways subjected on account of their complexion;—

That, in order to enable them to display their patriotic zeal and unwavering loyalty in the most effective manner in this trial-hour of the republic, and to relieve them from an odious proscription which has so long and so unjustly been directed against them, and all others complexionally identified with them, by an illegal act of Congress; they earnestly desire your honorable body to cause to be stricken forthwith from the militia law of the State the odious word "white," by which they are now precluded from being enrolled in the militia, and thus disabled as citizens from defending the Commonwealth against its enemies.

Your aggrieved petitioners further respectfully submit, that no law of Congress, however long submitted to, which is clearly unconstitutional, or of questionable legality, ought to be permitted to control the legislative action of your honorable body;—

That such is the Congressional law, enrolling only "white" persons in the militia, to the exclusion of all other citizens. . . .

Congress . . . has no more authority to establish a complexional rule in regard to the militia of the several States, than it has to require uniformity in political or religious opinion, or to establish a monarchy. . . . Your petitioners claim, as recognized citizens of Massachusetts, that they ought to be permitted to test the validity of the act of Congress complained of, before the proper judicial tribunals; and to this end they ask the obliteration of the word "white" from the militia law of the State.[5]

But in spite of Massachusetts' liberalism on racial matters, the legislature postponed action on these petitions. Other states and the federal government also spurned the offers of assistance from black men. The Secretary of War replied to Jacob Dodson's note, quoted above, that "this Department has no intention at present to call into the service of the Government any colored soldiers."[6] The militia commander in Ohio told the Negroes of Cleveland that "your patriotic letter of the 20th inst. is received, and in reply would say, the Constitution will not permit

*me to issue the order."[7] In New York City a group of black men
hired a public hall and began drilling in anticipation of a possible call to active service, but they were promptly told by the
chief of police that they must cease their activities or he could
not protect them from mob assault by the Negro-hating lower
classes of the city. The Negroes had no choice but to obey the
police order.[8] Patriotic black men in Cincinnati were also
threatened by mob violence. Writing about the incident in later
years, a Cincinnati Negro leader recalled that*

A meeting of the colored citizens of Cincinnati was called to
organize a company of "Home Guards." They did not propose
to invade the South, but merely desired to aid in the defense of
the city, should the necessity arise. The blood boils with indignation at the remembrance of the insults heaped upon them for
this simple offer. The keys of the school-house, in which a second meeting was proposed, were roughly demanded by the police. The proprietor of a place selected as a recruiting station
was compelled to take down an American flag which he had
raised over his door. The proprietors of another place were told
by the police: "We want you d—d niggers to keep out of this;
this is a white man's war."[9]

*"This is a white man's war!" Everywhere they turned,
Northern Negroes were confronted by such statements. The Lincoln administration and the Republican press, even antislavery
newspapers such as the New York* Tribune, *declared emphatically that the purpose of the war was the restoration of the
Union, and that the issues of slavery and the Negro had nothing
to do with the conflict. The Springfield* Republican *stated that
"if there is one point of honor upon which more than another
this administration will stick, it is its pledge not to interfere
with slavery in the states." Governor John Andrew of Massachusetts, seeking advice from Washington on the tone he should
take toward national affairs in his message to a special session
of the legislature, was bluntly told by Montgomery Blair to
"drop the nigger."[10] Some Northern generals returned fugitive
slaves who entered Union lines to their masters. These actions
dampened the enthusiasm of Negroes for the Union cause. On*

*May 9, 1861, the Rev. J. Sella Martin, a former slave who had
escaped to the North in 1855 and had become pastor of the Joy
Street Baptist Church in Boston and one of the best-known Negro ministers in the North, wrote to Frederick Douglass:*

Just think of Dimmick and Slemmer [Justin Dimmick and
A. J. Slemmer, Union officers] sending back the fugitives that
sought protection of them. They refuse to let white men sell the
Southerners food, and yet they return slaves to work on the
plantation to raise all the food that the Southerners want. They
arrest traitors, and yet make enemies of the colored people,
North and South; and if they do force the slave to fight for his
master, as the only hope of being benefited by the war, they
may thank their own cowardice and prejudice for the revenge
of the negro's aid and the retribution of his bullet while fighting
against them in the Southern States. I received a letter from
Mobile, in which the writer states that the returning of those
slaves by Slemmer has made the slaves determined to fight for
the South, in the hope that their masters may set them free after
the war, and when remonstrated with, they say that the North
will not let them fight for them.[11]

*As Martin's letter indicated, some Southern Negroes volun-
teered to aid the Confederate war effort. In the early weeks of
the war, free black men in several Southern communities formed
companies and offered their services to Confederate officials.
Some of these offers were accepted, and the Negroes were detailed to labor battalions for work on fortifications, earthworks,
and so on. In New Orleans the prosperous free Negro community declared that they were "ready to take arms at a moment's
notice and fight shoulder to shoulder with other citizens." Black
men in New Orleans formed a military organization known as
the "Native Guards," which was enrolled as part of the state
militia. But the "Native Guards" were never used by the Confederate government. When the Union forces captured New Orleans in the spring of 1862, the regiment of black men refused
to leave the city with the rest of the Confederate Army. Instead
they welcomed the conquering army and declared their allegiance to the Union.[12]*

Why did Southern black men offer their services to the Confederacy? In some cases, local patriotism and the hope of better treatment were the motivating factors. But there is also evidence that pressure from local officials and fear of impressment played a part in the decision of some Southern Negroes to volunteer. In 1862 General Benjamin Butler, commander of the Union forces occupying New Orleans, talked with the leaders of the city's free Negro community. "He asked them why they had accepted service under the Confederate government, which was set up for the distinctly avowed purpose of holding in eternal slavery their brethren and kindred. They answered, that they had not dared to refuse; that they had hoped, by serving the Confederates, to advance a little nearer to equality with whites; that they longed to throw the weight of their class into the scale of the Union, and only asked an opportunity to show their devotion to the cause with which their own dearest hopes were identified." These same men were later enrolled in the Union Army, and fought effectively for the North during the rest of the war.[13]

Wedded to the ideologies of slavery and Negro subordination, the Confederacy was incapable of treating the free Negro fairly or justly, even when he volunteered his support for the Confederate cause. Southern leaders suspected, with good reason, that the real loyalties of most Southern Negroes lay with the North. During the war most Confederate states enacted restrictive and repressive legislation against free Negroes, the purpose of which was to keep them under constant surveillance and in a condition closely resembling slavery. Six states passed laws providing for the impressment of free Negroes into Confederate labor battalions. Some states adopted legislation which actually remanded free Negroes to slavery, and several thousand free black men were forced to accept the status of slaves during the war. Under such conditions, it was little wonder that many free Negroes fled to Northern camps and declared their allegiance to the Union.[14]

During the war, slaves and free Negroes not only raised most of the food and fiber for the Confederate Army, but they did

much of the work on rebel fortifications and entrenchments as
well. The following documents are representative of hundreds
of items that can be found in the official Confederate war re-
cords:

R. H. Chilton, Assistant Adjutant General, to General J. B. Ma-
gruder at Yorktown, Virginia, Feb. 15, 1862:

The War Department finds it necessary to impress slaves and
free negroes to extend and complete the fortifications in the
Peninsula. You will therefore call upon the citizens of Dinwiddie
County, by direction of the Secretary of War, to send forthwith
one-half of their male slaves between the ages of sixteen and
fifty to execute this work on the Peninsula.

Jefferson Davis to Governor John Letcher of Virginia, Oct.
10, 1862:

In accordance with an act passed by the Legislature of Virginia October 3, 1862, I have the honor to call upon Your Excellency for 4,500 negroes to be employed upon the
fortifications. . . . It is unnecessary to call Your Excellency's attention to the importance of a prompt and efficient response to
this call, in view of the necessity of completing the works for
the defense of Richmond.[15]

Negroes who worked as teamsters, laborers, servants, cooks,
etc. in the Confederate Army were in a few instances actually
pressed into emergency service as soldiers during the heat of
battle. Throughout the war many Confederate Negroes deserted
to Union lines as soon as they got the chance. The following
story, written by a reporter for the Reading (Pennsylvania)
Journal, was taken down (and shorn of its plantation dialect)
from a slave who had been impressed during the Battle of
Bull Run to help service and load a Confederate artillery bat-
tery. The story illustrates both the Confederacy's occasional
use of black men in actual battle situations and the pen-
chant of Southern Negroes to desert to the Yankees whenever
possible.

My name is John Parker, I was born in King and Queen's
county Virginia, I do not know my age. My master's name was
Benjamin Wilson; he failed in business, and when he broke up

they seized 130 negroes—of which I was one—and sold them at
the auction market in Richmond. I was bought by Thomas Griggs,
a Colonel in the Rebel army for $1,000. . . . I stayed with my
new master until the war broke out, then he and his sons went
away to the war, leaving an overseer to manage us. In two weeks
our overseer also went to the war. We had good times then,
and eat up everything we could get. Not long after, our mistress
and her two daughters packed up and went off. Our master had
told us to stay at the plantation until he came back, and that if
any d—d Yankees showed themselves in his absence, to shoot
them. Our master had also before this sent us to Winchester and
Fredericksburg to work upon the batteries and assist at the
trenches. . . . Ten of us then went to Richmond and worked
for a considerable length of time upon batteries and breastworks
on James River. When they were done with us we returned to
the farm and found our overseer at home. We worked on
smoothly until the excitement about the expected battle at Bull
Run arose. They said that all the colored people must then come
and fight. I arrived at the Junction two days before the action
commenced. They immediately placed me in one of the batteries. There were four colored men in our battery, I don't know
how many there were in the others. We opened fire about ten
o'clock on the morning of Sunday the 21st; couldn't see the
Yankees at all and only fired at random. Sometimes they were
concealed in the woods and then we guessed our aim. . . . My
work was to hand the balls and swab out the cannon; in this we
took turns. The officers aimed this gun; we fired grape shot.
The balls from the Yankee guns fell thick all around. In one
battery a shell burst and killed twenty, the rest ran. . . . I felt
bad all the time, and thought every minute my time would come;
I felt so excited that I hardly knew what I was about, and felt
worse than dead. We wish to our hearts that the Yankees would
whip, and we would have run over to their side but our officers
would have shot us if we had made the attempt. I stayed at my
place till the order came for all to retreat, then every one ran
thinking that the Yankees were close upon their heels. I followed the retreat a good piece, but as soon as our officers found

out that the Yankees were also running as fast as we were, they ordered a halt, and the Black Horse Cavalry (which lost a great number in the fight) stopped all the fugitives and turned in pursuit of the United States troops but the general was a little "skittish" about following him, and they didn't care to press forward upon them very sharply. . . .

I stayed about here for two weeks, we worked until the next Friday burying the dead—we did not bury the Yankees and our men in the same hole, we generally dug a long hole 8 or 9 feet deep and threw in a hundred in each pit. . . .

We were afraid of another attack from the Yankees, and prepared ourselves as well as we could to meet them again, but they didn't come. I then left . . . with six of my master's men to go home. . . . When we got back we found all the cattle and mules gone, and corn all grown up with weeds, but we didn't care for that, all we wanted was a chance to escape. There were officers prowling round the neighborhood in search of all the negroes, but we dodged round so smartly, they didn't catch us. . . . I staid with my wife from Saturday night until Monday morning, and then returned to my master's; I was afraid to stay long in the neighborhood for fear of the officers, so I left and came nearer the American lines. I found the U.S. soldiers at Alexandria, who gave me two papers, one for myself and one for my wife; they asked me whether I could get my wife, I said I would try. I then went back, and finding her, I gave her the paper and told her she must try to get off, I told her to come to the Chain Bridge at a certain time and I would meet her, but I found out they wouldn't allow me to pass over there, so I fixed another plan to get my wife over, I was to meet her in a canoe and ferry her across, but I missed her though, and I think she must have gone too high up the river. When I had given her up I went along up the river and came up with some of the pickets in Gen. Banks' division, near Frederick, Md. I was afraid, but they welcomed me and shouted; "Come on! don't hurt him!" Some of the pickets were on horseback, they gave me a suit of clothes and plenty to eat, and treated me well. They wanted me to stay and go down into Virginia and tell them all about where

THE NEGRO'S CIVIL WAR

the batteries were, but I was afraid to try that country again, and said that I was bound for the North, I told them all I knew about the position of the other army, about the powder mill on the Rappahannock river, &c. They let me go. . . . I left at night and travelled for the star, I was afraid of the Secessionists in Maryland, and I only walked at night. I came to Gettysburg in a week, and I thought when I saw the *big barns*, that I was in another country. . . . I am going from here to New York where I hope to meet my wife, she has two girls with her; one of my boys is with my master, and the other, who is 14 years old, I think was taken to Louisiana. My wife and I are going to travel from New York to Canada.[16]

As this story indicates, some Union officers welcomed fugitives to their lines. In May 1861 Benjamin Butler had labeled three fugitives who had escaped from a Confederate labor battalion and had entered Butler's camp at Fortress Monroe, Virginia, as "contraband of war." By the end of July there were nine hundred such "contrabands" at Fortress Monroe, with more coming in every day. On August 6 the United States Congress passed a confiscation act providing for the seizure of all property used "in aid of the rebellion," including slaves. This bill applied only to those slaves who had actually worked on Confederate military fortifications, naval vessels, and so on, and it did not specifically emancipate such slaves, but it was nevertheless an important step in the direction of emancipation. Despite the Lincoln administration's efforts to keep slavery as an issue out of the war, the Negro by his own actions was making slavery an important issue.[17]

But in 1861 the Union government still refused to accept the proffered services of Negro soldiers. This refusal, plus the repeated official declarations that the war was not being waged against slavery, alienated many Northern Negroes and gave rise to a sharp debate within the Negro community concerning the attitude black men should adopt toward the war. This debate can be traced in the following documents.

At the beginning of May 1861 the leaders of Philadelphia's sizable Negro population issued a public statement:

Formidable difficulties prevent our service being made available to the country in this time of its extremity. First, the laws of this State debar 10,000 able-bodied colored citizens from bearing arms in defence of the State. . . .

The second is, that the . . . colored citizens of this State are not invited, at this stage, by the Government, to enroll themselves; still, in view of the present danger threatening the Commonwealth, we earnestly recommend that the colored citizens stand prepared, so that when officially solicited by the Government we may render such service as only men can render, who know how precious *Liberty* is.[18]

But another Philadelphia Negro, Henry Cropper, stated on May 4 that he would never fight for the Union unless the government accepted Negro volunteers on the same basis as whites:

We, the members of the first and only equipped military Company, have more knowledge of our duty, and also more dignity, than to offer our services to a Government, when knowing at the same time, that the laws call for none but white men to do military duty. . . . I, as the Captain, in behalf of the Company, am resolved never to offer or give service, except it be on equality with all other men.[19]

A black man in Chillicothe, Ohio, deplored the fact that Negroes were offering their services to the government even though they knew that such offers would be spurned.

Nevertheless, they say that when matters come to an adjustment, this offer of services can be used as a plea for our enfranchisement. But can it not be used as well against us? If the colored people, under all the social and legal disabilities by which they are environed, are ever ready to defend the government that despoils them of their rights, it may be concluded that it is quite safe to oppress them. . . . The truth is, if, in time of peace the fact of our having bled in defense of the country when it was struggling desperately for independence, avails nothing, it is absurd to suppose that the fact of tendering our services to settle a domestic war when we know that our services will be contemptuously rejected, will procure a practical acknowledgement of our rights.[20]

A group of Negroes in New York City held a meeting on May
1, at which the following resolution was discussed: "That sev-
eral of the Southern States, being in open rebellion against the
General Government, and the President, having called upon all
loyal citizens to rally to the defence thereof, Therefore, that we
tender our services to the Governor of this State, to serve during
the war, either as firemen, during the absence of those firemen
who may enlist for the war—to act as a Home Guard, or to go
South, if their services should be required." But several speak-
ers at the meeting opposed the resolution on the ground that
earlier offers by Negroes had been rejected, and they "did not
think that we should offer ourselves to be kicked and insulted,
as others had been. . . . The whites knew that we were willing
to fight, and therefore there was no need of laying ourselves
liable to insult, simply for the privilege of saying so." These
speakers prevailed, and the resolution was defeated.[21]

Nevertheless the Anglo-African, *a weekly Negro newspaper*
that circulated mainly among black people in New York City
and nearby areas, continued to urge black men to prepare them-
selves for any contingency:

Colored men whose fingers tingle to pull the trigger, or clutch
the knife aimed at the slave-holders in arms, will not have to
wait much longer. Whether the foe attack Washington and succeed, or whether they attempt Maryland and fail, there is equal
need for calling out the nation's "Reserve Guard"—the forlorn
hope which will march to "Liberty or Death." . . .

There are men among our people who look upon this as the
"white man's war," and such men openly say, let them fight it
out among themselves. It is their flag, and their constitution
which have been dishonored and set at naught. . . .

This is a huge fallacy. In proof of which let us ask ourselves
some questions. . . . What rights have we in the free States? We
have the "right to life, liberty and the pursuit of happiness."
We have the right to labor, and are secured in the fruits of our
labor; we have the right to our wives and our little ones; we
have to a large extent the right to educate our children. . . .

Are these rights worth the having? If they are then they are

worth defending with all our might, and at any cost. It is illog-
ical, unpatriotic, nay mean and unmanly in us to shrink from
the defence of these great rights and privileges. . . . But some
will say that these rights of *ours* are not assailed by the South.
Are they not? What in short is the programme or platform on
which the South would have consented to remain in the Union?
It was to spread slavery over all the States and territories. . . .

Hence, talk as we may, we *are* concerned in this fight and
our fate hangs upon its issues. The South must be subjugated,
or we shall be enslaved. In aiding the Federal government in
whatever way we can, we are aiding to secure our own liberty;
for this war can only end in the subjugation of the North or of
the South. We do not affirm that the North is fighting in behalf
of the black man's rights, as such—if this was the single issue,
we even doubt whether they would fight at all. But circumstances have been so arranged by the decrees of Providence,
that in struggling for their own nationality they are forced to
defend our rights. . . . Let us be awake, therefore brethren; a
generous emulation in a common patriotism, and a special call
to defend our rights alike bid us to be on the alert to seize arms
and drill as soon as the government shall be willing to accept
our services.[22]

A Negro whose initials were R.H.V. disagreed with the Anglo-
African:

No regiments of black troops should leave their bodies to rot
upon the battle-field beneath a Southern sun, to conquer a peace
based upon the perpetuity of human bondage. . . .

I claim that the raising of black regiments for the war would
be highly impolitic and uncalled for under the present state of
affairs, knowing, as we do, the policy of the Government in
relation to colored men. . . . Is this country ready and anxious
to initiate a new era for downtrodden humanity, that you now
so eagerly propose to make the sacrifice of thousands of our
ablest men to encourage and facilitate the great work of regeneration? No! no!! Your answer must be: No!!! No black regiments
unless by circumstances over which we have no option, no control; no initiatory war measures, to be adopted or encouraged

by us. Our policy must be neutral, ever praying for the success of that party determined to initiate first the policy of justice and equal rights.[23]

Alfred M. Green, a Negro schoolteacher in Philadelphia, rebuked R.H.V. for his counsel of inactivity:

This inactivity that is advocated is the principle that has ever had us left behind, and will leave us again unless we arouse from lethargy and arm ourselves as men and patriots against the common enemy of God and man. For six months I have labored to arouse our people to the necessity of action, and I have the satisfaction to say not without success. I have seen companies organized and under the most proficient modern drill in that time. I have seen men drilled among our sturdy colored men of the rural districts of Pennsylvania and New Jersey, in the regular African Zouave Drill, that would make the hearts of secession traitors, or prejudiced northern Yankees quake and tremble for fear. . . .

No nation ever has or ever will be emancipated from slavery . . . but by the sword, wielded too by their own strong arms. It is a foolish idea for us to still be nursing our past grievances to our own detriment when we should as one man grasp the sword. . . . We admit all that has or can be said about the meanness of this government towards us—we are fully aware that there is no more soul in the present administration on the great moral issues involved in the slavery question and the present war, than has characterized previous administrations; but what of that; it all teaches the necessity of our making ourselves felt as a people at this extremity of our national government worthy of consideration and of being recognized as a part of its own strength. . . .

God will help no one that refuses to help himself. . . . If ever colored men plead for rights or fought for liberty, now of all others is the time. The prejudiced white men North or South never will respect us until they are forced to do it by deeds of our own. . . . Without this we will be left a hundred years behind this gigantic age of human progress and development. . . .

The issue is here; let us prepare to meet it with manly spirit, let us say to the demagogues of the North who would prevent us even now from proving our manhood and foresight in the midst of all these complicated difficulties; that we will be armed, we will be schooled in military service; and if our fathers were cheated and disfranchised after nobly defending the country, we their sons have the manhood to defend the right and the sagacity to detest the wrong; time enough to secure to ourselves the primary interest we have in the great and moving cause of the great American Rebellion.[24]

A group of Northern Negroes sent a petition to President Lincoln:

We, the undersigned, respectfully represent to Your Excellency that we are native citizens of the United States, and that, notwithstanding much injustice and oppression which our race have suffered, we cherish a strong attachment for the land of our birth and for our Republican Government. We are filled with alarm at the formidable conspiracy for its overthrow, and lament the vast expense of blood and treasure which the present war involves. . . . We are anxious to use our power to give peace to our country and permanence to our Government.

We are strong in numbers, in courage, and in patriotism, and in behalf of our fellow countrymen of the colored race, we offer to you and to the nation a power and a will sufficient to conquer rebellion, and establish peace on a permanent basis. We pledge ourselves, upon receiving the sanction of Your Excellency, that we will immediately proceed to raise an efficient number of regiments, and so fast as arms and equipments shall be furnished, we will bring them into the field in good discipline, and ready for action.[25]

But a Colorado Negro denounced those black men who offered their active support to the Union cause:

I have observed with much indignation and shame, their willingness to take up arms in defence of this unholy, ill-begotten, would-be Republican government, that summons all its skill, energy, and might, of money, men, and false philosophy that a corrupt nation can bring to bear, to support, extend, and perpetuate that vilest of all vile systems, American slavery.[26]

And from Troy, New York, a Negro wrote:

We have nothing to gain, and everything to lose, by entering the lists as combatants. In the first place the authorities have not called upon us. . . . And suppose we were invited, what duty would we then owe to ourselves and our posterity? We are in advance of our fathers. They put confidence in the word of the whites only to feel the dagger of slavery driven still deeper into the heart throbbing with emotions of joy for freedom. We are not going to re-enact that tragedy. Our enslaved brethren must be made freedmen. . . . We of the North must have all rights which white men enjoy; until then we are in no condition to fight under the flag which gives us no protection.[27]

William H. Parham, a Negro public-school teacher in Cincinnati, wrote to his friend Jacob C. White, Jr., who taught at the Banneker Institute (a private Negro high school in Philadelphia):

You speak of several attempts having been made to organize military companies, all of which you state have proved ineffectual. If the aim of these attempted organizations be the acquiring a knowledge of the military drill simply, in order to be prepared for any emergency, I think it very commendable and hope they may yet be successful; but if it be with the intention of offering to this government, in this exigency, I am glad they have failed, and hope all similar efforts—whenever made—may meet with a like fate.

When Sumpter [sic] fell, the Northern heart was fired with indignation. . . . Some of the colored men thinking they were a part of this Northern heart alluded to, immagined [sic] themselves very indignant; and as all the rest of this heart was forming Home Guards etc. concluded they must do likewise. Whereupon meetings were held at which ardent speeches were made—all by black men—calling upon all Colored Americans to rally [sic] under the stars and stripes to protect their homes. These proceedings coming to the ears of the Municipal Authorities, judge the surprise of these patriotic individuals when waited upon by the Chief of Police, and informed by him that all that kind of thing must be stopped, that they had nothing to do with the fight, it was *white men's fight, with which niggers had nothing to do.* Although not of the parties concerned for I was opposed to it from first to last, so much so that I would not attend the meetings—yet as a black man, I regard it, (the information) as meant for me as well as all others, (Negroes). It being their fight I assure you they are welcome to it, so far as I am concerned.[28]

Despite this discouraging report, Negroes in several Northern cities succeeded in organizing and maintaining military companies. Moreover, there is evidence that several light-skinned Northern Negroes "passed" and joined white regiments.[29] In addition, hundreds of Northern Negroes served in white regiments from the beginning of the war as cooks and servants. One such Negro, William H. Johnson, who became prominent in New York State politics after the war, served in the Eighth Connecticut Volunteers in 1861. Johnson doubled as a war correspondent for the Boston Pine and Palm. *In November 1861, he reported to his newspaper from Annapolis, where the regiment was stationed, that*

the proscribed Americans (and there are many), attached to this regiment have, since their encampment here, formed themselves into a defensive association. They propose to cultivate a correct knowledge of the manual of arms and military evolutions, with a view to self-protection. The association is based upon the principles of military discipline, morality and literature; and they hope by a strict observance of the rules and regulations they have adopted, to do credit to their people, and honor to themselves. The name of the association is *Self-Defenders of Connecticut.* . . . In forming this association, we have been actuated by the conviction that the time is not far distant when the black man of this country will be summoned to show his hand in this struggle for liberty.[30]

In one way or another, many Northern Negroes participated in the Union war effort during the first year of the conflict. Meanwhile, on the home front, black orators and journalists were urging the Northern government and people to convert the War for the Union into a war of emancipation.

CHAPTER III

THE DRIVE FOR EMANCIPATION:

THE NORTHERN SCENE, 1861–65

Soon after the fall of Fort Sumter, the Anglo-African *proclaimed:*
No adjustment of the nation's difficulty is possible until the claims of the black man are first met and satisfied. . . . His prostrate body forms an impediment over which liberty cannot advance. . . . His title to life, to liberty and the pursuit of happiness must be acknowledged, or the nation will be forsworn; and being so, incur the dreadful penalty of permanent disunion, unending anarchy, and perpetual strife. . . . Men of the North, away with your Baalam-like proclivities, your trifling with truth and trafficking in principles. . . . Look upon us not as outcasts, pariahs, slaves, but as men whom the Almighty has endowed with the same faculties as yourselves, but in whom your cruelty has blurred His image and thwarted His intent. . . .

If you would restore the Union and maintain the government you so fondly cherish, make way for liberty, universal and complete. But the day of supplication is past—the hour of action is at hand. The black man, either with cooperation or without it, must be ready to strike for liberty whenever the auspicious moment comes.[1]

Frederick Douglass was one of the most eloquent and militant champions of the emancipation policy. In a series of editorials and speeches Douglass declared that
there is but one . . . effectual way to suppress and put down

the desolating war which the slaveholders and their rebel minions are now waging against the American Government and its loyal citizens. Fire must be met with water, darkness with light, and war for the destruction of liberty must be met with war for the destruction of slavery. *The simple way, then, to put an end to the savage and desolating war now waged by the slaveholders, is to strike down slavery itself*, the primal cause of that war. Freedom to the slave should now be proclaimed from the Capitol, and should be seen above the smoke and fire of every battle field, waving from every loyal flag. . . .

Not a slave should be left a slave in the returning footprints of the American army gone to put down this slaveholding rebellion. Sound policy, not less than humanity, demands the instant liberation of every slave in the rebel States. . . . Evade and equivocate as we may, slavery is not only the cause of the beginning of this war, but slavery is the sole support of the rebel cause. It is, so to speak, the very stomach of this rebellion. . . .

We talk the irrepressible conflict, and practically give the lie to our talk. We wage war against slaveholding rebels, and yet protect and augment the motive which has moved the slaveholders to rebellion. We strike at the effect, and leave the cause unharmed. Fire will not burn it out of us—water cannot wash it out of us, that this war with the slaveholders can never be brought to a desirable termination until slavery, the guilty cause of all our national troubles, has been totally and forever abolished.[2]

Negro and abolitionist spokesmen pointed out that slavery was a source of strength to the Confederacy. They quoted Southern statements such as the following article from the Montgomery Advertiser:

THE SLAVES AS A MILITARY ELEMENT
IN THE SOUTH

The total white population of the eleven States now comprising the Confederacy is 6,000,000, and, therefore, to fill up the ranks of the proposed army (600,000) about ten per cent of the entire white population will be required. In any other country than our own such a draft could not be met, but the Southern States can furnish that number of men, and still not leave the material interests of the country in a suffering condition. Those who are incapacitated for bearing arms can oversee the plantations, and the negroes can go on undisturbed in their usual labors. In the North the case is different; the men who join the army of subjugation are the laborers, the producers, and the factory operatives. Nearly every man from that section, especially those from the rural districts, leaves some branch of industry to suffer during his absence. The institution of slavery in the South alone enables her to place in the field a force much larger in proportion to her white population than the North. . . . The institution is a tower of strength to the South, particularly at the present crisis, and our enemies will be likely to find that the "moral cancer" about which their orators are so fond of prating, is really one of the most effective weapons employed against the Union by the South. Whatever number of men may be needed for this war, we are confident our people stand ready to furnish.[3]

Frederick Douglass agreed that slavery was "a tower of strength" to the Confederacy, and he urged the North to convert it into an element of weakness by proclaiming emancipation:
The slaveholders . . . boast that the slave population is a grand element of strength, and that it enables them to send and sustain a stronger body of rebels to overthrow the Government than they could otherwise do if the whites were required to perform the labors of cultivation; and in this they are unquestionably in the right, provided the National Government refuses to turn this mighty element of strength into one of weakness. . . . Why? Oh! why, in the name of all that is national, does our Government allow its enemies this powerful advantage? . . . The very stomach of this rebellion is the negro in the condition of a slave. Arrest that hoe in the hands of the negro, and you smite rebellion in the very seat of its life. . . . The negro is the key of the situation—the pivot upon which the whole rebellion turns. . . . Teach the rebels and traitors that the price they are

to pay for the attempt to abolish this Government must be the abolition of slavery. . . . Henceforth let the war cry be down with treason, and down with slavery, the cause of treason.[4]

William P. Powell, a Negro physician in New York City, maintained that preservation of the Union without the abolition of slavery was impossible. "What will the North do?" asked Powell.

Will the government prosecute this war of subjugation, and bring the rebel States,—slavery and all,—back to their allegiance? Ah! sir, if that is the sole aim of the government of President Lincoln and the federal army, they will be surely and shamefully beaten. This war, disguise it as they may, is virtually nothing more nor less than perpetual slavery against universal freedom, and to this end the free States will have to come. . . .

Never was there a greater opportunity for the American nation to put an everlasting end to negro slavery than now. . . . Without going into detail, I propose that Congress, at its next session, instantly abolish slavery by proclamation, without compensation, in all the rebel States . . . repeal the Fugitive Slave Law—form a new treaty with Great Britain, to effectually break up the African slave-trade—abolish slavery in Maryland and Virginia by compensation, and thereby make the capital free territory, as it should have been at the foundation of the government.[5]

The following petition was written by Dr. James W. C. Pennington, the minister of a Negro Presbyterian church in New York. Pennington had been an illiterate blacksmith when he escaped from slavery in the 1840s, but by 1851 he had achieved such eminence as a preacher and lecturer that he was honored with a degree of Doctor of Divinity from Heidelberg University. Pennington's petition was circulated widely among Negroes in the fall of 1861:

To the Hon. the Senate and House of Representatives of the United States, in Congress assembled:

The undersigned, Free Colored citizens of these United States, believing that African Slavery as it now exists at the South, is

the prime cause of the present Crisis and that permanent peace
cannot be restored until said cause be removed, most respectfully petition your honorable body to take such measures, or
enact such a law as may, in your wisdom seem best for the
immediate abolition of African Slavery.[6]

*On July 21 the North suffered a humiliating setback at the
Battle of Bull Run. Some Negroes discerned a ray of hope in
the defeat. They foresaw that it would compel the Northern people to revise their attitude toward the slavery issue. Frederick
Douglass wrote that the events at Bull Run had*
much changed the tone of Northern sentiment as to the proper
mode of prosecuting the war, in reference to slavery, the cause
of the war. Men now call not only for vengeance and righteous
retribution, but for the destruction of the cause of their great
national disaster. A cry has gone forth for the abolition of slavery. . . . If the defeat at Bull's Run shall have the effect to teach
the Government this high wisdom, and to distinguish between
its friends and its foes at the South, that defeat, terrible as it is,
will not have been entirely disastrous.[7]

*Congress passed the First Confiscation Act, noted in the pre-
vious chapter, on August 6. On August 30 General John C. Fremont, Commander of the Western Department, issued a bold
proclamation instituting martial law in Missouri and freeing
the slaves of every rebel in the state. Much of the North applauded this edict, but Lincoln was afraid that it would "alarm
our Southern Union friends and turn them against us; perhaps
ruin our rather fair prospect for Kentucky." On September 11
the President modified Fremont's proclamation to make it con-
form with the Confiscation Act of August 6, which confiscated
only those slaves who had directly aided the Confederate military forces.[8]*

*Negroes were profoundly depressed by Lincoln's action. One
black man who denounced the President's order was Robert
Hamilton, an experienced Negro journalist who had become
publisher and editor of the* Anglo-African *in August 1861. In
one of his early editorials Hamilton declared that*

the reverse at Bull Run was a slight affair compared with the letter of Abraham Lincoln which hurls back into the hell of slavery the thousands in Missouri rightfully set free by the proclamation of Gen. Fremont, which deprives the cause of the Union of its chiefest hold upon the heart of the public, and which gives to the rebels "aid and comfort" greater than they could have gained from any other earthly source. . . .

The forlorn hope of insurrection among the slaves may as well be abandoned. They are too well informed and too *wise* to court destruction at the hands of the combined Northern and Southern armies—for the man who has reduced back to slavery the slaves of rebels in Missouri would order the army of the United States to put down a slave insurrection in Virginia or Georgia.[9]

By the fall of 1861, many black men despaired of the future, for the reasons expressed by the Rev. J. P. Campbell of Trenton, a high official in the A.M.E. (African Methodist Episcopal) Church:

1st. The President is not now, and never was, either an abolitionist, or an anti-slavery man.

2nd. He has no quarrel whatever with the south, upon the slavery question.

3rd. He, his cabinet, and all of his official organs most steadily proclaim that this is not a war against slavery, but a war for the Union, to save slavery in the Union. . . .

4th. The President believes the Constitution of the United States to be a compromise, or an instrument of compromises between slavery and freedom.

5th. He holds the Dred Scott decision, which says that "Black men have no rights that white men are bound to respect," to be a part and parcel of the organic law of the land, which he is bound faithfully to execute. And for that very reason he would not treat slave property as suggested by General Butler, contraband of war, before the Special Congress took action upon the question. For that reason, after the Congress met and took action, and passed an act by which the slave property of rebels shall become confiscated to the United States, he interfered with the proclamation of General Fremont, when he attempted to carry into effect the intention of the act of Congress upon the slave property of rebels.[10]

But Harriet Tubman, the former slave whose forays into the South before the war to help other slaves escape had made her the "Moses" of her people, expressed a more optimistic view. "God's ahead ob Massa Linkum," she said at the end of 1861.

God won't let Massa Linkum beat de South till he do de right ting. Massa Linkum he great man, and I'se poor nigger; but dis nigger can tell Massa Linkum how to save de money and de young men. He do it by setting de niggers free. S'pose dar was awfu' big snake down dar, on de floor. He bite you. Folks all skeered, cause you die. You send for doctor to cut de bite; but snake he rolled up dar, and while doctor dwine it, he bite you agin. De doctor cut out dat bite; but while he dwine it, de snake he spring up and bite you agin, and so he keep dwine, till you kill him. Dat's what Massa Linkum orter know.[11]

The President began to fulfill Harriet Tubman's hopes in the spring of 1862. On March 6 he sent a message to Congress recommending passage of a joint resolution offering federal compensation to any state "which may adopt gradual abolishment of slavery."[12] Although nothing came of this plan because of border-state opposition, Negroes nevertheless welcomed it as a sign of a major shift in the administration's policy toward slavery. The Anglo-African *stated editorially:*

That the President of these United States sent a message to Congress proposing a means of securing the emancipation of the slaves, was an event which sent a thrill of joy throughout the North, and will meet with hearty response throughout christendom. The quiet manner in which this matter was laid before the national Legislature, and the utter unpreparedness of the public mind for this most important step, was a stroke of policy, grandly reticent on the part of its author, yet most timely and sagacious, which has secured for Abraham Lincoln a confidence and admiration on the part of the people, the whole loyal people, such as no man has enjoyed in the present era.

We could hardly believe the news. We dared not take up the

message for a day or two, satisfied with the simple glory of the announcement, yet fearful that a reading of the document might send some shuddering doubt through a willingly rejoicing spirit. . . . But any doubts, all doubts were removed on the third or fourth reading of the message—for it will bear a close scrutiny—and now, when it is more than a week old it seems better and stronger than ever. It is not only cased in impregnable armor, but gives half silent evidence of power and will to blast the institution of slavery at any moment. . . . It marks the grandest revolution of the ages, a revolution from barbarism to civilization, of darkness to light, of slavery into freedom.[13]

There was a great deal of antislavery activity in Washington in the spring of 1862. Congress passed a new article of war prohibiting army officers from returning fugitive slaves who entered their lines. Congress also enacted legislation prohibiting slavery in all the territories of the United States and providing for the effectual suppression of the African slave trade. Most dramatic of all, however, was the passage in April of an act abolishing slavery in the District of Columbia. Frederick Douglass was delighted. "I trust I am not dreaming," he wrote to Senator Charles Sumner in April, "but the events taking place seem like a dream."[14] A Negro resident of the capital wrote joyfully to a friend in Baltimore on the day after Congressional passage of the bill:

This indeed has been a happy day to me sights have I witnessed that I never anticipated one of which I will relate The Chambermaid at Smith's (my former place) . . . is a slave so this morning I went there to inform her of the passage of the Bill when I entered The cook her and another Slave woman who has a slave son were talking relative to the Bill expressing doubts of its passage & when I entered they perceived that something was ahead and emeadiately [sic] asked me "Whats the news?" The Districts free says I pulling out the "National Republican" and reading its editorial when I had finished the chambermaid had left the room sobbing for joy. The slave woman clapped her hands and shouted, left the house saying "let me go and tell my husband that Jesus has done all things well" While the cook who is free retired to another room to offer thanks for the blessing sent. Should I not feel glad to see so much rejoicing around me? Were I a drinker I would get on a jolly spree today but as a Christian I can but kneel in prayer and bless God for the privilege I've enjoyed this day. . . . Would to God that the Law applied also to Baltimore but a little patience and all will be well.[15]

The Anglo-African *declared editorially:*

It was a fitting celebration of the anniversary of Fort Sumter, that Congress should pass a bill to emancipate the Capital from the thrall of slavery forever. Henceforth, whatever betide the nation, its physical heart is freed from the presence of slavery. . . .

If we rejoice and give thanks to the Almighty for this great boon, we rejoice less as black men than as part and parcel of the American people: for it is clearly a greater boon to the nation at large than to the class more immediately concerned. There will not be set free by this act one tenth as many persons as were liberated by the guns of the Wabash at Port Royal.* . . . But to the nation at large the good wrought by this act is incalculable. . . . The heart once clear, the core once sound, there is no restraining the return of health and vigor and freedom to the whole national body. . . . It is an act of emancipation which frees a hundred thousand white men for every individual black man. . . . The man from Maine or the man from Massachusetts can each go to the Capital, and say aloud that his soul is his own. Members of Congress from the free North can take their seats and vote and speak without first bending their knees to Baal. . . . There will be one place at least in the national territory where slaves cannot breathe and where the old flag floats over freemen only. We can point to our Capital and say to all nations, "IT IS FREE!" Americans abroad can now hold up their heads when interrogated as to what the Federal Government is fighting for, and answer, "There, look at our Capital and see what we have fought for.[16]

But the day of total victory over slavery had not yet arrived.

* See below, p. 57.

On April 25 General David Hunter, commander of the Union forces occupying the islands off the coast of South Carolina, Georgia, and Florida, proclaimed martial law in the "Department of the South," comprising all of these three states. On May 9 he issued a second order stating that "Slavery and martial law in a free country are altogether incompatible" and declaring all slaves in the three states "forever free." But Lincoln feared the effect of such a sweeping edict on the border-state Unionists, and he revoked Hunter's order on May 19.[17]

This action of Lincoln's, coming after the events of the spring had raised antislavery hopes so high, had an even more depressing effect on Negroes than the President's earlier revocation of Fremont's proclamation. The Pacific Appeal, *a Negro newspaper in San Francisco edited by Philip Bell, a veteran champion of equal rights, published an editorial lamenting Lincoln's action:*

We thought from President Lincoln's confiscation messages, his emancipation recommendations and other liberal actions, that it was his intention to strike at the root of the tree of strife. We supposed he was possessed of judgment sufficient to know that it was useless to lop off the extraneous branches, and leave the trunk of the Upas of discord and disunion—slavery—still standing to branch forth again and diffuse its malignant and pestiferous poison over the land. . . . We fear the Administration is pursuing a course detrimental to the best interests of the country, and encouraging the Rebels in their efforts to overthrow the Union, and perpetuate slavery.[18]

And in a Fourth of July speech at Himrod's Corners, New York, Frederick Douglass savagely assailed Lincoln and General George B. McClellan, whom Douglass considered partly responsible for the administration's conservative policy toward slavery:

I feel quite sure that this country will yet come to the conclusion that Geo. B. McClellan is either a cold blooded Traitor, or that he is an unmitigated military Imposter. He has shown no heart in his conduct, except when doing something directly in favor of the rebels, such as guarding their persons and property and offering his services to suppress with an iron hand any attempt on the part of the slaves against their rebel masters.

I come now to the policy of President Lincoln in reference to slavery. . . . I do not hesitate to say, that whatever may have been his intentions, the action of President Lincoln has been calculated in a marked and decided way to shield and protect it from the very blows which its horrible crimes have loudly and persistently invited. . . . He has steadily refused to proclaim, as he had the constitutional and moral right to proclaim, complete emancipation to all the slaves of rebels who should make their way into the lines of our army. He has repeatedly interfered with and arrested the anti-slavery policy of some of his most earnest and reliable generals. . . . It is from such action as this, that we must infer the policy of the Administration. To my mind that policy is simply and solely to reconstruct the union on the old and corrupting basis of compromise, by which slavery shall retain all the power that it ever had, with the full assurance of gaining more, according to its future necessities.[19]

Douglass was attacked by the administration press for his statements about Lincoln, but the Negro orator held his ground and repeated his assertions in an editorial at the end of July:

ABRAHAM LINCOLN is no more fit for the place he holds than was JAMES BUCHANAN, and the latter was no more the miserable tool of traitors and rebels than the former is allowing himself to be. As to McClellan he still leaves us in doubt as to whether he is a military imposter, or a deliberate traitor. The country is destined to become sick of both McClellan and Lincoln, and the sooner the better. . . . The signs of the times indicate that the people will have to take this war into their own hands and dispense with the services of all who by their incompetency give aid and comfort to the destroyers of the country.[20]

In a calmer mood, John Rock declared on August 1:

I have never doubted but that the President was on the side of freedom and humanity, but I confess I do not understand how it is, that when the national life has been assailed, he has not availed himself of all the powers given him; and, more especially, why he has not broken every yoke, and let the oppressed go free. There may be many reasons why he should do as he has done; but I am puzzled to know why he, as a constitutional man and a patriot, has delayed enforcing laws recently enacted for the overthrow of rebellion. We all know that emancipation, if early proclaimed, would not only have saved many precious lives, but the nation itself. Why then delay, when delays are dangerous, and may prove fatal?[21]

From all quarters of the North came increasing pressures for emancipation. On July 17 Congress passed the Second Confiscation Act, declaring all slaves of rebel masters "forever free" as soon as they came into Union lines. But the Confiscation Act lacked the bold, dramatic sweep of a general emancipation proclamation, which many persons in the North were now demanding. The Act freed only one, a dozen, or a hundred slaves at a time, as they came within Union lines, and it left possible loopholes for lengthy litigation. Unknown to the public, Lincoln on July 22 submitted a draft of a general emancipation proclamation to his Cabinet, but was persuaded by Secretary of State William H. Seward to withhold it until Union arms won a victory.[22]

Meanwhile the despair of Northern Negroes increased. Union forces suffered a series of reverses in July and August. Defeatism was slowly creeping over the North. And on September 13 President Lincoln, despite the fact that he had privately decided to issue an emancipation edict when the time was right, publicly told a delegation of clergymen that an emancipation proclamation would be no more effective than the "Pope's bull against the comet."[23] In a letter to his friend Gerrit Smith, Frederick Douglass expressed the frustration of Northern Negroes with the course of events: "I think the nation was never more completely in the hands of the slave power. This government is now in the hands of the Army, and the Army is in the hands of the very worst type of American Democracy."[24]

But this mood of despondency was suddenly transformed into a chorus of elation by Lincoln's unexpected issuance of a preliminary Emancipation Proclamation on September 22. On September 17 the Union Army had finally won a victory at the

Battle of Antietam, and seizing upon the occasion, the President issued his Proclamation five days later. It was essentially a conservative document, but it contained a revolutionary promise. On January 1, 1863, all slaves in the rebellious states would be declared "forever free."[25]

Frederick Douglass was almost overcome by the Proclamation. "We shout for joy that we live to record this righteous decree," he wrote.

Border State influence, and the influence of half-loyal men, have been exerted and have done their worst. The end of these two influences is implied in this proclamation. . . . "Free forever" oh! long enslaved millions, whose cries have so vexed the air and sky, suffer on a few more days in sorrow, the hour of your deliverance draws nigh! Oh! Ye millions of free and loyal men who have earnestly sought to free your bleeding country from the dreadful ravages of revolution and anarchy, lift up now your voices with joy and thanksgiving for with freedom to the slave will come peace and safety to your country.[26]

Throughout the North, Negroes held meetings on January 1, 1863, to commemorate and celebrate the issuance of the final Emancipation Proclamation. One such meeting was held in the Israel Bethel Church (A.M.E.) in Washington. The pastor of the church was Henry M. Turner, a freeborn Negro who had migrated from his native South Carolina to Baltimore and finally to Washington, where he became a leader of the Negro community and a staunch fighter for racial justice in the capital. After the war Turner moved to Georgia, where he played a prominent part in Reconstruction politics, serving with distinction in the constitutional convention of 1867-68 and in the state legislature. He subsequently returned to the North and accepted an appointment as a bishop in the A.M.E. Church. In 1913, on the fiftieth anniversary of the Emancipation Proclamation, Turner recalled the events of January 1, 1863:

Seeing such a multitude of people in and around my church, I hurriedly went up to the office of the first paper in which the proclamation of freedom could be printed, known as the "Evening Star," and squeezed myself through the dense crowd that

was waiting for the paper. The first sheet run off with the proclamation in it was grabbed for by three of us, but some active
young man got possession of it and fled. The next sheet was
grabbed for by several, and was torn into tatters. The third sheet
from the press was grabbed for by several, but I succeeded in
procuring so much of it as contained the proclamation, and off
I went for life and death. Down Pennsylvania I ran as for my
life, and when the people saw me coming with the paper in my
hand they raised a shouting cheer that was almost deafening.
As many as could get around me lifted me to a great platform,
and I started to read the proclamation. I had run the best end
of a mile, I was out of breath, and could not read. Mr. Hinton,
to whom I handed the paper, read it with great force and clear-
ness. While he was reading every kind of demonstration and
gesticulation was going on. Men squealed, women fainted, dogs
barked, white and colored people shook hands, songs were sung,
and by this time cannons began to fire at the navy-yard, and
follow in the wake of the roar that had for some time been going
on behind the White House. . . . Great processions of colored
and white men marched to and fro and passed in front of the
White House and congratulated President Lincoln on his proclamation. The President came to the window and made responsive bows, and thousands told him, if he would come out of that
palace, they would hug him to death. Mr. Lincoln, however,
kept at a safe distance from the multitude, who were frenzied
to distraction over his proclamation. . . . It was indeed a time
of times, and a half time, nothing like it will ever be seen again
in this life.[27]

*In a letter dated January 4, 1863, Turner wrote the following
appraisal of the Proclamation:*

The time has come in the history of this nation, when the
downtrodden and abject black man can assert his rights, and
feel his manhood. . . . The proclamation of President Lincoln
reaches the most forlorn condition, in which our people are
placed. . . . The first day of January, 1863, is destined to form
one of the most memorable epochs in the history of the
world. . . . The seeds of freedom which are ever rejuvenescent

in themselves, have now been scattered where despotism and tyranny ranked and ruled, will be watered by the enlivening dews of God's clemency, till the reapers (abolitionists) shall shout the harvest home.[28]

Some Negroes noted that the Proclamation applied only to the Confederate states, and of these, Tennessee and parts of Louisiana and Virginia were exempted "for the present." All four of the loyal slave states (Kentucky, Missouri, Maryland, and Delaware) were exempted. But in spite of these shortcomings, Negroes were generally happy with the Proclamation. The Christian Recorder *praised Lincoln's action. The* Recorder *was a weekly newspaper edited in Philadelphia by the Rev. Elisha Weaver. Serving as the official organ of the A.M.E. Church and as a spokesman for Philadelphia Negroes, the* Recorder *circulated mainly among black Methodists in Pennsylvania, New Jersey, and New York. In an editorial entitled "The President's Proclamation," the* Recorder *stated:*

It will be seen that the President only makes provision for the emancipation of a *part* of an injured race, and that the Border States and certain parts of the rebel States are excepted from the relief offered to others by this most important document. We believe those who are not immediately liberated will be ultimately benefited by this act, and that Congress will do something for those poor souls who will still remain in degradation. But we thank God and President Lincoln for what has been done, "and take courage."[29]

A meeting of Negroes in Harrisburg, Pennsylvania, adopted the following resolutions:

Resolved, That we, the colored citizens of the city of Harrisburg, hail the 1st day of January, 1863, as a new era in our country's history—a day in which injustice and oppression were forced to flee and cower before the benign principles of justice and righteousness. . . .

Resolved, That if our wishes had been consulted we would have preferred that the proclamation should have been general instead of partial; but we can only say to our brethren of the "Border States," be of good cheer—the day of your deliverance draweth nigh—do not act contrary to the rules of propriety and good citizenship, for the rod of your oppressors will eventually be smitten by the omnipotence of truth—the "ark" of liberty will yet dwell within your borders and rest within your gates— the fires of freedom shall light your hill tops, and your valleys shall be made vocal with the songs of liberty. . . .

Resolved, That we are well aware that freedom and citizenship are attended with responsibilities; and that the success or failure of the proclamation depend entirely upon ourselves, as public sentiment will be influenced for or against that righteous decree, by our correct deportment and moral standing in this community.

Resolved, That although the proclamation was not made as an act of philanthropy, or as a great deed of justice due to those suffering in bonds, but simply as a war measure, still in it we recognize the hand of God; and for it we are constrained to say, roll forward the day when the American soil shall no more be polluted with that crime against God, American slavery; but all will be able to say, "Glory to God in the highest, on earth peace and good will to man."[30]

The subsequent course of the war insured the complete triumph of emancipation. On January 31, 1865, Congress adopted the Thirteenth Amendment abolishing slavery throughout the United States, and sent the Amendment to the states, where it was assured of ratification. On February 4 a mass meeting of Negroes and whites was held in Boston's Music Hall to celebrate the passage of the Amendment. Several speakers entertained and inspired the crowd, and the evening was concluded with the singing of "Sound the Loud Timbrel" by the Rev. Mr. Rue, pastor of the black Methodist church in Boston. On the second chorus a few members of the audience seated near the platform sang along with Mr. Rue, and in each succeeding chorus more and more of the huge throng joined in, swelling the refrain to triumphant heights of joyfulness. William Lloyd Garrison, Jr., described the scene in a letter to his wife:

It was a scene to be remembered—the earnestness of the singer, pouring out his heartfelt praise, the sympathy of the audience, catching the glow & the deep-toned organ blending the thousand voices in harmony. Nothing during the evening brought to my mind so clearly the magnitude of the act we celebrated, its deeply religious as well as moral significance than "Sound the loud timbrel o'er Egypt's dark sea, Jehovah has triumphed, His people are free."[31]

CHAPTER IV

EMANCIPATION IN THE SOUTH

1861–65

His people are free"! How did the slaves accept their freedom? Were they merely passive, insensate recipients of the boon of emancipation? Or did they comprehend the meaning of the war and take active steps to insure their freedom? There is no doubt that many, perhaps most, of the slaves had little realization of the great revolution going on around them during the Civil War. But on the other hand, hundreds of thousands of slaves had a distinct awareness of the course of the war and its meaning for their future. This chapter will examine the highlights of emancipation in the South as it affected those slaves who have left some record of their actions or feelings.

Northern and foreign observers in the South during the war punctured the myth of the contented, happy slave. William Howard Russell, correspondent of the London Times, a paper hostile to abolitionism and favorable to the South, traveled through the Confederate states in the early months of the war. He visited many plantations, and wrote from a large estate in Louisiana on June 2, 1861:

It struck me more and more . . . as I examined the expression on the faces of the slaves, that deep dejection is the prevailing, if not universal, characteristic of the race. Here there were abundant evidences that they were well treated; they had good clothing of its kind, food, and a master who wittingly could do them no injustice, as he is, I am sure, incapable of it. Still, they all looked sad, and even the old woman who boasted that she had held her old owner in her arms when he was an infant, did not smile cheerfully, as the nurse at home would have done at the sight of her ancient charge.[1]

George H. Hepworth, Chaplain of the Forty-seventh Massachusetts Regiment and Labor Superintendent of the Department of the Gulf, wrote from Louisiana in 1863 that
the slaves of the South are not a happy people. No one can travel from plantation to plantation, from county to county, as I have done, without being strangely impressed with the universal gloom of the negro character. You may talk of the light-hearted, merry slave as much as you will: it is all rhetoric, and has no foundation whatever in fact. They are a sombre race—a race who show that every effort has been made to crush them,—a race whose hearts have a chain and ball on them. Planters delight to tell you of the Saturday-afternoon dances, of the frolics when the day's work is over, and of the general hilarity which is noticed on a plantation. I have lived on plantations a week at a time; I have watched slaves under nearly all circumstances,—on the Saturday afternoon, in the evening, and at their balls; but I have been everywhere convinced that an unnatural gloom overspreads the negro's life. It is very seldom that you hear a good round laugh from a black man. He is timid and fearful, and seems like one walking in a dangerous place in the dark. But say, "Uncle, would you like to be free?" and notice the twinkle in his eye as he looks at you searchingly, and, after concluding that you are his friend, says, with an ominous shake of the head, "Yes master: all of us would *like* to be free; but we don't see the way yet."[2]

One of the estimated 500,000 slaves who escaped or came within Union lines during the war[3] was Susie King Taylor of Savannah, Georgia, who had been born a slave in 1848. In April 1862 she escaped with her uncle from Savannah to the Union lines at Fort Pulaski. Miss King (she later married a Negro soldier named Taylor) had secretly learned to read

and write while a slave, and during the remainder of the
war she served as a teacher of the freedmen and a laundress
at the Union encampments on the South Carolina Sea Is-
lands. Mrs. Taylor later recalled that in the early months of
the war she

had been reading so much about the "Yankees" I was very anxious to see them. The whites would tell their colored people not
to go to the Yankees, for they would harness them to carts and
make them pull the carts around, in place of horses. I asked
grandmother, one day, if this was true. She replied, "Certainly
not!" that the white people did not want slaves to go over to
the Yankees, and told them these things to frighten them. . . . I
wanted to see these wonderful "Yankees" so much, as I heard
my parents say the Yankee was going to set all the slaves free.
Oh, how those people prayed for freedom! I remember, one
night, my grandmother went out into the suburbs of the city to
a church meeting, and they were fervently singing this old
hymn,—

> "Yes, we all shall be free,
> Yes, we all shall be free,
> Yes, we all shall be free,
> When the Lord shall appear,"—

when the police came in and arrested all who were there, saying
they were planning freedom, and sang "the Lord," in place of
"Yankee," to blind any one who might be listening.[4]

In November 1861 a Union fleet and Northern soldiers cap-
tured and occupied Port Royal Island and the adjacent South
Carolina Sea Islands fifty miles southwest of Charleston. Most
of the white people on the islands fled to the mainland, leaving
behind scores of fertile long-staple cotton plantations and more
than eight thousand slaves. Northern philanthropists soon re-
cruited scores of missionaries, teachers, and plantation super-
intendents to go to the islands and help the Negroes in their
transition from slavery to freedom. One of these plantation su-

perintendents, Edward S. Philbrick, wrote of the Port Royal
freedmen in 1862:

I am surprised to find how little most of these people appreciate their present prospects. Once in a while you find an
intelligent man who does so, but the mass plod along in the
beaten track with little thought about the future and no sort
of feeling of responsibility. They feel a sense of relief that no
one stands to force them to labor, and they fall back with a
feeling of indifference as to whether they exert themselves
beyond what is necessary to supply the demands of necessity.[5]

But such descriptions of the Negroes' apathy toward freedom
were rare in the writings of Northerners who came to Port
Royal. Most of them testified to the slaves' eagerness for freedom
and their desire to make the best of their new opportunities.
Miss Charlotte Forten, a Northern Negro who came as a teacher
to Port Royal in 1862, had many conversations with the freedmen on the plantation where she taught, and they never tired
of telling her how "Massa" ran away when the Yankees came.
Harry, the foreman, told how "Massa" had tried to convince his
slaves to come with him. Miss Forten asked Harry why they did
not go. "Oh, Miss," he replied, "it wasn't 'cause Massa didn't
try to 'suade we. He tell we dat de Yankees would shoot we, or
would sell we to Cuba, an' do all de wust tings to we, when dey
come. 'Bery well, Sar,' says I. 'If I go wid you, I be good as dead.
If I stay here, I can't be no wust; so if I got to dead, I might's
well dead here as anywhere. So I'll stay here an' wait for de
"dam Yankees." ' Lor', Miss, I knowed he wasn't tellin' de truth
all de time.'"[6]

Harriet Tubman also came to the Sea Islands, where she
served as a nurse and scout for the Union forces. She recounted
the following story which had been told to her by one of the aged
slaves on the islands: he said

I'd been yere seventy-three years, workin' for my master widout even a dime wages. I'd worked rain-wet sun dry. I'd worked
wid my mouf full of dust, but would not stop to get a drink of

water. I'd been whipped, an' starved, an' I was always prayin',
"Oh! Lord, come an' delibber us!" All dat time de birds had
been flyin', and de rabens had been cryin', and de fish had been
sunnin' in de waters. One day I look up, an' I see a big cloud; it
didn't come up like as de clouds come out far yonder, but it
'peared to be right ober head. Der was tunders out of day, an'
der was lightnin's. Den I looked down on de water, an' I see,
'peared to me a big house in de water, an' out of de big house
came great big eggs, and de good eggs went on trou' de air, an'
fell into de fort; an' de bad eggs burst before dey got dar. . . .
Den I heard 'twas the Yankee ship [the *Wabash*] firin' out de
big eggs, and dey had come to set us free. Den I praise de Lord.
He come an' put he little finger in de work, an' dey Sesh Buckra
all go; and de birds stop flyin', and de rabens stop cryin', an'
when I go to catch a fish to eat wid my rice, de's no fish dar.
De Lord Almighty'd come and frightened 'em all out of de waters. Oh! Praise de Lord! I'd prayed seventy-three years, an'
now he's come an' we's all free.[7]

*One of the Port Royal planters, a Mr. Cuthbert, was captured
by the Federal forces, and while he was being rowed as a prisoner to a Union ship by his own slaves, the oarsmen burst into
a song, making up the verses as they went along:*

> De Norfmen dey's got massa now,
> De Norfmen dey's got massa now,
> De Norfmen dey's got massa now,
> Hallelujah.
>
> Oh! massa a rebel; we row him to prison.
> Hallelujah.
> Massa no whip us any more.
> Hallelujah.
> We have no massa now, we free.
> Hallelujah.
> We have de Yankees, who no run away.
> Hallelujah.
> Oh! all our old massas run away.
> Hallelujah.

Oh! massa going to prison now.
Hallelujah.[8]

Slaves began coming into Union lines in Virginia in the first month of the war, and they did not stop coming until the surrender at Appomattox four years later. The following report was written by T. Morris Chester, the only Negro war correspondent who wrote for a major Northern newspaper during the Civil War. Thirty years old in 1864 and a native of Pennsylvania, Chester had come to the attention of the managing editor of the Philadelphia Press *through his excellent report of the proceedings of the A.M.E. General Conference in 1864. In August of that year Chester was assigned to the Army of the James in Virginia, where he remained as the official* Press *correspondent for the rest of the war. Chester wrote the following account in the winter of 1864–65, but it could have been written at any period of the war:*

The underground railroad, from Richmond, seems to be thoroughly repaired, and is not only in running condition, but is doing an increasing business. . . . For some time past we have had an arrival from Richmond every day, and not unfrequently two or three times in the twenty-four hours. Notwithstanding this road is considered contraband by the rebel authorities, its officers thus far have been able to baffle the vigilance of their detectives, and fulfill the obligations which they have made to the public. Men, women, and children, of all colors, with their household effects, are daily coming into our lines and report at this place. . . . It is hardly necessary to inform our Southern brethren that what they consider as chattels, but what we regard as men, may be found industriously engaged about the quartermaster's department, or under the inspiration of martial air keeping step to the music of the Union.[9]

Not only on the Sea Islands and in Virginia, but in every part of the South penetrated by the Union armies, fugitive slaves flocked to the Federal lines and to freedom. On July 17, 1862,

*the Confederate Provost Marshal of Adams County, Mississippi,
wrote to the governor of the state: "There is a great disposition
among the Negroes to be insubordinate, and to run away and
go to the federals. Within the last 12 months we have had to
hang some 40 for plotting an insurrection, and there has been
about that number put in irons."[10] In October 1862, Federal
troops invaded the Lafourche district of south Louisiana. "What
shall I do about the negroes?" wrote General Godrey Weitzel to
Union Army headquarters on October 29.*

You can form no idea of the vicinity of my camp, nor can you
form an idea of the appearance of my brigade as it marched
down the bayou. My train was larger than an army train for
25,000 men. Every soldier had a negro marching in the flanks,
carrying his knapsack. Plantation carts, filled with negro women
and children, with their effects; and of course compelled to pil-
lage for their subsistence, as I have no rations to issue to them.
I have a great many more negroes in my camp now than I have
whites.[11]

*Confederate General Joseph Finegan wrote in the spring of
1863 that there was a communications network between Negroes
within Union lines in east Florida and the slaves behind Confederate lines. Many slaves escaped, because messages were
"conducted through swamps and under cover of the night, and
could not be prevented. A few weeks would suffice to corrupt the
entire slave population of East Florida." After a Union raid
along the Combahee River in South Carolina, Confederate General W. S. Walker wrote that "the enemy burned four fine res-
idences, and six mills, and took off with them about 700 negroes,
who are believed to have gone with great alacrity and to some
extent with pre-conceived arrangement."[12]*

*Many Southern Negroes learned of the Emancipation Proc-
lamation through the slave grapevine. Some literate slaves read
about the Proclamation in Southern newspapers. In Louisiana,
the newspaper L'Union, a bilingual journal (French and English) started by the free Negroes of New Orleans in September*

1862, spread the news of the Proclamation and urged all black men in Lousiana to make the best of their new opportunities in freedom:

Brothers! The hour strikes for us; a new sun, similar to that of 1789, should surely appear on our horizon. May the cry which resounded through France at the seizure of the Bastille resonate today in our ears. . . .

Compatriots! The epoch in which we live exhorts us in a loud voice to unite all our efforts for the cause of liberty and justice. Let us all be imbued with these noble sentiments which characterize all civilized people. . . . Let us be resolute. Let us rise up in all majesty and with the charity befitting Christians, let us preach by example to all men, so that they will follow the road which leads to liberty. . . .

Compatriots! May this new era fortify us, and be for us a rampart against persecution; and in sweet accord with our brothers, let us fill the air with these joyous cries: "vive la liberté! vive l'union! vive la justice pour tous les hommes!" . . .

Men of my blood! Shake off the contempt of your proud oppressors. Enough of shame and submission; the break is complete! Down with the craven behavior of bondage! Stand up under the noble flag of the Union and declare yourselves hardy champions of the right. Defend your rights against the barbarous and imbecile spirit of slavery; prove to the entire world that you have a heart noble enough to walk with civilization and to understand its benefits, and a spirit high enough to know and admire the imposing work of the Creator. . . . Fellow workers, plow in the vast field of the future the furrow of *Fraternité*; plant there firmly the tree of *Liberté*, whose fruits, collected by future generations, will be shared with the most perfect *Egalité* by the children of the same God.[13]

Many freedmen flocked to Washington during the war. On the evening of December 31, 1862, a meeting was held in one of the contraband camps to celebrate the issuance of the final Emancipation Proclamation. George Payne, a former slave from Virginia, addressed his fellow freedmen:

Friends, don't you see de han' of God in dis? Haven't we a

right to rejoice? You all know you couldn't have such a meetin'
as dis down in Dixie! Dat you all knows. I have a right to rejoice;
an' so have you; for we shall be free in jus' about five minutes.
Dat's a fact. I shall rejoice that God has placed Mr. Lincum in
de president's chair, and dat he wouldn't let de rebels make
peace until after dis new year. De Lord has heard de groans of
de people, and has come down to deliver! You all knows dat in
Dixie you worked de day long, an' never got no satisfacshun.
But here, what you make is yourn. I've worked six months; and
what I've made is mine! Let me tell you, though, don't be too
free! De lazy man can't go to heaven. You must be honest, an'
work, an' show dat you is fit to be free; an' de Lord will bless
you an' Abrum Lincum. Amen![14]

Another ex-slave told his brethren:

Onst the time was, dat I cried all night. What's de matter?
What's de matter? Matter enough. De nex mornin my child was
to be sold, an she was sold, and I neber spec to see her no more
till de day ob judgment. Now, no more dat! no more dat! no
more dat! Wid my hands agin my breast I was gwine to my work,
when de overseer used to whip me along. Now, no more dat! no
more dat! no more dat! When I think what de Lord's done for
us, an brot us thro' de trubbles, I feel dat I ought go inter His
service. We'se free now, bress de Lord! (Amens! were vocifer-
ated all over the building.) Dey can't sell my wife and child any
more, bress de Lord! (Glory! glory! from the audience.) No more
dat! no more dat! no more dat, now! (Glory!) Preserdun Lincum
have shot de gate![15]

*On the South Carolina Sea Islands the freedmen and their
Northern teachers also held a celebration on January 1, 1863.
Charlotte Forten wrote the following account:*

New-Year's-Day—Emancipation-Day—was a glorious one to
us. The morning was quite cold, the coldest we had experienced;
but we were determined to go to the celebration at Camp Saxton
. . . on this, "the greatest day in the nation's history." We enjoyed perfectly the exciting scene on board the Flora. There was
an eager, wondering crowd of the freed people in their holiday-
attire, with the gayest of head-hankerchiefs, the whitest of

aprons, and the happiest of faces. The band was playing, the flags streaming, everybody talking merrily and feeling strangely happy. . . . Long before we reached Camp Saxton we could see the beautiful grove, and the ruins of the old Huguenot fort near it. Some companies of the First Regiment* were drawn up in line under the trees, near the landing, to receive us. A fine, soldierly-looking set of men; their brilliant dress against the trees (they were then wearing red pantaloons) invested them with a semi-barbaric splendor. . . .

The celebration took place in the beautiful grove of live-oaks adjoining the camp. . . . I wish it were possible to describe fitly the scene which met our eyes as we sat upon the stand, and looked down on the crowd before us. There were the black soldiers in their blue coats and scarlet pantaloons, the officers of this and other regiments in their handsome uniforms, and crowds of lookers-on,—men, women, and children, of every complexion, grouped in various attitudes under the moss-hung trees. The faces of all wore a happy, interested look. The exercises commenced with a prayer by the chaplain of the regiment. . . . Colonel Higginson then introduced Dr. Brisbane, who read the President's Proclamation, which was enthusiastically cheered. Rev. Mr. French presented to the Colonel two very elegant flags, a gift to the regiment from the Church of the Puritans, accompanying them by an appropriate and enthusiastic speech. At its conclusion, before Colonel Higginson could reply, and while he still stood holding the flags in his hand, some of the colored people, of their own accord, commenced singing, "My Country, 'tis of thee." It was a touching and beautiful incident, and sent a thrill through all our hearts. The Colonel was deeply moved by it. He said that that reply was far more effective than any speech he could make.

After the meeting we saw the dress-parade, a brilliant and beautiful sight. An officer told us that the men went through

*The "First South Carolina Volunteers," a regiment of ex-slaves raised on the Sea Islands in the fall of 1862. It was commanded by Colonel Thomas Wentworth Higginson. See below, Chapter XI.

the drill remarkably well,—that the ease and rapidity with which
they learned the movements were wonderful. To us it seemed
strange as a miracle,—this black regiment, the first mustered
into the service of the United States, doing itself honor in the
sight of the officers of other regiments, many of whom, doubtless, "came to scoff." The men afterwards had a great feast,
ten oxen having been roasted whole for their especial benefit. . . .

It was the softest, loveliest moonlight; we seated ourselves
on the ruined wall of the old fort; and when the boat had got a
short distance from the shore the band in it commenced playing
"Sweet Home." The moonlight on the water, the perfect stillness around, the wildness and solitude of the ruins, all seemed
to give new pathos to that ever dear and beautiful old song. It
came very near to all of us,—strangers in that strange Southern
land. . . . Very unwilling were we to go home; for, besides the
attractive society, we knew that the soldiers were to have grand
shouts and a general jubilee that night. But the Flora was coming, and we were obliged to say a reluctant farewell to Camp
Saxton and the hospitable dwellers therein, and hasten to the
landing. We promenaded the deck of the steamer, sang patriotic
songs, and agreed that moonlight and water had never looked
so beautiful as on that night. At Beaufort we took the row-boat
for St. Helena; and the boatmen, as they rowed, sang some of
their sweetest, wildest hymns. It was a fitting close to such a
day. Our hearts were filled with an exceeding great gladness;
for, although the Government had left much undone, we knew
that Freedom was surely born in our land that day.[16]

*Negroes continued to pour into Union lines in growing num-
bers after the Proclamation. In September 1863, the venerable
industrialist and philanthropist Peter Cooper wrote:*

I learn direct from Mr. Dean, the provost-marshal of St. Louis,
that the Proclamation of Freedom has done more to weaken the
rebellion . . . than any other measure that could have been
adopted. On his late visit to my house he informed me that he
had brought on a large number of rebel officers and men to be
exchanged at Fortress Monroe. During their passage he took the

opportunity to ask the officers in a body what effect the President's Proclamation of Freedom had produced in the South. Their reply was . . . that "it had played hell with them." Mr. Dean then asked them how that could be possible, since the negroes cannot read. To which one of them replied that one of his negroes had told him of the proclamation five days before he heard it in any other way. Others said their negroes gave them their first information of the proclamation.[17]

The choice between remaining in slavery and escaping to freedom was not an easy one for some Negroes. The following story was told by an ex-slave who during the war had lived on a plantation near Dardanelle, Arkansas:

Them folks [Yankee soldiers] stood round there all day. Killed hogs and cooked them. Killed cows and cooked them. Took all kinds of sugar and preserves and things like that. Tore all the feathers out of the mattress looking for money. Then they put Old Miss and her daughter in the kitchen to cooking.

Ma got scared and went to bed. Directly the lieutenant come on down there and said, "Auntie, get up from there. We ain't a-going to do you no hurt. We're after helping you. We are freeing you. Aunt Dinah, you can do as you please now. You're free."

She was free!

They stayed round there all night cooking and eating and carrying on. They sent some of the meat in there to us colored folks.

Next morning they all dropped off going to take Dardanelle. You could hear the cannons roaring next day. They was all night getting away. They went on and took Dardanelle. Had all them white folks running and hiding.

The Secesh wouldn't go far. They would just hide. One night there'd be a gang of Secesh, and the next one, there'd come along a gang of Yankees. Pa was 'fraid of both of 'em. Secesh said they'd kill him if he left his white folks. Yankees said they'd kill him if he didn't leave 'em. He would hide out in the cotton patch and keep we children out there with him.[18]

But most slaves were happy to see the Yankee soldiers. Thou-

*sands of Negroes left their homes and joined Sherman's army
on its march from Atlanta to the sea. General Sherman wrote
in his memoirs:*

The next day [November 17, 1864, one day out of Atlanta on
his march to the sea] we passed through the handsome town of
Covington, the soldiers closing up their ranks, the color-bearers
unfurling their flags, and the bands striking up patriotic airs.
The white people came out of their houses to behold the sight,
spite of their deep hatred of the invaders, and the negroes were
simply frantic with joy. Whenever they heard my name, they
clustered about my horse, shouted and prayed in their peculiar
style, which had a natural eloquence that would have moved a
stone. I have witnessed hundreds, if not thousands, of such
scenes; and can now see a poor girl, in the very ecstasy of the
Methodist "shout," hugging the banner of one of the regiments,
and jumping up to the "feet of Jesus."[19]

*One of the climactic events of the war was the fall of Rich-
mond and President Lincoln's visit to the city on April 4, 1865.
T. Morris Chester, Negro correspondent of the Philadelphia
Press, entered Richmond soon after its evacuation by the Confederates, and wrote the following dispatches to his paper:*

Nothing can exceed the rejoicings of the negroes since the
occupation of this city. They declare that they cannot realize
the change; though they have long prayed for it, yet it seems
impossible that it has come. Old men and women weep and shout
for joy, and praise God for their deliverance through means of
the Union army. . . .

The great event after the capture of the city was the arrival
of President Lincoln in it. . . . There is no describing the scene
along the route. The colored population was wild with enthusiasm. Old men thanked God in a very boisterous manner, and old
women shouted upon the pavement as high as they had ever
done at a religious revival. . . .

Everyone declares that Richmond never before presented
such a spectacle of jubilee. It must be confessed that those who
participated in the informal reception of the President were
mainly negroes. There were many whites in the crowd, but they

were lost in the great concourse of American citizens of African descent. . . .

I visited yesterday several of the slave jails, where men, women, and children were confined, or herded, for the examination of purchasers. The jailers were in all cases slaves, and had been left in undisputed possession of the buildings. The owners, as soon as they were aware that we were coming, opened wide the doors and told the confined inmates they were free. The poor souls could not realize it until they saw the Union army. Even then they thought it must be a pleasant dream, but when they saw Abraham Lincoln they were satisfied that their freedom was perpetual. One enthusiastic old negro woman exclaimed: "I know that I am free, for I have seen Father Abraham and felt him."

When the President returned to the flag-ship of Admiral Porter, in the evening, he was taken from the wharf in a cutter. Just as he pushed off, amid the cheering of the crowd, another good old colored female shouted out, "Don't drown Massa Abe, for God's sake!" . . .

The highest degree of happiness attainable upon earth is now being enjoyed by the colored people of this city. They all declare that they are abundantly able to take care of themselves. Nothing can be more amusing than the efforts of some of the most violent rebels, who in other days never let an opportunity pass to show their love for Jeff Davis, or manifest their vindictive feelings against the negroes in every conceivable manner, to cultivate the friendship of the colored people, with the hope that the forgiving nature of the race may induce them to forget the wrongs of the past. . . . What a wonderful change has come over the spirit of Southern dreams.[20]

CHAPTER V

ANTI-NEGRO MOB VIOLENCE

IN THE NORTH, 1862–63

*W*hatever the change in the *spirit of Southern dreams may have been, the Negro had to overcome a great deal of hostility in the North before he could begin to exploit the potential opportunities for his race opened up by the Civil War. In an editorial on March 29, 1862, the* Anglo-African *declared that a "strong impediment" to Negro advancement was "the prejudice of the North."*

We may as well look this prejudice in the face as a disturbing element in the way of emancipation. Its manifest expression is, that setting black men free to be the equals of white men in the slave States is something more dreadful than rebellion or secession, or even a dismembered union. . . . The other form in which this prejudice is pronounced, is, in the fear expressed that the retaining of colored free laborers in the South will interfere with the domain of white laborers. . . . Poor, chicken-hearted, semi-barbarous Caucasians, when will you learn that "the earth was made for MAN"? You have arts and arms, and culture, and an overwhelming majority in numbers. . . . Must you die and give no sign that you have been able to surmount the prejudice of race, or your dread of the Negro?

The Anglo-African *had good reasons for its apprehensions, for the anti-Negro feeling in the North boiled over into several serious race riots in 1862–63. These riots were sparked by job competition between white and Negro laborers, by the white*

*workingman's fear that emancipation would loose a flood of
Negroes upon the labor market and drive down wages, and by
the inflammatory statements of the Democratic press and
Democratic politicians. In southern Illinois, Indiana, Ohio,
and Pennsylvania, a small influx of freedmen from the South
seeking employment lent reality to white fears of Negro competition. In other areas where violence occurred during the
war, there was a long tradition of racial friction—this was
especially true in New York City, Brooklyn, Philadelphia, and
Buffalo.[1]*

*Lorillard and Watson's tobacco factory in Brooklyn em-
ployed twenty-five black people, most of them women and children. In August 1862, a mob of Irish workers forced their way
into the factory and set it afire, hoping to burn down the building with the Negroes in it. Fortunately the police arrived in
time to extinguish the flames and rescue the employees, but the
murderous mood of the mob betokened ill for the future. The*
Anglo-African *published the following editorial concerning
the Brooklyn incident:*

Irishmen! the day will come that you will find out that you
are making a sad mistake in assisting to crush out our liberties.
Learn! O learn, that the protection of the feeblest of your fellow
beings, is the only guarantee you have of the protection for your
own liberty in this or any other land. We call upon the world to
bear witness to the dreadful effects which the system of slavery
has had upon the Irish people. In their own country they are
kind and hospitable to our poor and constantly abused race; but
here, so dreadfully corrupted do some of them become that they
are prepared for the vilest deed of diabolism which it is possible
for the brain of man to conceive, as is witnessed in their attempt
to roast alive a number of people who never did them the least
harm. Americans! we charge you before high Heaven and the
whole civilized world with being the authors of this great wickedness. It was you who first taught them to hate us. . . . Why,
our countrymen, will you not put away this great wickedness
from among you?[2]

*On March 6, 1863, a mob of white men marched into the Ne-
gro section of Detroit, destroyed thirty-two houses, killed several
Negroes, and left more than two hundred people homeless. The*
Christian Recorder, *official organ of the* A.M.E. *Church, declared in an editorial:*

We have to chronicle one of the most disgraceful, inhuman,
and heathen-like riots, ever recorded upon the pages of history.
It occurred in the city of Detroit, Mich. . . . What have the coloured people done that they should be thus treated? Even here,
in the city of Philadelphia, in many places it is almost impossible
for a respectable colored person to walk the streets without being insulted by a set of blackguards and cowards; and the very
lowest and most vulgar language that ever any human being
uttered, is addressed to our wives and daughters. How long shall
this state of things continue? For we solemnly declare that there
is not a more true and loyal people to the Union than the colored
people, and we hope that our city papers will come down on
such conduct.[3]

*On July 13, 1863, New York's lower-class white population
erupted into four of the bloodiest days of mob violence ever witnessed by the metropolis. The immediate object of the mob's
wrath was the draft enrollment office, but the city's helpless
Negro population bore the brunt of the violence. Dozens of Negroes were lynched in the streets or murdered in their homes.
The Colored Orphan Asylum was burned to the ground. Four
years later a Negro author published the following account
of the riots:*

The mob was composed of the lowest and most degraded of
the foreign population (mainly Irish), raked from the filthy cellars and dens of the city, steeped in crimes of the deepest dye,
and ready for any act, no matter how dark and damnable; together with the worst type of our native criminals. . . . Breaking
into stores, hotels, and saloons, and helping themselves to strong
drink, *ad libitum*, they became inebriated, and marched through
every part of the city. Calling at places where large bodies of
men were at work, and pressing them in, their numbers rapidly
increased to thousands, and their fiendish depredations had no

bounds. Having been taught by the leaders of the Democratic party to hate the negro, and having but a few weeks previous seen regiments of colored volunteers pass through New York on their way south, this infuriated band of drunken men, women, and children paid special visits to all localities inhabited by the blacks, and murdered all they could lay their hands on, without regard to age or sex. Every place known to employ negroes was searched: steamboats leaving the city, and railroad depots, were watched, lest some should escape their vengeance.

Hundreds of the blacks, driven from their homes, and hunted and chased through the streets, presented themselves at the doors of jails, prisons, and police-stations, and begged admission. . . .

Blacks were chased to the docks, thrown into the river and drowned; while some, after being murdered, were hung to lamp-posts. Between forty and fifty colored persons were killed [probably an exaggerated estimate], and nearly as many maimed for life.[4]

The Brooklyn correspondent of the Christian Recorder *wrote shortly after the riots that*
many men were killed and thrown into the rivers, a great number hung to trees and lamp-posts, numbers shot down; no black person could show their [sic] heads but what they were hunted like wolves. These scenes continued for four days. Hundreds of our people are in station houses, in the woods, and on Black-well's island. Over three thousand are to-day homeless and destitute, without means of support for their families. It is truly a day of distress to our race in this section. In Brooklyn we have not had any great trouble, but many of our people have been compelled to leave their houses and flee for refuge. The Irish have become so brutish, that it is unsafe for families to live near them, and while I write, there are many now in the stations and country hiding from violence. . . .

In Weeksville and Flatbush, the colored men who had manhood in them armed themselves, and threw out their pickets every day and night, determined to die defending their homes. Hundreds fled there from New York. . . . The mob spirit seemed to have run in every direction, and every little village catches the rebellious spirit. One instance is worthy of note. In the village of Flushing, the colored people went to the Catholic priest and told him that they were peaceable men doing no harm to any one, and that the Irish had threatened to mob them, but if they did, they would burn two Irish houses for every one of theirs, and would kill two Irish men for every colored man killed by them. They were not mobbed, and so in every place where they were prepared they escaped being mobbed. Most of the colored men in Brooklyn who remained in the city were armed daily for self-defence.[5]

William P. Powell, a Negro physician, barely managed to save himself and his family from the mob. He published the following account:

On the afternoon of [July 13] my house . . . was invaded by a mob of half grown boys. . . . [They] were soon replaced by men and women. From 2 P.M. to 8 P.M. myself and family were prisoners in my own house to king mob, from which there was no way to escape but over the roofs of adjoining houses. About 4 P.M. . . . the mob commenced throwing stones at the lower windows, until they had succeeded in making an opening. I was determined not to leave until driven from the premises. My family including my invalid daughter . . . took refuge on the roof of the next house. I remained till the mob broke in, and then narrowly escaped the same way. . . . We remained on the roof for an hour; still I hoped that relief would come. The neighbors, anticipating the mob would fire my house, were removing their effects on the roof—all was excitement. But as the object of the mob was plunder, they were too busily engaged in carrying off all my effects to apply the torch. . . .

How to escape from the roof of a five story building, with four females—and one a cripple—besides eight men, without a ladder, or any assistance from outside, was beyond my not excited imagination. But the God that succored Hagar in her flight, came to my relief in the person of a little deformed, despised Israelite—who, Samaritan-like, took my poor helpless daughter under his protection in his house, where I presume she now is, until friends send her to me. He also supplied me with a long rope. I then took a survey of the premises, and fortunately found a way to escape, and though pitchy dark, I took soundings with the rope to see if it would touch the next roof, after which I took a clove-hitch around the clothes line which was fastened to the wall by pulleys, and which led from one roof to the other over a space of about one hundred feet. In this manner I managed to lower my family down on to the next roof, and from one roof to another, until I landed them in a neighbor's yard. We were secreted in our friend's cellar till 11 P.M., when we were taken in charge by the Police and locked up in the Station house for safety. In this dismal place we found upwards of seventy men, women and children—some with broken limbs—bruised and beaten from head to foot. . . .

All my personal property, to the amount of $3,000, has been destroyed and scattered to the four winds. . . . As a devoted loyal Unionist, I have done all I could to perpetuate and uphold the integrity of this free government. As an evidence of this devotedness, my oldest son is now serving my country as a surgeon in the U.S. army, and myself had just received a commission in the naval service. What more could I do? What further evidence was wanting to prove my allegiance in the exigencies of our unfortunate country? I am now an old man, stripped of everything, . . . but I thank God that He has yet spared my life, which I am ready to yield in defence of my country.[6]

"*Great God! what is this nation coming to?*" *asked the* Christian Recorder *in an editorial on* "*The Riots in New York*":

These rioters of New York could not be satisfied with the resistance of the draft and doing all the damage they could against the government and those of the white citizens who are

friends to the administration, but must wheel upon the colored
people, killing and beating every one whom they could see and
catch, and destroying their property. . . . A gloom of infamy and
shame will hang over New York for centuries. . . . Our citizens
are expecting every day that a mob will break out here, in Philadelphia. . . . If so, we have only to say this to our colored citizens of Philadelphia and vicinity: Have plenty of powder and
ball in your houses, and use it with effect, if necessary, in the
protection of your wives and children; and even [boiling] water,
if need be; for any and every person has a perfect right to protect their [sic] homes.[7]

*Dr. J. W. C. Pennington discussed the lessons of the Draft
Riots in a speech at Poughkeepsie on August 24, 1863, which
deserves quotation at length:*

The elements of this mob have been centering and gathering
strength in New York, for more than two years. And, as soon as
the rebellion broke out, prominent colored men in passing the
streets, were often hailed as "Old Abe," or "Jeff. Davis," evidently to feel their loyal pulse, and as it became evident that
our sympathies were with the Federal government, we became
objects of more marked abuse and insult. From many of the
grocery corners, stones, potatoes, and pieces of coal, would often be hurled, by idle young loafers, standing about. . . . The
language addressed to colored men, not seemly to record on paper, became the common language of the street, and even of
some of the fashionable avenues. . . . In no other country in the
world would the streets of refined cities be allowed to be polluted, as those of New York have been, with foul and indecent
language, without rebuke from the press, the pulpit, or the authorities. . . . What has been the result? Why, just what we
might have expected,—the engendering of a public feeling unfriendly toward colored people. This feeling, once created, might
at any moment be intensified into an outbreak against its un-
offending objects. . . .

The opposition to the draft comes largely from that class of
men of foreign birth who had declared their intention to become
citizens, but who have not done so. They have been duly noti-

citizens, but who have not done so. They have been duly notified that they could leave the country within sixty days, or submit to the draft. . . . They do not wish to leave the country, and
they do not wish to fight. . . . Dishonest politicians aim to make
these men believe that the war has been undertaken to abolish
slavery; and so far as they believe so, their feelings are against
colored people. . . .

Let the greedy foreigner know that a part of this country
BELONGS TO US; and that we assert the right to live and labor
here: That in New York and other cities, we claim the right to
buy, hire, occupy and use houses and tenements, for legal con-
siderations; to pass and repass on the streets, lanes, avenues,
and all public ways. Our fathers have fought for this country,
and helped to free it from the British yoke. We are now fighting to help to free it from the combined conspiracy of Jeff.
Davis and Co.; we are doing so with the distinct understanding,
that WE ARE TO HAVE ALL OUR RIGHTS AS MEN AND AS CITIZENS, and,
that there are to be no side issues, no RESERVATIONS, either
political, civil, or religious. In this struggle we know nothing
but God, Manhood, and American Nationality, full and unim-
paired. . . .

How does the matter sum up? It sums up thus; for more than
a year, the riot spirit had been culminating, before it burst
forth. . . . The loss of life and property make only a small part
of the damage. The breaking up of families; and business relations just beginning to prosper; the blasting of hopes just dawning; the loss of precious harvest time which will never again
return; the feeling of insecurity engendered; the confidence destroyed; the reaction; and lastly, the gross insult offered to our
character as a people, sum up a weight of injury which can be
realized by the most enlightened and sensitive minds among
us. . . .

For all the purposes, therefore, of social, civil, and religious
enjoyment, and right, we hold New York solemnly bound to insure us, as citizens, permanent security in our homes. Relief,
and damage money, is well enough. But it cannot atone, fully,
for evils done by riots. It cannot bring back our murdered dead.

It cannot remove the insults we feel; and finally, it gives no proof that the people have really changed their minds, for the better towards us.[8]

In the end, the sympathy aroused for the black victims of the Draft Riots helped to better the status of Negroes not only in New York but all over the North. But the black man still had to face many decisions and trials before his position improved. One of these trials was the colonization issue.

CHAPTER VI

THE COLONIZATION ISSUE

In March 1862, the Tammany *Hall Young Men's Democratic Club resolved that "we are opposed to emancipating negro slaves, unless on some plan of colonization, in order that they may not come in contact with the white man's labor."[1] Colonization was the magic solution of the Negro question offered by many leading men in the early part of the Civil War. For more than forty years the American Colonization Society and its state auxiliaries, impelled by mixed motives, had sought to solve the race problem by colonizing freed Negroes in Africa. Opposed by abolitionists and by most Negroes, this project was a miserable failure. With the coming of war and the imminent possibility of large-scale emancipation, however, the colonization chimera gained new popularity among conservatives who foresaw the inevitability of emancipation but dreaded its social consequences.*

As fugitive slaves began to pour into Union army camps in the summer of 1861, colonization proposals blossomed forth in all parts of the North. Some suggestions envisaged voluntary colonization, others compulsory; still others were vague on the question whether emigration should be voluntary or compulsory. But all colonization plans had one thing in common: the belief that the negro and the white man could never live together peacefully as equals. Colonization, therefore, was the only possible solution of the vexing slavery and racial problems.

Embittered by their status as second-class citizens, some Northern Negroes favored emigration from America's hostile environment. In the 1850s a minority of black men, led by Henry Highland Garnet, Martin R. Delany, and James T. Holly, began to advocate the emigration of Negroes to Haiti or Central America. There they could escape the blighting prejudice of the white man and establish flourishing Negro republics that would disprove the myth of the black man's inability to govern himself.[2] James Redpath, a white, British-born radical, became the organizer of a spectacular but short-lived emigration movement to Haiti. Redpath visited Haiti three times as a reporter for the New York Tribune *in 1859 and 1860. He came away from the island deeply impressed by its beauty, fertility, and climate. A revolution in 1859 had brought a new president, Fabre Geffrard, to power in Haiti. Eager to develop the country's natural and human resources, Geffrard approached Redpath with a proposition to subsidize the emigration of American Negroes to the island. Geffrard finally won Redpath over to a vision of a powerful, prosperous Haiti which would exhibit the capacity and genius of the Negro race to a skeptical world.[3]*

Redpath returned to Boston with a commission as "General Agent of the Haytian Bureau of Emigration." With an initial grant of $20,000 from the Haitian government he opened a central office in Boston in the fall of 1860, and began to recruit agents and establish branch offices in several Northern cities. He published A Guide to Hayti *(which went through three editions), that described in glowing terms the physical and political characteristics of the island and urged American Negroes to emigrate there for a new and better start in life. Haiti, he told them, was the only country in the Western Hemisphere "where the Black and the man of color are undisputed lords ... where neither laws, nor prejudice, nor historical memories press cruelly on persons of African descent; where the people whom American degrades and drives from her are rulers, judges, and generals, ... authors, artists, and legislators." Redpath informed prospective emigrants that the Haitian government would pay fifteen dollars apiece toward their passage expenses,*

*and sell them land at low prices and long-term credits when
they arrived. They would be exempt from military service, and
eligible for citizenship after one year. Complete religious freedom for all immigrants was guaranteed.*[4]

*Redpath recruited several prominent Negroes as agents and
organizers for his Bureau: James T. Holly, Henry Highland
Garnet, William Wells Brown, H. Ford Douglass, and J. B.
Smith, to name only a few. He established in May 1861 an emigrationist newspaper, the* Pine and Palm, *which was published
in both Boston and New York. The New York editor was George
Lawrence, a Negro. Redpath's Negro allies gave scores of speeches
and published dozens of articles on behalf of the emigration
movement. The following selections are representative.*

The Anglo-African *of April 13, 1861, published a letter from
an anonymous supporter of emigration:*

Listen! We want our rights. No one is going to *give* them to
us, so perforce we must take them. In order to do this, we must
have a strong nationality somewhere—respected, feared. . . . We
can make of Hayti the nucleus of a power that shall be to the
black, what England has been to the white races, the hope of
progress and the guarantee of permanent civilization. Look at
her position; she is the centre of a circle in whose plane lie
Cuba, Central America, and the Southern Slave States. From
that centre, let but the fire of Freedom radiate until it shall
enkindle, in the whole of that vast area, the sacred flame of
Liberty upon the altar of every black man's heart, and you effect at once the abolition of slavery and the regeneration of our
race.

George Lawrence wrote:

Believing that "God hath made of one blood all nations of
men for to dwell on the face of the earth," we hold the idea of
the absolute inferiority of the negro to be a most damnable heresy, and that it is the bounden duty of those portions of the race
who have partially enjoyed the benefits of civilization, to refute
the heresy, and convince mankind of their error. . . .

To do it we must escape from the miasmatic influences of
prejudice, and the mephitic exhalations of mistaken philan-

thropy, and establish ourselves where our self-confidence will not be shaken either by the detraction of enemies, or the humiliating misgivings of friends. . . . [It is a] necessity, that we should demonstrate to the world by the upbuilding of black nationalities, our thorough capacity independently to compete with other peoples and our absolute equality to them. . . . Let us, then, not shirk the question, but meet it manfully, hopefully; let us say wherever there is a black man there is a brother, and that out of black men there *shall* arise a nation able to protect itself and defend the weaker portions of the race.[5]

A Washington Negro declared:.

In this city, the question is still discussed by the people of color—Shall we go to Hayti, and enjoy the blessings of citizenship in that free and independent Republic, or shall we remain in the United States, in ignorance and degradation? . . . Let us emigrate to Hayti, where we shall be free from the white man's contumely, and where we can secure for ourselves and our children after us, a home, a farm, and all the rights which citizenship confers. . . . If God ever opened a way for the poor despised African to escape from the bondage which he endures in this country, it is now—in the offer made to us by the Haytian Government. And if we, as a body, possess any desire to prove our manhood, let us go energetically to work, and demonstrate to the world that we can not only govern ourselves, but that we can only attain to true greatness when we cease to lean upon the white man for support.[6]

Another Negro advocate of emigration was J. Willis Menard. A college graduate, Menard later in the war became the first black man to hold a white-collar job in the national government, and during Reconstruction he played an active role in the politics of Louisiana and Florida. But in 1861 he was deeply discouraged by the lowly status of black men in America. He wrote that

two hundred and forty-two years of continued administration of injustice to our race on the North American Continent, ought home, as a race or as men and women, but their home only as "moveable chattels" and "saleable commodities." . . . Shall we always say, "O America, with thy many faults, we love thee still?" No! let us commit to the care of God the graves of our fathers, and of those who died by the cruel tortures of a slow fire, and go at once to our "promised land!" [Haiti] where we will yet be in hearing of the wails and groans of our enslaved brothers and sisters, and where we can at any time be summoned to help deal the last blow to slavery.

We need have no hope in the present conflict, for the atmosphere of North America is interwoven and vocal with the blasting breath of negro prejudice. It is the first lesson taught by white parents to their children, that the negro is a low, debased animal, not fit for their association nor their equal. . . .

> "Ho! children of the dusky brow!
> Why will ye wear the chain?
> A fairer home is waiting you,
> In isles beyond the main!"[7]

The opponents of emigration were as eloquent as its proponents. John Rock said in 1860 that
there are many reasons and much philosophy in abandoning a country and people who have so diligently sought to crush us. But, then, it must be remembered that there is no other country that is particularly inviting to us, and on this account the masses of the colored people, who *think* for themselves, have believed that the same effort made in working our way up in this country, and in civilizing the whites, would accomplish our object as certain and as easy as we could by emigrating to a foreign country, and overcoming the disadvantages of language, climate, low wages, and other obstacles which would tend to embarrass us in a strange country. This being our country, we have made up our minds to remain in it, and to try to make it worth living in.[8]

Frederick Douglass believed that "the place for the free colored people is the land where their brothers and sisters are held in slavery, and where circumstances might some day enable

them to contribute an important part to their liberation . . .
because we have seen that the habit of looking away from Amer-
ica for a home, induces neglect to improve such advantages as
are afforded by our condition here." Nevertheless, Douglass de-
clared at the end of 1860 that

while we have never favored any plan of emigration, and have
never been willing to concede that this is a doomed country,
and that we are a doomed race in it, we can raise no objection
to the present movement toward Hayti. . . . If we go any where,
let us go to Hayti. Let us go where we are still within hearing
distance of the wails of our brothers and sisters in bonds. Let us
not go to Africa, where those who hate and enslave us want us
to go; but let us go to Hayti, where our oppressors do not want
us to go, and where our influence and example can still be of
service to those whose tears will find their way to us by the
waters of the Gulf washing all our shores.[9]

But in June 1861, Douglass came out strongly against the
Haitian emigration movement:

Now, this simple overture of benevolence has hardened into
a grand scheme of public policy, and claims the acceptance of
the whole colored people and their friends. It has become eth-
nological, philosophical, political and commercial. It has its doc-
trines of races, of climates, of nationalities and destinies, and
offers itself as the grand solution of the destiny of the colored
people in America. In this aspect the Haytian Emigration movement challenges criticism, and leaves room to question its wisdom. . . . It has propagated the favorite doctrine of all those
who despise and hate the colored man, that the prejudice of the
whites is invincible, and that the cause of human freedom and
equality is hopeless for the black man in this country. . . . This
attitude of the Haytian Emigration movement compels me to
say, I am not an Emigrationist. . . .

We are Americans, speaking the same language, adopting the
same customs, holding the same general opinions, . . . and shall
rise or fall with Americans; upon the whole our history here has
been one of progress and improvement, and in all the likelihoods
of the case, will become more so; the lines of social and political

distinction, marking unjust and unnatural discriminations against us, are gradually being effaced; and that upon the fall of slavery, as fall it must, these discriminations will disappear still more rapidly. I hold that all schemes of wholesale emigration tend to awaken and keep alive and confirm the popular prejudices of the whites against us. They serve to kindle hopes of getting us out of the country. . . . I hold that there is no such thing as a natural and unconquerable repugnance between the varieties of men. All these artificial and arbitrary barriers give way before interest and enlightenment. . . . The hope of the world is in Human Brotherhood; in the union of mankind, not in exclusive nationalities.[10]

The emigration scheme gave rise to an intense and sometimes bitter debate among American Negroes in 1861. This debate can be traced in the following documents.

At the end of 1860 James McCune Smith wrote an open letter to Henry Highland Garnet, the foremost Negro clergyman in New York City, criticizing Garnet for his acceptance of a position in Redpath's Emigration Bureau. Dr. Smith's portly figure concealed a passionate and combative dedication to equal rights. After earning an M.D. degree at the University of Glasgow in 1837, Smith had returned to practice medicine in New York City, where he became a leader in the city's Negro community. In his public letter to Garnet he wrote:

More than a quarter of a century ago, you and others, among whom I was the humblest, pledged yourselves to devote life and energies to the elevation and affranchisement of the free colored people on this, the soil which gave them birth, and through their affranchisement, the emancipation of the slaves of the South. This may be called old-fashioned doctrine; but it is none the less sound, and our pledges are none the less binding on that account. We are bound by these pledges until one of two things occurs. Either the elevation and affranchisement of our brethren free and enslaved must be accomplished; or the attempt must be proven useless because impossible of accomplishment. . . .

So far from being released, we are more solemnly bound by

those pledges to-day than at any time since we made them: for we are hourly approaching that affranchisement for which we are bound to struggle. . . . Is it right, my dear Sir, or is it not rather a wanton shame, when the work goes so nobly on, while the goal is within our reach, is it not a shame that you should lend the weight of your name and the luster of your talents to divert us to other and distant fields of labor? . . . Is it right in you, my dear Sir, is it in accordance with the pledges of your youth to . . . [advise] us to leave the *white man's country*—which is our country before God? . . . Your duty to our people is to tell them to aim higher. In advising them to go to Hayti you direct them to sink lower. . . . We affirm by our lives and conduct that, if degraded, it is not by our innate inferiority, but by the active oppression of those who outnumber us. . . . Our people want to stay, and will stay, at home: we are in for the fight, and will fight it out here. Shake yourself free from these migrating phantasms, and join us with your might and main.[11]

Garnet was not convinced by Smith's argument. Born a slave in Maryland, Garnet was the son of an African chief who had been kidnapped and sold into American slavery. His father's entire family escaped to the North in 1822, where Henry was later educated at Oneida Institute in New York. He served as pastor of several churches in New York State and as a missionary to Jamaica before coming to New York as minister of the Shiloh Presbyterian Church. At the beginning of 1861 he replied to Smith's letter:

You anti-emigrationists seem to desire to see the hundreds of colored men and women who have good trades to stay here and be the drudges and menials of white men, who will not employ or work with them. Go to our hotels and private mansions of the rich, and on board of our steamboats, and you will find many skillful carpenters, masons, engineers, wheelwrights, and blacksmiths, millers, as well as female mechanics, who are wasting their talents for a mere pittance. You will see many of them borne down with discouragement, and they will tell you that the reason they do not work at their trades is, because they have been told over and over again when they have applied for work—"We don't employ niggers."[12]

A Negro woman from New York who agreed with Garnet wrote that "it is my firm conviction that we as a mass never can rise to any degree of eminence in this country. Our condition may be ameliorated, and individuals may by dint of severe struggling, manage to keep chin above water and that is about all."[13] The "Haytian Emigration Society" of Toledo adopted the following resolutions on January 14, 1861:

Whereas, It is common for man, wherever placed on the habitable globe, when deprived of his God-given rights, to devise some means to better his condition, . . . Resolved, That we view in Hayti the chief cornerstone of an Ethiopic empire, and that we see in her the elements of a future that are nowhere to be found on or adjacent to the American continent.

Resolved, That we appeal to the blacks and men of color to form this nucleus around the chief cornerstone in our political edifice of the Antilles, and ere long from that radiating point the sable arm of Africa will belt the tropical regions of the globe.[14]

But a Philadelphia Negro declared that "the idea of a great nationality in Hayti is all humbug; let us build up a nationality for ourselves here."[15] Opposition to colonization was very strong among Massachusetts Negroes, who enjoyed more rights than the black men of any other state. A meeting of Boston Negroes passed the following resolutions in November 1861:

Whereas, Strenuous efforts are now being made by certain intelligent, but misguided colored men and white men to induce free colored persons, resident in the United States and in the Canadas, to emigrate to Hayti under the mistaken policy of bettering their condition; and whereas, in the present crisis of the history of our race we deem such efforts pernicious, calculated to weaken our strength, by lessening our number, and removing our laboring and able-bodied men; Therefore,

Resolved, That we regard such men with suspicion, and deprecate both their counsel and advice; and we earnestly recommend that if they are sincere in their pretended love and admiration for Hayti, they immediately quit our shores and take up their abode in that country.

Resolved, That under no circumstances will we be induced or persuaded to emigrate from this our native country, until the last fetter has been struck from the limbs of the last slave on this continent, believing that in the accomplishment of this great work, which in our judgment is near at hand, we are to have a word to say and a blow to strike.[16]

Negro Baptists, meeting in New Bedford, resolved that
this Convention feel it to be their duty to protest against the operations and designs of those in charge of Haytian emigration, and that we look upon any body of men who seek our wholesale removal, as is contemplated by Mr. James Redpath and his co-adjutors, as being characterized by the same spirit which breathed into existence the old American Colonization Society.

Resolved, That we condemn the infamous doctrine . . . that the white and black races cannot live together upon this continent in a state of freedom and equality.

Resolved, That we feel a deep sense of regret that colored men in whom we have confided as our leaders should allow themselves to be the tools of a widespread evil, which is discouraging and dividing us just at the daybreak of our universal emancipation.[17]

William Wells Brown replied to the arguments of Redpath's critics:

All the objections to emigration appear to centre in the feeling that we ought not to quit the land of our birth, and leave the slave in his chains. This view of the case comes at the first glance with some force, but on a closer examination, it will be found to have but little weight. If it could be shown that our presence here was actually needed, and that we could exert an influence, no matter what position we occupied in the community, then I agree that duty would require us to remain.

But let us look at facts. It must be confessed that we, the colored people of this country, are a race of cooks, waiters, barbers, whitewashers, bootblacks, and chimney sweeps. How much influence has such a class upon a community? . . .

I hold that the descendants of Africa, in this country, will never be respected until they shall leave the cook shop and barber's chair and the white-wash brush. "They who would be free, themselves must strike the blow," means something more than appearing in a military attitude. To emigrate to Hayti, and to develop the resources of the Island, and to build up a powerful and influential government there, which shall demonstrate the genius and capabilities of the Negro, is as good an Anti-Slavery work as can be done in the Northern States of this Union.

Our opponents do not meet the subject fairly and honestly. To attempt to connect the Haytian emigration movement with the old and hateful colonization scheme, is only to create a prejudice in the minds of the people. Originated by a colored nation, in the interests of the colored race, conducted and sustained exclusively by the friends or members of that nation and that race, it is essentially and diametrically opposed to the colonization project, which was originated by slaveholders, in the interests of slavery, and conducted and sustained exclusively by the friends of bondage, and the haters of the Negro.[18]

And George Lawrence, the New York editor of the Pine and Palm, *stated that*
if this war should result in the abolition of slavery, as we hope it may, while it strikes the shackles from the slave, it will not ameliorate the condition of the free black man, one iota. Let none such, therefore, taking counsel of his desires, hope for a satisfactory recognition of his claims as the result, even under the most favorable of circumstances, of this war. He may be used (for Uncle Sam's chestnuts are roasting in a pretty hot fire), may be accorded a *quasi* recognition; but so soon as the purposes of the Federal Government may have been served through his instrumentality, he will be rewarded with a mockery of thanks, and unceremoniously thrust aside. Judging the future from the past, can any one doubt it? . . . The scanty pittance of social toleration which is here and there grudgingly doled out to

us is only exceptional, illustrating the more strikingly the rule which everywhere excludes us. And the only way in which we can reasonably expect to change this state of affairs is by assuming the separate position of an independent people, exacting social recognition, and able to enforce it. Why, then, refuse to look our condition fully in the face; why continue to hug a criminal delusion which only tends to deeper degradation?[19]

While the debate continued, Redpath went ahead with the work of recruiting emigrants and sending them to Haiti. Between December 1860 and October 1861, more than one thousand Negroes migrated from the United States to the island republic. But difficulties began to develop. Reports soon filtered back from Haiti of mismanagement, delays in the assignments of land grants, disease and death among unacclimated colonists, and hostility between the natives and the immigrants. A Pennsylvania Negro who had gone to Haiti in October 1861 returned home four months later and reported that "Hayti is not the place for a colored American, unless he is a capitalist, and it is utter folly for a poor man to go there and expect to make money or even procure as decent a living there as can be easily obtained here. The majority of the emigrants [are] . . . not doing well, earning but little money, enjoying miserable health, generally dissatisfied with the country, its prospects, its climate, soil, and the 'old fogy' modes in which business of all kinds are carried on."[20]

There were other reasons why the Haitian fever soon subsided among American Negroes. Despite the riots and discrimination to which black men were subjected in 1862-63, the war was opening up new opportunities for Negroes, and many of them exchanged their previous pessimism for the hope of a brighter future in America. For example, William Parham, the Cincinnati schoolteacher, had planned in 1862 to emigrate to Haiti or Jamaica. But by 1863 he had changed his mind, because "the present aspect of things in this country . . . —the injustice and outrage to which we are still subject, notwithstanding—gives evidence of the coming of a better and a brighter day."[21]

Reports of mismanagement and failure continued to come

*back from Haiti, and applications for emigration began to de-
cline. Finally in October 1862, Redpath suspended publication
of the* Pine and Palm *and resigned as agent of the Haytian Bureau of Emigration. His ill-starred colonization project was an
almost total failure. About two thousand emigrants went to
Haiti in 1861 and 1862. Most of them either died or returned to
the United States. An American commissioner who visited Haiti
in 1864 could find only two hundred of the original colonists
still living there. On May 5, 1863, a group of New York Negroes
held a meeting at Zion Church to welcome back from Haiti several families who had emigrated with high hopes, but who had
returned disillusioned and poverty-stricken. Emigration sentiment had been strong in New York in 1861, but now the meeting
gave the final burial to Redpath's movement by resolving that
"we view with contempt, as our fathers nobly did, the old Hag,
the 'American Colonization Society,' its pet daughter, the 'African Civilization Society,' also its deformed child, the Haytian
Emigration Movement, and their efforts to remove the colored
man from the United States."[22]*

    *But the demise of Redpath's Bureau did not mean the end of
the colonization issue. In the first two years of the war the Lincoln administration, supported by a large segment of Northern
public opinion, favored the gradual and voluntary colonization
of Negroes as the best possible solution of the race problem.
Aaron Powell, a lecturer for the American Anti-Slavery Society,
reported in 1862 that "unfriendly expressions against the colored people were never more common in my hearing. Many Republicans united with Democrats in cursing the 'niggers,' and
in declaring that the slaves, if possibly emancipated by the war,
must be removed from the country."[23]*

    *In his message to Congress on December 3, 1861, Lincoln rec-
ommended that "steps be taken" to colonize the slaves who had
come into Union lines plus any free Negroes who might wish to
emigrate. He urged Congress to appropriate money for the acquisition of colonial territory for this purpose.[24] During the
1861–62 Congressional session several colonization bills were*

introduced, and Congress actually appropriated $600,000 to help finance the voluntary emigration of Negroes freed by the District of Columbia Emancipation Act and the Second Confiscation Act.[25]

Whatever their attitude toward the Haitian movement, most Negroes were angrily opposed to the various colonization proposals advanced in the early war years whose general purpose was to rid the country of the troublesome Negro. The Anglo-African *labeled Lincoln's message to Congress "a speech to stir the hearts of all Confederates." Instead of colonizing black men, suggested this Negro newspaper, "any surplus change Congress may have can be appropriated 'with our consent' to expatriate and settle elsewhere the surviving slaveholders."*[26] *John Rock asked:*

Why is it that the white people of this country desire to get rid of us? Does any one pretend to deny that this is our country? or that much of the wealth and prosperity found here is the result of the labor of our hands? or that our blood and bones have not crimsoned and whitened every battle-field from Maine to Louisiana? Why this desire to get rid of us? Can it be possible that because the nation has robbed us for nearly two and a half centuries, and finding that she can do it no longer and preserve her character among nations, now, out of hatred, wishes to banish, because she cannot continue to rob us? . . .

This nation has wronged us, and for this reason many hate us. (Hear, hear.) The Spanish proverb is, *"Desde que te erre nunca bien te quise"*—Since I have wronged you, I have never liked you. This is true not only of Spaniards and Americans, but of every other class of people. When a man wrongs another, he not only hates him, but tries to make others dislike him. . . .

The black man is a good fellow while he is a slave, and toils for nothing, but the moment he claims his own flesh and blood and bones, he is a most obnoxious creature, and there is a proposition to get rid of him! He is happy while he remains a poor, degraded, ignorant slave, without even the right to his own offspring. While in this condition, the master can ride in the same carriage, sleep in the same bed, and nurse from the same bosom.

But give this same slave the right to use his own legs, his hands, his body and his mind, and this happy and desirable creature is instantly transformed into a miserable and loathsome wretch, fit only to be colonized. . . .

It is true, a great many simple-minded people have been induced to go to Liberia and to Hayti, but, be assured, the more intelligent portion of the colored people will remain here; not because we prefer being oppressed here to being freemen in other countries, but we will remain because we believe our future prospects are better here than elsewhere, and because our experience has proved that the greater proportion of those who have left this country during the last thirty years have made their condition worse, and would have gladly returned if they could have done so. You may rest assured that we shall remain here—here, where we have withstood almost everything. Now, when our prospects begin to brighten, we are the more encouraged to stay, pay off the old score, and have a reconstruction of things.[27]

And at a meeting on April 28, 1862, Boston's Negro leaders made their position perfectly clear in four sharply worded resolutions:

Resolved, That when we wish to leave the United States we can find and pay for that territory which shall suit us best.

Resolved, That when we are ready to leave, we shall be able to pay our own expenses of travel.

Resolved, That we don't want to go now.

Resolved, That if anybody else wants us to go, they must compel us.[28]

On August 14, 1862, President Lincoln met with five black men from the District of Columbia. This "interview" turned out to be a speech by Lincoln, a curious mixture of condescension and kindness. The President told his listeners that the broad racial differences between Negro and Caucasian made it impossible for them to live together as equals. "Whether it is right or wrong I need not discuss, but this physical difference is a great disadvantage to us both, as I think your race suffer very greatly, many of them by living among us, while ours suffer from your presence." Complete separation of the races was the only solution. "There is an unwillingness on the part of our people, harsh as it may be, for you free colored people to remain with us. . . . I do not propose to discuss this, but to propose it as a fact with which we have to deal. I cannot alter it if I would. . . . it is better for us both, therefore, to be separated." Lincoln urged the Negroes to recruit twenty-five, fifty, or a hundred black families for colonization in Central America, where they could find work in the new coal mines being developed there. He promised them government assistance. The delegation withdrew, telling Lincoln that they would have to think the matter over before replying.[29]

Accounts of this interview were widely publicized in the Northern press. The reaction by articulate Negroes was swift and angry. Frederick Douglass spared no adjectives in his denunciation of Lincoln's speech:

The President of the United States seems to possess an ever increasing passion for making himself appear silly and ridiculous, if nothing worse. . . . In this address Mr. Lincoln assumes the language and arguments of an itinerant Colonization lecturer, showing all his inconsistencies, his pride of race and blood, his contempt for negroes and his canting hypocrisy. . . . Mr. Lincoln takes care in urging his colonization scheme to furnish a weapon to all the ignorant and base, who need only the countenance of men in authority to commit all kinds of violence and outrage upon the colored people. . . . The tone of frankness and benevolence which he assumes in his speech to the colored committee is too thin a mask not to be seen through. The genuine spark of humanity is missing in it, no sincere wish to improve the condition of the oppressed has dictated it. It expresses merely the desire to get rid of them, and reminds one of the politeness with which a man might try to bow out of his house some troublesome creditor or the witness of some old guilt.[30]

A. P. Smith of Saddle River, New Jersey, published the following reply to Lincoln's proposal:

Let me tell you, sir, President though you are, there is but one race of men on the face of the earth:—One lord, one faith, one baptism, one God and Father of all, who is above all, and through all, and in all. Physical differences no doubt there are; no two persons on earth are exactly alike in this respect; but what of that? In physical conformation, you, Mr. President, may differ somewhat from the negro, and also from the majority of white men; you may even, as you indicate, feel this difference on your part to be very disadvantageous to you; but does it follow that therefore you should be removed to a foreign country? . . .

But were all you say on this point true, must I crush out my cherished hopes and aspirations, abandon my home, and become a pander to the mean and selfish spirit that oppresses me? Pray tell us, is our right to a home in this country less than your own, Mr. Lincoln? . . . Are you an American? So are we. Are you a patriot? So are we. Would you spurn all absurd, meddlesome, impudent propositions for your colonization in a foreign country? So do we. . . .

But say, good Mr. President, why we, why anybody should swelter, digging coal, if there be any in Central America? . . . But, say you: "Coal land is the best thing I know of to begin an enterprise." Astounding discovery! Worthy to be recorded in golden letters, like the Lunar Cycle in the temple of Minerva. "Coal land, sir!" Pardon, Mr. President, if my African risibilities get the better of me, if I do show my ivories whenever I read that sentence! Coal land, sir! If you please, sir, give McClellan some, give Halleck some, and by all means, save a little strip for yourself.

Twenty-five negroes digging coal in Central America! Mighty plan! Equal to about twenty-five negroes splitting rail in Sangamon! . . . Good sir, if you have any nearer friends than we are, let them have that coal-digging job.[31]

Isaiah Wears, a prominent Philadelphia Negro, expressed the opinion of most black men in his city:

To be asked, after so many years of oppression and wrong have been inflicted in a land and by a people who have been so largely enriched by the black man's toil, to pull up stakes in a civilized and Christian nation, and to go to an uncivilized and

barbarous nation, simply to gratify an unnatural wicked prejudice emanating from slavery, is unreasonable and anti-Christian
in the extreme. . . . If black men are here in the way of white
men, they did not come here of their own accord. Their presence is traceable to the white man's lust for power, love of oppression and disregard of the plain teachings of the Lord Jesus
Christ. . . . It is not the negro race that is the cause of the war;
it is the unwillingness on the part of the American people to do
the race simple justice. . . . The effect of this scheme of colonization, we fear, will be to arouse prejudice and to increase
enmity against us, without bringing with it the remedy proposed
or designed.[32]

*A mass meeting of black men at Newtown, Long Island, on
August 20 issued an eloquent rejection of Lincoln's colonization
proposal:*

We rejoice that we are colored Americans, but deny that we
are a "different race of people," as God has made of one blood
all nations that dwell on the face of the earth, and has hence
no respect of men in regard to color. . . .

This is our country by birth. . . . This is our native country;
we have as strong attachment naturally to our native hills, valleys, plains, luxuriant forests, flowing streams, mighty rivers,
and lofty mountains, as any other people. . . . This is the country of our choice, being our fathers' country. We love this land,
and have contributed our share to its prosperity and wealth. . . .

We have the right to have applied to ourselves those rights
named in the Declaration of Independence. . . . When our country is struggling for life, and one million freemen are believed
to be scarcely sufficient to meet the foe, we are called upon by
the President of the United States to leave this land. . . . But at
this crisis, we feel disposed to refuse the offers of the President
since the call of our suffering country is too loud and imperative
to be unheeded. . . .

In conclusion, we would say that, in our belief, the speech of
the President has only served the cause of our enemies, who
wish to insult and mob us, as we have, since its publication,
been repeatedly insulted, and told that we must leave the coun-

try. Hence we conclude that the policy of the President toward the colored people of this country *is a mistaken policy.*[33]

From all over the North came similar protests. But in spite of this cool reception of his colonization suggestion, Lincoln went ahead with plans to send a company of volunteer colonists to Central America. Four years earlier Ambrose W. Thompson, a free-lance American capitalist, had secured control by questionable means of a land grant of two million acres in the northern part of present-day Panama. Thompson incorporated the "Chiriqui Improvement Company" to develop the coal mines and other resources on his land. In 1861 he offered to sell to the American government coal for its navy at half the prevailing price if the government would supply him with Negro colonists to work the mines. Lincoln expressed interest in the offer, and in the summer of 1862 the President appointed Senator S. C. Pomeroy "United States Colonization Agent" to recruit colonists and arrange transportation. Pomeroy issued a pamphlet addressed to "The Free Colored People of the United States," praising the wonderful climate and opportunities for them in Chiriqui.[34]

Robert Purvis, the wealthy Negro abolitionist of Philadelphia, was not impressed by the pamphlet. He assured Pomeroy in a public letter that few Negroes wished to be colonized:

Sir, for more than twenty years the question of colonization agitated and divided this country. The "colored" people stamped it with the seal of their reprobation; the whites acquiesced in the justice of their decision, and the vexed and vexing question was put to rest. Now it is revived; the apple of discord is again thrown into the community, and as though you had not already enough to divide and distract you, a new scheme is hit upon, and deliberately sent upon its errand of mischief. . . .

But it is said this is a question of prejudice—of national antipathy and not to be reasoned about. The President has said, "Whether it is right or wrong, I need not now discuss it." Great God! is justice nothing? Is honor nothing? Is even pecuniary interest to be sacrificed to this insane and vulgar hate? . . .

Sir, we were born here and here we choose to remain. . . .

Don't advise me to leave, and don't add insult to injury by telling me it's for my own good. Of that I am to be the judge. It is in vain you talk to me about "two races" and their "mutal antagonism." In the matter of rights, there is but one race, and that is the *human* race. . . . Sir, this is our country as much as it is yours, and we will not leave it.[35]

In spite of this opposition to his scheme, Senator Pomeroy had by October 1862 secured five hundred Negro emigrants, purchased the necessary equipment, and chartered a ship. But members of Lincoln's Cabinet had begun to question the validity of Ambrose Thompson's title to the Chiriqui lands; scientist Joseph Henry of the Smithsonian Institution reported that the coal deposits in Chiriqui were virtually worthless; and several Latin American nations protested against any Yankee effort to establish a colony in Central America. Secretary of State Seward recommended that the whole Chiriqui project be abandoned. Lincoln adopted this recommendation, and Pomeroy's shipful of emigrants never sailed.[36] Frederick Douglass pronounced a fitting epitaph to the Chiriqui scheme: "A wise ending to a singularly foolish beginning."[37]

Lincoln, however, did not yet give up his cherished colonization ideas. In September 1862, another free-lance capitalist named Bernard Kock showed up in Washington and offered to provide employment for colonized Negroes on Ile à Vache, a small island off the southern coast of Haiti. Kock had leased the island from Haiti, agreeing to supply the Haitian government with 35 per cent of the timber he cut. He needed Negro labor to cut down the trees, and hoped to obtain it in Washington. Kock made a favorable impression on Lincoln, who signed a contract with him on December 31, 1862, to transport five hundred Negros to Ile à Vache for fifty dollars apiece. Subsequent investigation revealed Kock to be a rather shady character, so the government canceled the contract. A few months later the President authorized a similar contract with Paul S. Forbes and Charles K. Tuckerman, two New York businessmen. The two men promptly hired Kock as manager of the enterprise, and in

May 1863 a group of 453 Negroes from Washington and Hampton, Virginia, arrived at Ile à Vache.

The experiment of emigration to Ile à Vache was a disastrous failure. Kock confiscated the American dollars of the colonists and failed to provide them with adequate housing. Smallpox, mutiny, and actual starvation stalked the colony. Nearly a hundred Negroes died. Lincoln gave it up and in February 1864, he ordered a ship to return the surviving colonists to the United States. Congress gave the coup de grâce *to colonization in July 1864 by repealing all provisions of the legislation of 1862 appropriating funds for colonization purposes.*[38]

Negroes and abolitionists hoped that the government had learned something from the failure of its colonization schemes. The Anti-Slavery Standard, *official organ of the American Anti-Slavery Society, asserted in 1864 that the failure of emigration efforts proved colonization to be a "wild, delusive and impractical scheme," while immediate emancipation without expatriation had been entirely successful. "Thus does the boasted wisdom of 'Conservatism' turn out to be folly, while the 'fanaticism' of the 'crazy Radicals' is proved by experience to be the highest wisdom."*[39]

Colonization failed primarily because few Negroes wanted to be colonized. Lincoln and other proponents of colonization thought that black men would prefer to emigrate rather than remain in America as second-class citizens. But most Negroes were determined to stay in their native land and struggle their way upward to equality. The opportunities of the Civil War seemed to be opening a new and better future for the black man in America.

CHAPTER VII

THE NEGRO'S RESPONSE TO THE
CHARGE OF RACIAL INFERIORITY

Most white Americans in 1860 assumed that the Negro race was innately inferior in mental capacity to the Caucasian race. This assumption was one of the main props of slavery, and it also imposed a powerful obstacle to the advancement of free Negroes, in the North as well as in the South. Defenders of slavery reiterated ad nauseam that Negroes were by nature shiftless, slovenly, childlike, dull-witted, savage, and thus incapable of assimilation as equals or even as free men into white society. The belief in Negro inferiority underlay Lincoln's advocacy of colonization as a solution of the race problem, and it underlay most of the arguments against granting the freedmen equal opportunities in education, voting, and civil rights.[1]

Negro leaders realized that the common belief in the Negro's racial inferiority constituted one of the main justifications of slavery and discrimination. "In truth," said Frederick Douglass, "this question is at the bottom of the whole controversy." Robert Purvis wrote that

it has *everything* to do with the question—as at present discussed in this country in regard to the rights of the black man. "He has no rights, &c."—"He is an inferior order of being"— "No ancestral line, worthy of consideration"—"He is *not* of the Egyptian race, &c. &c."—Grounded upon these falsities and blasphemies the enslavers & haters of the black man seek their

apologies and defence. The conscience of the nation is de-
bauched and the work of Hell goes on.[2]

*Scarcely any articulate Negro subscribed to the notion of his
own inferiority. Black leaders argued that the degradations and
denials of slavery and discrimination, rather than inherent inferiority, were responsible for whatever defects of intellect the
Negro displayed. The following selections illustrate the Negro's
effort during the Civil War to destroy the myth of racial in-
equalities and pave the way for the emancipation and enfranchisement of his race.*

In 1860 Dr. John Rock said:

The unfortunate position which both the bond and the free
colored people have been forced to occupy in this country, has
not been favorable to the development of our higher faculties;
and, as a matter of course, we are not what we would have been
under more favorable circumstances. Our enemies have taken
every advantage of our unhappy situation, and attempt to prove
that, because we are unfortunate, we are necessarily an inferior
race, incapable of enjoying to a full extent the privileges of citizenship. The very unjust method of comparing the highest
grades of Anglo-American intellect with the lowest forms of negro sensuality is resorted to, to prove our inferiority, and that
the blessings of citizenship have been specially reserved by our
Heavenly Parent for those men who have white skins and
straight hair. . . .

It is not difficult to see that [this idea of Negro inferiority] is
a mere subterfuge, which is resorted to to bolster up the infamous treatment which greets the colored man everywhere in
this slavery-cursed land, where to us patriotism produces no
honor, goodness no merit, and intellectual industry no reward. . . .

I tell you, gentlemen, we have both physical and moral courage. I believe in the equality of my race. I will not admit, for a
moment, that we are inferior to you. We have always proved
ourselves your equals, when placed in juxtaposition with you.
We are the only oppressed people that advance in the country
of their oppression. Look at the sand-hillers of South Carolina,

the peasants and mendicants of Ireland, the beggars of the two Sicilies, the gipsy race that infest almost all Europe, the peasants of Hungary, and the serfs of Russia! These peoples, though possessing superior advantages to the negro, do not advance in the country of their oppression. Not so with the negro; his godlike intellect surmounts the difficulties which surround him, and he stands forth a man. This is certainly not a very strong argument in favor of our depravity.[3]

H. Ford Douglass declared later in the same year that we often hear, from this very platform, praise of the Saxon race. Now, I want to put this question to those who deny the equal manhood of the negro: What peculiar trait of character do the white men of this country possess, as a mark of superiority, either morally or mentally, that is not also manifested by the black man, under similar circumstances? ("Hear, hear.") You may take down the white and black part of the social and political structure, stone by stone, and in all the relations of life, where the exercise of his moral and intellectual functions is not restricted by positive law, or by the arbitrary restraints of society, you will find the negro the equal of the white man.

. . . You say to the German, the Hungarian, the Irishman, as soon as he lands here, "Go out on the highway of the world's progress, and compete with me, if you can, in the race for empire and dominion." You throw no fetters upon that ever-restless sea of energies that chafes our shores, saying "Thus far shalt thou go, but no further." . . . But no colored man can feel any of this inspiration. We are denied all participation in the government; we remember that that flag only covers us as slaves . . . and, feeling this, we can feel no inspiration when we look at the American flag. . . .

Now, I do not believe that the negro is inferior. Man's ability wholly depends upon surrounding circumstances. You may take all of those races that have risen from the lowest stage of degradation to the highest eminence of intellectual and moral splendor, and you will discover that no race has ever yet been able, by any internal power and will of its own, to lift itself into respectability, without contact with other civilized tribes. . . .

The men who justify slavery upon the assumed inferiority of the negro race, are very slow to admit these facts. They are just as tardy in admitting that the remains of ancient grandeur, which have been exhumed from beneath the accumulated dust of forty centuries, were wrought by the ingenuity and skill of the negro race, ere the Saxon was known in history. . . .

Now, friends, I am proud of the negro race, and I thank God to-day that there does not course in my veins a single drop of Saxon blood. . . . After all, I say that the negro is a man, and has all the elements of manhood, like other men; and, by the way, I think that, in this country, he has the *highest* element of manhood. . . . You may dwarf his manhood by the iron of bondage, you may dry up the fountain of his intellectual life, but you can never destroy his faith in God, and the ultimate triumph of His almighty purpose. Over a sea of blood and tears, he catches, in every lull of the midnight storm that breaks around him, the music of that "still, small voice," that bids him "Hope on, hope ever!"[4]

In 1861 the Anglo-African *told white Americans:*
if we are ignorant, it is you that have shut the light of knowledge from our souls and brutalized our instincts. If we are degraded, yours is the disgrace, for you have closed up every avenue whereby we might emerge from degradation and robbed us of all incentive to elevation. The enormity of your guilt, the immensity of the wrong does not appear in contemplating what you have made us, but in the consideration of what you have prevented us from being.[5]

A year later the Pacific Appeal, *a Negro newspaper in San Francisco, stated that*
facts recently brought to light have shown the slaves in their true character. That they are not all models of Christian virtue we will candidly admit: they have their faults, but also redeeming qualities, which far overbalance all their vices. Their faults are the effects of their condition; the besetting sins of their masters; their virtues, we are proud to say, are all their own. . . .

Can they be expected to be scrupulously honest where they are continually, and have been forever, robbed of everything—

time, labor, parents, children, the necessaries of life, nay, even life itself? Can they be truthful to those whose every look, every word, every action is a lie, as false as hell? Is it strange that licentiousness is the rule and chastity the exception, when the holy marriage-tie is disregarded (not of their choice) and dissolved at the will of another, and the female is taught, by force and example, that prostitution is the badge of all her race? How can they be otherwise than idle, when they are forced to toil that others may enjoy the fruits of their labor, and receive no remuneration but stripes?[6]

In 1860 Frederick Douglass wrote that

It has long been the misfortune of the colored people in the free States to be viewed indiscriminately by the ruling classes among whom they live. They are all bound in one bundle, the ignorant, lazy, thriftless, and unworthy, with the intelligent, industrious, thriving and worthy, and condemned to a common level of degradation. . . . While a part of us are engaged in our various useful occupations, seeking an honest livelihood—seen only by the few—large bodies in our cities, of idle, dissipated and worthless individuals, hang about the corners and dram shops, manufacturing their own ruin and a *bad reputation* for the whole race. . . . Prejudice, always blind to what it never wishes to see, and quick to perceive all it wishes, sees the whole race in the character of our worst representatives, while it has no eyes for our best.[7]

In 1862 Douglass argued that the Negro's "condition and circumstances for more than two centuries" were responsible for his degraded condition in America.

Take any race you please, French, English, Irish, or Scotch, subject them to slavery for ages—regard and treat them every where, every way, as property, as having no rights which other men are required to respect. Let them be loaded with chains, scarred with the whip, branded with hot irons, sold in the market, kept in ignorance, by force of law and by common usage, and I venture to say that the same doubt would spring up concerning either of them, which now confronts the negro. . . . No wonder, therefore, that the colored people in America appear stupid, helpless and degraded. The wonder is rather that they evince so much spirit and manhood as they do.[8]

Another eloquent spokesman for Negro equality was William Wells Brown, the black lecturer and author. Born a slave in Kentucky about 1815, Brown escaped to the North in 1834. He taught himself to read and write while making a living at odd jobs, and soon came to the attention of abolitionist leaders, who signed him on as a lecturer. For nearly twenty years before the Civil War he traveled as an antislavery agent, lecturer, and author in England and the United States. In 1863 Brown published a book entitled The Black Man: His Antecedents, His Genius, and His Achievements, *which contained brief biographies of fifty-seven prominent black men and women. Brown wrote the book in an effort to dispel popular notions about the Negro and to help mobilize public support for Lincoln's emancipation policy. The book was an immediate success; the first edition was sold out soon after publication, and in the next three years ten printings came off the presses. "Such a rapid sale of a book devoted entirely to an exhibition of the genius, the talent and the heroism of the hated Negro," said the* Anti-Slavery Standard *of August 1, 1863, "shows that a great change has come over the minds of the American people, and that justice to a long injured race is not far off."*

In the first chapter of his book, Brown wrote that
two and a half centuries of the negro's enslavement have created, in many minds, the opinion that he is intellectually inferior to the rest of mankind; and now that the blacks seem in a fair way to get their freedom in this country, it has been asserted, and from high authority in the government, that the natural inferiority of the negro makes it impossible for him to live on this continent with the white man, unless in a state of bondage. . . .

I admit that the condition of my race, whether considered in a mental, moral, or intellectual point of view, at the present time cannot compare favorably with the Anglo-Saxon. But it does not become the whites to point the finger of scorn at the blacks, when they have so long been degrading them. The negro has not always been considered the inferior race. The time was when he stood at the head of science and literature. . . .

It is the generally received opinion of the most eminent historians and ethnologists, that the Ethiopians were really negroes, although in them the physical characteristics of the race were exhibited in a less marked manner than in those dwelling on the coast of Guinea, from whence the stock of American slaves has been chiefly derived. That, in the earliest periods of history, the Ethiopians had attained a high degree of civilization, there is every reason to believe; and that to the learning and science derived from them we must ascribe those wonderful monuments which still exist to attest the power and skill of the ancient Egyptians. . . .

From whence sprang the Anglo-Saxon? For, mark you, it is he that denies the equality of the negro. . . . Hume says they were a rude and barbarous people, divided into numerous tribes, dressed in the skins of wild beasts. Druidism was their religion, and they were very superstitious. Such is the first account we have of the Britons. When the Romans invaded that country, they reduced the people to a state of vassalage as degrading as that of slavery in the Southern States. . . . This is not very flattering to the President's ancestors, but it is just . . . . I am sorry that Mr. Lincoln came from such a low origin; but he is not to blame. I only find fault with him for making mouths at me. . . .

But I do not despair; for the negro has that intellectual genius which God has planted in the mind of man, that distinguished him from the rest of creation, and which needs only cultivation to make it bring forth fruit. No nation has ever been found, which by its own unaided efforts, by some powerful inward impulse, has arisen from barbarism and degradation to civilization and respectability. There is nothing in race or blood, in color or features, that imparts susceptibility of improvement to one race over another. The mind left to itself from infancy, without culture, remains a blank. Knowledge is not innate. Development makes the man. As the Greeks, and Romans, and Jews drew knowledge from the Egyptians three thousand years ago, and the Europeans received it from the Romans, so must the blacks of this land rise in the same way. As one man learns from another, so nation learns from nation. . . .

It has been clearly demonstrated, I think, that the enslaved of the south are as capable of self-support as any other class of people in the country. It is well known that, throughout the entire south, a large class of slaves have been for years accustomed to hire their time from their owners. Many of these have paid very high prices for the privilege. Some able mechanics have been known to pay as high as six hundred dollars per annum, besides providing themselves with food and clothing; and this class of slaves, by their industry, have taken care of themselves so well, and their appearance has been so respectable, that many of the states have passed laws prohibiting masters from letting their slaves out to themselves, because, as it was said, it made the other slaves dissatisfied to see so many of their fellows well provided, and accumulating something for themselves in the way of pocket money. . . .

"What shall we do with the slave of the south? Expatriate him," say the haters of the negro. Expatriate him for what? He has cleared up the swamps of the south, and has put the soil under cultivation; he has built up her towns, and cities, and villages; he has enriched the north and Europe with his cotton, and sugar, and rice; and for this you would drive him out of the country! "What shall be done with the slaves if they are freed?" You had better ask, "What shall we do with the slaveholders if the slaves are freed?" The slave has shown himself better fitted to take care of himself than the slaveholder. He is the bone and sinew of the south; he is the producer, while the master is nothing but a consumer, and a very poor consumer at that. The slave is the producer, and he alone can be relied upon. He has the sinew, the determination, and the will; and if you will take the free colored people of the south as the criterion, take their past history as a sample of what the colored people are capable of doing, every one must be satisfied that the slaves can take care of themselves. . . .

But it is said, "The two races cannot live together in a state of freedom." Why, that is the cry that rung all over England thirty years ago: "If you liberate the slaves of the West Indies, they can't live with the whites in a state of freedom." Thirty years have shown the contrary. The blacks and the whites live together in Jamaica; they are all prosperous, and the island in a better condition than it ever was before the act of emancipation was passed. . . .

The majority of the colored people in the Northern States [are] descended from slaves: many of them were slaves themselves. In education, in morals, and in the development of mechanical genius, the free blacks of the Northern States will compare favorably with any laboring class in the world. And considering the fact that we have been shut out, by a cruel prejudice, from nearly all the mechanical branches, and all the professions, it is marvellous that we have attained the position we now occupy. Notwithstanding these bars, our young men have learned trades, become artists, gone into the professions, although bitter prejudice may prevent their having a great deal of practice. When it is considered that they have mostly come out of bondage, and that their calling has been the lowest kind in every community, it is still more strange that the colored people have amassed so much wealth in every state in the Union. If this is not an exhibition of capacity, I don't understand the meaning of the term.[9]

Most white Americans believed that Africa was hopelessly backward and barbaric compared with the progressive civilizations of Europe and America. This assumption played an important part in creating the image of the Negro as an inferior race. American Negroes admitted that West Africans of the coastal areas were indeed uncivilized and backward, but attributed this condition to the debasing influence of the slave trade. They asserted that travelers who had ventured into the interior of Africa had found a greater sophistication of social and political organization and a higher state of economic development. A New York Negro declared in 1860 that

for a long period public sentiment had judged of African character by the degraded standard of civilization on the low coast, where slavers visit and petty kings make merchandize of human flesh; but the fact is already becoming known to the world that the people of Africa possess a faculty for self-government, and are already developing those stamina of character which only wake to influences of Christianity. Already we can see three millions of her population engaged in self-government, pursuing the arts of industry, and conducting the affairs of a nation with a forecast and judgment of which we need not be ashamed.[10]

An anonymous Negro contributor to the Anglo-African *wrote in 1863 that*

the everlasting architecture of Africa resisting alike the ex-humations of time and the ravages of barbarism, exists to this day, though in ruins, the wonder of the world! Witness the pyramids of Egypt. The ruins of Thebus, and Hermopolis, of Alexandria and Jupiter Ammon. Look at the palace of the Ptolemus—the catacombs of Sycopolis—the ancient capitol of Abyssinia, where 40 pillars and 30 pedestals of granite, are still standing in gloomy magnificence to tell you what Africa once was! . . .

But I see the smile of disdain curling upon the lips of a pragmatic politician, and he points me to the intellect of modern Africa. . . . Yet the celebrated Blumenbach, the father of German naturalists, has a large library exclusively the productions of negroes, and he affirms, proudly and fearlessly, that there is no branch of science or literature, in which they have not excelled, have not distinguished themselves! And Gregory, ex-bishop of Blois, in France, has a large glass case filled with the works of negro authors exclusively, to which he points with exulting pride, as a refutation of all that can be said against the mental claims of Arica. Read her history and you will find a *thinking* story![11]

And in 1863, the Liberator *published a summary of a lecture by Martin R. Delany, who had traveled through West Central Africa in 1859–60. A short, wiry, full-blooded Negro, Delany had been born free in Virginia in 1812, moving to the North when he was ten years old. He had studied at Harvard Medical School and occasionally practiced medicine thereafter, but he was best known as a traveler and lecturer, and as a champion of black nationalism. Delany was later commissioned a major in the Union Army, and he was active in South Carolina's Reconstruction politics. The* Liberator*'s summary of his lecture in 1863 stated:*

He wanted to say what he knew of the negro race, not on the coast of Africa, but of the interior Africans, of whom so little is known—the Africans of the Niger Valley. The audience would be surprised to hear that even the Liberians had never until lately been ten miles beyond their territory; and so nothing could be expected from them. He was sorry to say, too, that American school-books inculcated, notwithstanding recent discoveries, very erroneous notions of the country. . . .

He had travelled three thousand miles in the country, and had seen it in all its phases of social organization. The language of a people is a good sign of its civility; and the African language is derived from fixed roots; it is not a jargon, but abounds in vowels, and is very melodious, and capable of expressing a wide range of feeling and sentiment. . . . The Doctor produced a grammar of the language, and made quotations from it. It was written by a native African, who had also composed numerous school-books, and made translations from the Bible. . . .

Alluding to the morals of the people, he said there was a mistake about it very current in these parts and elsewhere. It was thought that because polygamy was tolerated amongst them, there must be immorality also. Polygamy was an old and venerable institution, and had a genuine Oriental origin. Solomon was the arch-polygamist of the world, and the Africans who followed his example were no worse than he. It was the rich only, however, who had many wives; the poor could not afford to keep them. . . .

In these interior and remote regions, the people were ruled by a king, whom they elected themselves. Kings, and their sons and families, were all amenable to the law. Litigation begins always in the morning, and defendant's counsel has always the last speech.

Numerous examples of the industry of the Africans were given. They cultivated the lands, and made them as productive as gardens. All the staple cereals of a tropical clime were grown in abundance, and every species of fruit. They were workers in iron and other metals, and made excellent leather and glass. They were a religious people naturally; and he never met with a Pagan in all his travels.[12]

In the final analysis, wrote J. Anderson Raymond, a Philadelphia Negro, in 1864,
there is no *natural* difference existing between the two races. . . . Take a colored and a white child; rear them together; treat them precisely alike; show them the same advantages, and disadvantages; and at the end of ten years, show me which is the smarter child. Or, take them both, and turn them to the cares of the world, where they can have free access to all kinds of vice, then, at the end of ten years, tell me which can be the hardest, or endure the greater hardships. . . . If the white and the black man's conditions had been the same, no difference could have been found between the two races, as far as intellect is concerned.[13]

And the Pacific Appeal *stated:*
It is a fact known to every candid person that the mind of the negro in the United States has been chained. It has not been permitted to leave its resting place and explore the fields of science. The rights of his race have been perverted, crushed and prostrated by the degrading shackles of slavery; they have been deprived of schools, yet they have improved in knowledge, and many have attained the different arts and sciences. . . . The old-fashioned idea of the inferiority of the negro race has become obsolete, and it is time the newfangled notion of our superiority should be abolished. Let us assume a higher position. Let us place ourselves on the broad platform of the natural equality of mankind, and we will be invincible; behind that impregnable fortress we can safely combat, and finally overcome, prejudice and error.[14]

CHAPTER VIII

GOVERNMENT, PHILANTHROPY,

AND THE FREEDMEN

*In 1863 the Rev. Thomas Cala-
han, a missionary from the United Presbyterian Church serving among the freedmen in Louisiana, wrote that*
you have no idea of the state of things here. Go out in any
direction and you meet negroes on horses, negroes on mules,
negroes with oxen, negroes by the wagon, cart and buggy load,
negroes on foot, men, women and children; negroes in uniform, negroes in rags, negroes in frame houses, negroes living in
tents, negroes living in rail pens covered with brush, and negroes living under brush piles without any rails, negroes living
on the bare ground with the sky for their covering; all hopeful,
almost all cheerful, every one pleading to be taught, willing to
do anything for learning. They are never out of our rooms, and
their cry is for "Books! Books!" and "when will school begin?"
Negro women come and offer to cook and wash for us, if we
will only teach them to read the Bible. . . . And think of people
living in brush tents gathering for prayer meetings that last far
into the night. Every night hymns of praise to God and prayers
for the Government that oppressed them so long, rise around us
on every side—prayers for the white teachers that have already
come—prayers that God would send them more. These are our
circumstances.[1]

*At first there was no clear government policy toward these
thousands of "contrabands" who began pouring into Union*

lines in 1861. Gradually, during the second year of the war, some order began to emerge out of the chaos of contraband affairs. By the end of 1862 most army commanders had appointed a general superintendent of freedmen's affairs to organize and administer the contraband camps, to provide food, shelter, clothing, and medical care for the aged and helpless, and to put the able-bodied freedmen to work picking cotton on abandoned plantations or as laborers, teamsters, cooks, etc. in the Union army camps.[2]

In the fall and winter of 1861–62, the Washington correspondent of the Christian Recorder *reported that*

a great many colored people have escaped from rebel masters (in Virginia) and would-be masters, and are now quietly and successfully gaining a living in the district. . . . At Fortress Monroe the slaves who have managed to get within the federal lines, have evinced two things which set them in a most favorable light towards the world—*industry and a religious character*. Throughout the great circle of military camps that cover the hills as snowflakes, there is no place where God is as devoutly worshipped as by the "contraband" at Fortress Monroe. . . .

I trust that Congressmen and others have seen enough of the colored people recently freed to convince them that they can and *will* take care of themselves—of the many contrabands who have recently been "turned loose" from time to time, I venture to say no one has seen them begging or loafing. There exists the greatest demand for their labor, and they are anxious to supply the demand. They are kept at Government quarters till employed—they do not have to wait long for this. I have often visited them, and spoken words of cheer, and seen the kindling of aspiration—the development of manhood, as the prospect of freedom passed in review before them.[3]

All was not sweetness and light in freedmen's affairs, however. Union officers and soldiers frequently took advantage of the contraband's ignorance and inexperience. The government often failed to pay the Negroes their wages on time, and sometimes neglected to pay them at all. A missionary to the freedmen at Fortress Monroe, Virginia, wrote in 1862 that

there is an irrepressible foreboding, which seems to have fixed
itself upon the countenance of every one [of the Negroes]; and
it is not without good cause, for there has been, and is still,
meanness of every conceivable grade practised upon them. Officers take advantage of their ignorance in every way possible,
and torment them like fiends, while the government retains
them on its highways and public works, and the quartermaster
refuses to pay them. Thus these people have lived in this uncertain condition for nearly a year, and with this shameful and
glaring reproach to the government, open to all who wish to
know anything about the condition of the colored people here.[4]

*A newspaper reporter stationed on the South Carolina Sea
Islands declared that Union soldiers had shown*
some of the vilest and meanest exhibitions of human depravity
that it has ever been my lot to witness. Many, very many of the
soldiers, and not a few of the officers, have habitually treated
the negroes with the coarsest and most brutal insolence and in-
humanity; never speaking to them or of them but to curse and
revile them, to say all manner of evil against them, and to
threaten and imprecate all manner of evil upon them.[5]

*But not all Northerners acted with meanness toward the freed-
men. Many men and women gave up comfortable homes and
occupations in the North to come south and teach the freedmen
how to read and write, or to help supervise the Negroes' transition from slave labor to free labor. Nearly every Northern city
organized a freedmen's aid society; nearly every Northern
church helped to support Christian missionaries and teachers
of the freedmen. One of the most important and best publicized
of the freedmen's aid enterprises was undertaken on the South
Carolina Sea Islands, which were captured by Union forces in
November 1861. Because of their physical and cultural isola-
tion from the mainland, the slaves on these islands were among
the most backward in the entire South. If they proved themselves
capable of a productive and useful life in freedom, anti-
emancipation arguments based on the alleged innate inferiority of the Negro race would be seriously crippled.[6]*

A young lady from Boston, Elizabeth Botume, who came to

*the Sea Islands during the war to teach the freedmen, described
her first arrival in Beaufort, South Carolina:*

Negroes, negroes, negroes. They hovered around like bees in
a swarm. Sitting, standing, or lying at full-length, with their
faces turned to the sky. Every doorstep, box, or barrel was covered with them, for the arrival of a boat was a time of great
excitement. They were dressed—no, not dressed, nor clothed,
but partly covered with every conceivable thing which could be
put on the back of a biped. Some of the women had on old, cast-
off soldiers' coats, with "crocus bags," fastened together with
their own ravellings, for skirts, and bits of sailcloth for head-
handkerchiefs. Many of the men had strips of gay carpeting, or
old bags, or pieces of blanket, in which they cut arm-holes and
wore as jackets. Their pants were tied below and above the
knees and around the waist with pieces of rope to keep them
on. Words fail to describe their grotesque appearance. Fortunately they were oblivious to all this incongruity. They had not
yet attained distinct personality; they were only parts of a
whole; once "massa's niggers," now refugees and contrabands.
So all looked up with a smile, and put their hands to their fore-
heads in military fashion, with a "How d'ye, gineral? How d'ye,
missis?" as we passed along.[7]

*Another young teacher from the North was Charlotte Forten,
the granddaughter of James Forten, the famous Negro sail-
maker and abolitionist of Philadelphia. Miss Forten had moved
in 1854 from Philadelphia to Salem, Massachusetts, where she
graduated from the state normal school and became a teacher
in the Salem public schools. She came to the Sea Islands in 1862,
and later wrote the following account of her experiences:*

It was on the afternoon of a warm, murky day late in October
that our steamer, the *United States*, touched the landing at Hilton Head. A motley assemblage had collected on the wharf,—
officers, soldiers, and "contrabands" of every size and hue:
black was, however, the prevailing color. The first view of Hilton Head is desolate enough,—a long, low, sandy point, stretch-
ing out into the sea, with no visible dwellings upon it, except

the rows of small white-roofed houses which have lately been
built for the freed people. . . .

Little colored children of every hue were playing about the
streets, looking as merry and happy as children ought to look,—
now that the evil shadow of Slavery no longer hangs over them.
Some of the officers we met did not impress us favorably. They
talked flippantly, and sneeringly of the negroes, whom they
found we had come down to teach, using an epithet more offensive than gentlemanly. They assured us that there was great
danger of Rebel attacks, that the yellow fever prevailed to an
alarming extent, and that, indeed, the manufacture of coffins
was the only business that was at all flourishing at present. Although by no means daunted by these alarming stories, we were
glad when the announcement of our boat relieved us from their
edifying conversation.

We rowed across to Ladies Island, which adjoins St. Helena,
through the splendors of a grand Southern sunset. The gorgeous
clouds of crimson and gold were reflected as in a mirror in the
smooth, clear waters below. As we glided along, the rich tones
of the negro boatmen broke upon the evening stillness,—sweet,
strange, and solemn:

> "Jesus make de blind to see,
> Jesus make de cripple walk,
> Jesus make de deaf to hear.
> Walk in, kind Jesus!
> No man can hender me."

It was nearly dark when we reached the island, and then we
had a three-miles' drive through the lonely roads to the house
of the superintendent. We thought how easy it would be for a
band of guerrillas, had they chanced that way, to seize and hang
us; but we were in that excited, jubilant state of mind which
makes fear impossible, and sang "John Brown" with a will, as
we drove through the pines and palmettos. Oh, it was good to
sing that song in the very heart of Rebeldom! . . .

The next morning L. and I were awakened by the cheerful voices of men and women, children and chickens, in the yard below. We ran to the window, and looked out. Women in bright-colored handkerchiefs, some carrying pails on their heads, were crossing the yard, busy with their morning work; children were playing and tumbling around them. On every face there was a look of serenity and cheerfulness. My heart gave a great throb of happiness as I looked at them, and thought, "They are free! so long down-trodden, so long crushed to the earth, but now in their old homes, forever free!" And I thanked God that I had lived to see this day.

After breakfast Miss T. drove us to Oaklands, our future home. The road leading to the house was nearly choked with weeds. The house itself was in a dilapidated condition, and the yard and garden had a sadly neglected look. But there were roses in bloom. . . . The freed people on the place seemed glad to see us. After talking with them, and giving some directions for cleaning the house, we drove to the school, in which I was to teach. It is kept in the Baptist Church,—a brick building, beautifully situated in a grove of live-oaks. . . .

The school was opened in September. Many of the children had, however, received instruction during the summer. It was evident that they had made very rapid improvement, and we noticed with pleasure how bright and eager to learn many of them seemed. They sang in rich, sweet tones, and with a peculiar swaying motion of the body, which made their singing the more effective. . . .

The first day at school was rather trying. Most of my children were very small, and consequently restless. Some were too young to learn the alphabet. These little ones were brought to school because of the older children—in whose care their parents leave them while at work—could not come without them. We were therefore willing to have them come, although they seemed to have discovered the secret of perpetual motion, and tried one's patience sadly. But after some days of positive, though not severe treatment, order was brought out of chaos, and I found but little difficulty in managing and quieting the

tiniest and most restless spirits. I never before saw children so
eager to learn, although I had had several years' experience in
New-England schools. Coming to school is a constant delight and
recreation to them. They come here as other children go to play.
The older ones, during the summer, work in the fields from early
morning until eleven or twelve o'clock, and then come into
school, after their hard toil in the hot sun, as bright and as anxious to learn as ever.

Of course there are some stupid ones, but these are the minority. The majority learn with wonderful rapidity. Many of the
grown people are desirous of learning to read. It is wonderful
how a people who have been so long crushed to the earth, so
imbruted as these have been,—and they are said to be among
the most degraded negroes of the South,—can have so great a
desire for knowledge, and such a capability for attaining it. One
cannot believe that the haughty Anglo-Saxon race, after centuries of such an experience as these people have had, would
be very much superior to them. . . .

We found it rather hard to keep their attention in school. It
is not strange, as they have been so entirely unused to intellectual concentration. It is necessary to interest them every moment, in order to keep their thoughts from wandering. Teaching
here is consequently far more fatiguing than at the North. In
the church, we had of course but one room in which to hear all
the children; and to make one's self heard, when there were
often as many as a hundred and forty reciting at once, it was
necessary to tax the lungs very severely. . . .

In the evenings, the children frequently came in to sing and
shout for us. These "shouts" are very strange,—in truth, almost
indescribable. It is necessary to hear and see in order to have
any clear idea of them. The children form a ring, and move
around in a kind of shuffling dance, singing all the time. Four
or five stand apart, and sing very energetically, clapping their
hands, stamping their feet, and rocking their bodies to and
fro. . . . The grown people on this plantation did not shout, but
they do on some of the other plantations. . . . The shouting
of the grown people is rather solemn and impressive. . . . It is prob-

able that they are the barbarous expression of religion, handed down to them from their African ancestors, and destined to pass away under the influence of Christian teachings. The people on this island have no songs. They sing only hymns, and most of these are sad. . . .

The tiniest children are delighted to get a book in their hands. Many of them already know their letters. The parents are eager to have them learn. They sometimes said to me,—"Do, Miss, let de chil'en learn eberyting dey can. *We* nebber hab no chance to learn nuttin', but we wants de chil'en to learn."

They are willing to make many sacrifices that their children may attend school. One old woman, who had a large family of children and grandchildren, come regularly to school in the winter, and took her seat among the little ones. She was at least sixty years old. Another woman—who had one of the best faces I ever saw—came daily, and brought her baby in her arms.

Daily the long-oppressed people of these islands are demonstrating their capacity for improvement in learning and labor. What they have accomplished in one short year exceeds our utmost expectations. Still the sky is dark; but through the darkness we can discern a brighter future. We cannot but feel that the day of final and entire deliverance, so long and often so hopelessly prayed for, has at length begun to dawn upon this much-enduring race. An old freedman said to me one day, "De Lord make me suffer long time, Miss. 'Peared like we nebber was gwine to git troo. But now we's free. He bring us all out right at las'."[8]

The Northern teachers were confronted by a strange new situation when they set out to teach the freed children how to read and write. In her first day of teaching, Elizabeth Botume had difficulty in calling the roll because of the odd names, the lack of surnames, and the uncertainty of the children about their own first names. She finally enrolled the names of all fifteen present.

The next morning I called the roll, but no one answered, so I was obliged to go around again and make out a new list. I could not distinguish one from another. They looked like so many peas

in a pod. The woolly heads of the girls and boys looked just
alike. All wore indiscriminately any cast-off garments given
them, so it was not easy to tell "which was which." Were there
twenty-five new scholars, or only ten?

The third morning it was the same work over again. . . . I
now wrote down forty new names, and I began to despair of
ever getting regulated. . . . In time I began to get acquainted
with some of their faces. I could remember that "Cornhouse"
yesterday was "Primus" to-day. That "Quash" was "Bryan."
He was already denying the old sobriquet, and threatening to
"mash your mouf in," to any one who called him Quash.[9]

*Miss Laura Towne from Philadelphia described one of her
early classroom experiences: the pupils*
had no idea of sitting still, of giving attention or ceasing to talk
aloud. They lay down and went to sleep, they scuffled and
struck each other. They got up by the dozen, made their curt-
sies, and walked off to the neighboring field for blackberries,
coming back to their seats with a curtsy when they were ready.
They evidently did not understand me, and I could not understand them, and after two hours and a half of effort I was thoroughly exhausted.[10]

*Such difficulties discouraged many teachers, but most of them
stuck it out and soon adopted a more cheerful tone. Laura Towne
forgot her early discouragement, and in June 1862 she wrote to
a friend:*
I wish you were as free from every fret as I am, and as happy.
We found the people here naked, . . . afraid and discontented
about being made to work as slaves, and without assurance of
freedom or pay, of clothes or food,—and now they are jolly and
happy and decently fed and dressed, and so full of affection and
gratitude to the people who are relieving them that it is rather
too flattering to be enjoyed. It will not last, I dare say, but it
is genuine now and they are working like Trojans. . . . It is
such a satisfaction to an abolitionist to see that they are proving conclusively that they can and will even *like* to work
enough at least to support themselves and give something extra to Government.[11]

*Most participants in and observers of the "Post Royal Exper-
iment" concluded that the experiment had been a success. Edward S. Philbrick, a Boston businessman and engineer who had
come to the Sea Islands as a plantation superintendent in the
spring of 1862, and whose first impression of the freedmen was
unfavorable (see above, pp. 57–58), later changed his opinion.
In November 1862, Philbrick wrote:*

Just a year ago to-night I entered this house for the first time.
If our Northern croakers could only be made to realize as we do
here the ease with which we have reduced a comparative degree of order out of the chaos we found, and see how ready this
degraded and half-civilized race are to become an industrious
and useful laboring class, there would not be so much gabble
about the danger of immediate emancipation, or of a stampede
of negro labor to the North.

We found them a herd of suspicious savages who regarded
their change of condition with fear and trembling, looking at
the cotton-field as a life-long scene of unrequited toil, and hail-
ing with delight the prospect of ''no more driver, no more cotton, no more lickin'.'' They had broken up the cotton-gins and
hidden the iron-work, and nothing was more remote from their
shallow pates than the idea of planting cotton for "white folks"
again.

Now they have, without the least urging, prepared for planting some two hundred acres of cotton-land upon this plantation,
having spread on it sixteen hundred ox-cart-loads of manure,
and worked up every inch of the ground with their hoes. They
have also planted one hundred and thirty acres of corn. . . .

As a sample of the change of feeling in regard to working on
cotton, I will relate how I got the cotton ginned on this and the
various other plantations in this neighborhood. I walked through
the negro quarters one day in December and told the people I
would pay them three cents per pound of clean cotton if they
would gin, assort, clean, and pack their cotton ready for market.
They said in reply their gins were all broken up. I told them that
was their own fault, and that, if they wanted other people to
gin their cotton and get their seed away from the place, they

would do so, and so get all the money and leave them no good seed to plant. "Dat's so, Massa," said they, and I passed along. The next time I came they had hunted up the broken pieces of twenty-five gins, and patched them up, and had ginned and packed all their cotton, in two weeks.[12]

Charles Nordhoff, a Northern journalist who visited the Sea Islands in the spring of 1863, described the labor of black stevedores on the docks, black women in the cotton fields, and black children in the schoolroom, and commented:

By the time you have seen all this, you begin to lose faith in the person who assured you that the negroes of Port Royal are an idle, dissolute, worthless set of creatures, who are supported at an enormous expense by an abolition government, etc., etc. You see, on the contrary, that black men are usefully employed in the navy, in the army, and as laborers by the Quartermaster's Department. When you have looked around a little farther, you will find that in yet other useful work not only black men, but black women and children, are busily and profitably engaged. . . .

The South Carolina freedmen are not paupers. They receive no support of any kind from the Government, nor charity from any source. They have done almost all the work in the Quartermaster's Department; they have, besides this, raised on the plantations, during the past year of freedom, sufficient food to supply themselves. In the season they have sold garden vegetables, melons, etc. to the troops to a considerable amount; they have furnished a full regiment, and more, of soldiers; and besides this, they have raised, gathered, ginned and packed seventy-five thousand pounds of Sea Island cotton, which will presently come to market.[13]

Frederick A. Eustis, the son of a former planter and slaveowner on the Sea Islands, returned to cultivate his father's plantation with free Negro labor during the war. He told a government commission in 1863:

I never knew, during forty years of plantation life, so little sickness. Formerly, every man had a fever of some kind, and now the veriest old cripple, who did nothing under secesh rule, will row a boat three nights in succession to Edisto, or will pick up the corn about the corn house. There are twenty people whom I know who were considered worn out and too old to work under the slave system, who are now working cotton, as well as their two acres of provisions; and their crops look very well. I have an old woman who has taken six tasks (that is, an acre and a half), and last year she would do nothing.[14]

And John Murray Forbes, a Boston businessman who visited the Sea Islands in the spring of 1862, wrote in June of that year: "I used to think emancipation only another name for murder, fire and rape, but mature reflection and considerable personal observation have since convinced me that emancipation may, at any time, be declared without disorder."[15]

Reports from most other contraband camps confirmed the conclusion that with assistance, guidance, and a fair chance the Negro slave could be converted to a free laborer without violent social dislocation. Contraband camps and freedmen's labor colonies were established in every part of the South penetrated by Union armies. In November 1862, General Ulysses S. Grant, faced with the problem of caring for thousands of freedmen who had flocked to his lines, appointed the Rev. John Eaton as "General Superintendent of Freedmen, Department of the Tennessee," an area that eventually embraced western Tennessee, eastern Arkansas, northwestern Mississippi, and northern Louisiana. One of Eaton's assistants later described the early conditions in the contraband camps:

I hope I may never be called on again to witness the horrible scenes I saw in those first days of the history of the freedmen in the Mississippi Valley. Assistants were hard to get, especially the kind that would do any good in our camps. A detailed soldier in each camp of a thousand people was the best that could be done. His duties were so onerous that he ended by doing nothing. . . . In reviewing the condition of the people at that time, I am not surprised at the marvellous stories told by visitors who caught an occasional glimpse of the misery and wretchedness in these camps. . . . Our efforts to do anything for these people, as they herded together in masses, when founded on any expectation that they would help themselves, often failed; they had become so completely broken down in spirit, through suffering, that it was almost impossible to arouse them.[16]

Eaton introduced sanitation measures in the camps, provided food and medical care for the helpless, and put able-bodied freedmen to work on government and military installations. Union officers sometimes impressed Negro laborers into the service against their will. James E. Yeatman, an agent of the Western Sanitary Commission, visited the Department of the Tennessee in the fall of 1863, and reported:

Within the City of Memphis, not directly connected with any of the camps or with the colored Regiments, there are some *three thousand* freed men and women, mostly freed men, who are employed in various ways at various rates of compensation. Those employed by Government receive but $10 per month, while many could readily earn from $30 to $50 per month. . . .

I saw a number of colored men pressed into service (not military), to labor at the rate of $10 per month, one of whom petitioned to be released as he had a good situation at $30 per month. The firemen on the steamboat on which I was a passenger from St. Louis to Memphis were all colored, and were receiving $45 per month. These men were afraid to go ashore at Memphis, for fear of being picked up and forced into Government employment at less than one-fourth their existing wages. Besides the fact that men are thus pressed into service, thousands have been employed for weeks and months who have never received anything but promises to pay. This negligence and failure to comply with obligations have greatly disheartened the poor slave, who comes forth at the call of the President, and supposes himself a free man, and that by leaving his rebel master he is inflicting a blow on the enemy. . . . Thus he was promised freedom, but how is it with him? He is seized in the street and ordered to go and help unload a steamboat, for which he will be paid, or sent to work in the trenches, or to labor for some Quartermaster, or to chop wood for the Government. He labors for months, and at last is only paid with promises, unless perchance it may be with kicks, cuffs, and curses. Under such treatment he feels that he has exchanged one master for many masters.[17]

In 1863 the plantation-leasing system was introduced in the Mississippi Valley. Under this system the Union government leased captured or abandoned plantations to private individuals, who hired freedmen to plant and harvest the cotton. A few of the lessees were former planters who had taken the oath of allegiance; most were Yankees who had descended upon the lower Mississippi in the hope of making a fast dollar. The government established strict regulations for the conditions and terms of Negro employment on these plantations, but the regulations were haphazardly enforced and many of the freedmen were treated in much the same way as they had been under slavery. Yeatman visited many of the leased plantations, and reported:

The poor negroes are everywhere greatly depressed at their condition. They all testify that if they were only paid their little wages as they earn them, so that they could purchase clothing, and were furnished with the provisions promised they could stand it; but to work and get poorly paid, poorly fed, and not doctored when sick, is more than they can endure. Among the thousands whom I questioned none showed the least unwillingness to work. If they could only be paid fair wages they would be contented and happy. They do not realize that they are free men. They say that they are told they are, but then they are taken and hired out to men who treat them, so far as providing for them is concerned, far worse than their "secesh" masters did. . . .

The parties leasing plantations and employing these negroes do it from no motives either of loyalty or humanity. The desire of gain alone prompts them, and they care little whether they make it out of the blood of those they employ or from the soil. There are of course exceptions; but I am informed that the majority of these lessees were only adventurers, camp followers, "army sharks," as they are termed, who have turned aside from what they consider their legitimate prey, the poor soldier, to gather the riches of the land which his prowess has laid open to them. . . . Lessees are now allowed to lease as many plantations as their cupidity may lead them to grasp. . . . No one party should be permitted to lease over one. Lessees of more than one plantation are unable to give their personal supervision and so employ the old overseers whom the former masters had employed. Whether these men can ever be brought to regard as freemen those whom they had always known and treated as slaves is very doubtful.[18]

Late in the fall of 1864 the Rev. A. Severance Fisk, Assistant in Charge of Freedmen, Department of the Tennessee, made an inspection tour through part of the Department. He reported:

The inspection has covered ninety-five places leased by whites, and fifty-six plats of land worked by the blacks for themselves, in the Districts of Natchez, Vicksburg and Helena. . . .

TREATMENT FROM WHITE MEN ON PLANTATIONS: No complaint was made in forty-eight cases. On the remaining forty-seven plantations there was complaint of rough, or profane, or obscene, or insulting usage; while blows and kicks have been not infrequently administered on some; mainly . . . by the old Southern overseers. A certain roughness and severity of manner, however, has been used, foolishly, on almost all plantations. . . .

The ninety-five plantations examined embrace 45,745 acres of land, said to be cultivated, giving an average of 418 acres to the plantation. They have produced about 4,800 bales of cotton, and perhaps 18,000 bushels of corn. They have given labor and support to 8,588 people—about 90 people to a plantation. About twenty plantations I did not see. . . .

These one hundred and fifteen plantations, together with fifty-six plats of land cultivated by blacks, are what I find remaining of the four hundred and fifty leases, more or less, which have been taken for the year. From the ninety-five safest of these plantations, on which cultivation has been prosecuted for the season, there have been taken by the rebels 2,314 head of serviceable stock, and 967 blacks. . . . The blacks have been taken back into the interior of the State and resold into bondage. The mules have gone directly to the rebel service. Besides

this plunder, they have carried off with them how much supplies, both in dry-goods and in food, it is impossible to do more
than conjecture. Nor have I any means of ascertaining the
amount of stock or the number of hands taken from that greatly
larger outlying region, in which the planters have been utterly
broken up, and their all lost; from which white and black alike
fled for life, leaving behind them all things. Nor is it my sphere
to recite the horrible details of atrocious murders, perpetrated
upon both black and white, to which I have been a listener on
many of these places.[19]

*In an effort to provide the freedmen with a greater opportu-
nity to accumulate property and move ahead on their own, the
government leased many small farms to black men. Fisk visited
several of these Negro lessees:*

Their tracts of land ranged from five acres to one hundred
and fifty. There are many instances in which a family contrives
to get a good support from five acres, farmed with the hoe alone.
Many of these add to their resources by cutting wood. I doubt
if any of these five acre men have, for months, required or received any aid from the Government, or will ever require it in
the future; unless by some great failure of administrative wisdom they should be hindered from procuring land. . . . One old
man I found, who had himself, with his hoe only, made ten acres
of corn, on land newly cleared, and so a good year's wages. He
had lately married a wife, and wants, next year, twenty-five
acres; for, he says with pride, "She's a workin' woman, sah!"
He ought to have the land. There is no reason why, under supervision, this whole bend, from Young's upon the upper side,
to Brown and Johnson's upon the lower, may not be successfully tilled by the blacks, in such a way as to remove the support
of the people entirely from the shoulders of the Government. . . .

I cannot see that, in any particular, these colored men have
been less successful than the white planters alongside them.
Where they have employed hands, there is little, if any complaint against them, either in the matter of rations, wages, or
usage. Having undertaken small and manageable tracts of land,

working them in good part themselves, and employing but a small number of hands; their crops have been more fully worked, and so have produced more bountifully. Some of them, from small wood-yards have made the whole expenses of their enterprise. Many of them during the winter, will be making money in the same way. All of these are eager for the privilege of cultivating for themselves another year.[20]

In the fall of 1864 Superintendent Eaton submitted the following report for the Department of the Tennessee and the State of Arkansas:

This supervision, embracing the territory within the lines of our army, from Cairo down the Mississippi to the Red River, together with the State of Arkansas, numbered in its care during the past year 113,650 freedmen. These are now disposed as follows: In military service, as soldiers, laundresses, cooks, officers' servants, and laborers in the various staff departments, 41,150; in cities, on plantations, and in freedmen's villages and cared for, 72,500.

Of these, 62,300 are entirely self-supporting—the same as any industrial class anywhere—as planters, mechanics, barbers, hackmen, draymen, &c., conducting enterprises on their own responsibility, or as hired laborers. The remaining 10,200 receive subsistence from the government. 3,000 of them are members of families, whose heads are carrying on plantations, and have under cultivation 4,000 acres of cotton; and are to pay the Government for their subsistence from the first income of the crop.

The other 7,200 include the paupers (those over and under the self-supporting age, the crippled and sick in hospital) . . . and instead of being unproductive, have now under cultivation 500 acres of corn, 760 acres of vegetables, and 1,500 acres of cotton—besides the work done at wood chopping, etc.

There are reported in the aggregate something over 100,000 acres of cotton under cultivation. Of these, about 7,000 acres are leased and cultivated by the blacks. Some of these are managing as high as 300 or 400 acres. . . .

It would only be a guess to state the entire amount [of wood] cut by the people under this supervision; it must be enormous. The people have been paid from fifty cents to two dollars and fifty cents per cord for cutting. This wood has been essential to the commercial and military operations on the river.

Of the 113,650 blacks above mentioned, 13,320 have been under instruction in letters; about 4,000 have learned to read quite fairly, and about 2,000 to write.[21]

In December 1862, General Nathaniel P. Banks succeeded General Benjamin Butler as commander of the Department of the Gulf, comprising the Union-occupied portion of Louisiana south of the Red River. When he arrived in New Orleans, Banks found most of the contrabands crowded into filthy camps and huts, living on half-rations handed out by the army. He decided to get them back to work on the plantations, and issued a general order establishing rules and regulations for a system of labor on January 29, 1863, supplemented by an additional order on February 3, 1864. Louisiana planters within Banks's department who took the oath of allegiance were allowed to continue working their plantations with Negro labor, and Banks's officers encouraged the freedmen to go to work for their old masters. The order regulated the wage scale for freedmen by ability up to ten dollars a month, and stipulated that payment of half the wages should be reserved until the end of the year. Laborers were promised "just treatment, healthy rations, comfortable clothing, quarters, fuel, medical attendance, and instruction for children." But Negroes would not be allowed to leave the plantations without a pass, and provost marshals were ordered to enforce the "continuous and faithful service, respectful deportment, correct discipline and perfect subordination" of the freedmen. Whipping was prohibited, but laborers could be punished by loss of pay or rations for feigned sickness, laziness, disobedience, or "insolence."[22]

Northern radicals and Negroes charged that Banks's system was a form of serfdom scarcely distinguishable from slavery itself. Frederick Douglass said that Banks's labor policy "is our chief danger at the present moment; it practically enslaves the

*negro, and makes the Proclamation of 1863 a mockery and de-
lusion."*

What is freedom? It is the right to choose one's own employment. Certainly, it means that, if it means anything; and when
any individual or combination of individuals undertakes to decide for any man when he shall work, where he shall work, at
what he shall work, and for what he shall work, he or they
practically reduce him to slavery. He is a slave. That I understand Gen. Banks to do—to determine for the so-called freedman when, and where, and at what, and for how much he shall
work, when he shall be punished, and by whom punished. It is
absolute slavery. It defeats the beneficent intentions of the government, if it has beneficent intentions, in regard to the freedom of our people.[23]

*Articulate Negroes in Louisiana were also dissatisfied with
Banks's policy. The New Orleans Tribune, a triweekly, bilingual (French and English) newspaper established in July 1864
by the old free Negro-Creole community in New Orleans, complained about the fixed rate of low wages instituted by Banks's
orders:*

According to this, the condition of the slave is not materially
altered. The Eight, Six or Four dollars per month which they
have the promise of getting from their Employers, but which
perhaps in a great many instances they may never receive, is
scarcely enough to put an extra pair of boots upon their feet, to
say nothing of the hundred and one little incidental expenses,
which are not embraced, and could not be very well, in the
existing contract.[24]

*The Tribune compared Banks's labor code with the old Loui-
siana slave code:*

If we except the lash, which is not mentioned in these communications, one is unable to perceive any material difference
between the two sets of regulations. All the important prohibitions imposed upon the slave, are also enforced against the
freedman. The free laborer, as well as the slave, has to retire
into his cabin at a fixed hour in the evening; he cannot leave

on Sunday, even to visit friends or simply to take a walk in the neighborhood, unless he be provided with a written authorization. . . . It is true that the law calls him a freeman; but any white man, subjected to such restrictive and humiliating prohibitions, will certainly call himself a slave. . . . Our freedmen, on the plantations, at the present time, could more properly be called, mock-freedmen. . . . If we do not take care, slavery will never be practically abolished in Louisiana.[25]

In March 1865, Captain J. H. Ingraham, a prominent Louisiana Negro who had served in the Union Army, told a meeting of the Louisiana Equal Rights League:

No system of gradual elevation is needed to make us men. From Red River to the Gulf, we are told by this Banks oligarchy that we are subject to special rules and regulations in our affairs; we are told that we are not ready to assume the responsibility of citizens of the United States, and that it was essential to have a "free labor" system. . . . The defenders of such a system are not the friends we intend to have. (Applause.) . . .

I recently visited the parishes for the express purpose of inquiring about that system of "free labor." Hundreds of people assured me that the laborers were [worse] off under that new system, than they were under the old one. Let us eradicate Banks's system. (Applause.) You may rest assured that justice, equity, will never be our boon, so long as any friends of Gen. Banks remain here to carry out his system.[26]

In spite of these protests, Banks's system remained essentially unchanged until after the war.

Louisiana Negroes did praise one feature of Banks's administration. In March 1864 the General had issued an order creating a "Board of Education for the Department of the Gulf" with power to levy and collect a school tax, establish common schools, employ teachers, and erect schoolhouses. On October 23, 1864, the New Orleans Tribune stated editorially in its French section:

The members of the Board of Education have applied themselves industriously to their task. They have 78 colored schools,

attended by 7,900 students, with 125 teachers. . . . Of the 15,340
colored children who are inside Union lines in Louisiana, more
than half are already in these schools, and it is hoped that within
three or four months from now half of those who remain will
also receive instruction.

Although the schools have been open only a short time, one
can already find proof of the aptitude of the negro to receive
the elements of civilization. The children who began the alphabet three or four months ago are reading now in the first
Readers, and are doing easily the primary rules of arithmetic.

Intelligent men among the planters understand that everything which tends to elevate the intelligence and self-respect of
the worker is advantageous for themselves, and several of these
planters are helping the Board of Education to establish schools
on their plantations.

The schools of the city number fifteen, with 41 teachers and
an average attendance of 1,900 students. . . . These children are
aged from 5 to 18 years. There are also some adults of both
sexes, maids, workers, seamstresses, who arrange to take off
two hours daily from their work to attend school. Half of these
people did not know their letters last October. . . .

In the organization of these schools there are numerous difficulties to surmount, including racial prejudice. It was thought
that good teachers could not be secured without going to the
North for them. However, the white women of noble heart in
New Orleans put themselves swiftly to the task, and have continued courageously in the face of calumnies, mockeries, and
social proscription. One hundred of the teachers were born and
raised in the South, and 75 are from Louisiana. Honor to them!

The best days approach. The progressive successes of the arms
of the Union gradually purify the political atmosphere. Many of
those who were blind are beginning to see, and the community
is coming to the conclusion that since the Negro has become
free, it is preferable to have intelligent and enlightened workers
rather than uneducated drudges.[27]

*During the war, approximately 500,000 freedmen came
within Union lines. Many of them suffered severely from hun-*

ger, disease, and exposure; some were subjected to the cruelties and depredations of Union soldiers and rapacious civilians; a few found freedom more a curse than a boon. But most of them rejoiced in their newly won status as free men, and they went to work with the assistance of Northern teachers, missionaries, and army officers to prove themselves worthy of freedom. Negro free labor raised thousands of bales of cotton, earned hundreds of thousands of dollars, and accomplished millions of man-hours of work on Union military installations during the war. Most important of all, perhaps, it was estimated in August 1865, that more than 200,000 freedmen had received instruction in reading and writing during the past four years.[28] The Civil War did more than emancipate the slave; it started him on the long road to true freedom.

CHAPTER IX

NEGRO MISSIONS TO THE FREEDMEN

Most *of the organizers and teachers of the Northern freedmen's aid societies were white persons. But the Negroes themselves, in both North and South, did not shirk the duty of aiding and assisting their emancipated brethren. When philanthropic whites in the North began to form freedmen's aid societies in the spring of 1862, the* Christian Recorder, *organ of the A.M.E. Church, published an editorial on "Aid to the Contrabands":*

We say, and do recommend, to all of our people, as well as all others, to give to this cause, for we believe it to be a Christian act and a Christian duty. . . . Let us provide clothing and money to help to take care of them; let us send them kind teachers, both colored and white; let there be also persons to work with them, and let them till the ground, raise cotton, grain, and potatoes, as they understand the ground and climate. We recommend our people and churches to take hold of this matter, and appoint good and efficient committees who may be responsible for any amount that may be put into their hands.[1]

The Rev. Henry M. Turner, pastor of Israel Bethel Church in Washington, declared in October 1862 that
the time has arrived in the history of the American African, when grave and solemn responsibilities stare him in the face. The proclamation of President Lincoln . . . has opened up a new

series of obligations, consequences, and results, never known to our honored sires. . . .

The great quantity of contrabands (so-called), who have fled from the oppressor's rod, and are now thronging Old Point Comfort, Hilton Head, Washington City, and many other places, and the unnumbered host who shall soon be freed by the President's proclamation, are to materially change their political and social condition. The day of our inactivity, disinterestedness, and irresponsibility, has given place to a day in which our long cherished abilities, and every intellectual fibre of our being, are to be called into a sphere of requisition. The time for boasting of ancestral genius, and prowling through the dusty pages of ancient history to find a specimen of negro intellectuality is over. Such useless noise should now be lulled, while we turn our attention to an engagement with those means which must, and alone can, mould out and develop those religious, literary, and pecuniary resources, adapted to the grave expediency now about to be encountered.

Thousands of contrabands, now at the places above designated, are in a condition of the extremest suffering. We see them in droves every day perambulating the streets of Washington, homeless, shoeless, dressless, and moneyless. . . . Every man of us now, who has a speck of grace or bit of sympathy, for the race that we are inseparably identified with, is called upon by force of surrounding circumstances, to extend a hand of mercy to *bone of our bone and flesh of our flesh.* . . .

The proclamation of President Lincoln has banished the fog, and silenced the doubt. . . . We have stood still and seen the salvation of God, while we besought Him with teary eyes and bleeding hearts; but the stand-still day bid us adieu Sept. 22, 1862. A new era, a new dispensation of things, is now upon us—to action, to action, is the cry. We must now begin to think, to plan, and to legislate for ourselves.[2]

In 1864 the Rev. James Lynch, a Negro Methodist minister from Baltimore who had come to the South Carolina Sea Islands the previous year and had been appointed a "Missionary and Government Superintendent" at Beaufort, wrote that

you of the North, perhaps, under-estimate the influence and
power that can be wielded by colored men and women of character, intelligence and education. . . . I would no more let the
color of a man's skin determine my estimate of him than the
color of his coat; but I cannot see the entire work of the education of thousands of our black brethren being carried on entirely by the whites, without appealing to my colored friends to
be up and doing, and have "a lot and part in the matter." . . .

The white people are doing in the South an educational work
that shines forth as the greatest achievement of this world's six
thousand years. No one should find fault with it; every one
should rejoice at it, and be fired thereby with an heroic, self-
sacrificing zeal to go and do likewise.

The United States Direct Tax Commissioners have granted me,
for five years, a schoolfarm of one hundred and sixty-five acres
of improved land, with buildings erected thereon, and possessing the additional charm of having a number of orange trees,
the condition of tenure being the keeping of a school thereon.
On this spot I design to establish a school, to be under the entire
supervision of a colored lady or gentleman who may prove competent. On the borders of this farm a village for colored refugees
is in course of erection. . . .

Oh, this work among the freedmen has a charm about it! If
there is a soul in you, it is drawn out—any sympathy for your
fellow, it is enlarged and made the active instrument of his improvement. God is in the whole work, and in the man whose
heart is in it. It has its difficulties, but they may melt away
before a cool head and a warm heart.[3]

*In every Northern city with a sizable Negro population the
black churches and their secular leaders formed freedmen's aid
societies. Some of the larger and better known of these societies
were the Contraband Relief Association of Washington, the
Union Relief Association of the Israel Bethel Church in Washington, the Freedmen's Friend Society in Brooklyn, the African
Civilization Society in New York, the Contraband Aid Association of Cincinnati, and the Contraband Committee of the
Mother Bethel Church in Philadelphia.*

In the fall of 1862 the newly organized Union Relief Associ-
ation of the Israel Bethel Church (A.M.E.) in Washington pub-
lished the following appeal to the people of the North:

BRETHREN AND SISTERS: We appeal to you for aid in behalf of
our poor, destitute, and suffering people from the South, who
have come amongst us destitute of all the comforts of life. . . .
They have fled from the storm of battle, from the fire and the
sword, leaving everything behind them. . . . They have continued to come until they have increased from hundreds to thousands, and still they come, some almost naked, and many
without covering or a place to rest their heads upon at night,
except the cold earth, which has already produced considerable
sickness among them; and unless great exertion is made for their
relief, there will be the most dreadful suffering among our unhappy and disconsolate brethren that has ever been experienced
in the Capital of this one peaceful and happy nation. . . . We
have organized an Association, and enclosed a copy of our constitution, hoping that it will meet your approbation, and, in the
name of humanity, and the ties which bind us together in the
bonds of a common brotherhood, you will give us all the aid in
your power by contributing clothing for adults, or children of
both sexes. Bedding, or bed clothing, old or new, money, or any
nourishment for the sick will be thankfully received by the Association, and faithfully applied by the Executive Committee.[4]

In August 1862, Elizabeth Keckley, Mrs. Lincoln's mulatto
seamstress, organized the Contraband Relief Association of
Washington. Born a slave in Virginia, Mrs. Keckley had moved
to St. Louis in the 1840s, where she worked as a seamstress and
dressmaker to purchase freedom for herself and her son. She
later moved to Washington, where she came to the attention of
Mrs. Lincoln and was given a job as the First Lady's modiste in
1861. Intelligent, sensitive, and sympathetic, Mrs. Keckley soon
became a close friend and confidante of Mrs. Lincoln. In a book
about her experiences in the White House during the Civil War,
Mrs. Keckley described the founding of the Contraband Relief
Association in 1862:

In the summer of 1862, freedmen began to flock into Wash-

ington from Maryland and Virginia. They came with a great hope
in their hearts and with all their worldly goods on their
backs. . . . Many good friends reached forth kind hands, but the
North is not warm and impulsive. For one kind word spoken,
two harsh ones were uttered; there was something repelling in
the atmosphere, and the bright joyous dreams of freedom to the
slave faded—were sadly altered, in the presence of that stern,
practical mother, reality. . . .

One fair summer evening I was walking the streets of Washington, accompanied by a friend, when a band of music was
heard in the distance. We wondered what it could mean, and
curiosity prompted us to find out. . . . We approached the sen-
tinel on duty at the gate [of Mrs. Farnham's house], and asked
what was going on. He told us that it was a festival given for
the benefit of the sick and wounded soldiers in the city. This
suggested an idea to me. If the white people can give festivals
to raise funds for the relief of the suffering soldiers, why should
not the well-to-do colored people go to work to do something
for the benefit of the suffering blacks? I could not rest. The
thought was ever present with me, and the next Sunday I made
a suggestion in the colored church, that a society of colored
people be formed to labor for the benefit of the unfortunate
freedmen. The idea proved popular, and in two weeks "the
Contraband Relief Association" was organized, with forty working members.

In September of 1862, Mrs. Lincoln left Washington for New
York, and requested me to follow her in a few days, and join
her at the Metropolitan Hotel. I was glad of the opportunity to
do so, for I thought that in New York I would be able to do
something in the interests of our society. Armed with creden-
tials, I took the train for New York, and went to the Metropolitan, where Mrs. Lincoln had secured accommodations for me.
The next morning I told Mrs. Lincoln of my project; and she
immediately headed my list with a subscription of $200. I cir-
culated among the colored people, and got them thoroughly interested in the subject, when I was called to Boston by Mrs.
Lincoln, who wished to visit her son Robert, attending college

in that city. I met Mr. Wendell Phillips, and other Boston philanthropists, who gave me all the assistance in their power. We
held a mass meeting at the Colored Baptist Church, Rev. Mr.
Grimes, in Boston, raised a sum of money, and organized there
a branch society. The society was organized by Mrs. Grimes,
wife of the pastor, assisted by Mrs. Martin, wife of Rev. Sella
Martin. This branch of the main society, during the war, was
able to send us over eighty large boxes of goods, contributed
exclusively by the colored people of Boston. Returning to New
York, we held a successful meeting at the Shiloh Church, Rev.
Henry Highland Garnet, pastor. The Metropolitan Hotel, at that
time as now, employed colored help. I suggested the object of
my mission to Robert Thompson, Steward of the Hotel, who immediately raised quite a sum of money among the dining-room
waiters. Mr. Frederick Douglass contributed $200, besides lec-
turing for us. Other prominent colored men sent in liberal contributions. From England a large quantity of stores was received.
Mrs. Lincoln made frequent contributions, as also did the President. In 1863 I was re-elected President of the Association,
which office I continue to hold.[5]

*In its first two years the Association spent more than $1,600
and distributed nearly one hundred barrels and boxes of do-
nated clothing to needy contrabands. In 1864 the Association,
which had changed its name to "The Freedmen and Soldiers'
Relief Association of Washington," issued the following report:*

Two years ago, we pledged ourselves to do all we could towards ameliorating the condition of that class of suffering people, who by existing circumstances, have been released from the
tyranny of the oppressor, and cast in our midst in a state of utter
destitution. . . . Our efforts during the past year have been
crowned with success, and our appeals for aid to carry forward
the benevolent operations of this Association, have always met
a generous response.

. . . After the removal of the people from Camp Barker to
Freedmen's village, we directed our attention to those in and
around the city, we found many of them helpless, homeless, and
starving. Our work has been to provide shelter, food, clothing,

medicines and nourishments for them, we have also buried their dead, and in fact, done all we could, as far as means and circumstances would allow, to alleviate their sufferings, and help them on towards a higher plane of civilization. . . .

We return our sincere and heartfelt thanks to those of our friends in every city, who have reposed confidence in us and our plans, by so generously contributing means to carry them out, and we earnestly hope for a continuance of the same.[6]

Negroes were also active in the organization of schools for the freedmen. The first contraband school in the South was started by Mary Chase, a freedwoman of Alexandria, Virginia, on September 1, 1861. In subsequent months Alexandria Negroes established several additional schools for the freedmen.[7] Mrs. Mary Peake, a free Negro of Hampton, Virginia, started the first school for freedmen at Fortress Monroe on September 17, 1861. Washington Negroes organized several schools for their emancipated brethren. The African Civilization Society of New York, which had been founded in 1858 to promote American Negro missionary effort and settlement in Africa, reconstituted itself during the Civil War as a freedmen's aid society. The Society established six black schools in Washington between 1864 and 1867. The Negro Catholic parish of Blessed Martin de Porras also founded five schools in Washington between 1865 and 1872. In addition, twenty-two Negroes individually started private schools for contrabands and Negroes in Washington during the decade of the 1860s.[8] The Rev. James Lynch of Baltimore and the Rev. James D. Hall of New York went to South Carolina in May 1863 as the first missionaries to the freedmen from the A.M.E. Church. The Church also sent several black female teachers to the South during the war.[9]

Susie King Taylor, the young slave who had escaped to a Union blockade ship off the Georgia coast in 1862, later wrote in her memoirs:

After I had been on St. Simon's [Island] about three days, Commodore Goldsborough heard of me, and came to Gaston Bluff to see me. I found him very cordial. He said Captain Whitmore had spoken to him of me, and that he was pleased to hear

of my being so capable, etc., and wished me to take charge of a
school for the children on the island. I told him I would gladly
do so, if I could have some books. He said I should have them,
and in a week or two I received two large boxes of books and
testaments from the North. I had about forty children to teach,
beside a number of adults who came to me nights, all of them
so eager to learn to read, to read above anything else.[10]

*Mrs. Taylor was later transferred to Port Royal Island off the
South Carolina coast, where she served as a laundress and
teacher for the First South Carolina Volunteers, the first regiment of ex-slaves raised in the South. She recalled that*

I taught a great many of the comrades in Company E to read
and write, when they were off duty. Nearly all were anxious to
learn. My husband taught some also when it was convenient for
him. I was very happy to know my efforts were successful in
camp, and also felt grateful for the appreciation of my services.
I gave my services willingly for four years and three months
without receiving a dollar. I was glad, however, to be allowed
to go with the regiment, to care for the sick and afflicted comrades. . . .

I learned to handle a musket very well while in the regiment,
and could shoot straight and often hit the target. I assisted in
cleaning the guns and used to fire them off, to see if the car-
tridges were dry, before cleaning and reloading, each day. I
thought this great fun. I was able to take a gun all apart, and
put it together again. . . .

When at Camp Shaw, I visited the hospital in Beaufort, where
I met Clara Barton. There were a number of sick and wounded
soldiers there, and I went often to see the comrades. Miss Barton was always very cordial toward me, and I honored her for
her devotion and care of those men.[11]

*Mr. J. G. McKee, an agent of the Western Freedmen's Aid
Commission, wrote in 1863:*

In and about Nashville, nobody can tell the number of half-
naked contrabands that are crowded into the basements and
waste houses, for no white man so far as I can learn has taken
the trouble to look after them.

I conjecture there cannot be less than four thousand contrabands who need help and instruction about this city. I find over
40 crowded into one small house. Sometimes 5 or 6 families in
one room without fireplace or chimney, cooking their morsel on
a few bricks, the smoke filling the apartment and steaming out
at the door. I frequently propose to take them back to their
master. "Would you not feel better with him than here?" The
uniform answer is something like the following: "Ah, no, Massa.
Dese is hard times, sure, but de Lord'ie do somthin' for us."
There's a something in their very laugh that makes my heart
bleed for them.

The colored citizens of Nashville deserve great credit. They
organized a "Good Samaritan Society" during last winter to furnish clothing and medicine to the suffering in the colored hospital. Yet of the 1400 contrabands who died here I am credibly
informed that at least 700 perished from neglect through hun-
ger, cold, filth and vermin.

They are also making a great effort to learn. Since our army
arrived several colored schools have sprung up, taught by colored people who have got a little learning somehow. Most of the
pupils pay from $1 to $2 a month. . . . I visited all their schools.
Two of them had nearly 100 pupils each. The others were small
and taught in poor dark corners. One school of 15 was taught in
a corner under the stairs. Most of the pupils are residents of the
city. Their eagerness to have our mission schools opened here is
truly affecting. Continually I am met with the query "When will
you open school?" . . .

I then told them my object was to open a free school and
teach them. The proposition was hailed with almost frantic joy.
Such expressions as the following came from all sides: "Bress
de Lor!" "Oh if I can only learn to read de Bible. I don't care
for notin' more." "I'm too ole and can't see much no how; but
I would like to learn." "When will you come back?" "When
will de school begin?"[12]

*And the Rev. John Eaton, General Superintendent of the
Freedmen in the Department of Tennessee, wrote that*
an interesting illustration of the self-respecting and capable

qualities of the freedmen in [Arkansas] occurred in connection with the war-time schools. Until General Steele's occupation in 1863 the laws against a Negro's acquiring money had been particularly strict. Nevertheless, my officers reported that the Negroes of Little Rock formed a Freedmen's School Society in March, 1865, and by their own exertions made the city schools free for the rest of the year. To the best of my belief, these were the first free schools in Arkansas—whether for whites or blacks—to subscribe and pay in full the compensation of the teachers.[13]

These are but a few examples of the schools that were founded and taught by Negroes during the Civil War. After the war, of course, the scope of freedmen's education was much enlarged, and many schools, academies, and colleges were established in the South. These institutions had their origins in the desire for education that was awakened in the minds of the freedmen during the Civil War. The Negro societies, missionaries, and teachers who followed the Union armies southward played an important part in this awakening.

CHAPTER X

NEGRO CONTRIBUTIONS
TO THE UNION WAR EFFORT

The enlistment of Negro troops in the Union Army beginning in late 1862 was one of the most significant events of the Civil War. But even before black men were enrolled in the army, indeed all through the war, Negroes made a variety of important contributions to the Union war effort. The six chapters following this one will deal with the Negro as a soldier in the Union Army. This chapter will describe the nonmilitary and semimilitary activities of Negroes during the war.

Nearly 200,000 freedmen served as laborers, teamsters, cooks, carpenters, nurses, scouts, etc. for the Union forces. The Washington correspondent of the Anglo-African *described in 1861 the impact of the war on Negroes in the District of Columbia:*

Your readers probably would like to know how the war affects the colored people of Washington. This being the seat of war all classes here are benefited by it. Five hundred men find employment each day in the Quartermaster's department. . . . Business of every kind for males has increased fully ten per cent. Numbers of our young men have taken officers' messes. Some have staff officers of various commands. Others attend exclusively to the horses of the army officers. Large numbers find employment in our hotels, boarding-houses, and restaurants. Barbers and hackmen are doing a thriving business, and the Northern Sutlers' establishments give work to any number

as drivers, porters, assistant packers, and salesmen. Many are
engaged at the railroad depot unloading and storing the immense amount of freight that daily arrives here from the North
and West. Three or four thousand men are employed at cutting
wood in Virginia around the different fortifications, and on the
northern front of Washington. Laundresses are doing a fine
business. They have the exclusive wash of entire regiments and
the families of U.S. officers; also for the Hospital inmates. Many
females are securing a comfortable livelihood by peddling little
notions around the different camps. In a word, we are all doing
well as far as employment is concerned. None need be idle.[1]

*In the winter of 1861–62 the Federal forces captured and oc-
cupied several areas along the North Carolina coast. Vincent
Colyer, an agent of the Brooklyn Y.M.C.A., was appointed "Superintendent of the Poor for the Department of North Carolina"
on March 30, 1862. Colyer later described some of the activities
of black men in his department:*

In the four months that I had charge of them, the men built
three first-class earth-work forts: Fort Totten, at Newbern—a
large work; Fort Burnside, on the upper end of Roanoke Island;
and Fort——, at Washington, N.C. These three forts were our
chief reliance for defence against the rebels, in case of an attack; and have since been successfully used for that purpose by
our forces under Major-Generals Foster and Peck, in the two
attempts which have been made by the rebels to retake Newbern.

The negroes loaded and discharged cargoes, for about three
hundred vessels, served regularly as crews on about twenty
steamers, and acted as permanent gangs of laborers in all the
Quartermasters', Commissary and Ordinance Officers of the Department. A number of the men were good carpenters, blacksmiths, coopers, &c., and did effective work in their trades at
bridge-building, ship-joining, &c. A number of the wooden cots
in the hospital, and considerable of the blacksmith and wheel-
wright work was done by them. . . . The large rail-road bridge
across the Trent was built chiefly by them, as were also the
bridges across Batchelor's and other Creeks, and the docks at

Roanoke Island and elsewhere. Upwards of fifty volunteers of
the best and most courageous, were kept constantly employed
on the perilous but important duty of spies, scouts, and guides.
In this work they were invaluable and almost indispensable.
They frequently went from thirty to three hundred miles
within the enemy's lines; visiting his principal camps and most
important posts, and bringing us back important and reliable
information. . . . They were pursued on several occasions by
blood-hounds, two or three of them were taken prisoners; one
of these was known to have been shot, and the fate of the
others was not ascertained. The pay they received for this work
was small but satisfactory.[2]

Negro laborers were frequently exposed to danger and death.
Major J. W. Wallis, commander of the Union post at Elizabeth
City, North Carolina, reported in April 1863:

March 12 I sent a party of soldiers from the North Carolina
company into the woods for wood with 12 negroes. After being
there a short time they were attacked by about 40 guerrillas and
1 negro killed and 2 wounded and 3 of the soldiers taken and
carried away prisoners. . . .

Nothing more occurred until the 6th of April. Captain San-
ders, of the North Carolina company, with a detail of 7 soldiers
and 10 negroes, was sent down the river in a schooner after
wood; the wind blowing, they were not able to land that day;
he returned home and left the men on board; in the evening
they went on shore to see their families, and were all taken and
carried away to Richmond prisoners, leaving that company now
with only 14 men for duty.[3]

Noncombatant freedmen were occasionally called upon to
take up arms to protect Union outposts from rebel attack. Cap-
tain James B. Talbot, Superintendent of Contrabands at Pine
Bluff, Arkansas, described one such incident in October 1863:

When the skirmishing first commenced I received orders from
you [Colonel Powell Clayton, commander of the Post] to furnish
as many men as possible to roll out cotton-bales and form breastworks. I had 300 immediately brought from the camp, on double-
quick, and from the short space of time in which every street

opening was blockaded you may judge of their efficiency in that respect, especially when you consider that much of the work was accomplished under a heavy fire from the enemy's skirmishers.

By the time the breastworks were complete the fight had become general, and calls for water were urgent to supply the soldiers and quench the fire that had caught to the cotton-bales from our artillery. I immediately pressed every water-holding vessel within reach, and formed a chain of negroes with buckets from the top of the bank to the water's edge. At this time a galling fire that opened on them from the enemy killed 1, wounded 3, and for a moment threw them all into confusion; but they were soon rallied, and resumed their work with the most astonishing rapidity. . . . Fifteen of them had arms, and were ordered to hold the point along the river; which they did throughout the action, some of them firing as many as 30 rounds, and one actually ventured out and captured a prisoner. None of them had ever before seen a battle, and the facility with which they labored and the manly efforts put forth to aid in holding the place excelled my highest expectations, and deserves the applause of their country and the gratitude of the soldiers. Their total loss is five killed and twelve wounded.[4]

In his official report of November 3, 1864, Montgomery Meigs, Quartermaster General of the United States Army, wrote that this department has employed persons of African descent to perform the labor of teamsters, grooms, laborers upon docks and wharves, upon steam-boats, and generally in all the manual labor for which their previous training has fitted them. The supply has not been equal to the demand. . . .

Much distress, doubtless, attends the sudden change of condition of these people from slavery, in which their wants were provided for by their masters, to freedom, in which they must abandon their former homes and support and provide for themselves. But the fact that employment is ready for them all shows that this great social revolution is being accomplished with much less suffering to the oppressed and liberated race than was to be feared. . . .

In my annual report of 1862 this subject was referred to, and the experience of two years of war has confirmed the views then expressed. The negro is not an embarrassment, but a great aid, in the conduct of the war.[5]

Negroes also performed an important service as spies for the Union Army. Allan Pinkerton, the chief of the United States Secret Service during the first two years of the war, went to Memphis (posing as a Southerner) on a spying mission in 1861. He later stated:

Here, as in many other places, I found that my best source of information was the colored men, who were employed in various capacities of a military nature which entailed hard labor. The slaves, without reserve, were sent by their masters to perform the manual labor of building earthworks and fortifications, in driving the teams and in transporting cannon and ammunition . . . I mingled freely with them, and found them ever ready to answer questions and to furnish me with every fact which I desired to possess.[6]

One Negro, John Scobell, undertook several spying missions for Pinkerton in Virginia. Pinkerton described Scobell's work:

Among the many men thus employed, was a negro by the name of John Scobell, and the manner in which his duties were performed, was always a source of satisfaction to me and apparently of gratification to himself. From the commencement of the war, I had found the negroes of invaluable assistance, and I never hesitated to employ them when, after investigation, I found them to be intelligent and trustworthy. . . .

All refugees, deserters and contrabands coming through our lines were turned over to me for a thorough examination and for such future disposition as I should recommend. John Scobell came to me in this manner. One morning I was seated in my quarters, preparing for the business of the day, when the officer of the guard announced the appearance of a number of contrabands. Ordering them to be brought in, the pumping process was commenced, and before noon many stray pieces of information had been gathered, which, by accumulation of evidence, were highly valuable. Among the number I had especially noticed the

young man who had given his name as John Scobell. He had a
manly and intelligent bearing, and his straightforward answers
to the many questions propounded to him, at once impressed
me very favorably. He informed me that he had formerly been
a slave in the State of Mississippi, but had journeyed to Virginia
with his master, whose name he bore. His master was a Scotch-
man, and but a few weeks before had given him and his wife
their freedom. The young woman had obtained employment in
Richmond, while he had made his way to the Union lines, where,
encountering the Federal pickets, he had been brought to headquarters, and thence to me. . . .

I immediately decided to attach him to my headquarters, with
the view of eventually using him in the capacity of a scout,
should he prove equal to the task. . . . I resolved to send him
into the South, and test his ability for active duty. Calling him
into my quarters, I gave him the necessary directions, and dispatched him, in company with Timothy Webster, on a trip to
Virginia. Their line of travel was laid out through Centreville,
Manassas, Dumfries, and the Upper and Lower Accoquan.

John Scobell I found was a remarkably gifted man for one of
his race. He could read and write, and was as full of music as
the feathered songsters. . . . In addition to what seemed an almost inexhaustible stock of negro plantation melodies he had
also a charming variety of Scotch ballads, which he sang with a
voice of remarkable power and sweetness. . . . Possessing the
talents which he did, I felt sure, that he had only to assume the
character of the light-hearted, happy darky and no one would
suspect the cool-headed, vigilant detective, in the rollicking negro whose only aim in life appeared to be to get enough to eat,
and a comfortable place to toast his shins.

. . . Carefully noting everything that came in his way he traveled through Dumfries, Accoquan, Manassas and Centreville,
and after spending nearly ten days in those localities he finally
made his way to Leesburg, and thence down the Potomac to
Washington. His experiences on this trip were quite numerous
and varied, and only a lack of space prevents their narration.

Sometimes, as a vender of delicacies through the camps, a laborer on the earthworks at Manassas, or a cook at Centreville, he made his way uninterruptedly until he obtained the desired information and successfully accomplished the object of his mission.

His return to Washington was accomplished in safety and his full and concise report fully justified me in the selection I had made of a good, reliable and intelligent operative.[7]

Northern generals frequently obtained information on the location and size of enemy forces from "intelligent contrabands" who had entered Union lines. General Abner Doubleday, Commander of the Military Defences North of the Potomac, ordered that fugitive slaves should be encouraged to enter Union lines because "they bring much valuable information, which cannot be obtained from any other source . . . make excellent guides . . . [and] frequently have exposed the haunts of secession spies and traitors, and the existence of rebel organization." In 1864 the district attorney of Goochland County, Virginia, wrote that "it is a matter of notoriety in the sections of the Confederacy where raids are frequent that the guides of the enemy are nearly always free negroes and slaves."[8]

The information brought by freedmen, however, was not always accurate or reliable. A Northern journalist wrote from South Carolina in 1863 that

they have a habit or proneness to lying which is, I think, clearly one of the old effects of slavery. They can see no wrong in telling that story which shall seem in their judgment best calculated to produce any desired effect. . . . One of these blacks, fresh from slavery, will most adroitly tell you precisely what you want to hear. To cross-examine such a creature is a task of the most delicate nature; if you chance to put a leading question he will answer to its spirit as closely as the compass needle answers to the magnetic pole. Ask if the enemy had fifty thousand men, and he will be sure that they had at least that many; express your belief that they had not five thousand and he will laugh at the idea of their having more than forty-five hundred. "The intelligent and reliable contraband" is the dread of staff-officers, who pump him vainly for information on which they may depend.[9]

And George Hepworth, a labor superintendent in Louisiana, wrote of the freedmen that "we could trust them implicitly on all common points. They knew whether there were any rebels in that parish; and, if there were, where they were stationed. But we never could trust their estimate of distance or numbers. They do not seem to know the difference between one mile and six, and are as likely to say five hundred as fifty."[10]

Nevertheless, the information or assistance of the "intelligent contraband" was more often useful than not. General O. M. Mitchel, commander of the Union forces occupying north Alabama, reported to the Secretary of War in 1862 that "the negroes are our only friends, and in two instances I owe my own safety to their faithfulness. I shall very soon have watchful guards among the slaves on the plantations bordering the river from Bridgeport to Florence, and all who communicate to me valuable information I have promised the protection of my Government." And Secretary of State William H. Seward stated, in an official dispatch to Minister Charles Francis Adams in London, that "everywhere the American General receives his most useful and reliable information from the negro, who hails his coming as the harbinger of Freedom."[11]

Throughout the war Southern Negroes rendered valuable assistance to Northern soldiers who had escaped from Confederate prisons and were trying to find their way back to Union lines. One such escaped prisoner later said that "it would have been impossible for our men, held as prisoners in the South, to make an escape without the aid of Negroes."[12] The prison literature of the Civil War is full of stories about slaves who helped escaping Yankee soldiers. The following account by Lieutenant Hannibal Johnson of the Third Maine Infantry is typical of the genre. Johnson was captured during the Battle of the Wilderness in Virginia, on May 5, 1864. He was sent to a prison camp near Columbia, South Carolina, from which he and three other Union officers escaped on the night of November 20–21, 1864, by over-

powering the guard and running into the woods under cover of darkness. The four men struck out for the Union lines near Knoxville, Tennessee, more than two hundred miles away. Johnson chronicled the story of his escape in a diary:

Nov. 23. Struck the river again this morning, but have not found the proper road yet, or one that leads in the right direction. Came very near being captured by running on some white men, but saw them first, concealed ourselves, and escaped. For the past twenty-four hours have had nothing to eat but dry corn which we found in the fields. Must find some trusty negro who will feed us and put us on the right road. At night we approached a negro cabin for the first time; we did it with fear and trembling, but we must have food and help. Found a family of trusty negroes belonging to Colonel Boozier, who gave us a good supper, such as we had not had for many long months. . . . Here we remained till nearly morning, when we were taken to the woods and hid there to wait for a guide which these negroes say they would furnish at dark. . . .

Nov. 24. Still in the woods, the women coming to us twice during the day to bring us food and inform us that a guide will be ready at dark. God bless the poor slaves. At dark Frank took us seven miles, flanking Lexington Court House, striking the Augusta road five miles above. Traveled all night, making about twenty-two miles.

Nov. 25. Lay in the woods all day, and at night went to William Ford's plantation to get food. Here the negroes could not do enough for us, supplying us with edibles of a nice character.

Nov. 26. Remained in a corn house during the day, the blacks bringing us plenty of food. At night our guide informed us that he could not take the road with us until the following night, so we were obliged to wait one day longer. . . .

Nov. 28. Still at Ford's. . . . About midnight we got a guide by the name of Bob to take us seven miles on the Edgefield road, as the Augusta state road is too public to travel, and some of our officers were captured on that road to-day. Turned over by Bob to a guide by the name of George, who hid us in the woods.

Nov. 29. George has brought us food during the day, and will try to get us a guide to-night. At dark went to the negro quarters, where a nice chicken supper was waiting us. . . .

Dec. 1. Just comfortable for a winter's day. At night after eating the usual diet of chicken, Peter, our guide, told us he was ready for the road. Went about twelve miles when Joe took us in charge and Peter started for home again. Were then hidden in the woods for the day.

Dec. 2. As soon as daylight the negroes on this place commenced coming to where we were hidden, all having something for us in the way of food; they also promise us a guide for the night. If such kindness will not make one an Abolitionist then his heart must be made of stone. This is on the Mathews place. At dark were taken to the Widow Hardy's plantation, where chickens, etc., were served for our supper. Here Jim took us eight miles, and gave us into the care of Arthur, who, after going with us fifteen miles, gave us to Vance who hid us in the woods. At dark Vance brought us more chickens for our evening meal, then started on the road with us going eight miles, then Charles took us, he going five miles; then David took us four miles, he giving us into the care of Hanson who took us a short distance and left us at the Preston Brooks' plantation (late United States Congressman from South Carolina). . . .

Dec. 4. Early this morning the slaves brought us a nice breakfast, for everything is in first-class condition on this place; do not seem to have felt the effects of the war as the rest of the country we have passed through. . . .

Dec. 5. At dark we were taken four miles, when we found we were going in the wrong direction, retraced our steps, got another guide who took us to Colonel Frazier's. Distance in right direction about ten miles. During the night crossed the railroad above 96, and here Ned took us in charge. The boys on this place were good foragers, for while with them we lived on the fat of the land. At dark December 6th, two of the Frazier servants took us eighteen miles and then gave us into the hands of Ben and Harrison, who took us to Henry Jones' place. Just before we arrived at this plantation it commenced raining and we got as wet as if thrown into the Saluda River. Here we were put into a negro cabin with a fire and bed at our disposal, and took advantage of both. . . .

Dec. 9. We were hiding in the woods when it commenced snowing, the first of the season; soon a guide came for us and hid us for the day in a negro cabin. At night some negroes came six miles through the storm to bring us food. We were gaining in strength and weight, for we are eating most of the time when we are not on the road tramping. The snow being so deep it is not safe to travel to-night, so we are hidden in a fodder barn.[13]

After traveling and hiding for nearly four more weeks, Johnson's party finally reached the Union lines near Knoxville on January 5, 1865. Without the assistance, shelter, and food given them by scores of Negroes along the way, these Union soldiers and many others could not have made good their escape.

A Negro steward aboard the Yankee schooner S. J. Waring *was one of the first authentic Northern war heroes. The following account, accurate in nearly all respects, is from the pen of William Wells Brown:*

In the month of June, 1861, the schooner "S. J. Waring," from New York, bound to South America, was captured on the passage by the rebel privateer "Jeff. Davis," a prize-crew put on board, consisting of a captain, mate, and four seamen; and the vessel set sail for the port of Charleston, S.C. Three of the original crew were retained on board, a German as steersman, a Yankee who was put in irons, and a black man named William Tillman, the steward and cook of the schooner. The latter was put to work at his usual business, and told that he was henceforth the property of the Confederate States, and would be sold, on his arrival at Charleston, as a slave. Night comes on; darkness covers the sea; the vessel is gliding swiftly towards the South; the rebels, one after another, retire to their berths; the hour of midnight approaches; all is silent in the cabin; the captain is asleep; the mate, who has charge of the watch, takes his brandy toddy, and reclines upon the quarter-deck. The negro thinks of home and all its endearments: he sees in the dim future chains and slavery.

He resolves, and determines to put the resolution into practice upon the instant. Armed with a heavy club [hatchet], he proceeds to the captain's room. He strikes the fatal blow: he feels the pulse, and all is still. He next goes to the adjoining room: another blow is struck, and the black man is master of the cabin. Cautiously he ascends to the deck, strikes the mate: the officer is wounded but not killed. He draws his revolver, and calls for help. The crew are aroused: they are hastening to aid their commander. The negro repeats his blows with the heavy club: the rebel falls dead at Tillman's feet. The African seizes the revolver, drives the crew below deck, orders the release of the Yankee, puts the enemy in irons, and proclaims himself master of the vessel.

"The Waring's" head is turned towards New York, with the stars and stripes flying, a fair wind, and she rapidly retraces her steps. . . . Five days more, and "The S. J. Waring" arrives in the port of New York, under the command of William Tillman, the negro patriot.

"The New-York Tribune" said of this event,—

"To this colored man was the nation indebted for the first vindication of its honor on the sea." Another public journal spoke of that achievement alone as an offset to the defeat of the Federal arms at Bull Run. Unstinted praise from all parties, even those who are usually awkward in any other vernacular than derision of the colored man, has been awarded to this colored man. . . . The Federal Government awarded to Tillman the sum of six thousand dollars as prize-money for the capture of the schooner.[14]

Another spectacular naval exploit was performed in May 1862 by Robert Smalls, a slave living in Charleston, South Carolina. The following account is taken from a book about the Negro in the Civil War, Camp-Fires of the Afro-American, *published in 1889:*

When Fort Sumter was attacked, [Smalls] and his brother John, with their families, resided in Charleston, and saw with sorrow the lowering of its flag, but they were wise enough to think much, while saying little, except among themselves, and hoped for a time to come when they might again live under its Government.

The high-pressure side-wheel steamer *Planter*, on board which they were employed, Robert as an assistant pilot, and John as a sailor and assistant engineer, was a light-draught vessel, drawing only five feet when heavily ladened, and was very useful to the Confederates in plying around the harbor and among the islands near Charleston. . . .

On Monday evening, May 12, 1862, the *Planter* was lying at her wharf, the Southern, and her officers having finished their duties for the day, went ashore, first giving the usual instructions to Robert Smalls, to see that everything should be in readiness for their trip next morning. They had a valuable lot of freight for Fort Ripley and Fort Sumter, which was to be delivered the next day, but Robert thought to himself that perhaps these forts would not receive the articles after all, except as some of them might be delivered by the propulsion of powder out of Union guns. He did not betray his thoughts by his demeanor, and when the officers left the vessel he appeared to be in his usual respectful, attentive, efficient and obedient state of mind. He busied himself immediately to have the fires banked, and everything put shipshape for the night, according to orders.

A little after eight o'clock the wives and children of Robert and John Smalls came on board. As they had sometimes visited the vessel, carrying meals, nothing was thought of this circumstance by the wharf guard, who saw them. Somewhat later a Colored man from the steamer *Etowah* stepped past him, and joined the crew.

Robert Smalls, for some time, had been contemplating the move which he was now about to make. He had heard that Colored men were being enlisted in the United States service at his old home [Beaufort], and that General Hunter was foreshadowing the emancipatory policy, giving kindly treatment to all contraband refugees. Now he was more anxious to get within the Union lines, and to join its forces. He had seen from the pilot-house, at a long distance, the blockading vessels, and had thought over a plan to reach them with the *Planter*, and his desire was to run her away from the Confederates when she would have a valuable cargo. He had to proceed cautiously in the unfolding of his designs. First his brother was taken into confidence, and he at once approved the project. He, of course, could be trusted to keep the secret. Then the others were approached, gradually, after sounding with various lines the depths of their patriotism. . . .

The brave men knew what would be their fate in the event of failure, and so, in talking over the matter together, just before cutting loose, they decided not to be captured alive, but to go down with the ship if the batteries of Castle Pinckney, Forts Moultrie and Sumter, and other guns should be opened upon them. They also determined to use the *Planter*'s guns to repel pursuit and attack, if necessary. . . .

After midnight, when the officers ashore were in their soundest and sweetest slumbers, the fires were stirred up and steam raised to a high pressure, and between 3 and 4 o'clock Robert Smalls, the conceiver, leader and manager of this daring scheme, gave orders to "cast off," which was done quietly. To guard against a suspicion of anything being wrong in the movements of the *Planter*, he backed slowly from the wharf, blew her signal whistles, and seemed to be in no hurry to get away. He proceeded down the harbor, as if making towards Fort Sumter, and about quarter past 4 o'clock passed the frowning fortress, saluting it with loud signals, and then putting on all steam. Her appearance was duly reported to the officer of the day, but as her plying around the harbor, often at early hours, was not a strange occurrence, and she had become a familiar floating figure to the forts, she was not molested; and the heavy guns that easily could have sunk her, remained silent. Passing the lower batteries, also, without molestation, the happy crew, with the greater part of the strain removed from their minds, now jubilantly rigged a white flag that they had prepared for the next emergency, and steered straight on to the Union ships. They were yet in great danger, this time from the hands of friends, who, not knowing anything concerning their escape, and on the

lookout to sink at sight torpedo-boats and "rebel-rams," might
blow them out of the water before discovering their peaceful
flag.

An eye-witness of the *Planter*'s arrival, a member of the *Onward*'s crew, and a war correspondent, gave a good account of
it; and with some alterations it is here introduced: "We have
been anchored in the ship channel for some days, and have frequently seen a secesh steamer plying in and around the harbor.
Well, this morning, about sunrise, I was awakened by the cry of
'All hands to quarters!' and before I could get out, the steward
knocked vigorously on my door and called: 'All hands to quarter, sah! de ram am a comin', sah!' I don't recollect of ever
dressing myself any quicker, and got out on deck in a hurry.
Sure enough, we could see, through the mist and fog, a great
black object moving rapidly, and steadily, right at our port quarter. . . . Springs were bent on, and the *Onward* was rapidly
warping around so as to bring her broadside to bear on the
steamer that was still rapidly approaching us; and when the guns
were brought to bear, some of the men looked at the Stars and
Stripes, and then at the steamer, and muttered 'You——! if you
run into us we will go down with colors flying!' Just as No. 3
port gun was being elevated, some one cried out, 'I see something that looks like a white flag;' and true enough there was
something flying on the steamer that would have been *white* by
application of soap and water. As she neared us, we looked in
vain for the face of a white man. When they discovered that we
would not fire on them, there was a rush of contrabands out on
her deck, some dancing, some singing, whistling, jumping; and
others stood looking towards Fort Sumter, and muttering all sorts
of maledictions against it, and '*de heart of de Souf*,' generally.
As the steamer came near, and under the stern of the *Onward*,
one of the Colored men stepped forward, and taking off his hat,
shouted, 'Good morning, sir! I've brought you some of the old
United States guns, sir!' "[15]

Congress granted half of the prize money for the Planter *to
Smalls and his men. Smalls became one of the most valuable
assets of the Union blockade fleet in the South Atlantic. He*

brought much significant information to Union authorities, and during the rest of the war he served as pilot on the Planter *and other vessels operating along the South Carolina coastline. Smalls later played a prominent role in South Carolina's Reconstruction politics. Because of their intimate knowledge of the tortuous waterways of the South Atlantic coastline, several freedmen rendered important service as pilots for the navy.[16] In fact, Negroes had enlisted in the Union Navy from the beginning of the war. Unlike the army, the United States Navy had never followed a Jim Crow policy, and there were many black sailors in the prewar navy. It has been estimated that during the Civil War as many as 29,000 Negroes (one-fourth of the entire naval enrollment) served in the Union Navy. Four black sailors were awarded the Congressional Medal of Honor for outstanding bravery.[17]*

Some Negro mariners fought on land as well as on sea. The following account is from the pen of George W. Reed, a black sailor serving on the United States gunboat Commodore Reed, *Potomac Flotilla, and was dated May 4, 1864:*

Sir, having been engaged in the naval service nearly six years, I have never before witnessed what I now see on board this ship. Our crew are principally colored; and a braver set of men never trod the deck of an American ship. We have been on several expeditions recently. On the 15th of April our ship and other gunboats proceeded up the Rappahannock river for some distance, and finding no rebel batteries to oppose us, we concluded to land the men from the different boats, and make a raid. I was ordered by the Commodore to beat the call for all parties to go on shore. No sooner had I executed the order, than every man was at his post, our own color being the first to land. At first, there was a little prejudice against our colored men going on shore, but it soon died away. We succeeded in capturing 3 fine horses, 6 cows, 5 hogs, 6 sheep, 3 calves, an abundance of chickens, 600 pounds of pork, 300 bushels of corn, and succeeded in liberating from the horrible pit of bondage 10 men, 6 women, and 8 children. The principal part of the men have enlisted on this ship. The next day we started further up the river, when the gunboats in advance struck on a torpedo, but did no material damage. We landed our men again, and repulsed a band of rebels handsomely, and captured three prisoners. Going on a little further, we were surprised by 300 rebel cavalry, and repulsed, but retreated in good order, the gunboats covering our retreat. I regret to say we had the misfortune to lose Samuel Turner (colored) in our retreat. He was instantly killed, and his body remains in the rebel hands. He being the fifer, I miss him very much as a friend and companion, as he was beloved by all on board. We also had four slightly wounded.[18]

Black sailors played an important part in Northern victory, but the greatest amount of controversy, publicity, and glory was reserved for the black soldiers in the Union Army. The large-scale enlistment of Negro troops was one of the central issues of the Civil War, and it is to this issue that we turn next.

CHAPTER XI

NEGRO TROOPS IN THE UNION ARMY:

INITIATION OF A POLICY, 1862–63

In the first year of the war many Northern Negroes offered their services to the Union government as soldiers (see above, Chapter II). But the government and the Northern people considered it a "white man's war" and refused to accept the offers. Nevertheless, Negro leaders continued to urge the necessity of enrolling black troops. They knew that if the black man proved his patriotism and courage on the field of battle, the nation would be morally obligated to grant him first-class citizenship. As Frederick Douglass put it: "Once let the black man get upon his person the brass letters, U.S., let him get an eagle on his button, and a musket on his shoulder and bullets in his pocket, and there is no power on earth which can deny that he has earned the right to citizenship in the United States."[1]

Douglass was one of the most persistent and eloquent advocates of arming the Negro. In August 1861, when the war was more than four months old and the North had yet to win a major victory, Douglass chided the government in an editorial entitled "Fighting Rebels with Only One Hand":

What upon earth is the matter with the American Government and people? Do they really covet the world's ridicule as well as their own social and political ruin? What are they thinking about, or don't they condescend to think at all? So, indeed, it would seem from their blindness in dealing with the tremendous issue now upon them. Was there ever anything like it before? They are sorely pressed on every hand by a vast army of slave-holding rebels, flushed with success, and infuriated by the darkest inspirations of a deadly hate, bound to rule or ruin. . . .

Our Presidents, Governors, Generals and Secretaries are calling, with almost frantic vehemence, for men.—"Men! men! send us men!" they scream, or the cause of the Union is gone; . . . and yet these very officers, representing the people and Government, steadily and persistently refuse to receive the very class of men which have a deeper interest in the defeat and humiliation of the rebels, than all others. . . . What a spectacle of blind, unreasoning prejudice and pusillanimity is this! The national edifice is on fire. Every man who can carry a bucket of water, or remove a brick, is wanted; but those who have the care of the building, having a profound respect for the feeling of the national burglars who set the building on fire, are determined that the flames shall only be extinguished by Indo-Caucasian hands, and to have the building burnt rather than save it by means of any other. Such is the pride, the stupid prejudice and folly that rules the hour.

Why does the Government reject the negro? Is he not a man? Can he not wield a sword, fire a gun, march and countermarch, and obey orders like any other? . . . If persons so humble as we can be allowed to speak to the President of the United States, we should ask him if this dark and terrible hour of the nation's extremity is a time for consulting a mere vulgar and unnatural prejudice? . . . We would tell him that this is no time to fight with one hand, when both are needed; that this is no time to fight only with your white hand, and allow your black hand to remain tied. . . . While the Government continues to refuse the aid of colored men, thus alienating them from the national cause, and giving the rebels the advantage of them, it will not deserve better fortunes than it has thus far experienced.—Men in earnest don't fight with one hand, when they might fight with two, and a man drowning would not refuse to be saved even by a colored hand.[2]

Negroes and abolitionists pointed out that black men had

fought for America in the Revolution and the War of 1812. In February 1862, Douglass said sarcastically: "Colored men were good enough to fight under Washington. They are not good enough to fight under McClellan. They were good enough to fight under Andrew Jackson. They are not good enough to fight under Gen. Halleck. They were good enough to help win American independence, but they are not good enough to help preserve that independence against treason and rebellion."[3]

J. Madison Bell, a Negro poet in San Francisco and a former associate of John Brown, penned a poem in May 1862 entitled "What Shall We Do with the Contrabands?"

Shall we arm them? Yes, arm them! Give to each man
A rifle, a musket, a cutlass or sword;
   Then on to the charge! let them war in the van,
Where each may confront with his merciless lord,
And purge from their race, in the eyes of the brave,
The stigma and scorn now attending the slave.

I would not have the wrath of the rebels to cease,
   Their hope to grow weak nor their courage to wane,
Till the Contrabands join in securing a peace,
   Whose glory shall vanish the last galling chain,
And win for their race an undying respect
In the land of their prayers, their tears and neglect.

Is the war one for Freedom? Then why, tell me, why,
Should the wronged and oppressed be debarred from the fight?
Does not reason suggest, it were noble to die
   In the act of supplanting a wrong for the right?
Then lead to the charge! for the end is not far,
When the contraband host are enrolled in the war.[4]

There were two main objections to the enlistment of Negro troops. The first was the deep-seated racial prejudice of most Northerners. "We don't want to fight side and side with the nigger," wrote Corporal Felix Brannigan of the Seventy-fourth New York Regiment. "We think we are a too superior race for that." And in 1862 a writer in the New York Times *declared:*

I am quite sure there is not one man in ten but would feel

himself degraded as a volunteer if negro equality is to be the order in the field of battle. . . . I take the liberty of warning the abettors of fraternizing with the blacks, that one negro regiment, in the present temper of things, put on equality with those who have the past year fought and suffered, will withdraw an amount of life and energy in our army equal to disbanding ten of the best regiments we can now raise.[5]

Secondly, most people in the North believed that black men, especially the ex-slaves, were too servile and cowardly to make good soldiers. When General David Hunter proposed to raise a regiment of freedmen on the South Carolina Sea Islands in May 1862, many of the missionaries and teachers there were skeptical. One of them wrote: "I don't believe you could make soldiers of these men at all,—they are afraid, and they know it." Another said that "Negroes—plantation negroes, at least—will never make soldiers in one generation. Five white men could put a regiment to flight."[6] Lincoln summed up both types of opposition to Negro enlistment in two public statements. On August 4, 1862, an Indiana delegation offered the government two regiments of black men from their state, but the President declined the offer. "To arm the negroes," he said, "would turn 50,000 bayonets from the loyal Border States against us that were for us." And six weeks later Lincoln told another delegation that "if we were to arm [the Negroes], I fear that in a few weeks the arms would be in the hands of the rebels."[7]

Despite the government's official opposition to Negro soldiers, several Union generals tried to enlist black men in 1862. General Hunter proceeded with his organization of a regiment on the Sea Islands, although he had to resort to a draft to fill up his ranks. The War Department refused to sanction the regiment, however, and Hunter disbanded all but one company in August. Out in Kansas General James H. Lane raised two regiments of black men composed of fugitive slaves from Missouri and free Negroes from the North. Lane's black troopers were not officially recognized by the War Department until early in 1863, but in the meantime they had participated in several fights against rebel bushwhackers in Kansas and Missouri. Down in New Orleans the free Negroes, who had formed a Confederate regiment in 1861, offered their services to Union General Butler after the fall of the Crescent City in the spring of 1862. Butler refused the offer at first, but when he was threatened by a Confederate attack in August, the Massachusetts general hurriedly recruited three regiments of Negroes from southern Louisiana. These regiments took the field in November 1862, despite the fact that they had not yet been mustered in by the War Department.[8]

Meanwhile Northern public opinion was being gradually converted by the pressure of events to the idea of arming the Negroes. In the summer of 1862 the Union forces suffered a series of military defeats, which struck a sharp blow at Northern morale. War-weariness was beginning to sap the willingness of white men to join the army, and the administration began to consider more seriously the possibility of recruiting black men to supplement declining white manpower. On July 17, 1862, Congress passed two acts providing for the enlistment of Negroes as soldiers. The first was the Confiscation Act, which empowered the President "to employ as many persons of African descent as he may deem necessary and proper for the suppression of this rebellion." The second was a militia act repealing the provisions of the 1792 law barring black men, and authorizing the employment of free Negroes and freedmen as soldiers.[9]

There was still a considerable amount of opposition in the North to the enlistment of Negro soldiers, but on August 25 the War Department nevertheless authorized General Rufus Saxton, military governor of the South Carolina Sea Islands, to raise five regiments of black troops on the islands, with white men as officers. The teachers and missionaries on the islands had overcome their earlier skepticism about making soldiers out of freedmen, and they urged the Negroes to enlist to fight for their own freedom and to prove to the world that the black race deserved liberty. Volunteers came forward slowly at first, but by November 7 the regiment was filling up rapidly and was mustered in as the First South Carolina Volunteers.[10]

The Massachusetts abolitionist Thomas Wentworth Higginson was appointed colonel of the regiment in November. A few days after his arrival at Beaufort, Higginson wrote in his journal:

It needs but a few days to show the absurdity of doubting the equal military availability of these people, as compared with whites. There is quite as much average comprehension of the need of the thing, as much courage, I doubt not, as much previous knowledge of the gun, & there is a readiness of ear & of imitation which for purposes of drill counterbalances any defect of mental training.[11]

In January 1863, Higginson took part of his regiment on a raid along the St. Mary's River, which forms the boundary between Florida and Georgia. Upon his return, the Colonel submitted the following official report:

The expedition has carried the regimental flag and the President's proclamation far into the interior of Georgia and Florida. The men have been repeatedly under fire; have had infantry, cavalry, and even artillery arrayed against them, and have in every instance come off not only with unblemished honor, but with undisputed triumph.

At Township, Fla., a detachment of the expedition fought a cavalry company which met it unexpectedly on a midnight march through pine woods and which completely surrounded us. They were beaten off, with a loss on our part of 1 man killed and 7 wounded, while the opposing party admits 12 men killed, including Lieutenant Jones, in command of the company, besides many wounded. . . .

Nobody knows anything about these men who has not seen them in battle. I find that I myself knew nothing. There is a fiery energy about them beyond anything of which I have ever read, except it be the French Zouaves. It requires the strictest discipline to hold them in hand. During our first attack on the river, before I had got them all penned below, they crowded at the open ends of the steamer, loading and firing with inconceivable rapidity, and shouting to each other, "Never give it up." When collected into the hold they actually fought each other for places at the few port-holes from which they could fire on the enemy. Meanwhile the black gunners, admirably trained by Lieutenants Stockdale and O'Neil, both being accomplished artillerists, and Mr. Heron, of the gunboat, did their duty without the slightest protection and with great coolness amid a storm of shot. . . .

We found no large number of slaves anywhere; yet we brought away several whole families, and obtained by this means the most valuable information. I was interested to observe that the news of the President's proclamation produced a marked effect upon them, and in one case it was of the greatest service to us in securing the hearty aid of a guide, who was timid and distrustful until he heard that he was legally free, after which he aided us gladly and came away with us. . . .

No officer in this regiment now doubts that the key to the successful prosecution of this war lies in the unlimited employment of black troops. Their superiority lies simply in the fact that they know the country, while white troops do not, and, moreover, that they have peculiarities of temperament, position, and motive which belong to them alone. Instead of leaving their homes and families to fight they are fighting for their homes and families, and they show the resolution and the sagacity which a personal purpose gives. It would have been madness to attempt, with the bravest white troops, what I have successfully accomplished with black ones. Everything, even to the piloting of the vessels and the selection of the proper points for cannonading, was done by my own soldiers.[12]

A second Negro regiment was organized on the islands, with James Montgomery as its colonel. Higginson and Montgomery led their men on several successful raids into the interior of Georgia and Florida, and in March 1863 they captured and occupied Jacksonville.

On April 30, General David Hunter, Commander of the Department of the South, reported to Secretary Stanton:

I am happy to be able to announce to you my complete and eminent satisfaction with the results of the organization of negro regiments in this department. . . . In the field these regiments, so far as tried, have proved brave, active, docile, and energetic, frequently outrunning by their zeal and familiarity with the Southern country the restrictions deemed prudent by certain of their officers and . . . so conducting themselves, upon the whole, that even our enemies, though more anxious to find fault with these than with any other portion of our troops, have not yet been able to allege against them a single violation of any of the rules of civilized warfare.

I find the colored regiments hardy, generous, temperate, strictly obedient, possessing remarkable aptitude for military training, and deeply imbued with that religious sentiment (call it fanaticism, such as like) which made the soldiers of Oliver Cromwell invincible. They are imbued with a burning faith that now is the time appointed by God, in His All-wise Providence, for the deliverance of their race; and under the heroic incitement of this faith I believe them capable of courage and persistence of purpose which must in the end extort both victory and admiration. . . .

I am also happy to announce to you that the prejudices of certain of our white soldiers against these indispensable allies are rapidly softening or fading out.[13]

These enthusiastic official dispatches were written for the eyes of the Northern public as well as the Secretary of War, and most of the reports found their way into the newspapers. But the private reactions of those who watched the development of Higginson's regiment were almost as favorable as the public statements. One of the labor superintendents on the Sea Islands wrote in March 1863 that "these black men are slow about getting into the Army, but when they are once in they fight like fiends. . . . My faith is firm that the best thing that can be done for these men is to put them in the Army. They will learn there sooner than anywhere else that they are men. The improvement in the character & bearing of those who are now in the Army is so marked that every one notices it."[14]

The reports from South Carolina were beginning to convince the Republican press and the Lincoln administration of the wisdom and necessity of recruiting a large Negro army. On March 28, 1863, the New York Tribune *stated editorially:*

Facts are beginning to dispel prejudices. Enemies of the negro race, who have persistently denied the capacity and doubted the courage of the Blacks, are unanswerably confuted by the good conduct and gallant deeds of the men whom they persecute and slander. From many quarters comes evidence of the swiftly approaching success which is to crown what is still by some persons deemed to be the experiment of arming whom the Proclamation of Freedom liberates.

Two days earlier Lincoln had written to Andrew Johnson, War Governor of Tennessee:

I am told you have at least *thought* of raising a negro military force. In my opinion the country now needs no specific thing so much as some man of your ability and position to go to this work. . . . The colored population is the great *available* and yet *unavailed of* force for restoring the Union. The bare sight of 50,000 armed and drilled black soldiers upon the banks of the Mississippi would end the rebellion at once. And who doubts that we can present that sight if we but take hold in earnest?[15]

On April 1 Lincoln informed General Hunter that "I am glad to see the accounts of your colored force at Jacksonville, Florida. . . . It is important to the enemy that such a force shall not take shape, and grow, and thrive, in the South; and in precisely the same proportion, it is important to us that it shall."[16] The President had experienced a complete change of mind since the previous September when he had feared that arms placed in the hands of Negroes would soon find their way into the hands of rebels.

In the spring of 1863 General Nathaniel P. Banks began to recruit a "Corps d'Afrique" from the Negro population of Louisiana. The French-English Negro newspaper in New Orleans, L'Union, supported Banks's efforts with the following editorial:

To Arms! It is our duty. The nation counts on the devotion and the courage of its sons. We will not remain deaf to its call; we will not remain indifferent spectators, like strangers who attach no value to the land. We are sons of Louisiana, and when Louisiana calls us we march.

To Arms! It is an honor understood by our fathers who fought on the plains of Chalmette. He who defends his fatherland is the real citizen, and this time we are fighting for the rights of our race. . . . We demand justice. And when an organized, numerous, and respectable body which has rendered many services to the nation demands justice—nothing more, but nothing less—the nation cannot refuse.

To Arms! Who would think to save himself by neutrality? Would the enemies of the country and of our race have more respect for those who hold themselves timidly apart than for the brave who look them in the face? In what century and in what land has man made himself respected in wartime by cowardice? The scorn of the conqueror is the recompense of weakness.[17]

By the end of August Banks had recruited nearly fifteen thousand black soldiers in Louisiana.

In March 1863 Secretary of War Stanton had sent Adjutant General Lorenzo Thomas to the lower Mississippi Valley to recruit and organize as many Negro regiments as possible from among the freedmen in that area. On May 22 the Bureau of Colored Troops was established in the War Department to coordinate and administer the raising of Negro regiments in every part of the country.[18] The recruiting techniques of Union officers in the West were none too gentle. Robert Cowden, who eventually became colonel of the Fifty-ninth U.S. Colored Infantry, described the enlistment of that regiment in the vicinity of Memphis in May and June 1863:

The plan for "persuading" recruits while it could hardly be called the shot-gun policy was equally as convincing, and never failed to get the "recruit." . . . The cavalry of the division was continually employed as scouts and skirmishers, and almost daily brought into camp hundreds of animals and negroes as spoils. The former were used in replenishing the army and increasing its effectiveness for the summer campaign, and the latter were turned over to Colonel Bouton, whose recruiting agents accompanied all these excursions. . . . In this way, in the space of six weeks, the entire command was made up, without the expense of a single dollar to the Government, and on the 27th of June, 1863, was mustered into the United States military service.[19]

These hapless freedmen did not seem to be very promising material for soldiers. Cowden wrote:

The average plantation negro was a hard-looking specimen, with about as little of the soldier to be seen in him as there was of the angel in Michael Angelo's block of marble before he had applied his chisel. His head covered with a web of knotted cotton strings that had once been white, braided into his long, black, curly wool; his dress a close-fitting wool shirt, and pantaloons of homespun material, butternut brown, worn without suspenders, hanging slouchily upon him, and generally too short in the legs by several inches. . . . He had a rolling, dragging, moping gait and a cringing manner, with a downcast thievish glance that dared not look you in the eye. . . .

The first pass made at him was with a pair of shears, and his cotton strings and the excess of his black wool disappeared together. The next was to strip him of his filthy rags and burn them, and scour him thoroughly with soap and water. A clean new suit of army blue was now put on him, together with a full suit of military accoutrements, and a gun was placed in his hands, and, lo! he was completely metamorphosed, not only in appearance and dress, but in character and relations also. Yesterday a filthy, repulsive "nigger," to-day a neatly-attired man; yesterday a slave, to-day a freeman, yesterday a civilian, to-day a soldier. . . .

But he must be patiently taught to feel and to act what he is. All that he has ever learned except prompt, unquestioning obedience must be unlearned. The plantation manners, the awkward bowing and scraping, . . . with hat under arm, and with averted look, must be exchanged for the upright form, the open face, the gentlemanly address and soldierly salute. He must be taught to keep his person, clothes, arms and accoutrements clean. He must be shown how to stand and step; to carry and to handle his gun and bayonet, and how to shoot. He must be compelled to regular hours of rest. He had been accustomed, all his life, to stealing from his cabin at night and prowling around by the light of the stars to dances or to religious meetings, and it was one of the most difficult things to make him know that he *must* retire at nine at night and *stay retired* till reveille. Their singing, praying, and shouting in camp had to be arrested, sometimes, at the point of the bayonet. . . .

During the months of July and August, the condition of the health of the regiment was very discouraging,—more than forty dying in July, and nearly as many in August. The principal cause, doubtless, was that meal, from which the corn-bread to which they were accustomed was made, could not be obtained, and they were obliged to live on wheat-bread. Their superstitions may also have increased mortalities, for so frightened were they that, going to the regimental hospital was considered equivalent to death. As soon as corn-meal was obtained and the hot weather was past, health was restored. Meantime panic had seized upon many and they had absented themselves from camp for a time; but most of them returned, and after slight punishment were restored to duty.[20]

Despite this inauspicious beginning, Cowden's regiment later became an efficient and effective fighting force. By the first week of August 1863, there were fourteen Negro regiments in the field or ready for service, and twenty-four additional regiments were in the process of organization. Five of the fourteen battle-ready regiments had been recruited in the North.[21] Most Southern Negroes were illiterate and left little record of their feelings or experiences as they embarked upon their new lives as soldiers. Hence we must turn to the actions of Northern Negroes in 1863 for an account of how articulate black men viewed the experiment of a black army.

1. Mansion of J. Hopkinson on the South Carolina Sea Islands. One of the few photographs of blacks while still technically in slavery

2. Planting sweet potatoes, Edisto Island, South Carolina, 1862

3. Sorting cotton at Hilton Head, South Carolina, 1862

4. "An incident in the Battle of the Wilderness—the rebel Generals Bradley Johnson and E. Stuart taken to the rear by Negro cavalry"

5. "Army of the Potomac. Scene in camp of Negro regiments. Method of punishment of Negro Soldiers for various offenses." White soldiers were punished in the same way.

6. "The rebels preparing for the Union attack on Charleston. The confederates building fortifications on James Island, under the direction of General Beauregard, to repel the land attacks of the Union troops"

7. "The war on the Mississippi. Negro recruits taking the cars for Murfreesboro"

8. Portrait of Robert Smalls, captor of the ship *Planter*

9, 10 & 11. Contraband. Recruit. Veteran. Note the change in appearance and the loss of the "slave persona."

12 & 13. "The Escaped Slave." "The Escaped Slave in the Union Army." A slave who fled from Montgomery, Alabama, to Chattanooga, Tennessee, with the purpose of joining the Union Army, as he appeared before and after joining the ranks.

14, 15 & 16. "A typical Negro: Gordon under medical inspection; Gordon, as he entered our lines; Gordon in his uniform as a U.S. soldier." Sketches of a slave named Gordon who escaped his master and came into Union lines at Baton Rouge in March, 1863. The whipping which caused the scars had been given on Christmas Day, 1862.

17. "The Last Chattel"

18. "The war in Virginia. Contrabands coming in to the Union camp"

19. A group of Union officers recently escaped who received guidance, food, and protection from blacks living near Richmond

20. *U.S. Vermont.* Group of contrabands

21. Picture drawn from the liberation of slaves on Mr. Terrebee's plantation near Indiantown in Camden County on General Wild's raid into the North Carolina interior

22. "Mustered out. Colored soldiers at Little Rock, Arkansas." Based on an actual incident witnessed by the artist

23. "President Lincoln riding through Richmond, April 4, 1865, amid the enthusiastic cheers of the inhabitants"

24. "School girls—freed."
Freed children on the
South Carolina Sea
Islands

25. "Uncle." An old freedman
on the South Carolina Sea
Islands

CHAPTER XII

BLACK TROOPS FROM THE NORTH

In January 1863 the War Department authorized Governor John Andrew of Massachusetts to raise a regiment of Negro soldiers in his state. Massachusetts' Negro population was too small to fill up a regiment, so Andrew called upon the wealthy abolitionist George L. Stearns to form a committee of "prominent citizens" to raise money for the recruitment of men for the Fifty-fourth Massachusetts Regiment from all over the North. Stearns hired several Negro leaders as recruiting agents, including Frederick Douglass, William Wells Brown, Charles L. Remond, John Mercer Langston, Henry Highland Garnet, and Martin R. Delany. These men traveled all through the North and even into Canada, urging black men to join the army.[1]

But Northern Negroes seemed much less eager to flock to the colors now than they had been at the outbreak of the war. There were several reasons for this. In the first place, the booming war economy had created full employment and prosperity for Negroes in some parts of the North. A white Bostonian wrote in February 1863 that "the blacks here are too comfortable to do anything more than talk about freedom."[2] An Ohio Negro said, "I have no inclination to go to war. I had as soon pay three hundred dollars if I had it."[3] And William Parham of Cincinnati wrote that

an agent from "Mass." was here a few days since for the purpose of getting recruits for the 54th Massachusetts. A few of us met with him and selected a committee to see what could be done. I do not think, however, that more than 10 or 12 if so many, will go. The fact is, our men . . . are like the whites. At the beginning of the War when it was thought that there would be little, if any fighting every man you met with wanted to go to War; but now when they know that hard fighting is to be done, hardships to be suffered and privations endured, it is rather difficult, in fact impossible to get their courage screwed to the fighting pitch.[4]

In the second place, there were hints from Confederate sources that captured Negro soldiers would not be treated as ordinary prisoners of war. On May 1, 1863, the Confederate Congress authorized President Jefferson Davis to have captured officers of Negro regiments "put to death or be otherwise punished at the discretion" of a military tribunal. Black enlisted men were to "be delivered to the authorities of the State or States in which they shall be captured to be dealt with according to the present or future laws of such State or States."[5] This could mean death or sale into slavery. Few Northerners believed that the Confederacy would actually carry out such a barbarous policy wholesale, but in 1863 there were several reports, a few of them well authenticated, of the murder or sale into slavery of captured Negro soldiers.[6] Prospective black recruits naturally hesitated to sign up until they learned what measures the Union government meant to take to protect them if they were captured.[7]

In the third place, the authorization granted to Andrew by the War Department stipulated that all commissioned officers in the Negro regiment must be white men. Andrew wanted to grant a few commissions to qualified Negroes and give them opportunities for promotion, but Stanton and Lincoln feared the effect on Northern public opinion if black men became officers. The enlistment of Negro privates was an important step forward, they said, and the people must be allowed to digest this advance before any further progress could be made.[8] Intelligent and educated Northern Negroes resented the ineligibility of black men to become officers. Robert Purvis wrote:

Notwithstanding the advances made by the government in forming regiments of colored men, it argues a sad misapprehension of the character, aspirations and self-respect of colored men, to suppose that they would submit to the *degrading* limitations which the government imposes in regard to the officering of said regiments. From that position and error, the government *must* recede, or else . . . failure to secure the right kind of men will be the result.[9]

Because of these factors, recruiting agents had to call upon all of their eloquence to persuade black men to join the colors. Negro recruiters accepted the challenge. They blanketed Northern Negro communities with broadsides, editorials, and speeches. Henry M. Turner tried to shame his fellow Negroes into volunteering. The black man asked: "Do you suppose I am going to leave my home and comforts to be killed for nothing? I am not going to do any such thing." Turner replied:

Ah! That may do for that portion of our people who have no interest South; those who have no sympathy, no friends, no relations, no care, nor no desire for a triumph of freedom and our heaven-chartered rights. But those who have been taught by a God-blessed experience to abhor the monster slavery, and have felt its inhuman crushings, will look from a different standpoint. . . . The cry has long been, Give us the opportunity; show us a chance to climb to distinction, and we will show the world by our bravery what the negro can do, and then as soon as we are invited to stand on such a basis as will develop these interior qualities, for us to deride the idea and scornfully turn away, would be to argue a self-consciousness of incapacity.[10]

The Anglo-African *stated*:

Should we not with two centuries of cruel wrong stirring our heart's blood, be but too willing to embrace any chance to settle accounts with the slaveholders? . . . Why should we be alarmed at their threat of hanging us; do we intend to become their prisoners? Such is not the record our black fathers made in the revolutionary war . . . nor is such the record of those who fought under MacDonough and Jackson in the War of 1812. . . .

Can you ask any more than a chance to drive bayonet or

bullet into the slaveholders' hearts? Are you most anxious to be captains and colonels, or to extirpate these vipers from the face of the earth? The government has clothed you with citizenship, and has announced the freedom of all our brethren within the grasp of the rebellion, is there any higher, any nobler duty than to rush into the heart of the South, and pluck out from the grasp of the slaveholders the victims of their lust and tyranny?[11]

Frederick Douglass conceded privately that "it is a little cruel to say to the black soldier that he shall not rise to be an officer of the United States whatever may be his merits; but I see that though coupled with this disadvantage colored men should hail the opportunity of getting on the United States uniform as a very great advance."[12] Two of Douglass' sons were the first recruits from New York to join the Massachusetts Fifty-fourth. Douglass stated publicly:

Shall colored men enlist notwithstanding this unjust and ungenerous barrier raised against them? We answer yes. Go into the army and go with a will and a determination to blot out this and all other mean discriminations against us. To say we won't be soldiers because we cannot be colonels is like saying we won't go into the water till we have learned to swim. A half a loaf is better than no bread—and to go into the army is the speediest and best way to overcome the prejudice which has dictated unjust laws against us. To allow us in the army at all, is a great concession. Let us take this little the better to get more. By showing that we deserve the little is the best way to gain much. Once in the United States uniform and the colored man has a springing board under him by which he can jump to loftier heights.[13]

A California Negro wrote:

Our country, in her extremity, utters a piercing voice to her disfranchised children to come to the rescue. We discover in this invitation slight atonement for the past and cheerful promise for the future. It matters not now, in the hour of emergency, to inquire into the policy that has been pursued towards us for over eighty years. . . .

Colored men! a higher standard in the social world awaits

your grasp; ideality has destroyed all your concentration; this is not the moment to gaze back upon home and its endearments; the past belongs to history; that mighty volume has recorded you, through ages, as an inferior race of people; the charge has been assailed by industry and learning, but, in a collective sense, it has never been successfully removed. The present crisis, when it was unlooked for, affords you an opportunity, which comes but once in a lifetime, to engage into that contact which has so often rendered other races predominant and progressive. Will it be accepted? *Now* or *never*. We who have been obscured by darkness and inactivity, must seek every occasion to manifest our innate power. If we *fail* through cowardice, or remain immovable from apathy, the sunlight of philanthropy will never again unloosen the coldness of a cheerless despair.[14]

Many Negroes responded enthusiastically to such appeals. But others still held back. This was especially true in New York City, where Douglass, Henry Highland Garnet, and other speakers urged black men to enlist at a meeting in Shiloh Church on April 27. In spite of their eloquence, only one recruit came forward. Douglass was appalled, and told the audience that he was ashamed of them. A Mr. Robert Johnson rose and defended the Negroes of New York, and, according to the report of the affair, "by a few well-spoken words, [he] convinced the meeting that it was not cowardice which made the young men hesitate to enlist, but a proper respect for their own manhood. If the Government wanted their services, let it guarantee to them all the rights of citizens and soldiers, and, instead of one man, he would insure them 5,000 men in twenty days. Mr. J's remarks were received with tremendous and long-continued applause."[15]

The assemblage adjourned to meet again on April 30. Douglass, Garnet, and others repeated their exhortations, and George T. Downing introduced the following resolutions, which were adopted:

Resolved, That we are impressed with the fact, that the resolutions most in place *now* are those which will give force and efficacy to a determination, on our part, to stand by the Government in every way we may; with sympathy and succor, with loaded muskets and drawn swords, seeing that the very existence of our Government is imperilled; a Government which is daily endearing itself to us more and more, by an increasing willingness to respect and defend us as its equal subjects.

Resolved, That in determining to stand by the Government in this war, we are not only deciding to stand by good government, but against slavery, the parent and fosterer of the unjust prejudice we have been the subjects of here in the North; we believe that as we shall manifest competency and valor in the field, will rewards, acknowledgment and promotion be awarded us; and that the bugbear "Colonization," which has so troubled the American people, will not, out of respect for the feelings of loyal Americans, be ever again agitated.[16]

Several more men enlisted at this meeting, but New York Negroes still remained rather unenthusiastic. Nevertheless the response from the rest of the North was good. By the end of April recruits were coming in at the rate of thirty to forty per day, and Governor Andrew soon had enough men to form a second Negro regiment, the Fifty-fifth Massachusetts. Meanwhile a black regiment was being raised among the contrabands and free Negroes of Washington, D.C. The Rev. Henry M. Turner, pastor of the Israel Bethel A.M.E. Church, took the lead in recruiting this regiment and later became its chaplain, the first Negro chaplain in the Civil War. Enlistment proceeded slowly at first. The atmosphere in Washington, a Southern city, was still hostile to the idea of Negro soldiers. Loiterers and street bullies liked to beat up Negroes in uniform. A city policeman was reported to have said that he would put as many bullets through a "nigger" recruit as he would through a mad dog.[17] A correspondent of the Christian Recorder *wrote in June 1863:*

Passing along 7th Street, a few evenings ago, I saw an excited rabble pursuing a corporal belonging to the 1st Colored Regiment, District vols., named John Ross. Among the pursuers, was a United States police officer. Ross protested against being dragged away by these ruffians, at the same time expressing his willingness to accompany the police officer to whatever place he might designate; claiming at the same time his (the police officer's) protection from his assailants. But, shameful to say, that officer, after he had arrested Ross, permitted a cowardly villain to violently choke and otherwise maltreat him. After the melee, the corporal received some pretty severe bruises, whether from the policeman's club or from the stones that were thrown by the mob, I will not say. He quietly walked to the central guard house with this conservator of the peace, amidst the clamoring of the mob, their yells and shouts of "Kill the black . . . " &c., &c., "strip him, we'll stop this negro enlistment," &c., &c.[18]

Enlistment continued in spite of these harassments. At a meeting of black men in Asbury Church, Sayles Bowen of Washington said:

When we show that we are men, we can then demand our liberty, as did the revolutionary fathers—peaceably if we can, forcibly if we must. If we do not fight, we are traitors to our God, traitors to our country, traitors to our race, and traitors to ourselves. (Applause.) Richmond is the place for us, and we mean to go there. (Applause.) Our friend, Jeff. Davis, says we shall go there (laughter), and we will go; but they won't be glad to see us.

The regiment gained 140 recruits at this meeting.[19]

By mid-June the climate of opinion toward Negro soldiers had improved in Washington, and the regiment was rapidly filling up. The desperate courage of Louisiana Negroes at the battle of Port Hudson on May 27 had convinced many former skeptics of the value of black troops. A Washington Negro wrote on June 13 that

the bravery displayed before Port Hudson by the colored troops was applaudingly received here by persons who have not been looked upon as friendly to the movement, and that is another star whose looming lustre begins to aggrandize a frowning future. . . .

There never was, nor there never will be, a better opportunity for colored men to get what they want, than now. Suppose 500,000 colored men were under arms, would not the nation really be under our arms too? Would the nation refuse us our rights in such a condition? Would it refuse us our vote? Would it deny us any thing when its salvation was hanging upon us? No! never! . . .

We have had several fights this week between colored soldiers and white rowdies, or pretended citizens. But Mr. Colored Soldier has come out triumphant every time. . . . The soldiers all ride in the street cars or any other cars they want to ride in; and you might just as well declare war against them, as to declare that they can't ride there because they are colored.[20]

In the summer of 1863 the War Department authorized the governors of several Northern states to recruit Negro regiments to help fulfill their state troop quotas. The previous year John Mercer Langston, an Ohio Negro leader, had urged Governor David Tod to enlist black volunteers to be credited against Ohio's quota. Tod had rejected the suggestion with the words, "Do you not know, Mr. Langston, that this is a white man's government; that white men are able to defend and protect it? . . . When we want you colored men we will notify you." By June 1863 Tod had decided that he wanted black men. He notified Langston and gave him authority to enlist Negro soldiers. Langston and his assistants began to canvass the state.[21] They were encouraged by their reception in several Ohio towns, such as Xenia, where a meeting of black men adopted the following resolution:

We stand as ever on the side of the Government, and pledge to it "our lives, our property, and our sacred honor," in its efforts to subdue the rebellion of the slave oligarchy of the country, in its determination to emancipate the slaves of all rebels, to establish freedom in the District of Columbia and the National Territories, to welcome Hayti and Liberia to the great family of nations,* to recognize the citizenship of the native-born colored American, and to protect the colored soldiers, who, taking the American musket and bayonet, have gone

---

*In 1862 the United States government had extended diplomatic recognition to Haiti and Liberia.

forth at the call of their country to *do* and *die* for the Government and the Union.[22]
By November the Ohio regiment was ready for service.

Rhode Island, Connecticut, Maryland, and Pennsylvania also began to organize black regiments in the summer of 1863. Some of the most intensive recruiting took place in Philadelphia, which contained a larger Negro population than any other Northern city. By the first of August one Philadelphia regiment was ready for service and another was nearly half full. This rapid enlistment was encouraged by such editorials as the following, which appeared in the Christian Recorder:

We now appeal to the colored men of Philadelphia, and especially to the young and able-bodied. Gentlemen, you have often been heard talking about the freedom and rights which the colored man was entitled to in this country, but of which he has unfortunately been hitherto deprived. But now the Government has offered us a way by which we can secure all these advantages, if we choose. Will you do it? We believe you will. . . . We have been denounced as cowards. Arise and cast off the foul stigma. Shame on him who would hang back at the call of his country. Go with the view that you will return freemen. And if you should never return, you will die with the satisfaction of knowing that you have struck a blow for freedom, and assisted in giving liberty to our race in the land of our birth.[23]

At the end of October 1863 there were in existence fifty-eight regiments of Negro troops in the Union Army with a total strength, including white officers, of 37,482 men. These troops came from eight Northern states (including Maryland), seven Confederate states, and the District of Columbia.[24] A great expansion of recruiting activity would take place in 1864, but already in 1863 the policy of Negro enlistment had proved itself a success in both North and South. On July 11, 1863, the Anglo-African *issued an editorial manifesto to the American people:*

White Americans remember! that we know that in going to

the field we will neither get bounty, or as much wages even as you will receive for the performance of the same duty;—that we are well aware of the fact that if captured we will be treated like wild beasts by our enemies;—that the avenue to honor and promotion is closed to us; but for these things we care not.

We fight for God, liberty and country, not money. We will fight fearless of capture, as we do not expect quarter so we shall give none. It is infinitely more honorable to die upon the battle field, than to be murdered by the barbarians of the South. Promotion we will not ask, until we have earned it; and when we have, this nation shall know no rest until those in authority have crowned the brow of our heroes with wreaths of living green,—until the highway of advancement is open to the dusky sons of America, as well as those of paler hue.

The same sentiments were expressed in a lighter vein by the following song, written by a private in the Fifty-fourth Massachusetts Regiment:

Fremont told them, when it first begun,
How to save the Union, and the way it should be done;
But Kentucky swore so hard, and old Abe he had his fears,
Till every hope was lost but the colored volunteers.

   CHORUS.—O, give us a flag, all free without a slave,
   We'll fight to defend it, as our Fathers did so brave.
   The gallant Comp'ny "A" will make the rebels dance,
   And we'll stand by the Union if we only have a chance.

McClellan went to Richmond with two hundred thousand brave;
He said, "keep back the niggers," and the Union he would save.
Little Mac he had his way—still the Union is in tears—
Now they call for the help of the colored volunteers.

   CHORUS.—O, give us a flag, &c.

Old Jeff says he'll hang us if we dare to meet him armed,
A very big thing, but we are not at all alarmed,
For he has first got to catch us before the way is clear,
And "that is what's the matter with the colored volunteer."

   CHORUS.—O, give us a flag, &c.

So rally, boys, rally, let us never mind the past;
We had a hard road to travel, but our day is coming fast,
For God is for the right, and we have no need to fear,—
The Union must be saved by the colored volunteer.

   CHORUS.—O, give us a flag, &c.[25]

CHAPTER XIII

NEGRO SOLDIERS PROVE
THEMSELVES IN BATTLE, 1863

On May 1, 1863, the New York
Tribune *observed that most Northerners now approved of the
policy of arming Negroes, but that many still doubted whether
they would make good soldiers. "Loyal Whites have generally
become willing that they should fight," said the* Tribune, *"but
the great majority have no faith that they will really do so.
Many hope they will prove cowards and sneaks—others greatly
fear it."*

*Colonel Higginson's regiment had fought well in minor skir-
mishes, but as yet no Negro troops had been engaged in a major
battle. But on May 27, 1863, two regiments of New Orleans free
Negroes and Louisiana ex-slaves participated in an assault on
Port Hudson, a Confederate stronghold on the lower Mississippi.
The attack failed, but the Negroes fought heroically, advancing
over open ground in the face of deadly artillery fire. William
Wells Brown wrote the following account of the Port Hudson
assault. Brown's description contains some touches of the nov-
elist's pen, but in essence it is accurate:*

On the 26th of May, 1863, the wing of the army under Major-
Gen. Banks was brought before the rifle-pits and heavy guns of
Port Hudson. Night fell—the lovely Southern night—with its sil-
very moonshine on the gleaming waters of the Mississippi, that
passed directly by the intrenched town. The glistening stars appeared suspended in the upper air as globes of liquid light, while

the fresh soft breeze was bearing such sweet scents from the odoriferous trees and plants, that a poet might have fancied angelic spirits were abroad, making the atmosphere luminous with their pure presence, and every breeze fragrant with their luscious breath. The deep-run sun that rose on the next morning indicated that the day would be warm; and, as it advanced, the heat became intense. The earth had been long parched, and the hitherto green verdure had begun to turn yellow. Clouds of dust followed every step and movement of the troops. The air was filled with dust; clouds gathered, frowned upon the earth, and hastened away. . . .

The black forces consisted of the First Louisiana, under Lieut-Col. Bassett, and the Third Louisiana, under Col. Nelson. The line-officers of the Third were white; and the regiment was composed mostly of freedmen, many of whose backs still bore the marks of the lash, and whose brave, stout hearts beat high at the thought that the hour had come when they were to meet their proud and unfeeling oppressors. The First was the noted regiment called "The Native Guard," which Gen. Butler found when he entered New Orleans, and which so promptly offered its services to aid in crushing the Rebellion. The line-officers of this regiment were all colored, taken from amongst the most wealthy and influential of the free colored people of New Orleans. It was said that not one of them was worth less than twenty-five thousand dollars. . . . One of the most efficient officers was Capt. André Callioux, a man whose identity with his race could not be mistaken; for he prided himself on being the blackest man in the Crescent City. . . . This regiment petitioned their commander to allow them to occupy the post of danger in the battle, and it was granted. . . .

At last the welcome word was given, and our men started. The enemy opened a blistering fire of shell, canister, grape, and musketry. . . . At every pace, the column was thinned by the falling dead and wounded. . . . No matter how gallantly the men behaved, no matter how bravely they were led, it was not in the course of things that this gallant brigade should take these works by charge. Yet charge after charge was ordered and carried out under all these disasters with Spartan firmness. Six charges in all were made. . . . Shells from the rebel guns cut down trees three feet in diameter, and they fell, at one time burying a whole company beneath their branches. . . . The last charge was made about one o'clock. At this juncture, Capt. Callioux was seen with his left arm dangling by his side,—for a ball had broken it above the elbow,—while his right hand held his unsheathed sword gleaming in the rays of the sun; and his hoarse, faint voice was heard cheering on his men. A moment more, and the brave and generous Callioux was struck by a shell, and fell far in advance of his company. . . . Seeing it to be a hopeless effort, the taking of these batteries, the troops were called off. But had they accomplished anything more than the loss of many of their brave men? Yes: they had. The self-forgetfulness, the undaunted heroism, and the great endurance of the negro, as exhibited that day, created a new chapter in American history for the colored man.[1]

In his official report of the battle, General Nathaniel P. Banks said that

Whatever doubt may have existed heretofore as to the efficiency of organizations of this character, the history of this day proves conclusively to those who were in a condition to observe the conduct of these regiments, that the Government will find in this class of troops effective supporters and defenders. The severe test to which they were subjected, and the determined manner in which they encountered the enemy, leaves upon my mind no doubt of their ultimate success.[2]

A white officer of engineers who had witnessed the assault declared that "you have no idea how my prejudices with regard to negro troops have been dispelled by the battle the other day. The brigade of negroes behaved magnificently and fought splendidly; could not have done better. They are far superior in discipline to the white troops, and just as brave."[3] And the moderate New York Times, *commenting on the reports of the battle, said that "this official testimony settles the question that the negro race can fight. . . . It is no longer possible to doubt the bravery and steadiness of the colored race, when rightly led."[4]*

On June 7 two regiments of newly recruited freedmen beat back a Confederate attack on Milliken's Bend, a Union outpost on the Mississippi River above Vicksburg. The Negroes displayed great courage while driving the rebels back in a furious bayonet charge. Three days after the battle Captain M. M. Miller of the Ninth Regiment of Louisiana Volunteers of African Descent wrote to his aunt in Galena, Illinois:

Dear Aunt: We were attacked here on June 7, about 3 o'clock in the morning, by a brigade of Texas troops about 2,500 in number. We had about 600 men to withstand them—500 of them negroes. . . . Our regiment had about 300 men in the fight. . . . We had about 50 men killed in the regiment and 80 wounded; so you can judge of what part of the fight my company sustained. I never felt more grieved and sick at heart than when I saw how my brave soldiers had been slaughtered. . . . I never more wish to hear the expression, "the niggers won't fight." Come with me 100 yards from where I sit, and I can show you the wounds that cover the bodies of 16 as brave, loyal and patriotic soldiers as ever drew bead on a Rebel.

The enemy charged us so close that we fought with our bayonets, hand to hand. . . . It was a horrible fight, the worst I was ever engaged in—not even excepting Shiloh. The enemy cried "No quarter!" but some of them were very glad to take it when made prisoners. . . .

What few men I have left seem to think much of me because I stood up with them in the fight. I can say for them that I never saw a braver company of men in my life. Not one of them offered to leave his place until ordered to fall back; in fact very few ever did fall back. . . . So they fought and died defending the cause that we revere. They met death coolly, bravely—not rashly did they expose themselves, but all were steady and obedient to orders.[5]

Even the rebel general commanding the assault on Milliken's Bend gave a somewhat left-handed compliment to the Negro soldiers. "This charge was resisted by the negro portion of the enemy's force with considerable obstinacy," wrote General Henry McCulloch, C.S.A., "while the white or true Yankee portion ran

like whipped curs almost as soon as the charge was ordered."[6]
*Charles Dana, the Assistant Secretary of War, visited Milliken's
Bend a few days after the battle and later wrote that "the bravery of the blacks in the battle at Milliken's Bend completely rev-
olutionized the sentiment of the army with regard to the
employment of negro troops. I heard prominent officers who
formerly in private had sneered at the idea of the negroes fighting express themselves after that as heartily in favor of it.*"[7]
*And General Lorenzo Thomas, the War Department's official
recruiter of Negro troops in the Mississippi Valley, reported that
when he undertook his task "the prejudice against colored troops
was quite general, and it required in the first instance all my
efforts to counteract it; but finally it was overcome, and the
blacks themselves subsequently by their coolness and determination in battle fought themselves into their present high standing as soldiers.*"[8]

*The performance of Negro soldiers on the front lines in the
South helped make things easier for black civilians in the North.
A Philadelphia Negro wrote privately on June 11, 1863, that
"public sentiment has undergone a great change in the past
month or two, and more especially since the brilliant exploits
of the several colored regiments. It is the subject of conversation
of every crowd—but the infernal Copper-heads are incensed and
will not publish the true statements, let them wallow in the mire
and filth of their own pollution until damnation ends their career.*"[9]

*Part of the Negro soldier's desperate courage came from his
realization that he was fighting for the freedom of his race. A
Yankee teacher of the freedmen later wrote: "I think the men
understood what freedom meant for them much better than the
women did. They comprehended that they had rights, and this
alone would make heroes out of chattels. The women sang, 'We
must fight for liberty': the men had already fought for it.*"[10]
*And a middle-aged sergeant in a Louisiana Negro regiment told
his fellow soldiers in the summer of 1863:*

I had been a-thinkin' I was old man; for, on de plantation, I
was put down wid de old hands, and I quinsicontly feeled myself

dat I was a old man. But since I has come here to de Yankees, and been made a soldier for de United States, an' got dese beautiful clothes on, I feels like one young man; and I doesn't call myself a old man nebber no more. An' I feels dis ebenin' dat, if de rebs came down here to dis old Fort Hudson, dat I could jus fight um as brave as any man what is in the Sebenth Regiment. Sometimes I has mighty feelins in dis ole heart of mine, when I considers how dese ere ossifers come all de way from de North to fight in de cause what we is fighten fur. How many ossifers has died, and how many white soldiers has died, in dis great and glorious war what we is in! And now I feels dat, fore I would turn coward away from dese ossifers, I feels dat I could drink my own blood, and be pierced through wid five thousand bullets. I feels sometimes as doe I ought to tank Massa Linkern for dis blessin' what we has; but again I comes to de solemn conclusion dat I ought to tank de Lord, Massa Linkern, and all dese ossifers. 'Fore I would be a slave 'gain, I would fight till de last drop of blood was gone. I has 'cluded to fight for my liberty, and for dis eddication what we is now to receive in dis beautiful new house what we has. Aldo I hasn't got any eddication nor no book-learnin', I has rose up dis blessed ebenin' to do my best afore dis congregation. Dat's all what I has to say now.[11]

In May 1863, Governor John Andrew had said that his reputation would rise or fall with the success or failure of the Fifty-fourth Massachusetts. Rarely in history did a regiment so completely justify the faith of its founders. At twilight on July 18, 1863, the Fifty-fourth led an assault on Fort Wagner, a Confederate stronghold guarding the entrance to Charleston Harbor. Across the narrow spit of sand charged the Negro regiment led by its youthful white colonel, Robert Shaw. As the column approached the fort, the Confederates opened a murderous fire, cutting wide swaths in the ranks of the Fifty-fourth. Still they came, charging on to the parapets, swarming into the fort itself. Shaw was killed at the head of his regiment; his men fought on desperately until the failure of supporting white regiments to come up in time compelled a general retreat. George W. Williams, the Negro historian, described the battle in the following

*words. The Fifty-fourth had reached Morris Island, where Fort
Wagner was situated, by a forced march during the previous
night and day:*

All day they marched over the island under the exhausting
heat of a July sun in Carolina, with the uncertain sand slipping
under their weary tread. All night the march was continued
through darkness and rain, amid thunder and lightning, over
swollen streams, broken dikes, and feeble, shuddering, narrow
causeways. Now a halt for no apparent reason, and then the
column moved forward to lead in the dance of death. This
dreary, weary, and exhausting march was continued till six
o'clock in the morning of the 18th, when the Fifty-fourth
reached Morris Island. . . .

At 6 P.M. the Fifty-fourth Regiment reached General Geo. C.
Strong's headquarters, about the middle of the island, wet and
weary, hungry and thirsty; but there was no time for rest or
refreshments. Onward the Negro regiment marched several
hundred yards farther, and proudly took its place at the head
of the assaulting column. . . . After about thirty minutes' halt,
General Strong gave the order for the charge, and the column
advanced quickly to its perilous work. The ramparts of Wagner
flashed with small-arms, and all the large shotted guns roared
with defiance. Sumter and Cumming's Point delivered a destructive cross-fire, while the howitzers in the bastions raked
the ditch; but the gallant Negro regiment swept across it and
gained the parapet. Here the flag of this regiment was planted;
here General Strong fell mortally wounded; and here the brave,
beautiful, and heroic Colonel Shaw was saluted by death and
kissed by immortality.[12]

A Negro sergeant of the Fifty-fourth later wrote:

Regarding the assault on Fort Wagner, I recollect distinctly
that when our column had charged the fort, passed the half-
filled moat, and mounted to the parapet, many of the men clam-
bered over and some entered by the large embrasure in which
one of the big guns was mounted, the firing substantially ceased
there by the beach, and the rebel musketry firing steadily grew
hotter on our left. An officer of our regiment called out, "Spike

that gun." Whether this was done I do not know, for we fired our rifles and fought as hard as we could to return the fire on our right.

But the rebel fire grew hotter on our right, and a field piece every few seconds seemed to sweep along our rapidly thinning ranks. Men all around me would fall and roll down the scarp into the ditch. . . . Immediately after I heard an order, "Retreat!" Some twelve or fifteen of us slid down from our position on the parapet of the fort.

The men-of-war seemed to have turned their guns on the fort, and the fire of the Confederates on the right seemed to increase in power. The line of retreat seemed lit with infernal fire; the hissing bullets and bursting shells seemed angry demons.[13]

Two days after the battle Frederick Douglass' son Lewis, a sergeant in the Fifty-fourth, wrote to his future wife:

My Dear Amelia: I have been in two fights, and am unhurt. I am about to go in another I believe to-night. Our men fought well on both occasions. The last was desperate we charged that terrible battery on Morris Island known as Fort Wagoner [sic], and were repulsed with a loss of [many] killed and wounded. I escaped unhurt from amidst that perfect hail of shot and shell. It was terrible. I need not particularize the papers will give a better than I have time to give. My thoughts are with you often, you are as dear as ever, be good enough to remember it as I no doubt you will. As I said before we are on the eve of another fight and I am very busy and have just snatched a moment to write you. . . . Should I fall in the next fight killed or wounded I hope to fall with my face to the foe. . . .

This regiment has established its reputation as a fighting regiment not a man flinched, though it was a trying time. Men fell all around me. A shell would explode and clear a space of twenty feet, our men would close up again, but it was no use we had to retreat, which was a very hazardous undertaking. How I got out of that fight alive I cannot tell, but I am here. My Dear girl I hope again to see you. I must bid you farewell should I be killed. Remember if I die I die in a good cause. I wish we had a hundred thousand colored troops we would put an end to this war.[14]

The Fifty-fourth's assault on Fort Wagner was in a narrow sense a failure. But in a broader sense it was a significant triumph. In the face of heavy odds, black troops had proved once again their courage, determination, and willingness to die for the freedom of their race. The New York Tribune *later summarized the importance of the Fifty-fourth's performance at Wagner:*

It is not too much to say that if this Massachusetts Fifty-fourth had faltered when its trial came, two hundred thousand colored troops for whom it was a pioneer would never have been put into the field, or would not have been put in for another year, which would have been equivalent to protracting the war into 1866. But it did not falter. It made Fort Wagner such a name to the colored race as Bunker Hill has been for ninety years to the white Yankees.[15]

The Northern press publicized widely the exploits of the Fifty-fourth. The veteran abolitionist Angelina Grimké Weld asked a friend: "Do you not rejoice & exult in all that praise that is lavished upon our brave colored troops even by Pro-slavery papers? I have no tears to shed over their graves, because I see that their heroism is working a great change in public opinion, forcing all men to see the sin & shame of enslaving such men."[16]

It was not only the newspapers and orators who lavished praise upon Negro soldiers. On August 23, 1863, General Grant himself penned a private letter to Lincoln:

I have given the subject of arming the negro my hearty support. This, with the emancipation of the negro, is the heavyest [sic] blow yet given the Confederacy. . . . By arming the negro we have added a powerful ally. They will make good soldiers and taking them from the enemy weakens him in the same proportion they strengthen us. I am therefore most decidedly in favor of pushing this policy to the enlistment of a force sufficient to hold all the South falling into our hands and to aid in capturing more.[17]

On August 26 Abraham Lincoln wrote a public letter in which he reproved Northern opponents of emancipation and the use of Negro troops:

Some of the commanders of our armies in the field who have given us our most important successes, believe the emancipation policy, and the use of colored troops, constitute the heaviest blow yet dealt to the rebellion. . . . You say you will not fight to free negroes. Some of them seem willing to fight for you. . . . There will be some black men who can remember that, with silent tongue, and clenched teeth, and steady eye, and well-poised bayonet, they have helped mankind on to this great consummation; while, I fear, there will be some white ones, unable to forget that, with malignant heart, and deceitful speech, they have strove to hinder it.[18]

At the end of 1863 Christopher A. Fleetwood, a Baltimore free Negro who had joined the army, expressed the feelings of most black men as he wrote in his diary: "This year has brought about many changes that at the beginning were or would have been thought impossible. The close of the year finds me a soldier for the cause of my race. May God bless the cause, and enable me in the coming year to forward it on."[19]

CHAPTER XIV

THE STRUGGLE FOR EQUAL PAY

In spite of the courage and con-
tribution of Negro soldiers, the black troopers were subjected to
many indignities and injustices. As late as 1864, off-duty Negro
soldiers were sometimes assaulted by white bullies and mobs.
One such incident occurred at Zanesville, Ohio, in February
1864, and was described by a correspondent of the Anglo-
African:

A colored U.S. soldier who has been active and remarkably
successful in getting recruits to help put down this bloody rebellion, while in a barber shop relating some of his adventures
while transporting his men to their destination, and some of the
opposition he met by men whom he supposed to have been rebel
sympathizers, he was assaulted by one to whom he had not said
one word. The colored soldier showed no disposition whatever
to "back down," however, at the request of the barber he left
the shop, but was soon followed by this *bully* who was so cha-
grined at the idea of a negro expressing himself in severe language against traitors, that he was determined, with the
assistance of the crowd he had around him, to murder the soldier. So with a bludgeon in one hand, he laid hold of the soldier
with the other in the attitude of striking; the soldier told him
not to strike, but he did strike him; and the the soldier gave him
a bumper on the face, not far from the temple, which caused
him to tremble and fall as a withered leaf from a tree. : . . And

then, Mr. Editor, if you had been there and heard the hissing, hooting, yelling, and cry, "kill the nigger," you would not have thought it a misnomer when they gave this class of people the name of copperhead.

The soldier seeing the fearful odds against him attempted to retreat in the Zane House, but there he met with a heartless set of ruffians who thrust him out. He was pelted by stones from every direction as he backed across the street. He had no weapons but his hands and the crowds took good care not to come within reach of them. Some of the police finally came up and the soldier was enabled to pass through another barber shop, back from his pursuers, where he remained until his fellow-soldiers . . . came to him, then he washed off the blood from his wounds, and he and his comrades walked around unmolested.[1]

Negro soldiers were often assigned a disproportionate amount of heavy labor and fatigue duty. This stemmed in part from the government's original plan to use black soldiers mainly as garrison troops and labor battalions in order to release white troops for combat. After Negro soldiers had proved themselves in battle, such a policy made no sense. But it was continued nevertheless, in part because of the anti-Negro prejudices of many officers. The excessive fatigue duties performed by the men of the Fifty-fifth Massachusetts, for example, are described in the following letters from Charles P. Bowditch, a captain in the Fifty-fifth, to members of his family:

Folly Island, S.C., August 12, 1863: Details of men are made nearly every day for fatigue duty on Morris Island. They are erecting batteries on that island continually.

August 17, 1863: The negroes are kept at work digging trenches, hauling logs and cannon, loading ammunition, etc. . . . As I expected, I was sent off night before last on fatigue duty. We were sent to the marsh battery . . . I wrote you about in one of my former letters. We were set to work unloading sand bags and placing them on the fort where they were laid under the direction of the Engineers. . . . They kept us at work pretty steadily. I have been on fatigue duty about thirty hours out of the last seventy.

September 15, 1863: Heretofore once or twice the details for
fatigue work have been ordered to lay out camps, pitch tents,
dig wells, etc. for white regiments who have lain idle until the
work was finished for them. Gen. Wilde, hearing of this, sent
an order to Col. Hallowell, saying it was a grievance and requesting him to instruct the officers of the details to disregard
such orders in future on his (Gen. Wilde's) authority. This is a
very good idea, for if they want to keep up the self-respect and
discipline of the negroes they must be careful not to try to make
them perform the work of menials. . . . I must say that while
the agreement and harmony amongst the white and black privates are almost perfect, yet among the officers of white regiments the officers of the blacks are looked down upon.[2]

*On December 4, 1863, General Daniel Ullman, commander
of the Corps d'Afrique, wrote to Senator Henry Wilson, Chairman of the Senate Military Affairs Committee:*

The first point to settle is whether it be intended to make
these men soldiers or mere laborers; if the latter, the mode pursued is the right one, and I have nothing more to say. If the
former, then there are some vital changes to be made. I fear
that many high officials outside of Washington have no other
intention than that these men shall be used as diggers and
drudges. Now, I am well satisfied from my seven months' inter-
course with them that with just treatment they can be made
soldiers of as high an average as any in the world. . . . All that
is necessary is to give them a fair chance, which has not been
done. Since I have been in command such has been the amount
of fatigue work thrust upon the organization that it has been
with the utmost difficulty that any time could be set aside for
drill. . . . The amount of actual labor performed by these men
has been enormous. Most of it was done by them in the trenches
during the siege of this place [Port Hudson], whilst more exposed to the severe fire of the enemy than any other of our
troops. . . .

Then, again, I have been forced to put in their hands arms
almost entirely unserviceable, and in other respects their equipments have been of the poorest kind. . . . I assure you that these

poor fellows . . . are deeply sensible to this gross injustice. It
breaks down their "morale." My own judgment is, that in the
great future before us we shall have to draw largely from this
element for soldiers, and the sooner we set about it in earnest
the better.[3]

*After many similar complaints, the War Department finally
issued a directive, dated June 14, 1864:*

The incorporation into the Army of the United States of colored troops, renders it necessary that they should be brought as
speedily as possible to the highest state of discipline. Accordingly the practice which has hitherto prevailed, no doubt from
necessity, of requiring these troops to perform most of the labor
of fortifications, and the labor and fatigue duties of permanent
stations and camps, will cease, and they will only be required
to take their fair share of fatigue duty with white troops. This
is necessary to prepare them for the higher duties of conflict
with the enemy.[4]

*This order brought an end to excessive fatigue duty in some
regiments, but it was not consistently enforced. As late as November 1864, General Lorenzo Thomas told the Secretary of War
that "where white and black troops come together in the same
command, the latter have to do all the work. At first this was
always the case, and in vain did I endeavor to correct it."[5]*

*The most galling discrimination against black troops was in
the matter of pay. The South Carolina and Massachusetts regiments had enlisted under a War Department promise that they
would receive the same pay as white soldiers. But Secretary
Stanton had no legal authority to make such a promise. The
only law that applied specifically to black soldiers was the militia act of July 17, 1862, which provided that Negroes would
be paid ten dollars per month, three dollars of which could be
deducted for clothing. White privates received thirteen dollars
per month plus a clothing allowance of $3.50. At the time this
law was passed the government planned to enroll Negroes primarily as laborers rather than as combat soldiers. When Stanton formed the Bureau of Colored Troops in May 1863, he asked
the legal adviser of the War Department for a ruling on the pay*

*of black soldiers, and was informed that under the law their
pay would have to be ten dollars per month. Beginning in June
1863, all Negro soldiers were paid at this rate.*[6]

*Negroes were disheartened and angered by this decision. In
an interview with President Lincoln on August 10, 1863, Frederick Douglass protested against the inequality of pay. Lincoln
replied, as Douglass later recalled, that*

the employment of colored troops at all was a great gain to
the colored people—that the measure could not have been successfully adopted at the beginning of the war, that the wisdom
of making colored men soldiers was still doubted—that their enlistment was a serious offense to popular prejudice . . . that the
fact that they were not to receive the same pay as white soldiers
seemed a necessary concession to smooth the way to their employment at all as soldiers, but that ultimately they would receive the same.[7]

*In South Carolina the men of the Fifty-fourth and Fifty-fifth
Massachusetts were unwilling to wait for "ultimate" justice.
Deciding to meet the challenge directly, these two regiments refused on principle to accept any pay at all until they were
treated and paid as equals. Governor Andrew sympathized with
their stand, and called a special session of the state legislature
to appropriate funds to pay the Fifty-fourth and Fifty-fifth the
difference between their promised and actual wages. The legislature passed the law, but the regiments still refused to accept
any pay until Washington abolished the degrading distinction
between white and black troops. In fact, some Negroes resented
Massachusetts' action, which seemed to imply that the black soldiers were only holding out for more pay. On the contrary, they
were protesting the principle of unequal treatment. One soldier
of the Fifty-fourth wrote:*

A strange misapprehension exists as to the matter of pay, and
it pains us deeply. . . . Three times have we been mustered in
for pay. Twice have we swallowed the insult offered us by the
United States paymaster, contenting ourselves with a simple refusal to acknowledge ourselves different from other Massachusetts soldiers. Once, in the face of insult and intimidation such

as no body of men and soldiers were ever subjected to before, we quietly refused and continued to do our duty. For four months we have been steadily working night and day under fire. And such work! Up to our knees in mud half the time, causing the tearing and wearing out of more than the volunteer's yearly allowance of clothing, denied time to repair and wash . . . denied time to drill and perfect ourselves in soldierly qualities, denied the privilege of burying our dead decently. All this we've borne patiently, waiting for justice.

Imagine our surprise and disappointment on the receipt by the last mail of the Governor's address to the General Court, to find him making a proposition to them to pay this regiment the difference between what the United States Government offers us and what they are legally bound to pay us, which, in effect, advertises us to the world as holding out for *money* and not from *principle*, that we sink our manhood in consideration of a few more dollars. How has this come about? What false friend has been misrepresenting us to the Governor, to make him think that our necessities outweigh our self-respect?[8]

A soldier in the Massachusetts Fifty-fifth declared that a great deal has been said of the ungratefulness of the 55th. We would like to know if we must sacrifice our principle and manhood to keep our name from being slandered. . . . We did not come to fight for money, for if we did, we might just as well have accepted the money that was offered us; we came not only to make men of ourselves, but of our other colored brothers at home, and we do highly honor the generous-hearted people of the State of Massachusetts for their prompt and generous offer. It is not the money of 1863 that we are looking at! It is the principle: that one that made us men when we enlisted.[9]

And a private in the Fifty-fourth wrote to his sister:
My dear sister, it is with pleasure that I write these few lines, to let you know how we are getting along. When we enlisted we were to get $13 per month, clothing and rations, and treatment the same as white soldiers; and now they want to cheat us out of what is justly due us, by paying us off with $10 per month, and taking three dollars out of that for clothing. . . . Why are

we not worth as much as white soldiers? We do the same work they do, and do what they cannot. We fight as well as they do. Have they forgotten James Island? Just let them think of the charge at Fort Wagner, where the colored soldiers were cruelly murdered by the notorious rebels. Why is it that they do not want to give us our pay when they have already witnessed our deeds of courage and bravery? They say we are not United States Soldiers. They want to come around and say we are laborers. If we are laborers, how is it then we do soldiers' duty, such as stand guard, and do picket duty and form a line of battle when the long roll is beat? No, because we are men of color, they are trying to impose upon us. If we had staid at home with our fathers and mothers, wives and sisters, and dear ones at home, we could have received from $1.00 to $1.50 per day.[10]

In his annual report of December 1863, Stanton asked Congress for legislation to equalize the pay of white and black soldiers. Thaddeus Stevens introduced a bill to accomplish this object. Negroes expected quick approval of the bill, but the opposition of a considerable body of Northern opinion and the maneuverings of Democrats and conservative Republicans in Congress delayed the measure. Democrats argued that to pay Negroes the same wages as white soldiers would degrade the white man. The New York World *declared that "it is unjust in every way to the white soldier to put him on a level with the black."[11]*

While politicians argued and Congress delayed, the families of black soldiers were suffering. An officer of the Fifty-fourth Massachusetts wrote in March 1864: "There is Sergeant Swails, a man who has fairly won promotion on the field of battle. While he was doing the work of government in the field, his wife and children were placed in the poorhouse."[12] Even those soldiers who did not refuse the proffered wages found that ten dollars per month (minus the clothing deduction) was scarcely enough to support their families, especially when they were not paid on time. A soldier in the Eighth U.S. Colored Troops stationed in Jacksonville, Florida, wrote in March 1864:

Our families at home are in a suffering condition, and send

to their husbands for relief. Where is it to come from? The Government has never offered us a penny since we have been here. I have been from home since the 20th of October, and have never been able to send a penny or a penny's worth to them in that time. My wife and three little children at home are, in a manner, freezing and starving to death. She writes to me for aid, but I have nothing to send her; and, if I wish to answer her letter, I must go to some of our officers to get paper and envelopes.

With all this, they want us to be patriotic and good soldiers; but how can we when we see, in our minds, the agonies of our families? When we lie down to sleep, the pictures of our families are before us, asking for relief from their sufferings. How can men do their duty, with such agony in their minds?[13]

As Congress continued to debate whether the legislation equalizing the pay of black soldiers should be make retroactive to January 1, 1864, or to the date of enlistment, the mood of the soldiers themselves began to get ugly. Abram C. Simms, a corporal in the Massachusetts Fifty-fourth, wrote:

It is said that this regiment has a good name North, East, and West. Is that the only reward we are to receive for our services? Can our families live on glowing accounts of battles, and brave deeds, done by those who left their homes to fight for a free Union, and free institutions? It is the prevailing opinion here, that the United States Government wishes us to be as the rest of the colored troops now in the field; that is, *cheap soldiers*. . . . We have waited patiently for our pay, and continue to do so; but, Mr. Editor, that valuable trait in our character is nearly extinct. . . . The fact is, this regiment is bordering on demoralization.[14]

Charles P. Bowditch, a captain in the Fifty-fifth Massachusetts, related in February 1864 that
the other day Col. Hartwell received an anonymous letter from one of our men saying that if we were not paid by the 1st of March, the men would stack arms and do no more duty, and that more than half the regiment were of that way of thinking. . . . I should not be surprised if we had some trouble with

them within the next month. Little things show which way the wind blows and the men are rather given to talking about their non-receipt of pay. Of course there is nothing to be done, but it is very hard indeed for the men.[15]

There was a near-mutiny in the Fifty-fifth later in the year, and one soldier was court-martialed and executed. Officers of the Fifty-fourth were forced to shoot and wound slightly two soldiers who had refused to obey orders. More than twenty men of the Fourteenth Rhode Island Heavy Artillery (black) were thrown into jail. Sergeant William Walker of the Third South Carolina Volunteers, stationed in Jacksonville, marched his company to his captain's tent and ordered them to stack arms and resign from an army that broke its contract with them. Walker was court-martialed and shot for mutiny.[16]

Meanwhile Negroes, abolitionists, and radical Republicans in the North were exerting every possible pressure upon Congress in an effort to force passage of the equal pay bill. On February 29 the Rev. J. P. Campbell, a leader in the A.M.E. Church, said in Baltimore:

If we are asked the question, why it is that black men have not more readily enlisted in the volunteer service of the United States Government since the door has been opened to them? we answer, The door has not been fairly and sufficiently widely opened. It has been opened only in part, not the whole of the way. That it is not sufficiently and fairly opened, will appear from the action of the present Congress upon the subject of the pay of colored soldiers. It shows a strong disposition not to equalize the pay of soldiers, without distinction on account of color. . . .

We ask for equal pay and bounty, not because we set a greater value upon money than we do upon human liberty, compared with which, money is mere trash; but we contend for equal pay and bounty upon the principle, that if we receive equal pay and bounty when we go into the war, we hope to receive equal rights and privileges when we come out of the war.[17]

The Christian Recorder *issued the following editorial appeal:*
We are continually getting letters from our noble and brave

colored soldiers, who have perilled their lives for the sake of the Union cause, and, at the command of their leaders, have confronted the enemy, when their comrades would be shot down by their sides, and some of these men have been in the service of the Government for twelve or fifteen months, and have not received one red cent for their services. . . . Many of these men . . . have wives and children, who are wholly depending upon them for support. Now, in view of all of these facts, we, in the name of God and humanity . . . call upon Congress to at once pass a law, that these men shall at once be paid the same as all other soldiers are paid. . . . We ask that Congress will remember the words of the Lord God: "Thou shalt not muzzle the ox that treadeth out the corn." Will Congress violate that plain and positive language of the eternal Jehovah? We are frank to say, that God will not let us and our armies have success, until those who have it in their power to do right, do it.[18]

On June 15, 1864, Congress finally enacted legislation granting equal pay to Negro soldiers. The law was made retroactive to January 1, 1864, for all black soldiers, and retroactive to the time of enlistment for those Negroes who had been free on April 19, 1861.[19] The distinction between freemen and freedmen created a serious dilemma for some regiments. Most Northern black regiments had both free Negroes and ex-slaves in their ranks; even the Fifty-fourth and Fifty-fifth Massachusetts Regiments included a few men who had escaped from slavery after April 19, 1861. Morale in such regiments would be impaired if some of the men received more back pay than others. Colonel E. N. Hallowell of the Fifty-fourth worked out an inspired solution to the problem. The fact of freedom before April 19, 1861, was established by the soldier's oath. Hallowell invented the following oath: "You do solemnly swear that you owed no man unrequited labor on or before the 19th day of April, 1861. So help you God." This became known as the "Quaker Oath," and even those men of the Fifty-fourth who had been slaves took the oath in good conscience "by God's higher law, if not by their country's." Several other Northern Negro regiments imitated Hallowell's oath.[20]

The inequality in pay and the delays and vacillations in
remedying this inequality constituted one of the sorriest epi-
sodes of the Civil War. Many Negro soldiers and their families
suffered severe hardships because of the discrimination in
wages. Nevertheless, when the black troopers finally received
their full back pay, there was rejoicing and celebration. An of-
ficer of the Fifty-fourth Massachusetts wrote that
we had been eighteen months waiting, and the kaleidoscope was
turned,—nine hundred men received their money; nine hundred
stories rested on the faces of those men, as they passed in at
one door [of the paymaster's office] and out of the other. Wagner stared Readville in the face! There was use in waiting! Two
days have changed the face of things, and now a petty carnival
prevails. The fiddle and other music long neglected enlivens the
tents day and night. Songs burst out everywhere; dancing is incessant; boisterous shouts are heard, mimicry, burlesque, and
carnival; pompous salutations are heard on all sides. Here a
crowd and a preacher; there a crowd and two boxers; yonder,
feasting and jubilee.[21]

And James Ruffin, a sergeant in the Fifty-fifth, wrote to his
sister-in-law after the paymaster had visited the regiment: "We
had a glorious celebration, there was a procession, then a mass
meeting where speeches of various gentlemen were made, and
readings of resolutions to be published in the papers. In the
evening we had a Grand Supper. All passed off very credit-
able."[22]

CHAPTER XV

NEGRO SOLDIERS

IN THE UNION ARMY, 1863–64

F*ully convinced of the utility of a large Negro army, the Union government extended its recruiting activities to the border slave states in 1863–64. Although the brutality of impressment characterized the operations of some recruiters in these areas as it had elsewhere, most of the freedmen who joined the army in the border states did so voluntarily. The Negroes of Nashville held a meeting on October 20, 1863, where a black leader declared:*

Then let every able bodied descendant of Africa rally to arms, for arms alone will achieve our rights. God will rule over our destinies. He will guide us, for He is the friend of the oppressed and down-trodden. The God of battles will watch over us and lead us. We have nothing to lose, but everything to gain. (Applause.) Then why not enter upon the work with holy zeal, and throw ourselves with might and main into the breach? The decision of the great questions of the day rests with us. . . . Slavery can never be what it has been, but let us not sit supinely by, but rather take a share in the great events transpiring. Let us make a name for ourselves and race, bright as the noonday sun. Let us show, as Greece has done, a people bursting their bonds and rallying for freedom. . . . Present to the world a picture of manhood; show yourselves lion-hearted; be not afraid to die. (Cheering and applause.)

Jerry Sullivan, another black man, said:

God is in this war. He will lead us on to victory. Folks talk
about the fighting being nearly over, but I believe there is a
heap yet to come. Let the colored men accept the offer of the
President and Cabinet, take arms, join the army, and then we
will whip the rebels, even if Longstreet and all the Streets of
the South, concentrate at Chattanooga. (Laughter and applause.) Why, don't you remember how afraid they used to be
that we would rise? And you know we would, too, if we could.
(Cries of "that's so.") I ran away two years ago. . . . I got to Cincinnati, and from there I went straight to General Rosecrans' headquarters. And now I am going to be Corporal. (Shouts of laughter.)

Come, boys, let's get some guns from Uncle Sam, and go coon
hunting; shooting those gray back coons [Confederates] that go
poking about the country now a days. (Laughter.) Tomorrow
morning, don't eat too much breakfast, but as soon as you get
back from market, start the first thing for our camp. Don't ask
your wife, for if she is a wife worth having she will call you a
coward for asking her. (Applause, and waving of handkerchiefs
by the ladies.) I've got a wife and she says to me, the other day,
"Jerry, if you don't go to the war mighty soon, I'll go off and
leave you, as some of the Northern gentlemen want me to go
home to cook for them." (Laughter.) . . . The ladies are now
busy making us a flag, and let us prove ourselves men worthy
to bear it.[1]

*In September 1863, Elijah Marrs, a Kentucky slave, escaped
with some of his fellow slaves and went to Louisville, where they
joined the army. Marrs, who had been born in 1840, became a
teacher and a minister to his people in Kentucky after the war.
In his memoirs he described his escape from slavery in 1863:*

I remember the morning I made up my mind to join the United
States Army. I started to Simpsonville, and walking along I met
many of my old comrades on the Shelbyville Pike. I told them
of my determination, and asked all who desired to join my company to roll his coat sleeves above his elbows, and to let them
remain so during the day. I marshaled my forces that day and
night. I had twenty-seven men, all told, and I was elected their
captain to lead them to Louisville. Our headquarters were at the

colored church. During the day some one brought the news that
the rebels were in Simpsonville, and that they were preparing
to make a raid upon the church. For a time this news created a
panic—women screamed, jumped out the windows, crying
"Murder!"—strong men ran pell-mell over the women and took
to the woods. I, myself, crowded into the corner of the church,
and Captain Marrs was about, for the time being, to throw up
the sponge. But I did not despair. I picked up courage and rallied
my men, and news soon came that the report was false. . . .

Our arms consisted of twenty-six war clubs and one old rusty
pistol, the property of the captain. There was one place on our
route we dreaded, and that was in Middletown, through which
the colored people seldom passed with safety. When we got
within two miles of the place I ordered my men to circle to the
left until we got past the town, when we returned to the Pike,
striking it in front of Womack's big woods. At this place we
heard the rumbling of vehicles coming at full speed, as we supposed, towards us. I at once ordered the men to lie down in a
ditch by the roadside, where we remained some twenty-five
minutes, but hearing nothing further I ordered my men to arise
and we took up our line of march.

Day was now breaking, and in one half hour we were within
the lines of the Union Army, and by eight o'clock we were at
the recruiting office in the city of Louisville. Here we found Mr.
George Womack, the Provost Marshal, in whose dark woods we
had taken shelter the night before. By twelve o'clock the owner
of every man of us was in the city hunting his slaves, but we
had all enlisted save one boy, who was considered too young.[2]

*A drummer boy in one of the Kentucky Negro regiments com-
posed a delightful piece of doggerel in 1864:*

> Captain Fidler's come to town,
>   With his abolition papers;
> He swears he's one of Lincoln's men,
>   He's cutting almighty capers.
>
> Captain Fidler's come to town,
>   With his abolition triggers,

He swears he's one of Lincoln's men,
  "Enlisting all the niggers." . . .

You'll see the rebels on the street,
  Their noses like a bee gum;
I don't care what in thunder they say,
  I'm fighting for my freedom! . . .

My old massa's come to town,
  Cutting a Southern figure;
What's the matter with the man?
  Lincoln's got his niggers?

Some folks say this "almighty fuss
  Is getting worse and bigger";
Some folks say "its worse and worse,"
  Because I am a "nigger."

We'll get our colored regiments strung
  Out in a line of battle;
I'll bet my money agin the South
  The rebels will skedaddle.[3]

New York was one of the last Northern states to become active in the enlistment of Negro soldiers. Black men of New York held a convention at Poughkeepsie in July 1863 and formed a committee to recruit soldiers in the state.[4] The Union League of New York City also formed a recruiting committee. But Governor Horatio Seymour was strongly opposed to the idea of black soldiers, and he refused to allow any to be enrolled under state authority. New York advocates of Negro troops finally obtained permission from the War Department to recruit black regiments directly under national authority. The first New York regiment departed for the front in March 1864, and two more followed soon afterward.[5]

The parade of the Twentieth U.S. Colored Infantry down Broadway on March 5, 1864, was a mighty symbol of the revolution wrought in the Negro's status by the Civil War, and especially by the arming of black men. Eight months previously,

*Negroes in New York had been lynched in the streets by a mad-
dened and drunken mob. Now they marched proudly behind a
military band while thousands of spectators cheered from the
sidewalks. A correspondent of the* Christian Recorder *described
the occasion:*

I think that some of the same rabble, who were in the pro-
slavery melee of July 13, 1863, were made to shed tears of re-
pentance on beholding the 20th regiment of Colored Troops off
Riker's Island, as they marched through the streets of this great
city in glorious array, onward to the defence of their country,
God, and the right, notwithstanding the outrages they suffered
a few months past at the hands of the . . . copperheads. . . .

Saturday, then, was a great day; all seemed to be one grand
jubilee. A new era has been ushered in, colored soldiers glori-
ously welcomed in the streets of New York City, and protected
by the whole force of police; their columns headed, as they
marched down to the steam-boat landing, en route to New Orleans, by some one hundred of the most influential merchants
and business men of the city; also upwards of twelve hundred
of the most prominent colored men of the country, in the wake,
and with the two best brass bands of music the state could afford, next to them 1,000 strong of the brave 20th U.S. Colored
Troops, S.N.Y., and as they passed along see the white and colored ladies wave their handkerchiefs—see the wealthy merchant leave his desk and perplexed accounts, to behold the
scene; he claps his hands and smiles. The national ensign hung
out at every window; on they go, cheer after cheer. Ain't that
a victory? . . .

The colored people are getting along here very well; they will
soon shake off this tyranny, and stand forth bold, clothed with
courage. Go it Ethiopia, for when you get old you can't.[6]

*There were the beginnings of a revolution in the South as well
as in New York. The bottom rail was on top, at least temporar-
ily, in several Southern communities. A member of the Fourteenth Regiment of Rhode Island Heavy Artillery (black) wrote
in May 1864:*

In the city of New Orleans, we could see signs of smothered

hate and prejudice to both our color and present character as
Union soldiers. But, for once in his life, your humble correspondent walked fearlessly and boldly through the streets of a southern city! And he did this without being required to take off his
cap at every step, or to give all the side-walks to those lordly
princes of the sunny south, the planters' sons! Oh, chivalry! how
has thou lost thy potent power and charms! By what means,
pray tell me, hast thou so degenerated as to lose the respect and
admiration even of the sable sons of Africa? Methinks that the
spirit of thy charms is clothed in a strange and unwonted garb![7]

*In February 1865 the First U.S. Colored Infantry occupied
Smithville, North Carolina. The Rev. Henry M. Turner, chaplain of the regiment, went to visit one of the leading black
women of the town, and while he was there some white women
came into the yard*
and commenced a jabber about some wood, which the colored
lady was appropriating to her use. She told them it was Yankee
wood, and not theirs, and the tongue battle raged most furiously
for some minutes, when one of the white women called her a
liar, with another expression too vulgar to mention. To this the
colored woman responded, "I am no more a liar than you are."
This expression, from a negro wench, as they called her, was so
intolerable, that the white women grabbed up several clubs, and
leaped in the door, using the most filthy language in the vocab-
ulary of indecency. They had not yet observed me as being on
the premises. But at this juncture, I rose up, met them at the
door, and cried out, "Halt!" Said they, "Who are you?" "A
United States Officer," was my reply. "Well, are you going to
allow that negro to give us impudence?" "You gave her impudence first," was my reply. "What, we give a negro impudence!
We want you to know we are white, and are your superiors.
You are our inferior, much less she." "Well," said I, "all of you
put together would not make the equal of my wife, and I have
yet to hear her claim superiority over me." After that, I don't
know what was said, for that remark was received as such an
aggravated insult, that I can only compare the noise that fol-

lowed, to a gang of fice dogs, holding at bay a large cur dog, with a bow-wow-wow-wow. Finally, becoming tired of their annoying music, I told them to leave or I would imprison the whole party. They then went off, and dispatched one of their party to Head Quarters, to Colonel Barney, to induce him to send a file of men, and have me arrested. But the Colonel, I believe, drove her off, and that was the end of it. I afterwards learned that they were some of the Southern aristocracy.[8]

One feature of the revolution was the way in which thousands of Negro soldiers used their spare time to learn to read and write. Frances Beecher, wife of Colonel James Beecher, commander of the Thirty-fifth U.S. Colored Infantry, taught many men of this regiment to read and write while they were stationed at Beaufort and Jacksonville. She later recalled:

My mornings were spent in teaching the men of our regiment to read and write, and it became my pleasing duty and habit, wherever our moving tents were pitched, there to set up our school. Sometimes the chaplain assisted, and sometimes the officers; and the result was that when the men came to be mustered out each one of them could proudly sign his name to the pay-roll in a good legible hand. When enlisted, all but two or three of them were obliged to put a mark to their names as written by the paymaster, thus:

his

John X Jones

mark

while their eagerness to learn and the difficulty that many found in learning were very touching. One bright mulatto man particularly worked at his letters for two years, and then could only write his own name; while others learned at once. Whenever they had a spare moment, out would come a spelling-book or a primer or Testament, and you would often see a group of heads around one book.[9]

Robert Cowden, colonel of the Fifty-ninth U.S. Colored Infantry, wrote that soon after his regiment went into winter quarters near Memphis in 1863,

a commodious schoolhouse was built where the men, when off duty, were taught by the faithful chaplain and his no less devoted wife, to read, spell, and write. . . .

In the schoolhouse, not only the enlisted men, but the colored women and children of the neighborhood were gathered for instruction every day. It also served the purpose of a chapel where on Sabbaths especially during inclement weather, they were gathered for Bible instruction or Sabbath-school in the morning, and preaching-service in the afternoon. It was astonishing to note the eagerness with which these poor, ignorant creatures entered into the work of study, and also the rapid progress they made in learning. Their enthusiasm knew no bounds as one or another came out first or second best in the contests that secured prizes for best spelling, etc. Such intense interest was created that men going on duty were generally seen carrying their spelling-books or Testaments under their belts to their posts of duty and spending their time when off post in learning their lessons. In this way about two hundred and fifty of the enlisted men of this regiment learned to read and write.[10]

Joseph T. Wilson, a black trooper in the Fifty-fourth Massachusetts Regiment, later wrote in his history of Negro soldiers that "every camp had a teacher, in fact every company had some one to instruct the soldiers in reading, if nothing more. Since the war I have known of more than one who have taken up the profession of preaching and law making, whose first letter was learned in camp; and not a few who have entered college."[11] And James Monroe Trotter, a Negro who rose to the rank of lieutenant before the war was over, wrote many years later that

scattered here and there over this broad country to-day are many veteran soldiers who are good readers and writers, some of them even fair scholars, who took their first lessons from some manly officer or no less manly fellow-soldier in the manner mentioned, during such camp intervals as were allowed by the dread arbitrament of war. . . . But let it not be supposed for a moment that only officers and men of another race were engaged in this noble work of school-teaching in our colored army. Not a few of the best workers were colored chaplains, who wisely divided their time between preaching, administering to the sick by reason of wounds or otherwise . . . while many non-commissioned officers and private soldiers cheerfully rendered effective service in the same direction.[12]

Most Negro soldiers, even the illiterate ones, knew what they were fighting for. Corporal Thomas Long of Higginson's regiment, acting as chaplain one Sunday, told his fellow soldiers:

If we hadn't become sojers, all might have gone back as it was before; our freedom might have slipped through de two houses of Congress & President Linkum's four years might have passed by & notin been done for we. But now tings can never go back, because we have showed our energy & our courage & our naturally manhood.

Anoder ting is, suppose you had kept your freedom widout enlisting in dis army; your chilen might have grown up free, & been *well cultivated* so as to be equal to any business; but it would have been always flung in dere faces—"Your fader never fought for he own freedom"—and what could dey answer? *Neber can say that to dis African race any more,* (bringing down his hand with the greatest emphasis on the table). Tanks to dis regiment, never can say dat any more, because we first showed dem we could fight by dere side.[13]

A young Tennessee Negro boy who had joined the army when he was nineteen recalled much later:

I was in the Battle of Nashville, when we whipped old Hood. I went to see my mistress on my furlough, and she was glad to see me. She said, "You remember when you were sick and I had to bring you to the house and nurse you?" and I told her, "Yes'm, I remember." And she said, "And now you are fighting me!" I said, "No'm, I ain't fighting you, I'm fighting to get free."[14]

But not all Negro soldiers were heroically dedicated to the cause for which they were fighting. One black trooper related

that he had spent much of his time on the battlefield just pray-
ing for survival:

I prayed on the battle field some of the best prayers I ever prayed in my life. Why? Sometimes it looked like the war was about to cut my ears off. I would lay stretched out on the ground and bullets would fly over my head. I would take a rock and place it on top of my head, thinking maybe it would keep the bullet from going through my brain, for I knew that would kill me. I'd just lay out, and I was just as thin and looked like one of these old spreading-adder snakes. After a while they would say, "Forward March." They never say, "Get up." So I'd get up myself and move off and then they would tell me to commence firing. . . . The Chaplain or some one of them would pray some-times. . . . They would ask God to "give us the victory this day." Words of praise was not to the strong or to the swift, but to he who held out to the end. For my part, I said what I ever heard anybody else say. I wasn't giving God no heart. I was just saying what I heard the other people say. But I made God some of the finest promises that ever were made.[15]

And Thomas Cole, a slave who ran away from his plantation
in North Alabama in 1863, later recounted his subsequent ex-
periences:

I eats all the nuts and kills a few swamp rabbits and cotches a fish. I builds the fire and goes off 'bout a half a mile and hides in the thicket till it burns down to the coals, then bakes me some fish and rabbit. I's shaking all the time, 'fraid I'd get cotched, but I's nearly starve to death. I puts the rest of the fish in my cap and travels on that night by the North Star and hides in a big thicket the next day, and along evening I hears guns shoot-ing. I sure am scared this time, sure 'nough. I's scared to come in and scared to go out, and while I's standing there, I hears two men say, "Stick you hands up, boy. What you doing?" I says, "Uh-uh-uh, I dunno. You ain't gwine take me back to the plan-tation, is you?" They says, "No. Does you want to fight for the North?" I says I will, 'cause they talks like Northern men. Us walk night and day and gits in General Rosecrans' camp, and they thunk I's the spy from the South. They asks me all sorts of questions and says they'll whip me if I didn't tell them what I's spying 'bout. Finally they 'lieves me and puts me to work helping with the cannons. I feels 'portant then, but I didn't know what was in front of me, or I 'spects I'd run off 'gain.

I helps sot them cannons on this Chickamauga Mountain, in hiding places. I has to go with a man and wait on him and that cannon. First thing I knows—bang! bang! boom!—things has started, and guns am shooting faster than you can think, and I looks round for the way to run. But them guns am shooting down the hill in front of me and shooting at me, and over me and on both sides of me. I tries to dig me a hole and git in it. All this happen right now, and first thing I knows, the man am kicking me and wanting me to holp him keep that cannon loaded. Man, I didn't want no cannon, but I has to help anyway. We fit till dark, and the Rebels got more men than us, so General Rosecrans sends the message to General Woods to come help us out. When the messenger slips off, I sure wish it am me slipping off, but I didn't want to see no General Woods. I just wants to git back to that old plantation and pick more cotton. . . .

There was men laying wanting help, wanting water, with blood running out them and the top or sides their heads gone, great big holes in them. I just promises the good Lord if He just let me git out that mess, I wouldn't run off no more, but I didn't know then He wasn't gwine let me out with just that battle. He gwine give me plenty more, but that battle ain't over yet, for next morning the Rebels 'gins shooting and killing lots of our men, and General Woods ain't come, so General Rosecrans orders us to 'treat and didn't have to tell me what he said, neither. The Rebels comes after us, shooting, and we runs off and leaves that cannon what I was with setting on the hill, and I didn't want that thing nohow.

We kept hotfooting till we gits to Chattanooga, and there is where we stops. . . . There a long range of hills leading 'way from Lookout Mountain, nearly to Missionary Ridge. . . . They fights the Rebels on Orchard Knob Hill, and I wasn't in that, but I's in the Missionary Ridge battle. We has to come out the timber and run 'cross a strip or opening up the hill. They sure kilt lots

our men when we runs 'cross that opening. We runs for all we's
worth and uses guns or anything we could. The Rebels turns
and runs off, and our soldiers turns the cannons round what
we's capture and kilt some the Rebels with their own guns.

I never did git to where I wasn't scared when we goes into
the battle. This the last one I's in, and I's sure glad, for I never
seed the like of dead and wounded men. We picks them up, the
Rebels like the Unions, and doctors them the best we could. . . .

I sure wished lots of times I never run off from the plantation. I begs the General not to send me on any more battles, and
he says I's the coward and sympathizes with the South. But I
tells him I just couldn't stand to see all them men lying there
dying and hollering and begging for help and a drink of water
and blood everywhere you looks. . . .

Finally, the General tells me I can go back to Chattanooga
and guard the supplies in camp there and take the wounded
soldiers and prisoners. A bunch of men is with me, and we has
all we can do. We gits the orders to send supplies to some general, and it my job to help load the wagons or boxcars or boats.
A train of wagons leaves sometimes. We gits all them supplies
by boat, and Chattanooga am the 'stributing center. When winter comes, everybody rests awhile and waits for spring to open.
The Union general sends in some more colored soldiers. There
ain't been many colored men, but the last year the war there
am lots. The North and the South am taking anything they can
get to win the war.[16]

*Most Negro soldiers, however, had some comprehension of
why they were fighting and as much willingness as any other
race of men to die for their cause. In fact, it required more
courage for Negroes than for whites to become soldiers, because
the Confederacy had not revoked its stated intention to punish
captured Negroes as insurrectionists. The Richmond government never officially enforced this policy, but in some cases
rebel officers or soldiers refused to take black prisoners, or murdered such prisoners in cold blood after capture. The so-called
"Fort Pillow Massacre" was the most notable instance of the
murder of Negro prisoners after capture. Fort Pillow was a*

Union outpost on the Mississippi River, garrisoned by approx-
imately 570 troops, of whom slightly less than half were black.
On April 12, 1864, General Nathan Bedford Forrest led a rebel
attack on the fort and captured it. An undetermined number of
Union soldiers, mostly Negroes, were murdered in cold blood
after they had surrendered. A Congressional committee charged
that "at least 300" of the Union troops were massacred. Some
historians have denied that the alleged "massacre" took place
at all, and have claimed that the Unionists were killed during
the course of the battle. The most recent and objective studies,
however, have concluded that while the Congressional commit-
tee's report was distorted and exaggerated, nevertheless several
score Negro soldiers and some white troopers were indeed mur-
dered after they had surrendered.[17]

The Congressional committee interrogated twenty-one Negro
survivors of the Fort Pillow affair. The testimony of four of
these soldiers is excerpted below:

Sergeant Benjamin Robinson, (colored) company D, 6th United
States heavy artillery, sworn and examined. . . .

QUESTION. Were you at Fort Pillow in the fight there?

ANSWER. Yes, sir.

QUESTION. What did you see there?

ANSWER. I saw them shoot two white men right by the side of
me after they had laid their guns down. They shot a black man
clear over into the river. Then they hallooed to me to come up
the hill, and I came up. They said, "Give me your money, you
damned nigger." I told him I did not have any. "Give me your
money, or I will blow your brains out." Then they told me to lie
down, and I laid down, and they stripped everything off me.

QUESTION. This was the day of the fight?

ANSWER. Yes, sir.

QUESTION. Go on. Did they shoot you?

ANSWER. Yes, sir. After they stripped me and took my money
away from me they dragged me up the hill a little piece, and
laid me down flat on my stomach; I laid there till night, and
they took me down to an old house, and said they would kill me

the next morning. I got up and commenced crawling down the hill; I could not walk.

QUESTION. When were you shot?

ANSWER. About 3 o'clock.

QUESTION. Before they stripped you?

ANSWER. Yes, sir. They shot me before they said, "come up."

QUESTION. After you had surrendered?

ANSWER. Yes sir; they shot pretty nearly all of them after they surrendered. . . .

Major Williams, (colored) private, company B, 6th United States heavy artillery, sworn and examined.

By the chairman:

QUESTION. Where were you raised?

ANSWER. In Tennessee and North Mississippi.

QUESTION. Where did you enlist?

ANSWER. In Memphis. . . .

QUESTION. Were you in the fight at Fort Pillow?

ANSWER. Yes, sir. . . .

QUESTION. What did you see done there?

ANSWER. We fought them right hard during the battle, and killed some of them. After a time they sent in a flag of truce. . . .

QUESTION. When did you surrender?

ANSWER. I did not surrender until they all run.

QUESTION. Were you wounded then?

ANSWER. Yes, sir; after the surrender. . . .

QUESTION. Did you have any arms in your hands when they shot you?

ANSWER. No, sir; I was an artillery man, and had no arms. . . .

Eli Carlton, (colored) private, company B, 6th United States heavy artillery, sworn and examined.

By the chairman:

QUESTION. Where were you raised?

ANSWER. In East Tennessee.

QUESTION. Have you been a slave?

ANSWER. Yes, sir. . . .

QUESTION. Where did you join the army?

ANSWER. At Corinth, Mississippi, about a year ago.

QUESTION. Were you at Fort Pillow at the time it was taken?

ANSWER. Yes, sir.

QUESTION. State what happened there.

ANSWER. I saw 23 men shot after they surrendered; I made 24. 17 of them laid right around me dead, and 6 below me.

QUESTION. Who shot them?

ANSWER. The rebels; some white men were killed.

QUESTION. How many white men were killed?

ANSWER. Three or four.

QUESTION. Killed by the privates?

ANSWER. Yes, sir; I did not see any officers kill any. . . .

QUESTION. Where you shot with a musket or a pistol?

ANSWER. With a musket. I was hit once on the battle-field before we surrendered. They took me down to a little hospital under the hill. I was in the hospital when they shot me a second time. Some of our privates commenced talking. They said, "Do you fight with these God damned niggers?" they said, "Yes." Then they said, "God damn you, then, we will shoot you," and they shot one of them right down. They said, "I would not kill you, but, God damn you, you fight with these damned niggers, and we will kill you;" and they blew his brains out of his head. . . .

George Shaw, (colored) private, company B, 6th United States heavy artillery, sworn and examined.

By Mr. Gooch:

QUESTION. Where were you raised?

ANSWER. In Tennessee.

QUESTION. Where did you enlist?

ANSWER. At Fort Pillow.

QUESTION. Were you there at the fight?

ANSWER. Yes, sir.

QUESTION. When were you shot?

ANSWER. About four o'clock in the evening.

QUESTION. After you had surrendered?

ANSWER. Yes, sir.

QUESTION. Where were you at the time?

ANSWER. About ten feet from the river bank.

QUESTION. Who shot you?

ANSWER. A rebel soldier.

QUESTION. How near did he come to you?

ANSWER. About ten feet.

QUESTION. What did he say to you?

ANSWER. He said, "Damn you, what are you doing here?" I said, "Please don't shoot me." He said, "Damn you, you are fighting against your master." He raised his gun and fired, and the bullet went into my mouth and out the back part of my head. They threw me into the river and I swam around and hung on there in the water until night.

QUESTION. Did you see anybody else shot?

ANSWER. Yes, sir; three young boys, lying in the water, with their heads out; they could not swim. They begged them as long they could, but they shot them right in the forehead. . . .

QUESTION. How old were the boys?

ANSWER. Not more than fifteen or sixteen years old. They were not soldiers, but contraband boys, helping us on the breast-works.

QUESTION. Did you see any white men shot?

ANSWER. No, sir. I saw them shoot three men the next day.

QUESTION. How far from the fort?

ANSWER. About a mile and a half; after they had taken them back as prisoners.

QUESTION. Who shot them?

ANSWER. Private soldiers. One officer said, "Boys, I will have you arrested, if you don't quit killing them boys." Another officer said, "Damn it, let them go on; it isn't our law to take any niggers prisoners; kill every one of them." Then . . . two others came up, and said, "Damn you, we will kill you, and not be fooling about any longer." I said, "Don't shoot me." One of them said, "Go out and hold my horse." I made a step or two, and he said, "Turn around; I will hold my horse, and shoot you, too." I no sooner turned around than he shot me in the face. I fell down as if I was dead. He shot me again, and hit my arm, not my head. I laid there until I could hear him no more, and then I started back. I got back into Fort Pillow about sun up, and wandered about there until a gunboat came along, and I came up on that with about ten others.[18]

The Christian Recorder *commented editorially on "The Capture of Fort Pillow":*

It is needless, perhaps, for us to repeat to our readers, the butchery of black soldiers at Fort Pillow, for its sickening details have already been spread before them by the daily papers. We had hoped, however, that the first report might have been exaggerated; but, in this we have been doomed to disappointment. Every additional report only goes to confirm the first. We say, emphatically, that the massacre, at Fort Pillow, has been invited by the tardiness of the government, and the action of Congress. While they have professed to regard every man wearing the U.S. uniform, as being equal in theory, they have acted towards the black soldiers, in such a way, as to convince the Confederate government that they, themselves, do not regard the black soldiers as equal to the white. The rebels have taken advantage of this equivocation, to commit just such horrible butchery as that at Fort Pillow.[19]

One Northern Negro urged black soldiers to avenge the Fort Pillow Massacre:

We now call on our noble brethren in the army, to swear anew never to cease fighting, until they shall have made a rebel to bite the dust for every hair of those three hundred of our black brethren massacred in Fort Pillow; and, whenever you may be called upon to measure arms or bayonets, with the rebel horde, give no quarter; take no prisoners; make it dangerous to take the life of a black soldier by these barbarians; then, they will respect your manhood, and you will be treated as you deserve at the hands of those who have made you outlaws. . . . Warriors! remember that you fight for liberty! Remember the wives and children you have left behind! Remember, you from New York, the *July riots!* You from the South, who are soldiers of the Republic, remember your old gray-headed mothers, who are yet within the lines of rebeldom; remember your daughters, dishonored by those red-handed murderers of your race! Remember, that for two hundred and fifty years, your people have been sold and bartered like so many beasts, and then bow down before God, and swear anew to uphold your country's cause, and the cause of universal liberty.[20]

The Fort Pillow Massacre did indeed have the effect of making Negro troops fight more desperately, for they feared the consequences of capture. Negro troops at Memphis were reported to have taken an oath "on their knees" to avenge Fort Pillow and to show rebel troops no quarter.[21] An officer of one of the black regiments in the Army of the Potomac wrote from a Virginia battlefield in May 1864:

The real fact is, the rebels will not stand against our colored soldiers when there is any chance of being taken prisoners, for they are conscious of what they justly deserve. Our men went into these works after they were taken, yelling, "Fort Pillow!" The enemy well knows what this means, and I will venture the assertion that that piece of infernal brutality enforced by them there has cost the enemy already two men for every one they so inhumanly murdered.[22]

A white soldier in one of the Pennsylvania regiments fighting before Petersburg wrote home that "the Johnnies are not as much afraid of us as they are of the Mokes [black troops]. When they charge they will not take any prisoners, if they can help it. Their cry is, 'Remember Fort Pillow!' Sometimes, in their excitement, they forget what to say, when they catch a man they say: 'Remember what you done to us, way back, down dar!' "[23]

CHAPTER XVI

BLACK TROOPS

IN THE FINAL YEAR OF WAR

Although the reports of Negro determination to avenge Fort Pillow were probably exaggerated, it is true that in the last year of the war black troops fought in greater numbers and with greater efficiency than ever before. These troops played a major role in the final victory of Union arms. By October 20, 1864, there were 140 Negro regiments in the Federal service with a total strength of 101,950 men.[1] Fifteen Negro regiments served in the Army of the James and twenty-three in the Army of the Potomac during the massive Union invasion of Virginia in the summer of 1864.[2] Black troops participated in every other major Union campaign in 1864–65 except Sherman's invasion of Georgia.

It is obviously impossible to describe here all of the engagements in which Negro troops fought during 1864–65. Only a few of the battles can be discussed, and they must stand as representative of the whole. Negro soldiers played a vital role in the fighting around Petersburg, Virginia, in June 1864. Black regiments under General Edward Hinks assaulted and captured an important rebel entrenchment near the city. Secretary of War Stanton, referring to the battles near Petersburg, told a newspaper reporter that "the hardest fighting was done by the black troops. The forts they stormed were the worst of all. After the affair was over, General [William F.] Smith went to thank them, and tell them he was proud of their courage and dash. He says *they cannot be exceeded as soldiers, and that hereafter he will send them in a difficult place as readily as the best white troops."[3] An officer of the Twenty-second U.S. Colored Infantry wrote enthusiastically to a Philadelphia newspaper:*

The problem is solved. The negro is a man, a *soldier*, a hero. Knowing of your laudable interest in the colored troops, . . . I have thought it proper that I should let you know how they acquitted themselves in the late actions in front of Petersburg, of which you have already received newspaper accounts. If you remember, in my conversations upon the character of these troops. I carefully avoided saying anything about their fighting qualities till I could have an opportunity of trying them.

That opportunity came on [June 15th] and since, and I am now prepared to say that I never, since the beginning of this war, saw troops fight better, more bravely, and with more determination and enthusiasm. Our division, commanded by General Hinks, took the advance on the morning of the 15th inst., arrived in front of the enemy's works about 9 o'clock, A.M., formed line, charged them, and took them most handsomely. . . . We pushed on two and a half miles further, till we came in full view of the main defences of Petersburg. We formed line at about 2 o'clock P.M., reconnoitred and skirmished the whole afternoon, and we were constantly subject to the shells of the enemy's artillery. At sunset we charged these strong works, and carried them. Major Cook took one with the left wing of our regiment as skirmishers, by getting under the guns, and then preventing their gunners from using their pieces, while he gained the rear and redoubt, where there was no defence but the infantry, which, classically speaking, "skedaddled." We charged across what appeared to be an almost impassable ravine, with the right wing at the time subject to a hot fire of grape and cannister, until we got so far under the guns as to be sheltered, when the enemy took to their rifle-pits as infantry men. Our brave fellows went steadily through the swamp, and up the side of a hill, at an angle of almost fifty degrees, rendered nearly impassable by fallen timber. Here, again, our color sergeant was conspicuous in keeping far ahead of the most advanced, hanging on to the side of the hill, till he would turn about and wave the stars and stripes at his advancing comrades; then steadily advancing again, under the fire of the enemy, till he could almost have reached their rifle-pits with his flagstaff. How he kept from being killed I do not know. . . . We left forty-three men wounded, and eleven killed in the ravine over which our men charged the last time. Our loss in the whole day's operations was one hundred and forty-three, including six officers, one of whom was killed. Sir, there is no underrating the good conduct of these fellows during these charges; with but a few exceptions, they all went in as old soldiers, but with more enthusiasm. I am delighted that our first action resulted in a decided victory. . . .

Our men, unfortunately, owing to the irregular feature of the ground, took no prisoners. Sir, we can *bayonet* the enemy to terms on this matter of treating colored soldiers as prisoners of war far sooner than the authorities at Washington can bring him to it by negotiation. This I am *morally persuaded of.* I know further that the enemy won't fight us if he can help it. I am sure that the same number of white troops could not have taken those works on the evening of the 15th. . . . The real fact is, the rebels will not stand against our colored soldiers when there is any chance of their being taken prisoner.[4]

Thirteen Negro regiments fought at Chaffin's Farm in Virginia at the end of September, and of a total of thirty-seven Congressional Medals of Honor awarded to veterans of that battle, fourteen went to black soldiers.[5] Negro troops were not confined to infantry and artillery units alone. By October 1864 there were six black cavalry regiments in the service. One of these was the Third U.S. Colored Cavalry, composed mainly of freedmen recruited from Mississippi and Tennessee in 1863. In March 1864 the Third U.S. Colored Cavalry was garrisoned in a fort defending Yazoo City, Mississippi. A large Confederate force attacked the city on March 5. One of the officers of the Negro regiment wrote the following account of the battle:

The combined forces of Ross and Richardson, numbering between 4,000 and 5,000 men, formed a cordon around the city during the night of March 4th, and at daylight on the morning of March 5th, they were hurled against the Union troops, numbering but 1,217 men and officers all told.

. . . The gun-boats could render no assistance in this fight, as the city and the Union troops were between them and the enemy. The rebels opened the fight by first advancing on the Benton road, driving in the pickets of the Third U.S. Colored Cavalry. . . . The report of their carbines, volley after volley, as they met the attack, was the first sound to break the stillness of the early morning, denoting to the practiced ear that an attack in force was being made. Major Cook was at the fort, and hastened with a detachment of the regiment to support the picket, but the enemy came on with a rush that he could not check, and he was compelled to fall back and seek cover in the fort. . . .

The enemies [sic] batteries, from their commanding positions on the adjacent hills, rained shot and shell into and around the besieged fort, some of the shot bursting in the air over the fort, the pieces falling among the men, killing and wounding many, . . . while the rebel sharpshooters, crouching in gully and ravine, closed in around the besieged fort, in readiness for the final rush, which was to carry the fort by assault. Surely the little fort and its brave defenders seemed doomed. It was well known that the Texans took no "nigger" prisoners, therefore no quarter could be expected. . . . Thus the battle raged for several hours, the enemy all the time taking more advanced ground, when the firing ceased, and a flag of truce was seen approaching the fort. Major Cook sprang upon the parapet, where he was hailed by Colonel Mabry of the Third Texas Cavalry, bearing a message from General Ross, demanding the immediate and unconditional surrender of the forces holding the fort, to which demand Major Cook made this reply, "My compliments to General Ross, and say to him that if he wants this fort to come and take it." Colonel Mabry, bowing, returned to his command, and the firing was soon resumed. . . .

After the flag of truce incident, the attack was renewed with even more fury than before. . . . At this trying moment Major

McKee, Eleventh Illinois Infantry, reached the fort, having been sent by Colonel Coates, who was much concerned for the safety of those in it. . . . Maj. McKee ranked Maj. Cook by seniority of commission, and he at once assumed command. It being feared that the 9th Texas, which had secured a strong position west of the fort, and quite close to it, might attempt a charge across the intervening space, Major McKee ordered Companies A and B, Third U.S. Colored Cavalry, to take position outside the fort, in a deep ditch on the west side, bringing them face to face with the 9th Texas. . . . Major McKee accompanied these companies and remained with them, directing their movements. The enemy now formed a complete circle around the fort, ranging from 100 to 200 yards distant. They made repeated charges to carry the works by assault, but were as often beaten back, leaving the hill-side strewn with their dead and wounded. . . .

For a long time the issue trembled in the balance, it seeming that the Union soldiers must be overcome by sheer force of numbers, and it was only by their heroic bravery and bulldog tenacity that they maintained their ground. Communication between the Union forces in the city and those in the fort was now cut off, the fort being completely surrounded. The defeat of one meant the certain downfall of the other. . . . And so the fight raged, the yells of the combatants, the groans of the wounded and the prayers of the dying being drowned in the general tumult. At a moment when it seemed that the Union troops must yield to the great preponderance of numbers, one of those lucky incidents occurred that sometimes turn the tide of battle. It was brought about by a bold dash made by Lieutenants Farley and Carson of the Third U.S. Colored Calvary. Lieutenants Farley and Carson had been sent back to camp early that morning by Major Cook, to gather up all the men left in camp, and bring them to the fort, but on their return, they were cut off by the forces of General Richardson then entering the city. With the men they had gathered up, some 20 or 30, they fought their way back to the city, losing two men, killed by the enemy. Reaching the city, they put themselves at the command of Colonel Coates, doing gallant service. These officers . . . lead-

ing such men as they could rally, made a bold dash that turned
the enemy's left flank, which threw them into confusion. Sometimes it required but a trifle to start a panic, which once set in
motion is as uncontrollable as a drove of Texas steers when
stampeded. When the rebel line in the city broke, the 9th Texas,
rebel, occupying a position west of the fort, seeing the stampede
of their friends, and fearing that they too would be cut off, also
broke in disorder. This being the regiment confronting Major
McKee and the two companies of the Third U.S. Colored Cavalry, that officer sallied forth with these companies, dashed
down the hill, firing and yelling, which completed the rout of
the 9th Texas, which degenerated into a mad scramble to seek
shelter in gully and ravine. By these lucky and timely moves by
the officers named, the combined forces of Ross and Richardson
were defeated and put to flight. Thus the battle of Yazoo City
was fought and won. The enemy was in retreat, leaving their
dead and wounded where they fell.[6]

*One of the important engagements of 1864 was the Battle of
Nashville, December 15–16, in which General George Thomas's
Army of the Cumberland destroyed the Confederate Army of
Tennessee, commanded by John B. Hood. Eight black regiments
played a vital role in this victory. Thomas J. Morgan, Colonel
of the Fourteenth U.S. Colored Infantry and commander of a
brigade of four Negro regiments in the Battle of Nashville, gave
the following account of his regiment from the time it was organized in November 1863 until the Battle of Nashville more
than a year later:*

November 1st, 1863, by order of Major Stearns, I went to
Gallatin, Tennessee, to organize the 14th United States Colored
Infantry. . . . There were at that time several hundred negro
men in camp, in charge of, I think, a lieutenant. They were a
motley crowd,—old, young, middle aged. Some wore the United
States uniform, but most of them had on the clothes in which
they had left the plantations, or had worn during periods of
hard service as laborers in the army. . . .

As soon and as fast as practicable, I set about organizing the
regiment. . . . The colored men knew nothing of the duties of a

soldier, except a little they had picked up as camp-followers. . . .
We had no tents, and the men were sheltered in an old filthy
tobacco warehouse, where they fiddled, danced, sang, swore or
prayed, according to their mood.

How to meet the daily demands made upon us for military
duty, and at the same time to evoke order out of this chaos, was
no easy problem. The first thing to be done was to examine the
men. A room was prepared, and I and my clerk took our stations
at a table. One by one the recruits came before us *a la Eden,
sans* the fig leaves, and were subjected to a careful medical examination, those who were in any way physically disqualified
being rejected. Many bore the wounds and bruises of the slave-
driver's lash, and many were unfit for duty by reason of some
form of disease to which human flesh is heir. In the course of a
few weeks, however, we had a thousand able-bodied, stalwart
men. . . .

Acting upon my clerk's suggestion, I assigned them to companies according to their height, putting men of nearly the same
height together. When the regiment was full, the four center
companies were all composed of tall men, the flanking companies of men of medium height, while the little men were sand-
wiched between. The effect was excellent in every way, and
made the regiment quite unique. It was not uncommon to have
strangers who saw it parade for the first time, declare that the
men were all of one size. . . .

The complete organization of the regiment occupied about
two months, being finished by Jan. 1st, 1864. The field, staff
and company officers were all white men. All the non-
commissioned officers,—Hospital Steward, Quartermaster, Sergeant, Sergeant-Major, Orderlies, Sergeants and Corporals were
colored. They proved very efficient, and had the war continued
two years longer, many of them would have been competent as
commissioned officers. . . .

General George H. Thomas, though a Southerner, and a West
Point graduate, was a singularly fair-minded, candid man. He
asked me one day soon after my regiment was organized, if I
thought my men would fight. I replied that they would. He said

he thought "they might behind breastworks." I said they would fight in the open field. He thought not. "Give me a chance General," I replied, and I will prove it." . . .

While at Chattanooga, I organized two other regiments, the 42nd and the 44th United States Colored Infantry. In addition to the ordinary instruction in the duties required of the soldier, we established in every company a regular school, teaching men to read and write, and taking great pains to cultivate in them self-respect and all manly qualities. Our success in this respect was ample compensation for our labor. The men who went on picket or guard duty, took their books as quite as indispensable as their coffee pots. . . .

DALTON, GA.—August 15, 1864, we had our first fight at Dalton, Georgia. General Wheeler, with a considerable force of Confederate cavalry, attacked Dalton, which was occupied by a small detachment of Union troops belonging to the 2nd Missouri. . . . My regiment formed on the left of the 51st Indiana Infantry. . . . The fight was short, and not at all severe. The regiment was all exposed to fire. One private was killed, one lost a leg, and one was wounded in the right hand. Company B, on the skirmish line killed five of the enemy, and wounded others. To us it was a great battle, and a glorious victory. The regiment had been recognized as soldiers; it had taken its place side by side with a white regiment; it had been under fire. . . . After the fight, as we marched into town through a pouring rain, a white regiment standing at rest, swung their hats and gave three rousing cheers for the 14th Colored. . . .

PULASKI, TENN.—September 27th, 1864, I reported to Major-General Rousseau, commanding a force of cavalry at Pulaski, Tenn. As we approached the town by rail from Nashville, we heard artillery, then musketry, and as we left the cars we saw the smoke of guns. Forest [sic], with a large body of cavalry, had been steadily driving Rousseau before him all day, and was destroying the railroad. Finding the General, I said: "I am ordered to report to you, sir." "What have you?" "Two regiments of colored troops." Rousseau was a Kentuckian, and had not much faith in negro soldiers. By his direction I threw out a strong line of skirmishers, and posted the regiments on a ridge, in good supporting distance. Rousseau's men retired behind my line, and Forest's men pressed forward until they met our fire, and recognizing the sound of the minie ball, stopped to reflect.

The massacre of colored troops at Fort Pillow was well known to us, and had been fully discussed by our men. It was rumored, and thoroughly credited by them, that General Forest had offered a thousand dollars for the head of any commander of a "nigger regiment." Here, then, was just such an opportunity as those spoiling for a fight might desire. Negro troops stood face to face with Forest's veteran cavalry. The fire was growing hotter, and balls were uncomfortably thick. At length, the enemy in strong force, with banners flying, bore down toward us in full sight, apparently bent on mischief. Pointing to the advancing column, I said, as I passed along the line, "Boys, it looks very much like fight; keep çool, do your duty." They seemed full of glee, and replied with great enthusiasm: "Colonel, dey can't whip us, dey nebber get de ole 14th out of heah, nebber." "Nebber drives us away widout a mighty lot of dead men," &c.,&c.

When Forest learned that Rousseau was re-enforced by infantry, he did not stop to ask the color of their skin, but after testing our line, and finding it unyielding, turned to the east, and struck over toward Murfreesboro. . . .

NASHVILLE, TENN.—November 29, 1864, in command of the 14th, 16th, and 44th Regiments U.S.C.I., I embarked on a railroad train at Chattanooga for Nashville. On December 1st, with the 16th and most of the 14th, I reached my destination, and was assigned to a place on the extreme left of General Thomas' army then concentrating for the defence of Nashville against Hood's threatened attack. . . .

Soon after taking our position in line at Nashville, we were closely besieged by Hood's army; and thus we lay facing each other for two weeks. Hood had suffered so terribly by his defeat under Schofield, at Franklin, that he was in no mood to assault us in our works, and Thomas needed more time to concentrate and reorganize his army, before he could safely take the offensive. . . .

About nine o'clock at night December 14th, 1864, I was summoned to General Steadman's [sic] headquarters. He told me what the plan of battle was, and said he wished me to open the fight by making a vigorous assault upon Hood's right flank. This, he explained, was to be a feint, intended to betray Hood into the belief that it was the real attack, and to lead him to support his right by weakening his left, where Thomas intended assaulting him in very deed. The General gave me [four colored regiments], . . . a provisional brigade of white troops . . . and a section of Artillery . . . of the 20th Indiana Battery. . . .

As soon as the fog lifted, the battle began in good earnest. Hood mistook my assault for an attack in force upon his right flank, and weakening his left in order to meet it, gave the coveted opportunity to Thomas, who improved it by assailing Hood's left flank, doubling it up, and capturing a large number of prisoners.

Thus the first day's fight wore away. It had been for us a severe but glorious day. Over three hundred of my command had fallen, but everywhere our army was successful. . . . General Steadman congratulated us, saying his only fear had been that we might fight too hard. We had done all he desired, and more. Colored soldiers had again fought side by side with white troops; they had mingled together in the charge; they had supported each other; they had assisted each other from the field when wounded, and they lay side by side in death. The survivors rejoiced together over a hard fought field, won by a common valor. . . .

During that night Hood withdrew his army some two miles, and took up a new line along the crest of some low hills, which he strongly fortified with some improvised breast works and abatis. Soon after our early breakfast, we moved forward over the intervening space. My position was still on the extreme left of our line, and I was especially charged to look well to our flank, to avoid surprise.

The 2nd Colored Brigade, under Colonel Thompson, of the 12th U.S.C.I., was on my right, and participated in the first day's charge upon Overton's hill, which was repulsed. . . . When the

2nd Colored Brigade retired behind my lines to re-form, one of
the regimental color-bearers stopped in the open space between
the two armies, where, although exposed to a dangerous fire,
he planted his flag firmly in the ground, and began deliberately
and coolly to return the enemy's fire, and, greatly to our amusement, kept up for some little time his independent warfare.

When the second and final assault was made, the right of my
line took part. It was with breathless interest I watched that
noble army climb the hill with a steady resolve which nothing
but death itself could check. When at length the assaulting column sprang upon the earthworks, and the enemy seeing that
further resistance was madness, gave way and began a precipi-
tous retreat, our hearts swelled as only the hearts of soldiers
can, and scarcely stopping to cheer or to await orders, we
pushed forward and joined in the pursuit, until the darkness and
the rain forced a halt. . . .

When General Thomas rode over the battle-field and saw the
bodies of colored men side by side with the foremost, on the
very works of the enemy, he turned to his staff, saying: "Gentlemen, the question is settled; negroes will fight."[7]

*General James B. Steedman, an old Breckinridge Democrat
who had originally been opposed to the enlistment of Negro
troops, was in command of the left wing of the Army of the
Cumberland during the battle. He stated in his official report:*

The larger portion of these losses, amounting in the aggregate
to fully 25 per cent. of the men under my command who were
taken into action, it will be observed fell upon the colored
troops. The severe loss of this part of my troops was in their
brilliant charge on the enemy's works on Overton Hill on Friday
afternoon. I was unable to discover that color made any difference in the fighting of my troops. All, white and black, nobly
did their duty as soldiers.[8]

*Steedman's report reflected the growing respect for black
troops among persons who had once felt little but contempt or
pity for the Negro race. A government commission investigat-
ing the condition of the freedmen reported in May 1864 that*
the whites have changed, and are still rapidly changing, their

opinion of the negro. And the negro, in his new condition as freedman, is himself, to some extent, a changed being. No one circumstance has tended so much to these results as the display of manhood in negro soldiers. Though there are higher qualities than strength and physical courage, yet, in our present state of civilization, there are no qualities which command from the masses more respect.[9]

Lydia Maria Child recounted the following incident in the spring of 1864:

Capt. Wade, of the U.S. Navy, who bought a house for his wife in this town [Wayland, Mass.], has been a bitter pro-slavery man, violent and vulgar in his talk against abolitionists and "niggers." Two years ago, he was for having us mobbed because we advocated emancipating and arming the slaves. He has been serving in the vicinity of N. Orleans, and has come home on a furlough, an outspoken abolitionist. He not only says it in private; but has delivered three lectures in town, in which he has publicly announced the total change in his sentiments since he has had "an opportunity to *know* something on the subject." A few days ago, he was going in the cars from Boston to Roxbury, when a colored soldier entered the car. Attempting to seat himself, he was repulsed by a white man, who rudely exclaimed, *"I'm not going to ride with niggers."* Capt. Wade, who sat a few seats further forward, rose up, in all the gilded glory of his naval uniform, and called out, "Come here, my good fellow! I've been fighting along side of people of your color, and glad enough I was to have 'em by my side. Come and sit by me." Two years ago, I would not have believed such a thing possible of him. So the work goes on, in all directions.[10]

President Lincoln summarized the contribution of Negro soldiers and laborers to the Union cause in a letter of September 12, 1864: "We can not spare the hundred and forty or fifty thousand now serving us as soldiers, seamen, and laborers. This is not a question of sentiment or taste, but one of physical force which may be measured and estimated as horse-power and steam-power are measured and estimated. Keep it and you can save the Union. Throw it away, and the Union goes with it."[11]

The war also had its comic aspects. Elijah Marrs, an ex-slave from Kentucky who had become a sergeant in the Twelfth U.S. Colored Artillery, wrote the following account:

After Hood's defeat, and during the time our soldiers occupied Nashville, frequent furloughs were given to the colored soldiers to return to Kentucky to see their wives and families. One of them stopped at Bowling Green, his wife living about five miles distant, on the other side of Barren River. He informed our commanding officer, Col. Babcock, that the parties she belonged to had been treating her very cruelly, and to some extent on account of he, her husband, being in the army. The Colonel immediately sent for me, informed me of these facts, and ordered me to take a guard of ten men to accompany the soldier, who acted as our guide, and to bring the woman into camp; and further, that if the man who owned her had anything to say about it or offered any resistance, to put a ball into one ear so that it might come out of the other. When he said this I imagined that I was clothed with authority to do whatsoever I pleased on my trip. I got my men together as soon as possible, and crossed the Barren River, but instead of at once proceeding to the man's house on foot as we were ordered to do, I concluded that we would go by water, and at once commenced to look around for means of transportation. We soon discovered a small boat that was lying at the wharf, which we took possession of at once, and ordered the captain of the craft to take us nine miles down the river. This he refused to do, and as I did not propose to have my orders disobeyed, I concluded I would take charge of the boat myself, and at once placed myself at the wheel. I was not equal to the emergency, as the wheel refused to do my bidding. Some of the other boys tried it, but their failure equaled my own. I had determined, however, to make the journey by river, and as we could do nothing with the large boat, we "pressed" into service two skiffs, and started on our trip. We had not proceeded a great way before we were fired upon by the rebels from the southern side of the river. We at once, with great haste, rowed to the opposite shore, where we arrived in safety, abandoned the skiffs, and returned the enemy's fire at long range, the rebels being on one side of the river and we on the other. We remained out from camp until dark, when we made a forced march for our quarters.

We arrived in camp at about 10 o'clock. We claimed to have had a brush with the enemy, and that we had obtained a great and signal victory, but our victory was in beating a hasty retreat. The next morning I reported to the commander of the post as to the result of our expedition. But, unfortunately, advices had already reached his ears of our retreat, my attempt to capture the boat, which was already in the service of the Government, and of our taking the two skiffs. For these offenses I came very near losing my office, but luckily I escaped with a reprimand. From this time forward I was an obedient officer, and never attempted to do anything without [sic] I had special orders so to do from my superiors.[12]

The rebels evacuated Charleston on February 17, 1865, and the first Union troops to march into the city the next day were the men of the Twenty-first U.S. Colored Infantry, followed soon afterward by detachments of the Fifty-fourth and Fifty-fifth Massachusetts Regiments. Colonel Charles B. Fox of the Fifty-fifth described the entry of his regiment into Charleston:

Words would fail to describe the scene which those who witnessed it will never forget,—the welcome given to a regiment of colored troops by their people redeemed from slavery. As shouts, prayers, and blessings resounded on every side, all felt that the hardships and dangers of the siege were fully repaid. The few white inhabitants left in the town were either alarmed or indignant, and generally remained in their houses; but the colored people turned out *en masse*. . . . Cheers, blessings, prayers, and songs were heard on every side. Men and women crowded to shake hands with men and officers. Many of them talked earnestly and understandingly of the past and present.

. . . On through the streets of the rebel city passed the column, on through the chief seat of that slave power, tottering to its fall. Its walls rung to the chorus of manly voices singing "John Brown," "Babylon is Falling," and the "Battle-Cry of Freedom;'' while, at intervals, the national airs, long unheard there, were played by the regimental band. The glory and the triumph of this hour may be imagined, but can never be described. It was one of those occasions which happen but once in a lifetime, to be lived over in memory for ever.[13]

Negro troopers of the Fifth Massachusetts Cavalry were the first soldiers to enter Richmond after its evacuation on April 2, and close behind them came troops from General Godfrey Weitzel's XXVth Army Corps, an all-Negro corps of thirty-two regiments.

Official records show that a total of 178,985 enlisted men and 7,122 officers served in Negro regiments during the Civil War, nearly 10 per cent of the Union Army. These men fought in 449 engagements, of which thirty-nine were major battles. Approximately 37,300 Negroes lost their lives while serving in the Union Army. Seventeen black soldiers and four Negro sailors were awarded Congressional Medals of Honor.[14] Black men were understandably proud of their record in the Civil War, a record which made the continued denial of officers' commissions to deserving Negroes all the more galling. On July 26, 1864, a meeting of Philadelphia Negroes adopted the following resolutions:

Resolved, That there can be no good reason offered why colored men, especially those who have proved their availability in the field, may not be promoted to command colored troops, rather than [white] civilians. . . .

Resolved, That our duty to those men, *our brethren who are enlisted through our influence*, demands that we should not yield this point without an emphatic protest against its injustice to them, and its insulting endorsement of the old dogma of negro inferiority.

Resolved, That considered in the light of official reports from several battle-fields, we have now veteran colored troops, some of them deserving the highest acknowledgments from the nation, and while we battle for the country, and continue to swell the ranks of the army, we are determined to ask for those veterans the same treatment, promotion and emoluments that other veterans receive.[15]

In February 1865, a group of noncommissioned Negro officers in Louisiana sent the following petition to the Secretary of War:

In view of the recent Proclamation of the President calling for 300,000 volunteers, and appreciating the necessity of an immediate response to this call, we would respectfully petition that permission be given to raise a number of colored regiments, to be officered exclusively by colored men.

In regard to the policy of this measure, we would respectfully urge that while many of the noblest of our race have sprung to arms with alacrity in defense of the Government, many others, equally loyal, have hesitated because one of the greatest incentives to enlistment, and the greatest stimulant to the strict performance of a soldier's duty—the hope of promotion—has been denied them.

We confidently believe that the removal of this bar to a soldier's ambition would result in an uprising of the colored people, unsurpassed even by the enthusiastic response to the President's first call. In regard to the capability of colored men to perform the duties of commissioned officer, we would respectfully suggest that there are hundreds of non-commissioned officers in colored regiments who are amply qualified for these positions, both by education, and experience, and that others of our educated men, anticipating the granting of commissions to colored men by the Government, have applied themselves to the study of military tactics, in order that men properly educated might not be wanting to accept them.[16]

In spite of these appeals, very few Negroes were actually commissioned during the war. More than seventy-five black men had been commissioned in the three regiments raised by Butler in Louisiana in 1862, but General Banks later replaced most of these with white men. Six sergeants in the Massachusetts Fifty-fourth and Fifty-fifth Regiments were promoted to lieutenancies at the end of the war, and all three officers of an independent

*battery of light artillery in Kansas were black. Eight Negro sur-
geons were given medical commissions as majors, and in February 1865, Martin R. Delany was commissioned a Major of
Infantry and ordered to recruit an "armeé d'Afrique" in South
Carolina, but the end of the war put an end to Delany's project
before it had gotten fairly started. In all, not more than one
hundred Negroes (excluding chaplains) received officers' commissions during the war.*[17]

CHAPTER XVII

THE CONFEDERATE DECISION

TO RAISE A NEGRO ARMY, 1864–65

By 1864 the Northern example had convinced some Confederate leaders of the value of Negro soldiers. A few Southerners began to wonder out loud why the Confederacy did not take steps to utilize this powerful human resource. On January 2, 1864, a group of rebel officers in the Army of Tennessee, headed by General Patrick R. Cleburne, submitted the following report to their commanding general:

We have now been fighting for nearly three years, have spilled much of our best blood, and lost, consumed, or thrown to the flames an amount of property equal in value to the specie currency of the world. Through some lack in our system the fruits of our struggles and sacrifices have invariably slipped away from us and left us nothing but long lists of dead and mangled. . . . We can see three great causes operating to destroy us: First, the inferiority of our armies to those of the enemy in point of numbers; second, the poverty of our single source of supply in comparison with his several sources; third, the fact that slavery, from being one of our chief sources of strength at the commencement of the war, has now become, in a military point of view, one of our chief sources of weakness. . . .

Apart from the assistance that home and foreign prejudice against slavery has given to the North, slavery is a source of great strength to the enemy in a purely military point of view, by supplying him with an army from our granaries; but it is our most vulnerable point, a continued embarrassment, and in some respects an insidious weakness. . . . All along the lines slavery is comparatively valueless to us for labor, but of great and increasing worth to the enemy for information. It is an omnipresent spy system, pointing out our valuable men to the enemy, revealing our positions, purposes, and resources. . . .

Adequately to meet the causes which are now threatening ruin to our country, we propose . . . that we immediately commence training a large reserve of the most courageous of our slaves, and further that we guarantee freedom within a reasonable time to every slave in the South who shall remain true to the Confederacy in this war. As between the loss of independence and the loss of slavery, we assume that every patriot will freely give up the latter. . . .

The measure will at one blow strip the enemy of foreign sympathy and assistance, and transfer them to the South; it will dry up two of his three sources of recruiting; it will take from his negro army the only motive it could have to fight against the South, and will probably cause much of it to desert over to us. . . . The immediate effect of the emancipation and enrollment of negroes on the military strength of the South would be: To enable us to have armies numerically superior to those of the North, and a reserve of any size we might think necessary; to enable us to take the offensive, move forward, and forage on the enemy. . . . It would instantly remove all the vulnerability, embarrassment, and inherent weakness which result from slavery. The approach of the enemy would no longer find every household surrounded by spies. . . . There would be no recruits awaiting the enemy with open arms, no complete history of every neighborhood with ready guides, no fear of insurrection in the rear. . . . Apart from all other aspects of the question, the necessity for more fighting men is upon us. We can only get a sufficiency by making the negro share the danger and hardships of the war. . . .

Will the slaves fight? The helots of Sparta stood their masters good stead in battle. In the great sea fight of Lepanto where the Christians checked forever the spread of Mohammedanism over

Europe, the galley slaves of portions of the fleet were promised freedom, and called on to fight at a critical moment of the battle. They fought well, and civilization owes much to those brave galley slaves. The negro slaves of Santo Domingo, fighting for freedom, defeated their white masters and the French troops sent against them, . . . and the experience of this war has been so far that half-trained negroes have fought as bravely as many other half-trained Yankees. If, contrary to the training of a lifetime, they can be made to face and fight bravely against their former masters, how much more probable is it that with the allurement of a higher reward, and led by those masters, they would submit to discipline and face dangers?[1]

Jefferson Davis refused even to consider Cleburne's proposal, and issued instructions forbidding further discussion of the matter in the Confederate Army. But the subject would not die down. In the fall of 1864 the South suffered serious reverses in Georgia, Alabama, Virginia, and other areas; her resources were depleted, and she seemed on the verge of collapse. More and more men in the Confederacy were coming to the conclusion that defeat could only be averted by freeing and arming the slaves. Judah P. Benjamin, the Confederate Secretary of War, wrote to Fred A. Porcher of Charleston on December 21, 1864:

For a year past I have seen that the period was fast approaching when we should be compelled to use every resource at our command for the defense of our liberties. . . . The negroes will certainly be made to fight against us if not armed for our defense. The drain of that source of our strength is steadily fatal, and irreversible by any other expedient than that of arming the slaves as an auxiliary force.

I further agree with you that if they are to fight for our freedom they are entitled to their own. Public opinion is fast ripening on the subject, and ere the close of the winter the conviction on this point will become so widespread that the Government will have no difficulty in inaugurating the policy [of recruiting Negro soldiers].

. . . It is well known that General Lee, who commands so largely the confidence of the people, is strongly in favor of our

using the negroes for defense, and emancipating them, if necessary, for that purpose. Can you not yourself write a series of
articles in your papers, always urging this point as the true issue, viz, is it better for the negro to fight for us or against us?[2]

*But even as late as January 1865, there was still considerable
opposition in the South to the idea of arming the slaves. After
all, the Confederacy had gone to war to defend a social and
political system based on slavery, and to accept Benjamin's proposal would be to subvert the very cause for which the South
was fighting. General Howell Cobb wrote on January 8 that*
the proposition to make soldiers of our slaves is the most pernicious idea that has been suggested since the war began. . . .
My first hour of despondency will be the one in which that policy shall be adopted. You cannot make soldiers of slaves, nor
slaves of soldiers. . . . The day you make soldiers of them is the
beginning of the end of the revolution. If slaves will make good
soldiers our whole theory of slavery is wrong.[3]

*But in a letter of January 11 to a Confederate senator, Gen-
eral Robert E. Lee sanctioned the policy of arming slaves:*

If it ends in subverting slavery, it will be accomplished by
ourselves, and we can devise the means of alleviating the evil
consequences to both races. I think, therefore, we must decide
whether slavery shall be extinguished by our enemies and the
slave be used against us, or use them ourselves at the risk of the
effects which may be produced upon our social institutions. . . .
We should employ them without delay.[4]

*Lee's advice was decisive. On March 13 President Davis
signed a "Negro Soldier Law" which authorized the enlistment
of slaves as soldiers. Such slave soldiers could not be emancipated "except by consent of the owners and of the States in which
they may reside." The "Negro Soldier Law" was the dying ges-
ture of a crumbling nation. A few companies of black soldiers
were enrolled in Richmond and elsewhere, but before any regiments could be organized Richmond had fallen and the war was
over.[5]*

CHAPTER XVIII

CIVIL RIGHTS AND

DESEGREGATION IN THE NORTH

The Civil War accelerated the Negro's drive for civil rights and desegregation in the North. In most parts of the North in 1860, black men did not enjoy equal rights. Several states prohibited Negroes from testifying against whites in court: Indiana, Illinois, Iowa, California, and Oregon. These same states (except California) had constitutional or statute provisions barring the immigration of Negroes into the state, although these provisions were rarely enforced. Public accommodations, transportation facilities, restaurants, hotels, and theaters in some parts of the North were segregated. Negroes were effectually barred from jury service in every state except Massachusetts. Public schools were integrated in New England except for a few cities in Connecticut and Rhode Island. Negroes were also admitted to public schools on an integrated basis in Michigan, Wisconsin, and Minnesota, in the northern parts of Illinois and Ohio, and in some rural areas in New York, Pennsylvania, and New Jersey. But in the cities and larger towns of New York, New Jersey, Pennsylvania, and southern Ohio, where most of the Northern Negroes were concentrated, black children attended segregated public schools when they attended any at all. In southern Illinois and in Indiana Negroes were exempt from the school tax and excluded from the public schools entirely. In Iowa and California, black children attended separate schools. About twenty colleges and professional schools in the

North admitted Negroes; the rest closed their doors to black ap-
plicants. With only a few exceptions, Negroes suffered discrim-
ination in housing and jobs in every part of the North.¹

Edward Dicey, an English journalist who spent six months
traveling through the Northern states in 1862, wrote:

Everywhere and at all seasons the coloured people form a
separate community. In the public streets you hardly ever see a
coloured person in company with a white, except in the capacity of servant. Boston, indeed, is the only town I visited where
I ever observed black men and women walking about frequently
with white people. I never by any chance, in the Free States,
saw a coloured man dining at a public table, or mixing socially
in any manner with white men, or dressed as a man well to do
in the world, or occupying any position, however humble, in
which he was placed in authority over white persons. On board
the river steamboats, the commonest and homeliest of working
men has a right to dine, and does dine, at the public meals but,
for coloured passengers, there is always a separate table. At the
great hotels there is, as with us, a servants' table, but the coloured servants are not allowed to dine in common with the
white. At the inns, in the barbers' shops, on board the steamers,
and in most hotels, the servants are more often than not coloured people. . . . I hardly ever remember seeing a black employed as shopman, or placed in any post of responsibility. As a
rule, the blacks you meet in the Free States are shabbily, if not
squalidly dressed; and, as far as I could learn, the instances of
black men having made money by trade in the North, are very
few in number.

I remember one day in travelling through the State of Ohio
. . . that I was seated by one of the shrewdest and kindliest old
farmers it has been my lot to meet. He had been born and bred
in Ohio State, and dilated to me as a stranger, with not unnatural pride, on the beauty and prosperity of that rich garden
country:—"There is but one thing, sir," he ended by saying, "that
we want here, and that is to get rid of the niggers." I was rather
surprised at this illiberal expression of opinion . . . and I ques-

tioned him about the reasons of his antipathy towards the coloured people. I was answered by the old story. The free blacks did not work, and preferred doing nothing. Half the thefts and crimes in the State were committed by free negroes. Not content with having schools of their own, they wanted to have their children admitted to the free white schools. . . . But the great grievance seemed to his mind to be that, in defiance of the laws of Ohio, there had been recently some few inter-marriages between white men and black women. "It don't answer, sir," he concluded by saying; "it isn't right, you see, and it isn't meant to be."

These sentiments express, undoubtedly, the popular feeling of the Free States towards the free negro. Like most popular feelings, it has a basis of truth. In every Northern city, the poorest, the most thriftless, and perhaps the most troublesome part of the population, are the free negroes. . . . The free negro has not a fair chance throughout the North. The legislation of the country is as unfavourable to the status of free blacks, as the social sentiment of the people. . . . Certainly, as a matter of fact, a free negro citizen does not enjoy the full rights of citizenship.[2]

The segregated schools for Negro children in some parts of the North were in a sorry condition. Typical of many such schools was the one in Lockport, New York, about twenty-five miles northeast of Buffalo. Lockport had a Negro population of more than 250, but there were less than a dozen children in the school. A black man who visited the school wrote:

It may be said that the small attendance is the fault of the parents. Why don't they send their children to school? I will answer. It is a miserable house, about ten by fourteen feet square, to which no white person would send a child, were it a school for white children, and in which there is no stimulus nor encouragement to make a child study. . . . There are young men and women here who would attend school, but they have none in the village which they can attend, for they would feel degraded to be stuck up in one corner of a lumber yard, when their white brethren are drinking from fine, large founts of learning, from which they are excluded. But then we believe in fighting for our rights, and if we expect to get them we *must* fight.[3]

Even in Massachusetts, where Negroes enjoyed equal civil and political rights, where black children attended integrated schools and black men were admitted to the professions, and where John Rock was a justice of the peace in Suffolk County— even in Massachusetts, Negroes were subjected to many kinds of discrimination. John Rock said on August 1, 1862:

The present position of the colored man is a trying one; trying because the whole nation seems to have entered into a conspiracy to crush him. But few seem to comprehend our position in the free States. The masses seem to think that we are oppressed only in the South. This is a mistake; we are oppressed everywhere in this slavery-cursed land. Massachusetts has a great name, and deserves much credit for what she has done, but the position of the colored people in Massachusetts is far from being an enviable one. While colored men have many rights, they have few privileges here. To be sure, we are seldom insulted by passersby, we have the right of suffrage, the free schools and colleges are opened to our children, and from them have come forth young men capable of filling any post of profit or honor. But there is no field for these young men. Their education aggravates their suffering. . . . The educated colored man meets on the one hand, the embittered prejudices of the whites, and on the other the jealousies of his own race. . . . You can hardly imagine the humiliation and contempt a colored lad must feel by graduating the first in his class, and then being rejected everywhere else because of his color. . . .

No where in the United States is the colored man of talent appreciated. Even in Boston, which has a great reputation for being anti-slavery, he has no field for his talent. Some persons think that, because we have the right of suffrage, and enjoy the privilege of riding in the cars, there is less prejudice here than there is farther South. In some respects this is true, and in others it is not true. We are colonized in Boston. It is five times as difficult to get a house in a good location in Boston as it is in

Philadelphia, and it is ten times more difficult for a colored me-
chanic to get employment than in Charleston. Colored men in
business in Massachusetts receive more respect, and less patron-
age than in any place that I know of. In Boston we are proscribed in some of the eating-houses, many of the hotels, and
all the theatres but one. . . .

The laboring men who could once be found all along the
wharves of Boston, can now be found only about Central wharf,
with scarcely encouragement enough to keep soul and body together. You know that the colored man is proscribed in some of
the churches, and that this proscription is carried even to the
grave-yards. This is Boston—by far the best, or at least the most
liberal large city in the United States. . . .

We desire to take part in this contest [the Civil War], and
when our Government shall see the necessity of using the loyal
blacks of the free States, I hope it will have the courage to recognize their manhood. It certainly will not be mean enough to
force us to fight for your liberty, . . . and then leave us when
we go home to our respective States to be told that we cannot
ride in the cars, that our children cannot go to the public schools,
that we cannot vote; and if we don't like that state of things,
there is an appropriation to colonize us. We ask for our rights.[4]

*The Civil War produced great changes in the status of North-
ern Negroes. Some of the more important gains for civil rights
during the war were made on the national level. The State Department ignored Chief Justice Roger Taney's dictum in the
Dred Scott case that a Negro could not be an American citizen,
and granted a passport in August 1861 to Henry Highland Garnet. The passport explicitly stated that Garnet was a "citizen of
the United States."[5] In 1862 an American revenue cutter de-
tained a vessel in the coastwise trade because the captain was
a black man. Under the Dred Scott decision, Negroes were not
citizens and hence were not eligible to command ships flying
the American flag. Secretary of the Treasury Salmon P. Chase
seized this opportunity to address a formal inquiry regarding
the citizenship of black men to Attorney General Edward Bates.
Bates replied with a lengthy statement which denied the prin-*

ciples of the Dred Scott decision and affirmed that every free
person born in the United States was, "at the moment of birth,
prima facie *a citizen."*[6]

Under the leadership of Charles Sumner, Congress passed
several antidiscrimination measures during the war. In 1862
the Senate repealed an 1825 law barring black persons from
carrying the mail. Democrats and conservative Republicans
killed the bill in the House, but it finally passed both Houses
and became law on March 3, 1865. In 1862 Congress decreed
that in all proceedings of District of Columbia courts there must
be no exclusion of witnesses because of race, and in 1864, this
legislation was broadened to cover every federal court in the
nation.[7]

Negro leaders were active in several states in the movement
to end discrimination and segregation at the state level. The
following statement is from the salutatory editorial of the Pacific Appeal, *a Negro newspaper in San Francisco edited by*
Philip Bell from 1862 to 1864:

We have nothing to disguise; we enter the field boldly, fearlessly, but with dignity and calmness to *Appeal* for the rights of
the Colored Citizens of this State.

As we say in our Prospectus, our paper "is devoted to the
interests of the Colored People of California and to their moral,
intellectual and political advancement."

It will advocate their rights, their claims to humanity and
justice; it will oppose the wrongs inflicted on them, and the
disabilities under which they labor. It will urge the repeal of all
oppressive laws, particularly that law which deprives them of
the right to testify in courts, in cases in which a white person is
a party.

Such laws are disgraceful to the statutes of our State, are
relics of barbarism and slavery, retard the wheels of justice,
degrade our manhood, and inflict irreparable injury on our rights
and liberties.

We shall *Appeal* to the hearts and consciences of our rulers,
not to their passions and prejudices; we shall *Appeal* to their

sense of right and justice; not to their feelings of pity and com-
miseration.[8]

*The California law barring Negroes from testifying against
whites gave free license to whites to rob and beat black persons
without fear of arrest. As the* Pacific Appeal *stated: "As long as
those unjust laws which exclude our testimony in courts remain
on the Statute books of California, so long will we be fitting
subjects for assaults on our persons and property, by knavish
and brutal white men, who, knowing we have no protection in
law, think they can rob and murder us with impunity."[9] California Negroes worked hard to obtain repeal of the testimony
law. They circulated petitions and gave speeches. In 1862 the
legislature defeated a repeal motion by a narrow margin. The*
Pacific Appeal *stated editorially:*

Let our failure this year, be but the incentive to renewed
exertion. Be active! Be vigilant! . . . Be not discouraged! Say not
"it is useless, the whites will never grant us our legal rights."
Be not governed by any such fallacy. Show the white man it is
not only an act of justice and humanity, but it is one of deep
interest to the community.

Another year, and the people of California will be convinced
that it is no longer to their interest to yield obedience to the
demands of the Slave Oligarchy. Chivalry will then be an extinct
institution, and our State will be freed from the domineering
influence of Secessionists.[10]

One California Negro wrote in the fall of 1862:

Everything around us indicates a change in our condition,
and the revolution of events, and the change in the public sentiment toward us, all go to prove the necessity for us to prepare
to act in a different sphere from that in which we have heretofore acted. . . . Our relation to this Government is changing
daily. . . . Our relation to this Government and our position in
the history of the country will, in future, be entirely different
to that which we formerly occupied. . . . The only place the
American historian could find for the colored man was in the
background of a cotton-field, or the foreground of a cane-brake

or a rice swamp, to adorn the pages of geography. . . . But . . . old things are passing away, and eventually old prejudices must follow. The revolution has begun, and time alone must decide where it is to end. Meanwhile, there is a work for us to do. . . . We must learn to concentrate our strength and influence, to be united, to work shoulder to shoulder, for the accomplishment of a common end.[11]

Buoyed up by such optimism, California Negroes stepped up their petition campaign. Their efforts were rewarded in 1863 when the California legislature repealed the testimony law. Black men could henceforth testify in any court case.[12]

In Illinois, Negroes could not testify in any case to which a white person was a party. But the most severe feature of the Illinois "black laws," as they were called, was the law barring Negro immigration. Every black person entering the state with intent to settle was subject to a heavy fine; in default of payment he could be sold at public auction to the person bidding the shortest period of service in return for payment of the fine. This law was seldom enforced, and Negroes continued to move into Illinois after the statute was enacted in 1853. But the influx of freedmen during the war prompted the courts to begin enforcing the law: in 1863 eight Negroes were convicted of entering the state illegally, and seven of them were sold into temporary slavery to pay the fine.[13]

This was an intolerable situation, and Chicago Negroes, under the leadership of John Jones, a wealthy black man, formed a "Repeal Association" in 1864. One of the wealthiest Negroes in America, Jones had been born free in North Carolina, where he taught himself to read and write and served as a tailor's apprentice. He came to Chicago in 1845 with $3.50 in his pocket. In the next fifteen years he made a small fortune out of his tailoring business, and became a militant race leader in Illinois. He was twice elected Cook County Commissioner after the war. In November 1864 Jones made the following appeal to Governor Richard Yates of Illinois:

Your petitioner, though humble in position, and having no political status in your State, notwithstanding I have resided in

it for twenty-years, and to-day am paying taxes on thirty thousand dollars, most humbly beseech you to recommend in your
Message to the Legislature . . . the repeal of the Black Laws of
this your State.

Jones also addressed an appeal to the legislature:

Gentlemen, we appeal directly to you. Our destiny is in your
hands. Will you lift us out of our present degradation, and place
us under the protection of wholesome laws, and make us responsible for the abuse of them as other citizens are? I beseech
you, in behalf of seven thousand colored inhabitants of your
State, try the experiment. In the States before mentioned, this
experiment has been tried and there is no disposition in those
States to return to their former unjust discrimination between
their respective inhabitants. The petitions that will be presented
to you this winter from all parts of your State will be signed by
your most respected and influential citizens.

*The Repeal Association circulated a petition in northern Il-
linois calling for repeal of the "black laws," and obtained eleven
thousand signatures. Jones went to Springfield and made the
following speech to a legislative committee:*

We, the colored people of Illinois, charge upon that enactment, and lay at the doors of those who enacted it, our present
degraded condition in this our great State. Every other nation,
kindred and tongue have prospered and gained property, and
are recognized as a part of the great Commonwealth, with the
exception of our own: we have been treated as strangers in the
land of our birth. . . . To-day a colored man cannot buy a
burying-lot in the city of Chicago for his own use. All of this
grows out of the proscriptive laws of this State, against our poor,
unfortunate colored people. And, more than this, the cruel
treatment that we receive daily at the hands of a portion of your
foreign population, is all based upon these enactments. . . . They
think we have no rights which white men are bound to respect,
and according to your laws they think right. Then, fellow-
citizens, in the name of the great Republic, and all that is dear
to a man in this life, erase those nefarious and unnecessary laws,
and give us your protection, and treat us as you treat other

citizens of the State. We ask only even handed justice, and all
of our wrongs will be at an end by virtue of that act. May God
in His goodness assist you to do the right. Will you do it?[14]

*The contribution of black soldiers to Union victory had pro-
duced a favorable climate for Jones's appeal, and the legislature
in February repealed the "black laws" barring Negro immigration and testimony.[15] By the spring of 1865 Indiana was the
only Northern state that retained such restrictions. Indiana's
Negroes had also worked for repeal of the black laws during the
Civil War. A short-lived monthly newspaper published by Negroes in Spartanburg, Indiana, the* Students' Repository, *urged
the state legislature in 1863 to put an end to a radical discrimination:*

Look at the barbarous code of black laws with which the Constitution and Statute books . . . are disgraced! by the provisions
of these barbarous laws, colored emigration [sic] into the State
is entirely prohibited, and twelve thousand of the population of
Indiana is wholly disfranchised. We are denied the right of suffrage, denied the right of holding office, denied the right of
testifying in courts of justice, denied the benefit of the schools
funds and at the same time compelled to pay taxes for the support of the government. . . .

The worst and most deplorable feature of those proscriptive
laws is, that they shut us out from the public schools, and leave
us (so far as the State is concerned) entirely without the means
of education; and numbers of families that live in white settle-
ments, are growing up without education.

Republicans, how long! Oh! how long will this be the case?
When you support, by your votes and by your influence, the
other proscriptive laws of this State, you indeed commit a crime
against God and humanity of great magnitude; but when you
deprive us of the means of education, you commit an outrage
upon *the SOUL; a war upon THE IMMORTAL PART!* . . .

The question of the colored man's rights in this country has
got to be met and settled before long. It may be delayed, but it
cannot be evaded.[16]

Indiana's black laws against Negro immigration and testi-

*mony were struck down by court decision and legislative repeal
in the winter of 1865–66.*[17]

*Legal barriers fell rapidly in most parts of the North during
or immediately after the Civil War, but other forms of discrimination proved more resistant. One of the most rigidly segregated cities in America was Philadelphia, the City of Brotherly
Love. Frederick Douglass visited Philadelphia at the beginning
of 1862, and wrote:*

There is not perhaps anywhere to be found a city in which
prejudice against color is more rampant than in Philadelphia.
Hence all the incidents of caste are to be seen there in perfec-
tion. It has its white schools and colored schools, its white
churches and its colored churches, its white Christianity and its
colored Christianity, its white concerts and its colored concerts,
its white literary institutions and its colored literary institutions,
. . . and the line is everywhere tightly drawn between them.
Colored persons, no matter how well dressed or how well behaved, ladies or gentlemen, rich or poor, are not even permitted
to ride on any of the many railways through that Christian city.
Halls are rented with the express understanding that no person
of color shall be allowed to enter, either to attend a concert or
listen to a lecture. The whole aspect of city usage at this point
is mean, contemptible and barbarous. The colored man is compelled to occupy only what are called the servile positions in life
. . . and yet, despite the restrictions laid upon them and the
discrimination to bind them into one common bundle of degradation, we could name many comparatively rich men among
them. . . .

The colored people of Philadelphia have had a narrow and
thorny path to tread for many years; but we predict for them a
brighter and better future. If they have made bricks without
straw, they will do better when the present restrictions and em-
barrassments are removed, as they certainly will be.[18]

*Most of Philadelphia's streetcars allowed Negroes to ride only
on the front platform; some refused to admit black people at all.
Under the leadership of William Still, a prosperous Negro coal
merchant and an active agent of the Underground Railroad,*

Philadelphia's Negroes mounted an attack on streetcar segregation in 1859—an attack that increased in scope and intensity during the Civil War until it finally achieved success in 1867. The Philadelphia struggle is discussed at length below because in many ways it was a microcosm of the Negro's battle for equal rights and human dignity.

In the winter of 1861–62 Still obtained the signatures of 360 prominent white Philadelphians to the following petition requesting the Board of Presidents of the City Railways to end segregation on their lines:

The colored citizens of Philadelphia suffer very serious inconvenience and hardship, daily, by being excluded from riding in the city passenger cars. In New York City, and in all the principal northern cities, except Philadelphia, they ride;* even in New Orleans (although subject to some proscription), they ride in the cars. Why then should they be excluded in Philadelphia,— in a city standing so preeminently high for its benevolence, liberality, love of freedom, and Christianity, as the city of brotherly love?

Colored people pay more taxes here than is paid by the same class in any other northern city. . . . Therefore, the undersigned respectfully petition that the various Boards of the city passenger cars rescind the rules indiscriminately excluding colored persons from the inside of the cars.[19]

In December 1863 Still wrote the following letter to the Philadelphia Press, *the city's leading Republican newspaper. The letter was widely reprinted. It appeared in the London* Times, *and it was reported by an American correspondent in London to have done more harm to the Union cause in England than a military defeat.*[20]

* This statement was not quite accurate. In New York city, Negroes were subject to occasional discrimination on some of the streetcar lines, and were required to ride in a Jim Crow car on the Sixth Avenue line. Segregation also existed in streetcars in Cincinnati and San Francisco. The Jim Crow policy was abandoned in New York and San Francisco in 1864, and segregation on Cincinnati streetcars was abolished after the Civil War. *See* James M. McPherson, *The Struggle for Equality: Abolitionists and the Negro in the Civil War and Reconstruction* (Princeton, 1964), pp. 231–33.

Being under the necessity of going out to Camp William Penn, to-day, on business, I took the North Pennsylvania Railroad, and reached the ground about 11 o'clock. Remembering that pressing duties required my presence at my store by a certain hour in the early part of the afternoon, I promptly attended to my business at the camp, but as I could not return by the way I came without waiting two and a half hours . . . I decided to take the city passenger cars. Soon one came along with but few passengers in it, and into it I walked. . . . Quickly the conductor approached me and I tendered him the fare. . . . The conductor very cordially received the money, but before he took time to hand me the change that was due to me, invited me to "step out on the platform." "Why is this?" I remarked. "It is against the rules," he added. "Who objects?" I inquired. "It is the aristocracy," he again added. "Well, it is a *cruel rule!* and I believe this is the only city of note in the civilized world, where a decent colored man cannot be allowed to ride in a city passenger car. . . ."

Riding on the platform of a bitter cold day like this I need not say is almost intolerable, but to compel persons to pay the same as those who enjoy comfortable seats inside by a good fire, seems quite atrocious.

Yet I felt, under the circumstances, compelled to submit to the wrong, for the sake of arriving at my place of business in due time. But before I arrived at my destination it began to snow, which, as I was already thoroughly chilled with the cold, made the platform utterly intolerable; hence, I concluded to walk the rest of the distance, and accordingly got off, feeling satisfied that no where in Christendom could be found a better illustration of Judge Taney's decision in the Dred Scott case. . . .

Every colored man, woman, and child of the 25,000 inhabitants of this city, many of whom are tax payers, and as upright as any other class of citizens, are daily liable to this treatment. The truth is, so far as my case is concerned, I fared well, compared with the treatment some have received. A long catalogue of injuries and outrages could be recounted.[21]

Negro and abolitionist organizations repeatedly petitioned

the Board of Railway Presidents and the state legislature to end
streetcar segregation in Philadelphia, but to little avail. In July
1864 the Rev. William J. Alston, rector of St. Thomas's Episco-
pal Church (black), sent the following letter to the Philadelphia
Press:

TO THE CHRISTIAN PUBLIC OF PHILADELPHIA.—Within the past
week, my only living child having been at death's door, by our
physician we were directed to take him over the Delaware river
as often as convenient. On our return to the Philadelphia side,
on one occasion, the child became completely prostrated. I held
my ear to his mouth three several times to ascertain whether
he was still alive. Such a death-like appearance came over him,
I felt the necessity of reaching home as soon as possible, and to
my satisfaction (for the time being), I saw one of the Lombard
and South street cars approaching, which I hailed, and was in
the act of entering, when the conductor arrested my progress
by informing me that I could not enter—*being colored.* I referred
him to the condition of my child, but all to no purpose; he ordered the driver to go on, regardless of our humble plea. . . .
Had the cars been overloaded, that would have been excuse
sufficient; but the fact of the case is, that the only persons on
the cars referred to were the conductor and the driver.

In the face of these facts, we ask the Christian public of Philadelphia, can you look on in silence, and see respectable colored
citizens excluded from the privilege of availing themselves of
the *public* facilities for going from one extreme of the city to
the other? We ask, where is the superiority of Philadelphia over
New York city? Yet the latter has opened all of her railroad lines
to the public, irrespective of caste. . . .

Is it humane to exclude respectable colored citizens from your
street cars, when so many of our brave and vigorous young men
have been and are enlisting, to take part in this heaven-ordained
slavery extermination, many of whom have performed commendable service in our army and navy—in the former of which
your humble subscriber has two brawny-armed and battle-tried
brothers? Finally, we ask, is it in accordance with Christian civilization to thrust out of your street car the dying child of an

humble servant of Christ, in whose congregation there exists an active auxiliary to the Pennsylvania branch of the Women's Sanitary Committee of the United States?

We beg you to remember the words of Him by whom soon you and I are to be judged . . . : "Verily, I say unto you, inasmuch as ye have done it unto one of the least of these, my brethren, ye have done it unto me."[22]

Angry Negroes held a mass meeting five days after this letter was published and pledged to "employ all just and lawful means to agitate the public mind, that a righteous public sentiment may exist on this subject."[23] They raised money to carry on the work of agitation, but the immediate future only brought new examples of discrimination. A Negro woman published an account of another incident in August:

There are now in the Summit House Hospital, West Philadelphia, about six miles from the city, a very large number of colored soldiers wounded in the sanguinary battles before Petersburg. These men displayed great courage and bravery, and hundreds of their associates lost their lives in the desperate struggle, while endeavoring to sustain the Federal Government.

They have been sent here, and it is naturally to be supposed that their wives, children, friends, and relatives, are anxious to see them, administer to their wants, and alleviate their suffering as much as they possibly can; but in a large number of cases they find it utterly impossible to do so, being unable to afford a private conveyance at an expense of six or seven dollars, the city passenger cars refusing to carry colored persons except on the front platform, a position every woman should refuse to occupy who has self-respect. . . .

We have in this city three societies of ladies for the relief of the sick and wounded soldiers. . . . These ladies, whenever they desire to visit their brethren at the hospitals, either to minister to their wants or attend them when dying, are constrained to pay for carriage hire, thus expending money that would be otherwise appropriated to the soldiers were they permitted to ride in the cars. . . .

Now we do think this is a great outrage, not only upon us but upon the men who, regardless of the prejudice they have always encountered in this the land of their birth, have at the call of their country rushed forth to aid in putting down the rebellion, and now they are wounded, many disabled for life, are deprived of seeing those dear to them, because the directors of the city passenger cars refuse to let colored people ride, which, to say the least, is a stigma upon the city of Philadelphia. We do hope it will not be long before this distinction will be removed.[24]

In March 1865 a white minister was angered by the ejection of two black soldiers from a Philadelphia streetcar:

Sir: A few minutes before six o'clock on Monday evening two non-commissioned officers of the United States army, belonging to a regiment now forming at Camp William Penn, stepped on the front platform of a Fifth street car . . . on their way to the Berks-street depot of the North Pennsylvania Railroad. It was the last car by which they could reach the train to convey them out to their camp that night. When these well-dressed and well-behaved colored soldiers stepped on the platform there was no one else on it except the driver. They were almost immediately seen by the conductor, who rushed through the car and ordered the men to "get off." One of the soldiers replied, "We want to reach the train to get out to camp tonight." "I can't help that, you can't ride on this car," was the answer. As the men did not move at once, the conductor put his hand on the one nearest to him, to put him off. The men without resistance, but with an indignation they could not repress were forced from the platform. . . .

The men were then on the sidewalk, within a short distance of us, but the conductor would not listen to their being allowed to stand on the vacant platform. . . . We reached the Berks-street station just in time to take the train on the North Pennsylvania Railroad, and the two soldiers were left behind. . . .

I have seen colored soldiers on the battle field. I have seen them defending fortifications, which, a few hours before, they had taken from Southern rebels, at the point of a bayonet. I have seen them suffering in their wounds received in our defence, but I never before saw them forcibly driven from the privilege of standing on the platform of a railway car.[25]

The Negro's contribution to Union victory on the battlefield made the cruelty and injustice of the Jim Crow policy more and more obvious, and by the winter of 1864–65 the Republican party and the Republican press in Philadelphia were backing the drive to end streetcar segregation. A meeting of prominent white citizens on January 13, 1865, appointed a committee to negotiate with the railroad presidents for an end to discrimination. The committee also made a direct appeal to the Democratic mayor of Philadelphia, who rebuffed them with the statement that he did not wish "the ladies of his family to ride in the cars with colored people."[26] Stymied at the city level, the advocates of equal rights turned hopefully to the state legislature, where Senator Morrow B. Lowry, an abolitionist from northwestern Pennsylvania, had been urging the adoption of a state law to prohibit segregation in public transportation. In March 1867 Lowry's bill finally passed both Houses and became law. It forbade discrimination in every form of public transportation in the entire state.[27] It was an impressive victory for equal rights, and the Negroes of Philadelphia deserve much of the credit for the triumph. It was they who initiated the battle and kept up the pressure until the white people of Pennsylvania could no longer ignore the moral cancer in Philadelphia.

At the beginning of the Civil War, most of the streetcar lines in the national capital were segregated. In 1863 Senator Charles Sumner began introducing amendments to the charter renewal grants of several Washington street railroad companies prohibiting them from excluding or segregating passengers on account of race. On February 1, 1864, Major A. T. Augusta, a Negro army surgeon, arrived late at a court-martial where he was an important witness. Augusta explained the reason for his tardiness in a letter to the judge advocate:

Sir: I have the honor to report that I have been obstructed in getting to the court this morning by the conductor of car No. 32, of the Fourteenth street line of the city railway.

I started from my lodgings to go to the hospital I formerly had charge of to get some notes of the case I was to give evidence in, and hailed the car at the corner of Fourteenth and I streets. It was stopped for me and when I attempted to enter the conductor pulled me back, and informed me that I must ride on the front with the driver, as it was against the rules for colored persons to ride inside. I told him I would not ride on the front, and he said I should not ride at all. He then ejected me from the platform, and at the same time gave orders to the driver to go on. I have therefore been compelled to walk the distance in the mud and rain, and have also been delayed in my attendance upon the court.[28]

Augusta's letter added a strong impetus to Sumner's anti-segregation drive. Sumner read it into the Congressional Globe, *and introduced a resolution instructing the Senate District of Columbia Committee to frame a law barring streetcar discrimination in the District. Such a law was finally passed in March 1865.[29] In an effort to test the effectiveness of this statute, Sojourner Truth, the fearless and legendary ex-slave, abolitionist, and advocate of women's rights who was now working among the freedmen in Arlington, rode on the streetcars of several Washington lines. Olive Gilbert, Sojourner Truth's friend and biographer, recounted the story:*

Not long after [passage of the law], Sojourner, having occasion to ride, signaled the car, but neither conductor nor driver noticed her. Soon another followed, and she raised her hand again, but they also turned away. She then gave three tremendous yelps, "I want to ride! *I want to ride!!* I WANT TO RIDE!!!" Consternation seized the passing crowd—people, carriages, go-carts of every description stood still. The car was effectually blocked up, and before it could move on, Sojourner had jumped aboard. Then there arose a great shout from the crowd, "Ha! ha! ha!! She has beaten him," &c. The angry conductor told her to go forward where the horses were, or he would put her out. Quietly seating herself, she informed him that she was a passenger. "Go forward where the horses are, or I will throw you out," said he in a menacing voice. She told him that she was neither

a Marylander nor a Virginian to fear his threats; but was from
the Empire State of New York, and knew the laws as well as he
did.

Several soldiers were in the car, and when other passengers
came in, they related the circumstance and said, "You ought to
have heard that old woman talk to the conductor." Sojourner
rode farther than she needed to go; for a ride was so rare a
privilege that she determined to make the most of it. She left
the car feeling very happy, and said, "Bless God! I have had a
ride." . . .

At another time, she was sent to Georgetown to obtain a nurse
for the hospital, which being accomplished, they went to the
station and took seats in an empty car, but had not proceeded
far before two ladies came in, and seating themselves opposite
the colored women began a whispered conversation, frequently
casting scornful glances at the latter. The nurse, for the first
time in her life finding herself in one sense on a level with white
folks and being much abashed, hung her poor old head nearly
down to her lap; but Sojourner, nothing daunted, looked fearlessly about. At length one of the ladies called out, in a weak,
faint voice, "Conductor, conductor, does niggers ride in these
cars?" He hesitatingly answered, "Ye-yea-yes," to which she
responded, " 'Tis a shame and a disgrace. They ought to have a
nigger car on the track." Sojourner remarked, "Of course colored people ride in the cars. Street cars are designed for poor
white, and colored, folks. Carriages are for ladies and gentlemen. There are carriages [pointing out of the window], standing
ready to take you three or four miles for sixpence, and then you
talk of a nigger car!!!" Promptly acting upon this hint, they arose
to leave. "Ah!" said Sojourner, "now they are going to take a
carriage. Good-by, ladies."

Mrs. Laura Haviland, a widely known philanthropist, spent
several months in the same hospital and sometimes went about
the city with Sojourner to procure necessaries for the invalids.
Returning one day, being much fatigued, Mrs. Haviland proposed to take a car. . . . "A man coming out as we were going
into the next car [Sojourner recalled], asked the conductor if

'niggers were allowed to ride.' The conductor grabbed me by the shoulder and jerking me around, ordered me to get out. Mrs. Haviland took hold of my other arm and said, 'Don't put her out.' The conductor asked if I belonged to her. 'No,' replied Mrs. Haviland, 'She belongs to humanity.' 'Then take her and go,' said he, and giving me another push slammed me against the door. I told him I would let him know whether he could shove me about like a dog, and said to Mrs. Haviland, 'Take the number of this car.'

"At this, the man looked alarmed, and gave us no more trouble. When we arrived at the hospital, the surgeons were called in to examine my shoulder and found that a bone was misplaced. I complained to the president of the road, who advised me to arrest the man for assault and battery. The [Freedmen's] Bureau furnished me a lawyer, and the fellow lost his situation. It created a great sensation, and before the trial was ended, the inside of the cars looked like pepper and salt. . . . A little circumstance will show how great a change a few weeks had produced: a lady saw some colored women looking wistfully toward a car, when the conductor, halting, said, 'Walk in, ladies.' Now they who had so lately cursed me for wanting to ride, could stop for black as well as white, and could even condescend to say, 'Walk in, ladies.' "³⁰

*During the Civil War, Congress admitted Negroes to its visitors' galleries for the first time.*³¹ *Public lectures at the Smithsonian were opened to Negroes in 1862. Also for the first time, black people were welcomed to the President's public reception on New Year's Day in 1864. Black troops marched in the Inauguration Day parade on March 4, 1865.*³² *Frederick Douglass wrote the following account of his attendance at the Inaugural reception on the evening of March 4:*

For the first time in my life, and I suppose the first time in any colored man's life, I attended the reception of President Lincoln on the evening of the inauguration. As I approached the door I was seized by two policemen and forbidden to enter. I said to them that they were mistaken entirely in what they were

doing, that if Mr. Lincoln knew that I was at the door he would
order my admission, and I bolted in by them. On the inside I was
taken charge of by two other policemen, to be conducted as I
supposed to the President, but instead of that they were conducting me out the window on a plank.

"Oh," said I, "this will not do, gentlemen," and as a gentleman was passing in I said to him, "Just say to Mr. Lincoln that
Fred Douglass is at the door."

He rushed in to President Lincoln, and almost in less than a
half a minute I was invited into the East Room of the White
House. A perfect sea of beauty and elegance, too, it was. The
ladies were in very fine attire, and Mrs. Lincoln was standing
there. I could not have been more than ten feet from him when
Mr. Lincoln saw me; his countenance lighted up, and he said in
a voice which was heard all around: "Here comes my friend
Douglass." As I approached him he reached out his hand, gave
me a cordial shake, and said: "Douglass, I saw you in the crowd
to-day listening to my inaugural address. There is no man's opinion that I value more than yours: what do you think of it?" I
said: "Mr. Lincoln, I cannot stop here to talk with you, as there
are thousands waiting to shake you by the hand;" but he said
again: "What did you think of it?" I said: "Mr. Lincoln, it was
a sacred effort," and then I walked off. "I am glad you liked
it," he said.[33]

*In February 1865 Charles Sumner presented the Boston law-
yer John Rock as a candidate to argue cases before the Supreme
Court. Chief Justice Salmon P. Chase accepted Rock and swore
him in, making him the first Negro ever to be accredited as a
Supreme Court lawyer. This event could stand as a symbol of
the great revolution in the Negro's status since 1857, when the
Supreme Court had denied the citizenship of black men.[34]*

*The Northern Negro's drive for improved and/or desegregated
education was also stepped up during the war, and the more
favorable attitude toward black people produced by the war resulted in some solid achievements. In 1862, San Francisco Negroes were not yet prepared to ask for integrated education, but*

they did feel that it was time the city gave them a decent school building. They drew up the following petition to the school board and presented it on September 23, 1862:

GENTLEMEN—The undersigned, residents of the city and county of San Francisco . . . respectfully represent to your honorable body that the condition of the school appropriated to the children is such that we deem it our duty to call your attention thereto.

There are about fifty pupils in attendance, at the present time, of both sexes. The room in which they are taught is unsuitable, for the following reasons: It is a basement and below the grade of the street. It is badly ventilated—the air from the west and north sides comes laden with the effluvia of cellars, sinks and vaults contiguous, and is foul and unhealthful.

The hall above the school-room is occupied by a military company. The loud sounds arising from their exercises, at times, greatly disturb those of the schoolroom.

The plastering is broken and falling from the ceiling, so that the water from above runs through the floor upon the desks and floor of the school-room beneath. . . .

At a time when your honorable board is doing so much to improve the public schools; for the health and advancement of pupils; the character, convenience and efficiency of teachers, we respectfully ask you to consider and provide for the pressing wants of the colored children. . . .

We are willing—have ever been willing—to bear our share of the public burdens, and when the time shall come, we shall be ready to stand in the place assigned to us, to help defend the laws and uphold the government of our country.

Our children—as yours—are passing on to manhood and womanhood; they will be virtuous or vicious, respectable or disreputable, educated or ignorant. . . . While you are making such wise and liberal provision for the schooling of the youth, deeming your labors and money so expended good economy, because children are the true jewels of the state, . . . permit us to suggest what, no doubt, you have felt deeply in your own hearts, that the same arguments apply to colored children.[35]

*The appeal was successful, and in 1863 the school board ordered
the construction of a new school building for Negroes.*[36]

*In 1861, five New England cities still maintained segregated
public schools: Hartford and New Haven in Connecticut; and
Providence, Newport, and Bristol in Rhode Island. Rhode Island
Negroes were dissatisfied with segregated education for their
children, and under the leadership of George T. Downing they
began a campaign for desegregation as early as 1857. Downing
was a successful businessman and a militant crusader for racial justice. By 1845, when he was only twenty-six years old, he
had established a catering business in New York serving the
cream of Broadway society. In 1846 he opened a restaurant and
catering service at Newport, and in the 1850s he purchased real
estate and established a thriving business in Providence. In 1865
Downing took over the restaurant serving the House of Representatives in Washington. When his children were refused admission to the Newport schools, Downing launched a drive to
break down racial barriers in Rhode Island's public schools.
The war gave an added impetus to the movement, and every
year the Negroes sent petitions to school boards, city councils,
and the state legislature. In 1864 the drive seemed to be on the
verge of success when the legislature's committee on education
recommended passage of a desegregation law. But the general
assembly tabled the recommendation. In 1865 the assembly was
prepared to pass a compromise measure which would guarantee
Negroes equal facilities in separate schools.*[37] *But the black leaders would have none of this, and Downing prepared and sent
the following petition to the governor:*

Honored Sir: The anxiety of a father, who loves his seven
children, is my apology for personally addressing you. You are
soon to decide whether the rights and feelings of my God-given
little ones shall be cared for in law. You are soon to decide
whether they shall grow up in your midst with manly and un-
trammeled, or with depressed, dejected feelings. A great responsibility is involved. I . . . entreat you not to regard the
unholy prejudice against color which was triumphant when
slavery was triumphant,—which should die with slavery. Dis-

regard it; do in the matter, what your heart and head tell you is just. . . .

Our case is simple. Being acknowledged by the Constitution of the State as citizens and as equals, the fact of our being colored not being allowed in the Constitution to have any weight in judging of our rights and privileges as well as our burdens, should any local authority in the State be allowed to discriminate between us and other citizens in the matter of education because of our color, simply to gratify a prejudice which existed to favor slavery? This is the question. Is not such a distinction invidious; does it not amount to a civil incapacitation?

You have two reports before you. Both of them fully concede that we have just cause of complaint; that something should be done. One gives us bread, the other a stone. . . . The majority report *legalizes any local proscription that may be forced upon us.* . . . The local authorities who proscribe us have all along declared that they give us as good schools, &c., as they do others; but they, almost with the same breath, unconsciously contradict themselves. . . .

The law [recommended by the majority report] proposes that the teachers, and everything else connected with these proposed schools, shall be as good as the other schools. Let us try this proposition by my city, Newport. After the city shall have erected the necessary five school houses, with recitation rooms, all the costly incidentals of the same, with all the modern regard for conveniences, for ventilation, &c., true of Newport schools, . . . and then a costly high school which will be needed, with many expenses which I will not stop to mention, . . . we would have to be taxed annually in addition to all of the above, at least five thousand dollars for principal teachers. For the colored schools, to be as good as the others, must have as good teachers as the others, who command the highest salaries. But if the colored children go into the present schools of their district the expense will not be as great as the present expense. Notice that the present schools can accommodate all of them. We protest against this proposition as taxpayers.

The Government at Washington; the Western States, which have been disgraced with black laws on their statute books, are repealing them rapidly. Rhode Island is free from this disgrace; shall it now as the proposition of the majority proposes, blot her fair name by enacting *for the first time in her history, a pro-slavery, black law,* making a distinction among its citizens?[38]

This petition helped to defeat the compromise measure, and in 1866 the Rhode Island legislature outlawed school segregation in the entire state. The Connecticut legislature followed the example of its neighbor and abolished segregated public education in the Nutmeg State in 1868.[39] Public schools in Chicago and scattered places elsewhere in the North were also desegregated during or immediately after the war.[40]

The desire for desegregation was also voiced by intelligent Southern Negroes. The New Orleans Tribune *declared editorially in February 1865:*

If we have done with slavery, not so with the aristocracy of color. The negroes are set free, say the pro-slavery men of old, as our horses or cattle could be turned loose. Free and freed persons of color are not, for that party, real and complete men, made in the image of their Creator. They are held as a kind of bastard race, half-way between man and ape, a race that the law has to protect in some form, but that men of Caucasian, and particularly of Anglo-Saxon descent, can only look upon with disdain. . . .

[Segregated schools] perpetuate from childhood the infatuation of the white, and prompt the black to retaliate by enmity or envy, [and] . . . draw a line between two elements of one and the same people, from the cradle itself up to the time of manhood and throughout life. . . .

[Slavery is dead, but] we see . . . that some persons still imagine that we need two separate legislations. They intend to have a statute-book for the whites and another one for the blacks; they want two laws in one and the same country: the black law and the white law. This will be no less than a reminiscence of slavery; it springs only from narrow-minded people, who understand nothing of legislation. Policy, as well as history, warns the American people to listen not to these shortsighted counsels. . . . Shall we make two peoples with one people, two nations with one nation? This will be impossible. The strength of the United States will require that the dictates of equity and justice be heeded. A country cannot be powerful unless the people be made one nation. We want to have one country; let us therefore have one law.[41]

Northern Negroes broke down many forms of legal and social discrimination during the war, and the impetus provided by the war paved the way for several later advances. Massachusetts enacted the first comprehensive public accommodations law in America in 1865, forbidding the exclusion of any person because of race or color from restaurants, inns, theaters, and places of amusement. Several other states adopted similar legislation in the decades after the Civil War. In the thirty years following the war, public-school segregation and discrimination in public transportation was ended almost everywhere in the North.[42] But many kinds of inequality and segregation remained in the North. The battle was not won in 1865, nor even in 1900. It is not won yet.

CHAPTER XIX

WARTIME DISCUSSIONS OF RECONSTRUCTION AND NEGRO SUFFRAGE

By the end of 1863 the problem of reconstruction had emerged as one of the major political issues in the North. Most Negro leaders urged that the Union be reconstructed only on the basis of full civil and political equality for all men, in the North as well as in the South. At a commemorative meeting of the American Anti-Slavery Society in December 1863, Frederick Douglass said that

our work will not be done until the colored man is admitted as a full member in good and regular standing in the American body politic. . . . It is said that the colored man is ignorant, and therefore he shall not vote. In saying this, you lay down a rule for the black man that you apply to no other class of your citizens. I will hear nothing of degradation or of ignorance against the black man. . . . If he knows an honest man from a thief, he knows much more than some of our white voters. If he knows as much when sober as an Irishman knows when drunk, he knows enough to vote. If he knows enough to take up arms in defence of this Government, and bare his breast to the storm of rebel artillery, he knows enough to vote. (Great applause.) . . . All I ask, however, in regard to the blacks, is that whatever rule you adopt, whether of intelligence or wealth, as the condition of voting, you shall apply it equally to the black man. . . .

Men talk about saving the Union, and restoring the Union as

it was. . . . What business . . . have we to fight for the old
Union? . . . We are fighting for something incomparably better
than the old Union. We are fighting for unity, . . . in which
there shall be no North, no South, no East, no West, no black,
no white, but a solidarity of the nation, making every slave free,
and every free man a voter. (Great applause.)[1]

*Equal voting rights was the key issue of Reconstruction. But
for Northern Negroes, equal voting rights had been an important issue for decades, and continued to be so during the war.
Negroes in 1860 could vote on equal terms with whites in only
five states (Maine, New Hampshire, Vermont, Massachusetts,
and Rhode Island), and these states contained only 7 per cent of
the Northern Negro population. Black men stepped up their
drive for equal suffrage in the North and South alike during
the war, and although no final successes were achieved in the
war years, the activities of Negroes during those years helped
pave the way for the adoption of the Fifteenth Amendment in
1870.*

*In New York State, Negroes could vote only if they owned
$250 worth of property (about 21 per cent of the state's adult
male Negroes qualified under this provision). No such restriction was placed on white suffrage. New York abolitionists and
Negroes had tried for many years to get this degrading distinction removed from the Constitution. In 1860 the legislature
adopted a constitutional amendment abolishing the $250 prop-
erty qualification for black men, subject to the approval of the
voters in November. New York Negroes organized suffrage committees in nearly every city and large town in the state in an
effort to get out a favorable vote on the amendment.[2] The most
important of these committees, The New York City and County
Suffrage Committee of Colored Citizens, issued in September the
following broadside on "The Suffrage Question," written by
James McCune Smith:*

FELLOW CITIZENS: We have had, and still have, great wrongs
of which to complain. A heavy and cruel hand has been laid
upon us. As a people, we feel ourselves to be not only deeply
injured, but grossly misunderstood. Our white countrymen do

not know us. They are strangers to our characters, ignorant of our capacity, oblivious to our history and progress, and are misinformed as to the principles and ideas that control and guide us, as a people. The great mass of American citizens estimate us as being a characterless and purposeless people; and hence we hold up our heads, if at all, against the withering influence of a nation's scorn and contempt. . . .

What stone has been left unturned to degrade us? What hand has refused to fan the flame of popular prejudice against us? What American artist has not caricatured us? What wit has not laughed at us in our wretchedness? What songster has not made merry over our depressed spirits? What press has not ridiculed and condemned us? . . .

The colored people have not only taken good care of themselves in this state, notwithstanding the prejudice of color which limits their sphere of occupation, by amassing real and personal estate of large amount, but they are no greater, if so great a burden to the State in almshouses and prisons than other classes of citizens. . . . Principles of justice to the individuals who compose the State, and thereby of justice to the State itself, require that the basis of voting should be equal to all. No one class can be depressed and made unequal without injury to the other classes, and to the whole State. And are not these patriotic, industrious, provident, exemplary citizens deserving equal right at the ballot-box? . . .

We respectfully request you voters of the State of New York, irrespective of party, that you will give your attention to the proposed Amendment to the Constitution. The question is one, not of party, but humanity and right. We appeal with equal confidence to Democrats and Republicans. We feel assured that if you will examine the question in the light of reason and justice and Christianity, you will not hesitate to vote for the proposed Amendment in relation to the Suffrage.[3]

Thousands of copies of this broadside were printed and scattered throughout the state. But even though Lincoln carried New York State in 1860, the voters defeated the suffrage amendment by a margin of 337,934 to 197,505.[4]

In 1863 a convention of Kansas Negroes issued an "Address of the Colored Convention to the Citizens of Kansas":

Citizens of Kansas, we appeal to you on a subject dear to us. We ask of you the right of suffrage. . . . This Government was founded in the interest of Freedom, the founders thereof appealing to the fundamental principles of Liberty, Justice and Equality, as their warrant for what they did. We therefore hold that to deprive any portion of the native population of this country of so essential a right as that of suffrage, is to do violence to the genius of American Institutions, and is a departure from the aims of the illustrious founders of the Republic. . . .

This nation has long turned a deaf ear to the cry of the black man. . . . Happily the nation's conscience, schooled by misfortune, is becoming aroused to the necessity of repairing the many wrongs which it has inflicted on the black man. In the progress of this war, destructive of so many prejudices and fruitful of so many new ideas, it will doubtless be discovered that it is as necessary to make the black man a voter, as it was to make him a soldier. He was made a soldier to RESTORE the Union. He must be made a voter to preserve it.

How else can you restore the Union on any desirable basis? If left in exclusive possession of the machinery of the State governments, will not the white population of the seceded States, humiliated by defeat, estranged beyond hope of reconciliation, burning for revenge, and maddened by the recollection of a thousand injuries, suffered and inflicted, seek to renew the strife on the first opportunity, when, perhaps, the nation is engaged in a foreign war of gigantic proportions?

The restoration of the Union and the elevation of the black man, will go hand in hand. The nation will need the black man to vote for her, therefore it will make him a voter. . . . The argument that black men should not vote, because ignorant, is met by the observation that many ignorant white men vote— the want of intelligence among them not working a forfeiture of a *natural* and *inherent* right. We contend that *our* right to vote is natural and inherent; resting it upon the fact of our being born in this country, and upon the form of government under which we live. . . .

Citizens of Kansas, shall your black veterans return victorious from the war, proud of dangers past, of many toils cheerfully borne, and of honorable scars bravely won, to find themselves still denied the rights of a manhood so nobly vindicated? . . . No! still obedient to the voice of liberty and honor, you will continue to lead the van of progress. You will not stop to listen to the voice of slavery, whilst yet your soil is wet with blood of martyrs, slain in defence of liberty. . . . If there are any still enchained by the hateful spirit of caste, we beg you to take counsel of your courage, and conquer your prejudices. Anticipate the fruition of time, and grant us to-day, what you will certainly grant us in a few short years at most.[5]

Southern Negroes were also active in the movement for equal suffrage. A delegation of five black men from North Carolina called upon Lincoln at the White House in May 1864, and presented to him the following petition:

WE, the colored citizens of North Carolina, composed alike of those born in freedom and those whose chains of bondage were severed by your gracious proclamation, cherishing in our hearts and memories that ever to be remembered sentence, embodied in the Declaration of Independence, that "all men are created free and equal," being well aware that the right of suffrage was exercised, without detriment, by the colored freemen of this State previous to 1835, . . . do most earnestly and respectfully petition your Excellency to finish the noble work you have begun, and grant unto your petitioners that greatest of privileges, when the State is reconstructed, to exercise the right of suffrage, which will greatly extend our sphere of usefulness, redound to your honor, and cause posterity, to the latest generation, to acknowledge their deep sense of gratitude. We feel proud in saying that we have contributed moral and physical aid to our country in her hour of need, and expect to do so until every cloud of war shall disappear.[6]

No action was taken on any of these petitions during the war.

But the suffrage question in Louisiana became a major political issue in 1864–65. When the Union Army and Navy captured New Orleans in April 1862, the population of the city was approximately 170,000, of whom about 13,000 were slaves and 10,000 were free Negroes. Descendants of generations of Creole planters and their Negro mistresses, the free black population of New Orleans was more prosperous and better educated than any other Negro community, North or South. New Orleans Negroes established a bilingual (French and English) newspaper in September 1862, L'Union (The Union), which was published triweekly for nearly two years. In July 1864 La Tribune de la Nouvelle Orléans *(The New Orleans* Tribune*), also bilingual, was founded as a spokesman for Negroes not only in New Orleans but in all of Louisiana. The paper was published triweekly until October 1864, when it began daily publication.*

Before the war, of course, free black men in Louisiana had not possessed the franchise. But the intelligent and articulate leaders of New Orleans' Negro community were determined to obtain equal suffrage as one of the conditions of Louisiana's restoration to the Union. In its salutatory editorial, L'Union *clearly indicated that the black men of Louisiana would be satisfied with nothing less than equal justice:*

We inaugurate today a new era in the destiny of the South. We proclaim the Declaration of Independence as the basis of our platform. . . . You who aspire to establish true republicanism, democracy without shackles, gather around us and contribute your grain of sand to the construction of the Temple of Liberty! . . . Let all friends of Progress unite! The hour has come for the struggle of the great humanitarian principles against a vile and sordid interest which gives birth to pride, ambition, hypocrisy, and lying, and silences the conscience, that voice of the heavens which cries endlessly to a man: "You were born for liberty and happiness! Do not deceive yourself in this and do not deceive your brother!"[7]

A white newspaper in New Orleans branded the desire of Negroes for equal rights "a sick vanity." L'Union *replied:*

A *sick vanity* of the men of color! It is the white aristocracy of this country that is in a state of chronic sickness—this aristocracy which arrogates to itself all rights and privileges. Are we vain because we believe that this revolution should produce a change in the abject condition your selfishness and injustice have made for us? Is it vanity to believe that we are like you sons of God, and that, as such, we have a right just as well as you to a place in the sun? Is it vanity for us . . . to hope for a future more in harmony with the institutions of true democracy and republicanism? . . .

Full of confidence in the justice of our cause . . . we want to work without hate and without passion for our rehabilitation. No power can arrest the *élan* summoned forth by this revolution. Foolish men! You have not yet seen that this revolution is the work of God, and that it would be as insane to try to return the waters of this great river to their source as to try to stop progress in its incessant march.[8]

There was much talk about the reconstruction of Louisiana in 1863. New Orleans Negroes held a mass meeting on November 5 and agreed to petition George F. Shepley, military governor of the state, for the right to vote. "If we cannot succeed with the authorities here," they declared, "we will go to President Lincoln."[9] *But Lincoln soon disappointed them. As a supplement to his annual message to Congress on December 8, 1863, the President announced his reconstruction policy. He offered a full pardon with restoration of property rights to all Confederates (with a few prominent exceptions) who would take an oath of allegiance to the Constitution and swear to abide by all acts of the Executive and Congress relative to slavery. When a number of white voters equal to one-tenth of those who had voted in 1860 took this oath, they would be allowed to re-establish a state government.*[10] *Lincoln subsequently ordered General Banks, Commander of the Department of the Gulf, to proceed with the reconstruction of Louisiana under the policy announced in the proclamation of December 8. With the approval of Lincoln, Banks scheduled an election for state officials on February 22,*

*1864, with a view toward drawing up a new constitution for
Louisiana after the elected officials had taken office. Only white
men who took the oath of allegiance would be eligible to vote.*[11]

*The elections of February 22 resulted in the choice of Michael
Hahn, a moderate who opposed Negro suffrage, as governor.
Frustrated at the state level, New Orleans Negroes had mean-
while decided to take their case directly to the President. On
January 5, 1864, they drew up a petition for the franchise and
addressed it to both President Lincoln and the Congress. The
petition bore the signatures of more than one thousand men,
twenty-seven of whom had fought under Andrew Jackson at the
Battle of New Orleans in 1815. Two of the signers, Jean Baptiste
Roudanez and Arnold Bertonneau, carried the petition to
Washington where they presented it to Lincoln on March 12.
Senator Sumner presented it to the Senate on March 15. The
petition stated:*

The undersigned respectfully submit the following:

That they are natives of Louisiana, and citizens of the United
States; that they are loyal citizens, sincerely attached to the
Country and the Constitution, and ardently desire the maintenance of the national unity, for which they are ready to sacrifice their fortunes and their lives.

That a large portion of them are owners of real estate, and
all of them are owners of personal property; that many of them
are engaged in the pursuits of commerce and industry, while
others are employed as artisans in various trades; that they are
all fitted to enjoy the privileges and immunities belonging to the
condition of citizens of the United States, and among them may
be found many of the descendants of those men whom the illustrious Jackson styled "his fellow citizens" when he called
upon them to take up arms to repel the enemies of the country. . . .

Notwithstanding their forefathers served in the army of the
United States, in 1814–15, and aided in repelling from the soil
of Louisiana the haughty enemy, over-confident of success, yet
they and their descendants have ever since, and until the era
of the present rebellion, been estranged, and even repulsed—

excluded from all franchises, even the smallest. . . . During this period of forty-nine years, they have never ceased to be peaceable citizens, paying their taxes on an assessment of more than fifteen millions of dollars.

At the call of General Banks, they hastened to rally under the banner of Union and Liberty; they have spilled their blood, and are still pouring it out for the maintenance of the Constitution of the United States; in a word, they are soldiers of the Union, and they will defend it so long as their hands have strength to hold a musket. . . .

Your petitioners aver that they have applied in respectful terms to Brig. Gen. George F. Shepley, Military Governor of Louisiana, and to Major Gen. N. P. Banks, commanding the Department of the Gulf, praying to be placed upon the registers as voters, to the end that they might participate in the reorganization of civil government in Louisiana, and that their petition has met with no response from those officers, and it is feared that none will be given; and they therefore appeal to the justice of the Representatives of the nation, and ask that all the citizens of Louisiana of African descent, born free before the rebellion, may be, by proper orders, directed to be inscribed on the registers, and admitted to the rights and privileges of electors.

After arriving in Washington, Roudanez and Bertonneau were persuaded by radical Republicans that the phrase "born free before the rebellion" created a caste distinction between free *Negroes and* freed *Negroes, so they added a final paragraph to the petition:*

Your memorialists pray that the right of suffrage may be extended not only to natives of Louisiana of African descent, born free, but also to all others, whether born slave or free, especially those who have vindicated their right to vote by bearing arms, subject only to such qualifications as shall equally affect the white and colored citizens.[12]

Lincoln was impressed by the petition. The day after he received it he wrote a private note to Governor Hahn, who was preparing for the Louisiana constitutional convention scheduled to meet early in April. "I barely suggest for your private consideration," said the President, "whether some of the colored people may not be let in [to the suffrage]—as, for instance, the very intelligent, and especially those who have fought gallantly in our ranks."[13]

Republican leaders in Massachusetts invited Roudanez and Bertonneau to a complimentary dinner in Boston on April 12. Several speakers supported their petition, and Mr. Roudanez told the diners:

We ask that, in the reconstruction of the State Government, the right to vote shall not depend on the color of the citizen; that the colored citizen shall have and enjoy every civil, political and religious right that white citizens enjoy; in a word, that every man shall stand equal before the law. (Applause.) To secure these rights, which belong to every free citizen, we ask the aid and influence of every true loyal man all over the country. . . .

In order to make our State blossom and bloom as the rose, the character of the whole people must be changed. As slavery is abolished, with it must vanish every vestige of oppression. The right to vote must be secured; the doors of our public schools must be opened, that our children, side by side, may study from the same books, and imbibe the same principles and precepts from the Book of Books—learn the great truth that God "created of one blood all nations of men to dwell on all the face of the earth"—so will caste, founded on prejudice against color, disappear. . . .

Mr. President, when we return to New Orleans, we shall tell our friends that, in Massachusetts, we could ride in every public vehicle; that the colored children not only were allowed to attend public schools with white children, but they were compelled by law to attend such schools (applause)—that we visited your courts of justice, and saw colored lawyers defending their clients; and we shall tell them, too, of this most generous welcome extended to us by you. It will prove most grateful to their feeling, animate them with new hopes and desires, and, will prove a grand stimulus to renewed efforts for the requisition of every right that can be guaranteed to them by law.[14]

*But the new constitution, although it officially abolished
slavery in Louisiana and ordained a system of public schools
(segregated) for all children, failed to grant equal suffrage to
black men. Louisiana Negroes were disappointed, and they
stepped up their drive to obtain the ballot. Conservatives raised
the cry of "radicalism" against the movement for Negro suffrage, but L'Union was not frightened by this label:*

It is really curious to see what pitiable diatribes against radicalism certain publications inflict on their readers each day. . . .
These days, the great crime, the grand malediction, the eternal
scapegoat, is radicalism.

Let us shed a little light on these absurd charges. To say that
a man is a radical is to say nothing of his character except that
he is an energetic man. . . . Radical methods get at the root, at
the source of a problem; they involve the entire achievement of
a work, and opposition to half measures. . . . The man who is
not radically honest is nothing but a disguised cheat. Each man
ought to be radically true and sincere; if he is not, he is but a
deceiver. All virtue is radical, because it must go to the root of
character, or it is not a virtue. The very essence of morality
consists in its radicalism. . . .

The true friends of liberty should not allow themselves to be
intimidated by the denunciations of a false conservatism that
wants to conserve nothing except the inalienable rights of traitors and despots. Our revolutionary ancestors were radicals
when they undertook to overthrow British despotism. Jefferson
and those who aided him were radicals, and they drafted the
most radical political document in the history of mankind—the
Declaration of Independence. If we really believe that the grand
principles of this Declaration are the only sane base for republican liberty, we cannot be too radical in defending them. The
truth has no need of halfway believers nor of temporizing dis-
ciples.[15]

L'Union *argued that the courageous fighting of Negro troops
had earned the right of suffrage for their race:*

From the day that bayonets were placed in the hands of the
blacks . . . the Negro became a citizen of the United States.

Schools have been established for the instruction of freedmen, and all reports say that they have learned to read and write so rapidly that the black sergeants, after three months' study, have mastered their books as well as the most pure Caucasians placed in the same circumstances. . . . How does one explain, then, the hesitancy of the American people to grant the right to vote to these black men, who have as much intelligence, energy, and vigor as the average white man and much more patriotism than the traitors who have dared to place their bloodstained hands on the federal Constitution? This war has broken the chains of the slave, and it is written in the heavens that from this war shall grow the seeds of the political enfranchisement of the oppressed race. . . .

We believe that in spite of traitors and copperheads, the time is not far distant when the American people, who said to the men of color during a crucial moment for the Republic: "Come help us maintain the integrity of the Republic of our Fathers," will say to them also: "Fellow citizens, come help us elect pure men and patriots to govern a nation which has been delivered from the shameful mark of human slavery."[16]

Some white leaders in New Orleans tried to drive a wedge between the light-skinned free Negro element in the city and the darker-skinned freedmen of the country districts by proposing to grant equal rights to the former while denying them to the latter. L'Union *denounced this scheme:*

To achieve their ends, the oppressors ceaselessly flatter the unjust passions and prejudices of the class they wish to exploit. In this state, where the issues of liberty and equality are being debated, the oppressors represent the free colored population which has sacrificed so much for the noble cause of liberty as being the enemy of black men who have been held in slavery until now. Why do they falsely represent the free colored people? Read the history of St. Domingo and you shall understand that the germ of discord which they sowed among the diverse colored populations of the island did more harm to our race than slavery itself. They try to renew here their criminal designs, but success is not so easy for them as they first believed. They were

able to succeed for a moment with their infernal enterprise. But
. . . harmony among all the descendants of the African race hastened to retake the place which had been marked for it by logic,
reason, prudence, and the need of union among all those of our
race who have understood that:

> United, we stand!
> Divided, we fall![17]

*In November 1864 a Mr. Smith introduced in the Louisiana
legislature a bill which specified that any man with one-fourth
or less Negro blood would be considered a white man for voting
purposes. Many of the old free Negro class in New Orleans fell
into this quadroon category, and the proposed law would have
given them the right to vote. Nevertheless the New Orleans* Tribune (La Tribune de la Nouvelle Orléans), *which was financed
and edited largely by the quadroon element, came out squarely
against this attempt to create a caste system among the black
people. Said the* Tribune:

Although we were convinced at the outset that the odious
distinction which M. Smith wants to make among the children
of the same race could not be adopted, it is, we believe, a duty
of our population to protest against the narrow views which the
thinking of the Senator from St. Mary's Parish illustrates. Colored men desire political advancement and equal rights, but they
do not desire the humbling of their brothers to serve as foot-
walks for the attainment of privileges that are denied to the
men of our race who are presently spilling their blood for the
defense of the country. There may be among our population a
few "aristocrats of light skin," but they are in the minority. The
majority of us, who have admired the principles of '93, know
by experience that caste distinctions can only create bitterness
and weakness. . . . We understand too well that if we wish the
sympathies of all friends of progress and men of good will, our
first duty is to place ourselves at a high level of civilization and
to demand for all colored men what we claim for ourselves. To
do aught else would be a scandal in the eyes of reason, a great

joy for the enemies of the black man, and a triumph for the
sophisms of the planters who are trying to establish the inferiority of the negro race. Therefore, we tell M. Smith and those
who think as he does that this bill is simply ridiculous. . . . We
are in a century of progress, this revolution is being fought for
the benefit of all, and in this Republic where our brothers spill
waves of precious blood for the common defense, all should be
recognized equally as children of the same fatherland. May narrow minds not forget that the tranquillity of the country and
the security of the future demand that the American Republic
regenerate itself by proclaiming loudly and firmly the sacred
principles of the Declaration of Independence which admit of
no distinction of race or color. . . . Recognize all the children of
the black race as members of the great American family, and
while accomplishing an act of justice you will have assured a
peaceful and prosperous future, which will make of the United
States one of the greatest nations on earth.[18]

The bill was defeated, in part because of the Tribune's *strong
opposition to it.*[19]

*Another proposition suggested in the legislature was a liter-
acy qualification for Negro voters (though there was no such
qualification for white voters in Louisiana). The* Tribune *was
opposed to this idea also:*

Now we are willing to abide by the laws governing the white
voters. . . . But we must confess that we cannot perceive the
propriety or justice of exacting a higher intellectual status from
a negro than from a white man. Is a white voter required to
know how to read and write? To be a moral, a religious or a
temperance man? Not in the least. . . . We care not for incomplete justice; we do not press any personal claims; we advocate
a general right.

The objections, which are now presented against extending
the right of suffrage to the black and colored, are exactly the
same arguments that the pro-slavery men brought forth against
emancipation. They talked of preparing and educating the
blacks, so as to qualify them for liberty; but at the same time
they were careful that the slaves should not educate or elevate

themselves. If we admit the objection, it will hold good for ever. . . .

The actual enjoyment of new rights is the only way to get accustomed to and become fit for their exercise. . . . It is certainly desirable that our brethren recently redeemed from bondage and called to the blessings of freedom should have a certain degree of education. . . . However, we can only see in this subject a distinct and collateral question, which has no direct bearing upon the right of voting. We claim the electoral franchise as an act of justice, as an application of a general principle; we do not claim it for a few individuals, but for all.[20]

At the same time, Frederick Douglass was telling the white people of Maryland, who had just voted for emancipation in their state, that

if you would be consistent, you will not stop here. If you would be true to the great principles of Liberty and Justice, you must make Maryland thoroughly and practically free. You must wipe out all those black laws that disgrace your statutes. You must give us the right to vote, to hold office, testify in courts and sit in jury boxes. . . . What we want is perfect civil, religious and political equality. We do not ask for social equality. There is no such thing. That is something that will settle and regulate itself. . . .

Why should you be afraid to permit us to enter the race of competition with you? Is our degradation necessary to your elevation? Must our hands be tied in order that you may thrive? I cannot believe it. . . . I know that you contend that negroes are too ignorant to vote understandingly. But is ignorance confined to negroes alone? How many thousands of whites are there who are unable to read the tickets they deposit in the ballot-box? . . . Away with your conditions to freedom. There can be no stopping halfway. All we ask is a fair and equal chance, and we are willing to abide the results. If we fail then, we are willing to go down. And I confidently believe the good work will go on until the obstacles which now confront us will be swept away, and every inhabitant clothed with the rights of freemen.[21]

On October 4–7, 1864, 144 Negroes from eighteen states, in-

*cluding seven slave states, met in Syracuse, New York, for a
"National Convention of Colored Citizens of the United States."
The convention adopted several resolutions calling for equal
rights and justice in the reconstruction of the Union, and issued
an "Address to the People of the United States," written by Frederick Douglass, which stated in part:*

We want the elective franchise in all the States now in the
Union, and the same in all such States as may come into the
Union hereafter. We believe that the highest welfare of this
great country will be found in erasing from its statute-books all
enactments discriminating in favor of or against any class of its
people, and by establishing one law for the white and colored
people alike. Whatever prejudice and taste may be innocently
allowed to do or to dictate in social and domestic relations, it is
plain, that in the matter of government, the object of which is
the protection and security of human rights, prejudice should
be allowed no voice whatever. In this department of human
relations, no notice should be taken of the color of men; but
justice, wisdom, and humanity should weigh alone, and be all-
controlling.

Formerly our petitions for the elective franchise were met
and denied upon the ground, that, while colored men were protected in person and property, they were not required to perform military duty. Of course this was only a plausible excuse;
for we were subject to any call the Government was pleased to
make upon us, and we could not properly be made to suffer
because the Government did not see fit to impose military duty
upon us. The fault was with the Government, not with us.

But now even this frivolous . . . apology for excluding us from
the ballot-box is entirely swept away. Two hundred thousand
colored men, according to a recent statement of President Lincoln, are now in the service, upon field and flood, in the army
and the navy of the United States; and every day adds to their
number. . . .

In a republican country, where general suffrage is the rule,
personal liberty, the right to testify in courts of law, the right
to hold, buy, and sell property, and all other rights, become

mere privileges, held at the option of others, where we are excepted from the general political liberty. . . . The possession of that right is the keystone to the arch of human liberty: and, without that, the whole may at any moment fall to the ground; while, with it, that liberty may stand forever,—a blessing to us, and no possible injury to you. If you still ask us why we want to vote, we answer, Because we don't want to be mobbed from our work, or insulted with impunity at every corner. We are men, and want to be as free in our native country as other men.[22]

This convention organized a National Equal Rights League, with John Mercer Langston of Ohio as president. Born free in Virginia in 1829, Langston had graduated from Oberlin, and was admitted to the bar and practiced law in Oberlin, Ohio, before the war. He recruited three Negro regiments during the war, and later became dean of law and acting president of Howard University. In 1888 he was the first and only Negro elected to Congress from Virginia. The purpose of the League he headed in 1865 was to work for equal rights and equal opportunities for Negroes everywhere in the United States. In an address "To the Colored People of the United States," Langston urged Negroes in every state with an appreciable black population to form state auxiliaries of the National Equal Rights League.[23] Within four months such state auxiliaries were organized in New York, Pennsylvania, Ohio, Michigan, North Carolina, Tennessee, and Louisiana.[24] These state leagues lost no time in presenting their demands to the people. The Pennsylvania League held a convention at Harrisburg in February 1865, and resolved:

1st, It is the duty of every colored citizen to obtain a repeal of the law which disfranchises him on the soil on which he was born. 2d, Colored people should adopt the motto that self-reliance is the sure road to independence. . . . 5th, As the nation has cast off slavery, let them destroy restrictions which prevent colored people from entering libraries, colleges, lecture rooms, military academies, jury boxes, churches, theatres, street cars, and from voting. 6th, It is the duty of Pennsylvania to do justice to her colored men in the field. 7th, Colored men at home should secure indemnity for the past, compensation for the present, and security for the future. 8th, We ask of the people a patient hearing and admission to our common brotherhood, the human race.²⁵

The Colored Citizen, *a Negro newspaper in Cincinnati that had been designated as the official organ of the Ohio Equal Rights League, stated at the end of 1864:*

The times demand united action on the part of the colored man. . . . American society is in a state of revolution. The armed slave confronts his master on the field of battle. They whom the highest judicial authority in the country pronounced aliens in the land of their birth, are solemnly declared citizens, and invited to share in the perils of those who are striving to maintain the Union, which happily has become, to us and our children, the bulwark of liberty.

This much the dire pressure of war has brought about. Much more remains to be gained. The same Congress which decreed that colored men should be enrolled in the militia of the nation, refused to open the way to promotion for such gallant sons of our State as Beatty, Holland, Brandon, and others, who have so nobly demonstrated the equal manhood of our race. . . . The policy of the Government as foreshadowed in the Amnesty Proclamation, and the reorganization of the State of Louisiana, indicates, that our brethren in the revolted States, are, after the war, to be subjected to the tender mercies of the fiends who have made Port Hudson, Fort Pillow and Olustee forever infamous.

. . . In nearly all of the States we are denied the elective franchise. . . . Against these national and State wrongs it is our duty to protest. . . . For once let the colored men of the nation speak with one voice. Let California and Maine, Ohio and Louisiana join hands in demanding that in the new order of things which shall arise from this war, when the nation shall again clothe itself in the garments of peace, that there shall be no distinction on account of color in all our broad land.²⁶

The Ohio League held a state convention in Xenia, January 10–12, 1865, and adopted resolutions embodying the demands expressed by the Colored Citizen. *Article 2 of the League's constitution stated that "The object of this League shall be to secure, by political and moral means as far as may be, the repeal of all laws and parts of laws, State and National, that make distinctions on account of color."*[27]

The convention of the Louisiana Equal Rights League met in New Orleans from January 9 through January 14. After the meetings were over, the New Orleans Tribune *commented:*

The day of the meeting of this Convention has inaugurated a new era. It was the first political move ever made by the colored people of the State acting in a body. . . . There were seated side by side the rich and the poor, the literate and educated man, and the country laborer, hardly released from bondage, distinguished only by the natural gifts of the mind. There, the rich landowner, the opulent tradesman, seconded motions offered by humble mechanics and freedmen. Ministers of the Gospel, officers and privates of the U.S. Army, men who handle the sword or the pen, merchants and clerks, all classes of society were represented, and united in a common thought: the actual liberation from social and political bondage.[28]

One of the most eloquent appeals for equal rights was uttered by the Rev. Henry Highland Garnet, Negro pastor of Shiloh Presbyterian Church in New York, in a sermon which he gave in the chamber of the national House of Representatives on February 12, 1865. Garnet said:

It is often asked when and where will the demands of the reformers of this and coming ages end? It is a fair question, and I will answer.

When all unjust and heavy burdens shall be removed from every man in the land. When all invidious and proscriptive distinctions shall be blotted out from our laws, whether they be constitutional, statute, or municipal laws. When emancipation shall be followed by enfranchisement, and all men holding allegiance to the government shall enjoy every right of American citizenship. When our brave and gallant soldiers shall have justice done unto them. When the men who endure the sufferings and perils of the battle-field in the defence of their country,

THE NEGRO'S CIVIL WAR ...

and in order to keep our rulers in their places, shall enjoy the well-earned privilege of voting for them. When in the army and navy, and in every legitimate and honorable occupation, promotion shall smile upon merit without the slightest regard to the complexion of a man's face. When there shall be no more class-legislation, and no more trouble concerning the black man and his rights, than there is in regard to other American citizens. When, in every respect, he shall be equal before the law, and shall be left to make his own way in the social walks of life.[29]

As the war neared its end, the Christian Recorder *urged Negroes to redouble their efforts for equality:*

There never was a period in the history of our race in this country more favorable to universal, individual action on our part, than the present. The thermometer of public feeling has been down to the zero of cold-hearted indifference against us, ever since the first African slave-trader crossed the Atlantic with her cargo of human beings, until a few months ago, when the mercury ran up to BLOOD—heat!! Black men were accepted to help shed the blood of slave-traders—and the mercury is still rising! Slavery is abolished; public feeling changing. And now, those among us who were disposed to wait for opportunities of improving their condition, are left without an excuse, if they still refuse to ACT!

Colored Men! Fellow Citizens of America! AWAKE TO ACTION!! . . . Lay claim to every available opportunity of amassing property, increasing wealth, becoming stockholders, merchants and mechanics, that our foothold may be strengthened upon the soil of our native land. Let us, en masse, make rapid strides in literary culture and moral improvement, ever remembering that domestic happiness depends, in a great measure, upon moral impetus. . . . As tax-payers, and loyal subjects of a Free Republican Government, let us contend lawfully, rightfully and perseveringly for our political rights, in common with other men, who cannot boast of greater loyalty, and whom the Painter slighted when giving out the sable hue. . . .

We have feasted on celebrations enough to go on and do a

little more work. . . . *No shouting yet! Go on and complete the victory!*[30]

And in its French-language section, the New Orleans Tribune *proclaimed:*

Emancipation is one fact, and effective liberty is another. Man does not have all his rights and privileges, he does not have free exercise of his faculties and skills by the simple consequence of the abolition of slavery. Old attitudes survive the proclamation of liberty, and old interests persist through the changes brought about by a new regime. After slavery has disappeared from the law, the former rulers seem to want to preserve slavery in fact. . . . This party accepts emancipation, it is true; but it wants the black to be happy with an empty liberty. Such liberty would be but a word; we want true liberty. . . .

Does America want to hold the black suspended between slavery and freedom, in a sphere where he possesses neither the right to live according to his wishes, nor the power to act by himself? No Pariahs in America! Such is the cry that should arise from every throat. Liberty is one and there is only one way to exercise it. Liberty must be the same for all men. If liberty is qualified, those who possess the least rights are not really free. We demand, therefore, like all other citizens, and on the same footing as they:

The right to go and to come;

The right to vote;

The right to public instruction;

The right to hold public office;

The right to be judged, treated and governed according to the common law.

This is our program. May all those who are worthy of exercising these rights join us in fighting for them.[31]

CHAPTER XX

LAND FOR THE LANDLESS

Many Negroes argued that education and equal rights were not enough to give the freedmen a solid new start in life. Unless some kind of economic assistance were granted to the ex-slave, they said, he would remain a sharecropper or laborer on the land of his former master. Political equality and education would mean little to the freedmen without a secure foundation of economic independence. From the outset of the war, some Negroes called for the breakup of large Southern plantations and their redistribution among the landless farmers, black and white. Such action would accomplish two important objectives: it would foster democracy in the South by destroying the economic basis of the "landed aristocracy"; and it would insure the creation of a prosperous and independent black yeomanry.

In November 1861 the Anglo-African published an editorial entitled "What Shall Be Done with the Slaves?"

When the war is ended, there will be few, if any slaves, for the government to dispose of. There will be four million of free men and women and children, accustomed to toil, who have by their labor during sixty years past supported themselves, and in addition, an extravagant aristocracy. . . . Besides these laborers, lands will be confiscated to the government, and turned into public lands. . . . What course can be clearer, what course more politic, what course will so immediately restore the equilibrium of commerce, what course will be so just, so humane, so thoroughly conducive to the public weal and the national advancement, as that the government should immediately bestow these lands upon these freed men who know best how to cultivate them, and will joyfully bring their brawny arms, their willing hearts, and their skilled hands to the glorious labor of cultivating as their OWN, the lands which they have bought and paid for by their sweat and blood.[1]

In 1862 John Rock asked:

Why talk about compensating masters? Compensate them for what? What do you owe them? What does the slave owe them? What does society owe them? Compensate the master? . . . It is the slave who ought to be compensated. The property of the South is by right the property of the slave. You talk of compensating the master who has stolen enough to sink ten generations, and yet you do not propose to restore even a part of that which has been plundered. . . . Restore to the [freedman] the wealth of the South, and he will engage to take care of the master well, as he has always been obliged to do, and make a good speculation by the transaction. (Applause.) This you owe to the slave; and if you do your duty, posterity will give to you the honor of being the first nation that dared to deal justly by the oppressed.[2]

A North Carolina Negro wrote in June 1863 that "if the strict law of right and justice is to be observed, the country around about me, or the Sunny South, is the entailed inheritance of the Americans of African descent, purchased by the invaluable labor of our ancestors, through a life of tears and groans, under the lash and the yoke of tyranny."[3] Prince Rivers, a black sergeant in the First South Carolina Volunteers, said in November 1863 that "every colored man will be a slave, & feel himself a slave until he can raise him own bale of cotton & put him own mark upon it & say dis is mine!"[4] And Daniel Foster, an old-line abolitionist who had been appointed colonel of the Third North Carolina Colored Volunteers, wrote in January 1864: "The slaves, with almost entire unanimity, long for a little land, that they may own a home of their own. I trust the Government will make provision for them to buy land when they wish. Let

*these immense plantations in the South be cut up, and the soil
sold at a low rate, to industrious freedmen.''*[5]

In New Orleans, the black editors of the Tribune *denounced
the policy of leasing abandoned plantations to white men of the
North and former planters of the South. Said the* Tribune:

The National Government takes possession of both lands and
slaves; and after declaring the slaves to be freemen and citizens,
proceeds to cultivate the plantations in a way most justly calculated to bring down upon it the jibing and jeers of its enemies
and the regret of all good men. . . . The Government should have
taken possession of the lands, divided them out into five-acre
lots, and distributed them among those persons who had, by
dint of daily and long continued toil, created all the wealth of
the South. . . .

No such plan was adopted. . . . The plantations were leased out
to avaricious adventurers from the North, whose sole desire was
to *exploit* the services of the freedmen, and make out of their labor
as much money as possible. The slaves were made serfs and chained
to the soil. . . . Such was the boasted freedom acquired by the
colored man at the hands of the "Yankees." . . .

It is not too late for the Government to adopt the correct
policy in this matter. Sooner or later, this division of property
must come about; and the sooner, the better. The land tillers
are entitled by a paramount right to the possession of the soil
they have so long cultivated. . . . If the Government will not
give them the land, let it be rented to them. It is folly now to
deny the Rebellion and not accept all its logical results. Revo-
lutions never go backward. . . . Give the men of color an equal
chance; and this is all they ask. . . . Let us create a new class of
landholders, who shall be interested in the permanent establish-
ment of a new and truly republican system—the prize for which
we are now fighting—and we are sure to succeed.[6]

*Congress and the Lincoln administration were unresponsive
to the more extreme demands for confiscation. But a limited
degree of expropriation was accomplished during the Civil War.
The Confiscation Act of July 17, 1862, provided for the expropriation of all property belonging to traitors. Lincoln objected,*

*however, that this provision violated the constitutional prohi-
bition of bills of attainder that worked forfeiture of property
beyond the life of offenders, and Congress passed a joint resolution stating that nothing in the act should be construed to
work a forfeiture of real estate beyond the life of the offender.
This meant that when the original Confederate owner died, his
confiscated property would revert to his heirs. No effectual land
reform could be based on this legislation, and in fact only a
relatively small amount of property was expropriated and sold
to new owners under the act of July 1862. Later Congressional
efforts to modify or amend the act to provide for permanent
confiscation failed of passage.[7]*

*Meanwhile, a small degree of expropriation was accom-
plished through confiscatory taxation. In August 1861 Congress
levied a direct tax on every state to raise revenue for the war
effort. Of course this tax could not be collected in most parts of
the South, and an act of June 7, 1862, authorized the President
to appoint tax commissioners to determine the amount of taxes
owed by occupied areas of the Confederacy and to offer the land
of delinquent taxpayers for sale at public auction. This policy
was actually carried out on a large scale on the South Carolina
Sea Islands. In March 1863, 16,749 acres of abandoned plantation lands were put up for general sale. About two thousand
acres were purchased by freedmen who had laboriously saved
their wages and pooled their savings. The rest of the land was
bought by Northern investors and speculators. The sale of nearly
90 per cent of the auctioned property to well-heeled outsiders
created considerable dissatisfaction among the freedmen and
their Northern teachers on the islands. The government still held
60,000 acres of land on the islands for nonpayment of taxes,
and on December 31, 1863, these teachers and missionaries
managed to obtain a government order allowing Negro heads of
families to pre-empt any of this land up to forty acres apiece
for a nominal price of $1.25 per acre. But the tax commission-
ers rebelled at this order, and with the aid of wealthy Northern
investors they secured its rescindment. At a second public auc-*

tion on February 18, 1864, the freedmen were able to buy only about 2,750 acres.[8]

Some Negroes who had saved a little money but who were unable to pay competitive prices for the land on which they had worked most of their lives were sadly disappointed by this turn of events. One of them, Don Carlos Butler, dictated the following letter to President Lincoln on May 29, 1864:

I Hope my letter will find you and your family in perfect health. Will you please to be so kind, Sir as to tell me whether the land will be sold from under us or no, or whether it will be sold to us at all. I should like to buy the very spot where I live. It ain't but six acres, and I have got cotton planted on it, and very fine cotton too; and potatoes and corn coming on very pretty. If we colored people have land I know we shall do very well—there is no fear of that. Some of us have as much as three acres of corn, besides ground-nuts, potatoes, peas, and I don't know what else myself. If the land can only be sold we can buy it all, for every house has its cotton planted, and doing well, and planted only for ourselves. We should like to know how much we shall have to pay for it—if it is sold.

I am pretty well struck in age Sir, for I waited upon Mrs. Alston that was Theodosia Burr, daughter of Aaron Burr, and I remember well when she was taken by pirates.—but I can maintain myself and my family well on this land. My son got sick on the Wabash (Flagship at Hilton Head) and he will never get well, for he has a cough that will kill him at last. He cannot do much work, but I can maintain him. I had rather work for myself and raise my own cotton than work for a gentleman for wages for if I could sell my cotton for [illegible] cents a pound it would pay me.

Whatever you say I am willing to do and I will attend to whatever you tell me.[9]

Another freedman on the islands dictated a letter to a former teacher who had returned to Philadelphia. The writer of the letter put down the words exactly as dictated, retaining the peculiar Sea Island dialect:

MY DEAR YOUNG MISSUS: I been a elder in de church, and sper-
etual fader to a hep of gals no older dan oona [you]. I know dat
womens has feelin' hearts, and dat de men will heardy de voice
of a gal when dey too hard head for mind dose dat has more
wisdom. So I bin a beg one of dese yere little white sisters in
the church, dat de Lord sends from the Nort for school we chilen, to write to oona for me to ax of oona if oona so please an'
will be so kind, my missus, to speak to Linkum and tell him for
we how we po' folks tank him and de Lord for we great privilege
to see de happy day when we can talk to de white folks and
make known to de Gov'ment what we wants. *Do*, my missus,
tell Linkum dat we wants land—dis bery land dat is rich wid de
sweat ob we face and de blood ob we back. We born here; we
parents' graves here; we donne oder country; dis yere our home.
De Nort folks hab home, antee? What a pity dat dey don't love
der home like we love we home, for den dey would neber come
here for buy all way from we.

Do, my missus, beg Linkum for lef us room for buy land and
live here. We don't ask for it for notins. We too tankful. We too
satisfy to pay just what de rich buckra pay. But dey done buy
too much a'ready, and lef we no chance. We could a bin buy all
we want, but dey make de lots too big, and cut we out.

De word cum from Massa Linkum's self, dat we take out
claims and hold on ter um, an' plant um, and he will see dat we
get um, every man ten or twenty acre. We too glad. We stake
out an' list, but fore de time for plant, dese missionaries [tax
commissioners] sells to white folks all de best land. Where
Linkum? We cry to him, but he too far for hear we. Dey keep
us back, and we can't tell him self. Do missus speak ter um for
we, an' ax Linkum for stretch out he hand an' make dese yer
missionaries cut de land so dat we able for buy. Dey good and
wise men, may be, but ax Linkum for send us *his* word, and den
we satisfy. Our men—ebery able bodied man from we island—
bin a fight for dere country in Florida, at Fort Wagner; any
where dat Govment send um. But his dere country. Dey want
land *here*, for dere wives to work. Look at de fiels! No more but
womens and chilens, all de men gone to fight, and while dey

gone de land sold from dere families to rich white buckra to
scrape, and neber live on. Dey runs to de Nort; dey can't live
here. What dey want to carry from we all de witeness of de
land, and leave we for Govment to feed.

I tell you all stinctually and punctually. Speak softly next
time you meets Massa Linkum. Talk him bout me, and de Lord
will keep you warm under he feathers, he will gather oona to
he breast, for he love dem what help de poor. My best respects,
and ober huddy from Uncle Smart X his mark.[10]

*Lincoln was unable to satisfy these requests, but Sea Island
Negroes did manage in subsequent years to buy several thousand acres from the original Northern wartime purchasers.
Black people on the Sea Islands probably owned more land per
capita in 1870 than Negroes in any other part of the South.
Meanwhile the possibility of a truly revolutionary land reform
program had been created by General William T. Sherman's
famous "Order No. 15" of January 16, 1865. As Sherman
marched through Georgia in the last weeks of 1864, thousands
of ragged and destitute freedmen fell in behind his troops. When
the army reached Savannah the problem of taking care of these
refugees became critical. General Sherman and Secretary of
War Stanton held a conference on January 12 with twenty Negro ministers and church officials of Savannah, fifteen of whom
were former slaves. In response to one of Stanton's questions,
the spokesman for the Negroes replied:*

The way we can best take care of ourselves is to have land,
and turn in and till it by our labor—that is, by the labor of the
women, and children, and old men—and we can soon maintain
ourselves and have something to spare; and to assist the Government, the young men should enlist in the service of the Government, and serve in such manner as they may be wanted. . . .
We want to be placed on land until we are able to buy it, and
make it our own.[11]

*Four days after this conference, Sherman issued his "Special
Field Order No. 15," which designated the coastline and river-
banks thirty miles inland from Charleston to Jacksonville as
an area for exclusive Negro settlement. Freedmen settling in*

this area could take up not more than forty acres of land per family, to which they would be given "possessory titles" until Congress "shall regulate the title." General Rufus Saxton was authorized to supervise the settlement of the Negroes on the land, and by the end of June 1865, more than forty thousand freedmen had moved onto their new farms. But this great experiment was destroyed by President Andrew Johnson, who in August 1865 issued orders of pardon and restoration of property to the former Confederate owners of these lands. Most of the forty thousand freedmen were turned off their farms, some of them at bayonet point, and although Congress passed legislation granting the evicted Negroes an option to purchase other government-owned land in the South, most of these freedmen were compelled by circumstances to go to work for the white plantation owners. It was a tragic end to a hopeful experiment.[12]

Fifteen years after the end of the war, Frederick Douglass surveyed the failure of Reconstruction and the subordinate position of his people in the South. He cited the refusal of the government to provide the freedmen with an opportunity to obtain good land of their own as the main reason for the Negro's helplessness in 1880. Said Douglass:

Could the nation have been induced to listen to those stalwart Republicans, Thaddeus Stevens and Charles Sumner [who had favored the confiscation of Confederate estates], some of the evils which we now suffer would have been averted. The negro would not today be on his knees, as he is, supplicating the old master class to give him leave to toil. . . . He would not now be swindled out of his hard earnings by money orders for wages with no money in them . . . as is now the case because left by our emancipation measures at the mercy of the men who had robbed him all his life and his people for centuries.[13]

CHAPTER XXI

THE NEGRO'S ATTITUDE

TOWARD LINCOLN, 1864–65

In September 1863 the Brooklyn correspondent of the Christian Recorder *declared:*

I am of the opinion that it is the duty of every colored man to uphold the present administration, because it is doing more for his race than has ever been done since the organization of the government. Never has a President, or cabinet officer stood forth to vindicate the rights of black men before. Never before have black men been recognized as citizens by the Secretary of State, and the giving of passports to them when embarking for foreign ports. Then the recognition of the republics of Liberia and Hayti, the acceptance of ambassadors from these countries, all demonstrate that this administration is the friend of the black race, and desires its prosperity no less than the good of all the races of men.[1]

Even though they could not vote in the presidential election, a mass meeting of San Francisco Negroes unanimously adopted a resolution on New Year's Day, 1864, endorsing Lincoln's re-election to the presidency. In an editorial supporting the resolution, the Pacific Appeal *stated:*

The nomination of Mr. Lincoln by acclamation, at the celebration held on January 1st . . . in commemoration of the Emancipation Proclamation . . . was a tribute of respect and the high appreciation felt by the colored citizens of San Francisco for him. They were made happy in this opportunity to bestow a humble mark of their approbation. He is the man who, of all others who have occupied the Presidential chair, since the formation of the Government or the adoption of the Constitution, has stood up in defiance of the slave-power, and dared officially to maintain the doctrine, by his official actions, that we are citizens, though of African descent—that the army and navy shall protect and defend such citizens in common with all others—that provision ought to be made for the education of freedmen. . . . For these, and other more weighty reasons, we have duly considered him to be the right man in the right place in the present crisis, and also the man to fill the Presidential chair in 1864.[2]

These statements probably expressed the feelings of a majority of American Negroes toward Lincoln. But a militant minority of black leaders in the North and in New Orleans were critical of the President because of his seemingly conservative approach to the questions of Reconstruction and Negro suffrage. The New Orleans Tribune *was bitter toward Lincoln because of the President's support of General Banks and of the Louisiana constitution of 1864, which excluded black men from the suffrage. "The history of Louisiana for the past year," said the* Tribune *on August 13, 1864,*

shows conclusively what the truly loyal men of the State have to expect, from a reorganization under the auspices of the Executive and his martial law. . . . The Constitution they have made was conceived in the fraudulent design of getting up a sham electoral ticket in Louisiana; carried through by military violence against the will of the people; had root in no lawful authority, *being based on Executive usurpation*; contrary to the expressed will of Congress [Congress had tried to controvert Lincoln's "ten per cent" plan by passage of the Wade-Davis bill, which Lincoln vetoed], and framed by men who had no higher principle of action than hatred of their fellows of African descent.

Two weeks later the Tribune *denounced Lincoln in strong editorial language:*

If "our Southern Brethren" had desired a conservative President in 1860, neither North nor South of the Potomac could they have found one who would have more zealously protected their rights of property in man; no one who would have lent the whole weight of the executive of the nation to the rigid enforcement of the Fugitive Slave Act; no one who would have preserved more inviolate the rights of the people of the Southern States under the Constitution than Abraham Lincoln. As for proof, we refer to his conduct in the executive chair from the 4th of March, 1861, down to the present time.

But perhaps of all the instances of this "Conservatism" which is now deluging the country with blood and continuing indefinitely the duration of the war, when bold, decisive, thoroughgoing measures would long since have ended it, the most remarkable one is that which took place in [August], 1862, in Washington. A delegation of free people of color waited upon the President at the White House. After a polite reception, the following extraordinary language was addressed to these representatives of citizens touching the colonization of Chiriqui: "Had it not been for the presence of your race upon this Continent, there would have been no war between the North and the South."

The editorial concluded that if the black people wanted justice, they would have to find another president.[3]

Some Northern Negroes concurred with the Tribune. *They pointed to Lincoln's reluctance to take decisive action against slavery in 1861–62, his suppression of emancipation edicts issued by his generals, his efforts to colonize the Negroes, the injustices to black troops, and Lincoln's reconstruction policy which would restore the former rebels to power and leave the freedman little more than a peon on the soil of his old master. A few white radicals agreed with the Negro militants, and these radicals met in Cleveland on May 31, 1864, to nominate John C. Fremont for the presidency on a platform of equal rights for the Negroes of the South. Frederick Douglass endorsed the Cleveland convention in a public letter:*

I mean the complete abolition of every vestige, form and modification of Slavery in every part of the United States, perfect equality for the black man in every State before the law, in the jury box, at the ballot-box and on the battle-field; ample and salutary retaliation for every instance of enslavement or slaughter of prisoners of color. I mean that in the distribution of offices and honors under this Government no discrimination shall be made in favor of or against any class of citizens, whether black or white, of native or foreign birth. And supposing that the Convention which is to meet at Cleveland means the same thing, I cheerfully give my name as one of the signers of the call.[4]

Several other prominent Negroes supported the Fremont nomination, but most black men probably agreed with William Howard Day of Brooklyn, who admitted that Lincoln was not quite up to the radical mark, but believed nevertheless that he should be re-elected. "I feel," said Mr. Day,

that much of the failure of Mr. Lincoln to do [his] duty is owing to the failure of the people of the land whose agent he is. Do we complain that Mr. Lincoln and the government do not recognize the manhood of the negro? Let us find the cause of that in the people at home. Just so long as citizens of New York exclude respectable colored persons from railway cars on the streets; just so long as the people of the city exclude the colored children from the ward schools, and force the colored children from several wards together, on the ground of color merely; just so long as even in some of the churches of the city there are negro pews—just so long as there is evidence that the people themselves do not recognize the manhood of the black man of this country.[5]

Democrats were happy about Fremont's nomination, for it opened up the possibility of a Democratic victory over a divided Republican party in the presidential election in November. Negroes realized this, and many of them agreed with the Rev. J. Sella Martin, who said in June:

I am for Mr. Lincoln against Copperheadism, as threatened in a coalition with Mr. Fremont. . . . As a negro, I am for the man whose party and policy have given us a free capital, a confiscation law, and a proclamation of freedom, as against the man who, with honest enough intentions, expects to drive out devils by Beelzebub.[6]

*Though they could not vote, Baltimore Negroes expressed their
sympathy and support for the President in September by the
presentation to Lincoln of an elegantly bound Bible as a gift
from the black people of Baltimore. The Bible had cost $580.75,
and on the cover was a design showing Lincoln in a cotton field
striking the shackles from the wrists of a slave. The Bible was
presented to the President on September 7 by the Rev. S. M.
Chase, who said:*

Mr. President: The loyal colored people of Baltimore have
entrusted us with authority to present this Bible as a testimonial
of their appreciation of your humane conduct towards the people of our race. . . . Since our incorporation into the American
family we have been true and loyal, and we are now ready to
aid in defending the country, to be armed and trained in military
matters, in order to assist in protecting and defending the star
spangled banner.

Towards you, sir, our hearts will ever be warm with gratitude. We come to present to you this copy of the Holy Scrip-
tures, as a token of respect for your active participation in
furtherance of the cause of the emancipation of our race. This
great event will be a matter of history. Hereafter when our children shall ask what mean these tokens, they will be told of your
worthy deeds, and will rise up and call you blessed.

The loyal colored people of this country everywhere will remember you at the Throne of Divine Grace. May the King Eternal, and all wise Providence protect and keep you, and when
you pass from this world to that of eternity, may you be borne
to the bosom of your Savior and your God.[7]

*Two events at the end of August and the beginning of Septem-
ber radically changed the political situation and caused all Republicans and Negroes, no matter what their previous opinion
of Lincoln, to unite behind the President. On August 30 the
Democrats nominated George B. McClellan for president on an
anti-emancipation peace platform. And on September 3 the
prestige of the Lincoln administration, which had sunk to an
all-time low in August, rocketed to a new high upon receipt of
the news of the fall of Atlanta to Sherman's army. Lincoln was*

now head of a victorious nation, and McClellan symbolized defeatism and despair. Lincoln stood for emancipation; McClellan stood for the continuance of slavery. All factions of the Republican party united behind Lincoln as the only alternative to McClellan and disaster. Fremont withdrew from the race. Frederick Douglass came out for Lincoln in a public letter dated September 17:

While there was, or seemed to be, the slightest possibility of securing the nomination and election of a man to the Presidency of more decided anti-slavery convictions and a firmer faith in the immediate necessity and practicability of justice and equality for all men, than have been exhibited in the policy of the present administration, I, like many other radical men, freely criticized, in private and in public, the actions and utterances of Mr. Lincoln, and withheld from him my support. That possibility is now no longer conceivable; it is now plain that this country is to be governed or misgoverned during the next four years, either by the Republican Party represented in the person of Abraham Lincoln, or by the (miscalled) Democratic Party, represented by George B. McClellan. With this alternative clearly before us, all hesitation ought to cease, and every man who wishes well to the slave and to the country should at once rally with all the warmth and earnestness of his nature to the support of Abraham Lincoln.[8]

Douglass stated privately in October: "I now look upon the election of Mr. Lincoln as settled. When there was any shadow of a hope that a man of more decided anti-slavery conviction and policy could be elected, I was not for Mr. Lincoln. But as soon as the Chicago convention, my mind was made up, and it is made still. All dates changed with the nomination of Mr. McClellan."[9]

Robert Hamilton, publisher of the Anglo-African, *told Northern Negroes in September:*

You and we may have thought that Mr. Lincoln has not done what *we think* he could have done for the overthrow of oppression in our land; *but that is not the question now.* The great and overshadowing inquiry is, *do you want to see the many noble acts which have been passed during Mr. Lincoln's administration repealed, and slavery fastened again upon Maryland, Louisiana, Tennessee, Virginia and portions of States now free?* This is the only question now, and if you are a friend of liberty you will give your influence and cast your vote for Abraham Lincoln, who, under God, is the only hope of the oppressed.[10]

James Ruffin, a Negro soldier stationed in South Carolina, wrote to his sister on October 16: "We are all for Old Abe. I hope he will be elected. Let the colored men at home do their duty."[11] Nearly every Northern Negro who possessed the franchise cast his ballot in November for Abraham Lincoln. If Southern Negroes could have voted, they would have done the same. Black men in Nashville held a mock election in November, and the result was: Lincoln, 3,193 votes; McClellan, 1 vote.[12]

After Lincoln's re-election some black men continued to worry about the President's conservatism on the Reconstruction issue. But there were signs in the spring of 1865 that the flexible, pragmatic Lincoln would go at least halfway to meet the demands of Negroes and radicals on this matter. The President's assassination on April 14 came as a shattering blow to every black man in America. Freedmen on the South Carolina Sea Islands were filled with despair and disbelief when they heard of Lincoln's death. One of them, Jack Flowers, who had taken great risks to escape from slavery, told a Northern teacher after the assassination: "I 'spect it's no use to be here. I might as well stayed where I was. It 'pears we can't be free, nohow. The rebs won't let us alone. If they can't kill us, they'll kill all our frien's, sure."[13] The Negroes of Mitchelville, a freedmen's village on Hilton Head Island, South Carolina, adopted the following resolutions:

Resolved, That we, the representatives of Mitchelville, look upon the death of the Chief Magistrate of our country as a national calamity, and an irrepressible loss beyond the power of words to express, covering the land with gloom and sorrow, mourning and desolation. An event so appalling as the assassination of our beloved President we feel to be a fitting memento of the bloody times in which we live. . . .

Resolved, That viewing the wisdom and Christian patriotism displayed by the President in the management of the terribly bloody conflict in which the nation has been engaged during the past four years, and of that most memorable act proclaiming *Liberty* to our race, we would not fail to acknowledge the hand of Almighty God, who has crowned the career of this great and good man with a blessed immortality, sealed by his blood, and embalmed him in the memory of future generations.[14]

The New Orleans Tribune, *which had been sharply critical of Lincoln the previous summer, now expressed heartfelt sorrow at the loss of a great leader:*

Brethren, we are mourning for a benefactor of our race. Sadness has taken hold of our hearts. No man can suppress his feeling at this hour of affliction. Lincoln and John Brown are two martyrs, whose memories will live united in our bosoms. Both have willingly jeopardized their lives for the sacred cause of freedom.[15]

And Edgar Dinsmore, a Negro soldier from New York stationed at Charleston, summed up the feelings of his race in a letter to his fiancée:

We mourn for the loss of our great and good President as a loss irreparable. Humanity has lost a firm advocate, our race its Patron Saint, and the good of all the world a fitting object to emulate. . . . The name Abraham Lincoln will ever be cherished in our hearts, and none will more delight to lisp his name in reverence than the future generations of our people.[16]

CHAPTER XXII

THE NEGRO FACES THE FUTURE

Except for the sorrow pro-
duced by Lincoln's assassination, the mood of the Negro at the
end of the war was optimistic. Ever since 1862, when it became
apparent that the war would work a revolution in the status of
American Negroes, the hopes of black men had been building
up until they reached a crescendo of fervent expectations in
1865. As early as August 1862, Philip Bell, editor of the Pacific
Appeal, *said that*

we are . . . filled with joy in view of the future which is now
dawning on our hitherto benighted prospects. . . . We feel that
there is some happiness yet in store for us: our countrymen are
repenting of the great sin they have committed against us for
centuries, and the good time is coming when the colored American will be recognized as one of the free institutions of the
land; when it will no longer be a disgrace to own that we have
African blood in our veins.[1]

In May 1863 Robert Purvis declared that
this is a proud day for the "colored" man. For the first time
since this [American Anti-Slavery] Society was organized, I stand
before you a recognized citizen of the United States. (Applause.)
And, let me add, for the first time since your government was
a government, it is an honor to be a citizen of the United States!
Sir, old things are passing away, all things are becoming new.
Now a black man has rights, under this government, which every

white man, here and everywhere, is bound to respect. (Applause.) The damnable doctrine of the detestable Taney is no longer the doctrine of the country. The Slave Power no longer rules at Washington. The slaveholders and their miserable allies are biting the dust. . . .

Sir, I know very well that this government is not yet all that it ought to be. . . . But, sir, these gentlemen have in a signal manner recognized my rights, and the rights of my oppressed countrymen. They have officially invested us with the prerogatives of which we have been basely robbed, and I would be false to my nature, false to my convictions, false to my best feelings, did I not thus publicly testify my sense of respect and heartfelt gratitude. . . .

You know, Mr. Chairman, how bitterly I used to denounce the United states as the basest despotism the sun ever shone upon; and I take nothing back that ever I said. When this government was, as it used to be, a slaveholding oligarchy . . . I hated it with a wrath which words could not express, and I denounced it with all the bitterness of my indignant soul. . . . I was a victim, stricken, degraded, injured, insulted in my person, in my family, in my friends, in my estate; I returned bitterness for bitterness, and scorn for scorn. . . . [But now] I forget the past; joy fills my soul at the prospect of the future.

. . . The good time which has so long been coming is at hand. I feel it, I see it in the air, I read it in the signs of the times; I see it in the acts of Congress, in the abolition of slavery in the District of Columbia, in its exclusion from the Territories, in solemn treaties for the effectual suppression of the infernal foreign slave trade, in the acknowledgement of the black republics of Hayti and Liberia. I see it in the new spirit that is in the army; I see it in the black regiment of South Carolina—(applause); I see it in the 54th Regiment of Massachusetts; I see it in the order of Adjutant-General Thomas, forming a black brigade at Memphis; I see it, above all, and more than all, in THE GLORIOUS AND IMMORTAL PROCLAMATION OF ABRAHAM LINCOLN ON THE FIRST OF JANUARY, 1863. (Cheers.) . . . In *spirit* and in *purpose*, thanks to *Almighty God!* this is no longer a slaveholding republic. The fiat has gone forth which, when this rebellion is crushed, . . . in the simple but beautiful language of the President, "will take all burdens from off all backs, and make every man a freeman."[2]

James F. Jones, a soldier in the Fourteenth Rhode Island Heavy Artillery (black), wrote in June 1864:

I think, Mr. Editor, that, under God, this will yet be a pleasant land for the colored man to dwell in, the declarations of colonizationists to the contrary, notwithstanding. Step by step we are emerging from darkness into light. One by one the scales that have so long blinded our race—ignorance and superstition— are falling off; prejudice, with all its concomitant evils, is fast giving way; men begin to reason and think of us in a rational and religious way. As a people, we begin to think of our race as something more than vassals, and goods, and chattels; and with this increasing good opinion of ourselves, we will make all people respect us.[3]

And in February 1865 the Christian Recorder *published an editorial entitled "Retrospect":*

When we reflect upon the condition and position of the African race, at the present time, contrasted with that presented to the inquisitive gaze of a world four years ago, well may we boast of being in the ascendant. Having been weighed in the balance and found not wanting, the opportunity was allowed us to make advancement in a moral, social, and political point of view, and with what rapid strides have we progressed.

Within two years the standard of "Justice" has been raised in our favor; an admission of our valor, our manhood, our courage, has been made by our former oppressors; *partial* equality has been extended to us, and our rights as citizens have been recognized, in a great measure. . . . The white soldiers of our army find us an indispensable acquisition to their numbers, and fear not to fight upon the same ground with us. . . .

A retrospective view of the past satisfies me that we are on the *advance*, in a military point of view, and I am convinced by force of circumstances, that it remains with ourselves to further the cause of universal Freedom and Justice. Let every man then "bear a hand" an be united, and by untiring effort on our parts, we may yet behold Ethiopia stretch forth her hands.[4]

But in the next four decades these hopes were destined to turn sour and the expectations to become bitter. After the withdrawal of Federal troops from the South and the end of Reconstruction in the 1870s, the white people of the South proceeded to segregate, subordinate, disfranchise, and frequently to lynch Negroes. By 1900 the militancy, determination, and courage that had characterized black men of the Civil War generation seemed to have been crushed out of Southern Negroes. In 1902 Susie King Taylor, who had escaped from slavery in 1862 and had served during the rest of the war as a laundress and teacher in Higginson's Negro regiment, wrote an analysis of the race issue in America which can perhaps stand as the best conclusion to a book on the Negro in the Civil War:

My dear friends! do we understand the meaning of war? Do we know or think of that war of '61? No, we do not, only those brave soldiers, and those who had occasion to be in it, can realize what it was. I can and shall never forget that terrible war until my eyes close in death. The scenes are just as fresh in my mind to-day as in '61. I see now each scene,—the roll-call, the drum tap, "lights out," the call at night when there was danger from the enemy, the double force of pickets, the cold and rain. How anxious I would be, not knowing what would happen before morning! . . . It was mostly at night that our men went out for their scouts, and often had a hand to hand fight with the rebels, and although our men came out sometimes with a few killed or wounded, none of them ever were captured.

We do not, as the black race, properly appreciate the old veterans, white or black, as we ought to. I know what they went through, especially those black men, for the Confederates had no mercy on them. . . . I have seen the terrors of that war. I was the wife of one of those men who did not get a penny for eighteen months for their services. . . .

I look around now and see the comforts that our younger generation enjoy, and think of the blood that was shed to make these comforts possible for them, and see how little some of them appreciate the old soldiers. . . . There are only a few of them left now, so let us all, as the ranks close, take a deeper interest in them. Let the younger generation take an interest also, and remember that it was through the efforts of these veterans that they and we older ones enjoy our liberty to-day. . . .

Living here in Boston where the black man is given equal justice, I must say a word on the general treatment of my race, both in the North and South, in this twentieth century. I wonder if our white fellow men realize the true sense or meaning of brotherhood? For two hundred years we had toiled for them; the war of 1861 came and was ended, and we thought our race was forever freed from bondage, and that the two races could live in unity with each other, but when we read almost every day of what is being done to my race by some whites in the South, I sometimes ask, "Was the war in vain? Has it brought freedom, in the full sense of the word, or has it not make our condition more hopeless?"

In this "land of the free" we are burned, tortured, and denied a fair trial, murdered for any imaginary wrong conceived in the brain of the negro-hating white man. There is no redress for us from a government which promised to protect all under its flag. It seems a mystery to me. They say, "One flag, one nation, one country indivisible." Is this true? Can we say this truthfully, when one race is allowed to burn, hang, and inflict the most horrible torture weekly, monthly, on another? No we cannot sing, "My country, 't is of thee, Sweet land of Liberty"! It is hollow mockery. The Southland laws are all on the side of the white, and they do just as they like to the negro, whether in the right or not. . . .

I may not live to see it, but the time is approaching when the South will again have cause to repent for the blood it has shed of innocent black men, for their blood cries out for vengeance. . . . All we ask for is "equal justice," the same that is accorded to all other races who come to this country, of their free will (not forced to, as we were), and are allowed to enjoy every privilege, unrestricted, while we are denied what is rightfully our own in a country which the labor of our forefathers helped to make what it is. . . .

I read an article, which said the ex-Confederate Daughters

had sent a petition to the managers of the local theatres in Tennessee to prohibit the performance of "Uncle Tom's Cabin," claiming that it was exaggerated (that is, the treatment of the slaves), and would have a very bad effect on the children who might see the drama. I paused and thought back a few years of the heart-rending scenes I have witnessed; I have seen many times, when I was a mere girl, thirty or forty men, handcuffed, and as many women and children, come every first Tuesday of each month from Mr. Wiley's trade office to the auction blocks. . . .

Do these Confederate Daughters ever send petitions to prohibit the atrocious lynchings and wholesale murdering and torture of the negro? Do you ever hear of them fearing this would have a bad effect on the children? . . . It does not seem as if our land is yet civilized. It is like times long past, when rulers and high officers had to flee for their lives, and the negro has been dealt with in the same way since the war by those he lived with and toiled for two hundred years or more. . . .

There are still good friends to the negro. Why, there are still thousands that have not bowed to Baal. . . . Man thinks two hundred years is a long time, and it is, too; but it is only as a week to God, and in his own time—I know I shall not live to see the day, but it will come—the South will be like the North, and when it comes it will be prized higher than we prize the North to-day. God is just; when he created man he made him in his image, and never intended one should misuse the other. All men are born free and equal in his sight.[5]

APPENDICES

NOTES

A NOTE ON SOURCES

AN AFTERWORD
ON BIBLIOGRAPHY

INDEX

APPENDIX A: NEGRO AND WHITE POPULATION OF THE UNITED STATES IN 1860
(Compiled from the Census Returns of 1860)

STATE	NEGRO		WHITE	TOTAL
	Slave	*Free*		
UNITED STATES	3,953,760	488,070	26,922,537	31,364,367
FREE STATES	18	225,224	18,512,183	18,737,425
SLAVE STATES	3,950,511	250,787	7,936,619	12,127,977
NEW ENGLAND		24,711	3,110,480	3,135,191
Maine		1,327	626,947	628,274
New Hampshire		494	325,579	326,073
Vermont		709	314,369	315,078
Massachusetts		9,602	1,221,432	1,231,034
Rhode Island		3,952	170,649	174,601
Connecticut		8,627	451,504	460,131
MIDDLE ATLANTIC	18	131,272	7,327,548	7,458,838
New York		49,005	3,831,590	3,880,595
New Jersey	18	25,318	646,699	672,035
Pennsylvania		56,949	2,849,259	2,906,208
EAST NORTH CENTRAL		63,699	6,855,644	6,919,343
Ohio		36,673	2,302,808	2,339,481
Indiana		11,248	1,338,710	1,350,138
Illinois		7,628	1,704,291	1,711,919
Michigan		6,799	736,142	742,941
Wisconsin		1,171	773,693	774,864
WEST NORTH CENTRAL	114,931	4,900	1,906,583	2,026,414
Minnesota		259	169,395	169,654
Iowa		1,069	673,779	674,848
Missouri	114,931	3,572	1,063,409	1,181,912
SOUTH ATLANTIC	1,837,260	196,622	3,144,344	5,178,226
Delaware	1,798	19,829	90,589	112,216
Maryland	87,189	83,942	515,918	687,049
Virginia	490,865	58,042	1,047,299	1,588,206
North Carolina	331,059	30,463	629,942	991,464
South Carolina	402,406	9,914	291,300	703,620
Georgia	462,198	3,500	491,550	957,248
Florida	61,745	932	77,746	140,423

STATE	NEGRO		WHITE	TOTAL
	Slave	*Free*		
EAST SOUTH CENTRAL	1,372,913	21,447	2,626,376	4,019,736
Kentucky	225,483	10,684	919,484	1,155,651
Tennessee	275,719	7,300	826,722	1,108,741
Alabama	435,080	2,690	526,271	964,041
Mississippi	436,631	773	353,899	791,303
WEST SOUTH CENTRAL	625,407	19,146	1,102,490	1,727,043
Arkansas	111,115	144	324,143	435,402
Louisiana	331,726	18,647	357,456	708,002
Texas	182,566	355	420,891	603,812
PACIFIC		4,214	375,337	379,451
Oregon		128	52,160	52,188
California		4,086	323,177	327,263
DISTRICT OF COLUMBIA	3,185	11,131	60,763	75,079
TERRITORIES	46	928	310,316	311,290
Nebraska	15	67	28,696	28,778
Kansas	2	625	106,390	107,017
Colorado		46	34,231	34,277
New Mexico		85	82,924	83,009
Utah	29	30	40,125	40,184
Nevada		45	6,812	6,857
Washington		30	11,138	11,168

APPENDIX B: NEGRO AND WHITE POPULATION OF SELECTED AMERICAN CITIES IN 1860
(Compiled from the Census Returns of 1860)

STATE	NEGRO		WHITE	TOTAL
	Slave	*Free*		
Baltimore	2,218	25,680	184,520	212,418
Boston		2,261	175,579	177,840
Brooklyn		4,313	262,348	266,661
Buffalo		809	80,320	81,129
Charleston, S.C.	13,909	3,237	23,376	40,522
Chicago		955	108,305	109,260
Cincinnati		3,731	157,313	161,044
Cleveland		799	42,168	42,967
Columbus		997	17,557	18,554
Detroit		1,403	44,216	45,619
Harrisburg		1,321	12,084	13,405
Louisville	4,903	1,917	61,213	68,033
Memphis	3,684	198	18,741	22,623
Mobile	7,587	817	20,854	29,258
Nashville	3,226	719	13,043	16,988
New Bedford, Mass.		1,515	20,785	22,300
New Haven		1,488	37,779	39,267
New Orleans	13,385	10,689	144,601	168,675
New York		12,472	793,186	805,658
Newark		1,287	70,654	71,941
Philadelphia		22,185	543,344	565,529
Pittsburgh		1,154	48,063	49,217
Providence		1,537	49,129	50,666
Richmond	11,699	2,576	23,635	37,910
St. Louis	1,542	1,755	157,476	160,773
San Francisco		1,176	52,866	54,042
Savannah	7,712	705	13,875	22,292
Wilmington, Del.	4	2,210	19,044	21,258

NOTES

PREFACE TO THE FIRST EDITION

1. W. E. Woodward, *Meet General Grant* (New York, 1928), p. 237.

2. Stephens' speech was reprinted in Edward McPherson, *The Political History of the United States of America, during the Great Rebellion* (Washington, 1865), pp. 103–4.

3. *Principia*, June 11, 1863.

4. *Congressional Globe*, 38 Cong., 1 Sess., p. 1444.

CHAPTER I
THE ELECTION OF 1860 AND THE COMING OF WAR

1. James M. McPherson, *The Struggle for Equality: Abolitionists and the Negro in the Civil War and Reconstruction* (Princeton, 1964), pp. 223–24.

2. *Ibid.*, pp. 10–13, 16–19, 23–25; Greeley's statement quoted from the New York *Tribune*, September 7, 1860.

3. *Anglo-African*, March 17, 1860.

4. Rock's speech to the annual convention of the Massachusetts Anti-Slavery Society, January 27, 1860, printed in the *Liberator*, February 3, 1860.

5. *Liberator*, July 13, 1860.

6. *Douglass' Monthly*, III (June, 1860), 276.

7. *Ibid.*, III (August, 1860), 305.

8. *Ibid.*, III (October, 1860), 338.

9. *Ibid.*, III (October, 1860), 339–40. Gerrit Smith received an undetermined but very small number of votes for the presidency.

10. *Anglo-African*, February 4, 1860; *Douglass' Monthly*, III (August,

1860), 314; *Liberator*, October 19, 1860. See also the *Principia*, September 8, 1860.

11. *Students' Repository*, I (July, 1863), 4. This was originally written in the summer of 1860.

12. *Douglass' Monthly*, III (December, 1860), 370–71.

13. Douglass quoted in the Chicago *Daily Times and Herald*, November 20, 1860; *Anglo-African*, January 19, 1861.

14. *Liberator*, May 18, 1860.

15. *Douglass' Monthly*, III (January, 1861), 392.

16. *Ibid.*, III (January, 1861), 388.

17. *Congressional Globe*, 36 Cong., 2 Sess., pp. 112–14, 237, 1093–94, 1259–61, 1368, 1405.

18. *Liberator*, February 22, 1861.

19. *Ibid.*

20. William Howard Russell, *My Diary North and South* (2 vols., London, 1863), I, 115.

21. *Douglass' Monthly*, III (May, 1861), 451–52.

22. *Ibid.*, III (May, 1861), 450.

23. *Anglo-African*, April 20, 27, 1861.

CHAPTER II
THE NEGRO'S RESPONSE TO THE WAR, 1861

1. Dodson to Simon Cameron, April 23, 1861, in *War of the Rebellion: . . . Official Records of the Union and Confederate Armies* (128 vols., 1880–1901) (hereinafter cited as *O.R.*), Ser. 3, Vol. I, p. 106.

2. Pittsburgh *Gazette*, April 18, 1861.

3. *Liberator*, May 10, 1861.

4. *Ibid.*, April 26, 1861.

5. *Ibid.*, May 17, 1861.

6. Cameron to Dodson, April 29, 1861, *O.R.*, Ser. 3, Vol. I, p. 133.

7. *Liberator*, May 10, 1861.

8. Horace Greeley, *The American Conflict* (2 vols., New York, 1864–67), II, 514–15.

9. Peter H. Clark, *The Black Brigade of Cincinnati* (Cincinnati, 1864), pp. 4–5.

10. Springfield *Republican*, June 8, 1861; Henry Greenleaf Pearson, *The Life of John Andrew* (2 vols., Boston, 1904), I, 248–49.

11. Martin to Douglass, May 9, 1861 in *Douglass' Monthly*, IV (June, 1861), 469.

12. Benjamin Quarles, *The Negro in the Civil War* (Boston, 1953), pp. 35–41; Charles H. Wesley, *The Collapse of the Confederacy* (Washington, 1937), pp. 140–42; James Parton, *General Butler in New Orleans* (Boston, 1864), p. 265.

13. Quarles, *The Negro in the Civil War*, pp. 38–39; quotation from Parton, *Butler in New Orleans*, p. 517.

14. Bernard H. Nelson, "Legislative Control of the Southern Free Negro, 1861–1865," *Catholic Historical Review*, XXXII (April, 1946), 28–46.

15. *O.R.*, Ser. 1, Vol. LI, Pt. ii, pp. 472–73, 633.

16. Reading *Journal*, quoted in *Douglass' Monthly*, IV (March, 1862), 617.

17. James M. McPherson, *The Struggle for Equality: Abolitionists and the Negro in the Civil War and Reconstruction* (Princeton, 1964), pp. 69–70, 72.

18. *Christian Recorder*, May 4, 1861.

19. *Pine and Palm*, May 25, 1861.

20. *Ibid.*

21. *Ibid.*

22. *Anglo-African*, August 24, September 14, 1861.

23. *Ibid.*, September 28, 1861.

24. *Ibid.*, October 12, 1861.

25. *Pine and Palm*, October 12, 1861.

26. Wesley W. Tate of Denver to the editor of the *Pine and Palm*, printed in *ibid.*, November 23, 1861.

27. *Anglo-African*, October 19, 1861.

28. Parham to White, October 12, 1861, Jacob C. White Papers, Howard University Library.

29. Joseph T. Wilson, *The Black Phalanx* (Hartford, 1888), pp. 179–80; Herbert Aptheker, "Negro Casualties in the Civil War," *Journal of Negro History*, XXXII (January, 1947), 49.

30. *Pine and Palm*, November 23, 1861.

CHAPTER III
THE DRIVE FOR EMANCIPATION:
THE NORTHERN SCENE, 1861–65

1. *Anglo-African*, May 11, 1861.

2. *Douglass' Monthly*, III (May, 1861), 451: IV (July, 1861), 486. IV (August, 1861), 502.

3. Montgomery *Advertiser*, November 6, 1861.

4. *Douglass' Monthly*, IV (July, 1861), 481–82.

5. *Liberator*, August 30, 1861.

6. *Anglo-African*, August 17, 1861.

7. *Douglass' Monthly*, IV (August, 1861), 498.

8. Roy P. Basler, ed., *The Collected Works of Abraham Lincoln* (9 vols., New Brunswick, 1955), IV, 506–7, 517–18.

9. *Anglo-African*, September 21, 1861.

10. *Christian Recorder*, October 12, 1861.

11. Quoted in a letter from Lydia Maria Child to John G. Whittier, January 21, 1862, in *Letters of Lydia Maria Child* (Boston, 1883), p. 161. See also Mrs. Child to Gerrit Smith, December 29, 1861, Gerrit Smith Papers, Syracuse University Library.

12. Basler, *Collected Works of Lincoln*, V, 144–46.

13. *Anglo-African*, March 22, 1862.

14. Douglass to Sumner, April 8, 1862, Sumner Papers, Houghton Library, Harvard University.

15. Unknown to Christopher A. Fleetwood, April 12, 1862, Christopher A. Fleetwood Papers, Library of Congress.

16. *Anglo-African*, April 19, 1862.

17. T. Harry Williams, *Lincoln and the Radicals* (Madison, Wis., 1941), pp. 137–38.

18. *Pacific Appeal*, June 14, 1862.

19. *Douglass' Monthly*, V (August, 1862), 692–93.

20. *Ibid.*, V (August, 1862), 694.

21. *Liberator*, August 15, 1862.

22. James M. McPherson, *The Struggle for Equality: Abolitionists and the Negro in the Civil War and Reconstruction* (Princeton, 1964), pp. 110–111.

23. Basler, *Collected Works of Lincoln*, V, 420.

24. Douglass to Smith, September 8, 1862, Smith Papers, Syracuse University Library.

25. Basler, *Collected Works of Lincoln*, V, 433–36.

26. *Douglass' Monthly*, V (October, 1862), 721–22.

27. Henry M. Turner, *The Negro in Slavery, War and Peace* (Philadelphia, 1913), pp. 6–7.

28. *Christian Recorder*, January 10, 1863. Turner was at this time the Washington correspondent of the *Recorder*.

29. *Ibid.*, January 3, 1863.

30. Published in *ibid.*, February 7, 1863.

31. William Lloyd Garrison, Jr., to E. W. Garrison, February 5, 1865, William Lloyd Garrison, Jr., Papers, Smith College Library.

CHAPTER IV
EMANCIPATION IN THE SOUTH, 1861–65

1. William Howard Russell, *My Diary North and South* (2 vols., London, 1863), I. 373.

2. George H. Hepworth, *The Whip, Hoe, and Sword* (Boston, 1864), pp. 159–60.

3. This estimate was made by Herbert Aptheker, *The Negro in the Civil War* (New York, 1938), p. 23.

4. Susie King Taylor, *Reminiscences of My Life in Camp* (Boston, 1902), pp. 7–8.

5. Elizabeth Ware Pearson, ed., *Letters from Port Royal, Written at the Time of the Civil War* (Boston, 1906), p. 63.

6. Charlotte Forten, "Life on the Sea Islands," *Atlantic Monthly*, XIII (May, 1864), 593.

7. Sarah Bradford, *Scenes in the Life of Harriet Tubman* (Auburn, N.Y., 1869), pp. 44–46.

8. Printed in *Anglo-African*, March 1, 1862.

9. Philadelphia *Press*, January 12, 1865.

10. A. K. Farrar to Governor Pettus, July 17, 1862, quoted in Herbert Aptheker, "Notes on Slave Conspiracies in Confederate Mississippi," *Journal of Negro History*, XXIX (January, 1944), 76.

11. Quoted in James Parton, *General Butler in New Orleans* (Boston, 1864), p. 580.

12. Finegan to Gen. Thomas Jordan, March 14, 1863, *O.R.*, Ser. 1, Vol. XIV, p. 228; Walker to Gen. Thomas Jordan, June 17, 1863, *ibid.*, p. 291.

13. *L'Union*, October 18, December 6, 1862. Translated by Roger Des Forges.

14. Quoted in William Wells Brown, *The Negro in the American Rebellion* (Boston, 1867), p. 114.

15. *Liberator*, January 16, 1863.

16. Charlotte Forten, "Life on the Sea Islands," *Atlantic Monthly*, XIII (June, 1864), 668–70.

17. Cooper to Horatio Seymour, September 28, 1863, Seymour Papers, Library of Congress.

18. Story told by Matilda Hatchett in the 1930s, published in B. A. Botkin, ed., *Lay My Burden Down: A Folk History of Slavery* (Chicago, 1945), p. 217.

19. William T. Sherman, *Memoirs of General William T. Sherman* (2 vols., New York, 1886), II, 180.

20. Philadelphia *Press*, April 11, 12, 1865.

CHAPTER V
ANTI-NEGRO MOB VIOLENCE IN THE NORTH, 1862–63

1. See Williston Lofton, "Northern Labor and the Negro during the Civil War," *Journal of Negro History*, XXXIV (July, 1949), 251–73.

2. *Anglo-African*, August 9, 1862.

3. *Christian Recorder*, March 14, 1863.

4. William Wells Brown, *The Negro in the American Rebellion* (New York, 1867), pp. 192–97.

5. *Christian Recorder*, July 25, 1863.

6. Letter to the New Bedford *Standard*, reprinted in the *Pacific Appeal*, August 22, 1863.

7. *Christian Recorder*, July 18, 1863.

8. Published in the *Principia*, January 7, 14, 1864.

CHAPTER VI
THE COLONIZATION ISSUE

1. *Liberator*, May 16, 1862.

2. Leon F. Litwack, *North of Slavery* (Chicago, 1961), pp. 257-62.

3. James Redpath, *A Guide to Hayti* (Boston, 1st ed., 1860, 2nd and 3rd eds., 1861), pp. 9-11.

4. *Ibid.*, p. 9 and *passim*.

5. *Pine and Palm*, June 22, 1861.

6. *Ibid.*

7. *Ibid.*, September 10, 1861.

8. *Liberator*, February 3, 1860.

9. *Douglass' Monthly*, III (January, 1861), 386-87.

10. *Ibid.*, IV (July, 1861), 484.

11. *Anglo-African*, January 5, 12, 1861.

12. *Ibid.*, January 19, 1861.

13. *Ibid.*, January 26, 1861.

14. *Ibid.*, February 16, 1861.

15. *Ibid.*, March 16, 1861.

16. *Ibid.*, November 16, 1861.

17. *Liberator*, October 25, 1861.

18. *Pine and Palm*, June 2, 1861.

19. *Ibid.*, November 16, 1861.

20. *Anglo-African*, March 15, 1862.

21. Parham to Jacob C. White, Jr., August 7, 1863, Jacob C. White Papers, Howard University Library. See also Parham to White, March 5, September 7, 1862, and March (?), 1863, White Papers.

22. *Liberator*, June 12, 1863. See also Willis D. Boyd, "James Redpath and American Negro Colonization in Haiti, 1860-1862," *The Americas*, XII (1955), 169-82.

23. *National Anti-Slavery Standard*, June 28, 1862.

24. Roy P. Basler, ed., *The Collected Works of Abraham Lincoln* (9 vols., New Brunswick, 1955), V, 48.

25. *U.S. Statutes at Large*, XII, 376-78, 582.

26. *Anglo-African*, December 7, 1861.

27. Speech by Rock to the annual convention of the Massachusetts Anti-Slavery Society in Boston, January 23, 1862, printed in the *Liberator*, February 14, 1862.

28. *Ibid.*, May 2, 1862.

29. Basler, *Collected Works of Lincoln*, V, 370–75.

30. *Douglass' Monthly*, V (September, 1862), 707–8.

31. *National Anti-Slavery Standard*, September 6, 1862.

32. *Christian Recorder*, August 23, 1862. Philadelphia Negroes addressed a long Appeal to the President urging him to abandon his colonization ideas. See *An Appeal from the Colored Men of Philadelphia to the President of the United States* (Philadelphia, 1862).

33. *National Anti-Slavery Standard*, September 13, 1862.

34. Paul J. Scheips, "Lincoln and the Chiriqui Colonization Project," *Journal of Negro History*, XXXVII (1950), 419–30.

35. Purvis to Pomeroy, August 28, 1862, printed in the New York *Tribune*, September 20, 1862.

36. Scheips, "Lincoln and Chiriqui Colonization," *loc. cit.*, 430–35.

37. Douglass to Theodore Tilton, October 21, 1862, Douglass Papers, Misc. MSS, New York Historical Society.

38. Willis Boyd, "Negro Colonization in the National Crisis, 1860–1870" (Ph.D. dissertation, UCLA, 1953), pp. 180–208.

39. *National Anti-Slavery Standard*, March 19, 1864.

CHAPTER VII
THE NEGRO'S RESPONSE
TO THE CHARGE OF RACIAL INFERIORITY

1. See James M. McPherson, *The Struggle for Equality: Abolitionists and the Negro in the Civil War and Reconstruction* (Princeton, 1964), Chap. 6.

2. Philip S. Foner, *Life and Writings of Frederick Douglass* (4 vols., New York, 1950–55), II, 294; Purvis to J. Miller McKim, December 2, 1860, J. M. McKim Papers, Cornell University Library.

3. *Liberator*, March 2, 1860.

4. *Ibid.*, July 13, 1860.

5. *Anglo-African*, May 11, 1861.

6. *Pacific Appeal*, May 31, 1862.

7. *Douglass' Monthly*, III (October, 1860), 337.

8. *Ibid.*, IV (March, 1862), 614–15.

9. William Wells Brown, *The Black Man: His Antecedents, His Genius, and His Achievements* (Boston, 1863), pp. 31–50. Brown repeated the substance of these assertions in several lectures during the war.

10. *Anglo-African*, March 17, 1860.

11. *Ibid.*, February 14, 1863.

12. *Liberator*, May 1, 1863.

13. *Christian Recorder*, July 16, 1864.

14. *Pacific Appeal*, October 24 (misdated October 25) and October 31, 1863.

CHAPTER VIII
GOVERNMENT, PHILANTHROPY, AND THE FREEDMEN

1. *Liberator*, January 8, 1864.

2. See George R. Bentley, *A History of the Freedmen's Bureau* (Philadelphia, 1955), pp. 1–29.

3. *Christian Recorder*, October 5, 1861, April 26, 1862.

4. *Liberator*, September 26, 1862.

5. From the Hilton Head correspondent of the New York *Evening Post*, quoted in the Boston *Commonwealth*, October 4, 1862.

6. For an excellent study of the Sea Islands during the Civil War, see Willie L. N. Rose, *Rehearsal for Reconstruction: The Port Royal Experiment* (New York, 1964).

7. Elizabeth Botume, *First Days Amongst the Contrabands* (Boston, 1893), pp. 31–32.

8. Charlotte Forten, "Life on the Sea Islands," *Atlantic Monthly*, XIII (May, 1864), 587–94; (June, 1864), 667, 676.

9. Botume, *First Days Amongst the Contrabands*, pp. 46–49.

10. Rupert S. Holland, ed., *Letters and Diary of Laura M. Towne* (Cambridge, Mass., 1912), pp. xiv-xv.

11. *Ibid.*, p. 68.

12. Elizabeth Ware Pearson, ed., *Letters from Port Royal, Written at the Time of the Civil War* (Boston, 1906), pp. 180–82.

13. Charles Nordhoff, *The Freedmen of South Carolina* (New York, 1863), pp. 2–4.

14. "Preliminary Report of the Freedmen's Inquiry Commission," June 30, 1863, in *O.R.*, Ser. 3, Vol. III, p. 435.

15. Sarah Forbes Hughes, ed., *Letters and Recollections of John Murray Forbes* (2 vols., Boston, 1899), I, 317–18.

16. Quoted in John Eaton, *Grant, Lincoln, and the Freedmen* (New York, 1907), p. 19.

17. James E. Yeatman, *A Report on the Condition of the Freedmen of the Mississippi* (St. Louis, 1864), pp. 4–5.

18. *Ibid.*, pp. 7–9.

19. *Report of the General Superintendent of Freedmen, Department of the Tennessee and State of Arkansas, for 1864* (Memphis, 1965), pp. 43–49.

20. *Ibid.*, pp. 49–51.

21. Quoted in *Liberator*, November 18, 1864.

22. Fred H. Harrington, *Fighting Politician: Major General N. P. Banks* (Philadelphia, 1948), pp. 104–5; Banks's orders were published in *O.R.*, Ser. 1, Vol. XV, pp. 666–67, and Vol. XXXIV, Pt. ii, pp. 227–31.

23. Speech by Douglass in Boston, January 25, 1865, published in the *Liberator*, February 10, 1865.

24. New Orleans *Tribune*, August 13, 1864.

25. *Ibid.*, December 8, 1864.

26. *Ibid.*, March 18, 1865.

27. *La Tribune de la Nouvelle Orléans*, October 23, 1864. Translated by Roger Des Forges.

28. Philadelphia *Ledger*, August 10, 1865.

CHAPTER IX
NEGRO MISSIONS TO THE FREEDMEN

1. *Christian Recorder*, March 22, 1862.

2. *Ibid.*, October 4, 1862.

3. *Ibid.*, February 27, 1864.

4. *Ibid.*, November 8, 1862.

5. Elizabeth Keckley, *Behind the Scenes: Or, Thirty Years a Slave, and Four Years in the White House* (New York, 1868), pp. 111–16.

6. *Second Annual Report of the Freedmen and Soldiers' Relief Association (Late Contraband Relief Association), Organized, August 12, 1862* (Washington, 1864).

7. *Special Report of the Commissioner of Education on the Condition and Improvement of Public Schools in the District of Columbia* . . . (Washington, 1871), pp. 285–87.

8. Lewis C. Lockwood, *Mary S. Peake, the Colored Teacher at Fortress Monroe* (Boston, 1862); Lillian G. Dabney, *The History of Schools for Negroes in the District of Columbia, 1807–1947* (Washington, 1949), pp. 26–28, 58–59, 99–100; for the work of the African Civilization Society, see the *Anglo-African*, November 16, 1861, March 14, 1863, September 24, 1864, and the *Christian Recorder*, February 20, April 2, 1864.

9. *Christian Recorder*, May 30, June 20, 1863.

10. Susie King Taylor, *Reminiscences of My Life in Camp* (Boston, 1902), p. 11.

11. *Ibid.*, pp. 21, 26, 30.

12. *The Colored Citizen* (Cincinnati), November 7, 1863.

13. John Eaton, *Grant, Lincoln, and the Freedmen* (New York, 1907), p. 200.

CHAPTER X
NEGRO CONTRIBUTIONS TO THE UNION WAR EFFORT

1. *Anglo-African*, November 30, 1861.

2. Vincent Colyer, *Report of the Services Rendered by the Freed People to the United States Army, in North Carolina* (New York, 1864), p. 9.

3. *O.R.*, Ser. 1, Vol. XVIII, p. 675.

4. *Ibid.*, Ser. 1, Vol. XXII, pp. 724–25.

5. *Ibid.*, Ser. 3, Vol. IV, pp. 893–94.

6. Allan Pinkerton, *Spy in the Rebellion* (New York, 1883), p. 194.

7. *Ibid.*, pp. 344–46, 366.

8. *O.R.*, Ser. 2, Vol. I, p. 815; Ser. 2, Vol. VI, p. 1053.

9. Charles Nordhoff, *The Freedmen of South Carolina* (New York, 1863), pp. 24–25.

10. George H. Hepworth, *The Whip, Hoe, and Sword* (Boston, 1864), pp. 259–60.

11. Mitchel to Stanton, May 4, 1862, *O.R.*, Ser. 1, Vol. X, Pt. ii, p. 162; Seward to Adams, May 28, 1862, in *Papers Relating to Foreign Affairs, Communicated to Congress, December 1, 1862* (Washington, 1862), p. 104.

12. Quoted in Herbert Aptheker, *The Negro in the Civil War* (New York, 1938), p. 17.

13. Hannibal A. Johnson, *The Sword of Honor* (Providence, R.I., 1903), pp. 25–35.

14. William Wells Brown, *The Negro in the American Rebellion* (Boston, 1867), pp. 74–76. For a modern account of the Tillman episode, see Benjamin Quarles, *The Negro in the Civil War* (Boston, 1953), pp. 32–34.

15. James M. Guthrie, *Camp-Fires of the Afro-American* (Philadelphia, 1889), pp 306–13. For official reports of the *Planter* episode, see the *Official Records of the Union and Confederate Navies in the War of the Rebellion*, Ser. 1, Vol. XII, pp. 820–25.

16. Quarles, *The Negro in the Civil War*, pp. 91–93.

17. Herbert Aptheker, "The Negro in the Union Navy," *Journal of Negro History*, XXXII (April, 1947), 169–200.

18. *Christian Recorder*, May 21, 1864.

CHAPTER XI
NEGRO TROOPS IN THE UNION ARMY;
INITIATION OF A POLICY, 1862–63

1. *Douglass' Monthly*, V (August, 1863), 852.

2. *Ibid.*, IV (September, 1861), 516.

3. Speech at Cooper Union, February 12, 1862, reported in New York *Tribune*, February 13, 1862.

4. *Pacific Appeal*, May 24, 1862.

5. Brannigan quoted in Benjamin Quarles, *The Negro in the Civil War* (Boston, 1953), p. 31; the writer in the *New York Times* quoted by the New York *Tribune*, August 16, 1862.

6. Elizabeth Ware Pearson, ed., *Letters from Port Royal, Written at the Time of the Civil War* (Boston, 1906), pp. 42–43.

7. Roy P. Basler, ed., *The Collected Works of Abraham Lincoln* (9 vols., New Brunswick, N.J., 1955), V, 357–423.

8. Dudley T. Cornish, *The Sable Arm: Negro Troops in the Union Army, 1861–1865* (New York, 1956), pp. 32–78.

9. *U.S. Statutes at Large*, XII, 589–92.

10. Cornish, *The Sable Arm*, pp. 80–84, 92–93.

11. Higginson, Journal, entry of November 27, 1862, Higginson Papers, Houghton Library, Harvard University.

12. *O.R.*, Ser. 1, Vol. XIV, pp. 195–98.

13. *Ibid.*, Ser. 3, Vol. III, p. 177.

14. Reuben Tomlinson to J. M. McKim, March 16, 1863, McKim Papers, Cornell University Library.

15. Basler, *Collected Works of Lincoln*, VI, 149–50.

16. *Ibid.*, p. 158.

17. *L'Union*, June 2, 1863. Translated by Roger Des Forges.

18. Cornish, *The Sable Arm*, pp. 110–30.

19. Robert Cowden, *A Brief Sketch of the Organization and Services of the Fifty-Ninth Regiment of United States Colored Infantry* (Dayton, Ohio, 1883), pp. 38–40.

20. *Ibid.*, pp. 44–48.

21. Cornish, *The Sable Arm*, p. 234.

CHAPTER XII

BLACK TROOPS FROM THE NORTH

1. James M. McPherson, *The Struggle for Equality: Abolitionists and the Negro in the Civil War and Reconstruction* (Princeton, 1964), pp. 202–3, 205.

2. Charles Russell Lowell to his mother, February 4, 1863, in Edward W. Emerson, ed., *Life and Letters of Charles Russell Lowell* (Boston, 1907), pp. 233–34.

3. J. B. Moore to his brother, March 3, 1863, Moore Papers, Howard University Library.

4. Parham to Jacob C. White, Jr., February or March, 1863, White Papers, Howard University Library.

5. *O.R.*, Ser. 2, Vol. V, pp. 940–41.

6. Dudley T. Cornish, *The Sable Arm* (New York, 1956), pp. 158–73; Allan Nevins, *The War for the Union: War Becomes Revolution, 1862–1863* (New York, 1960), pp. 520–22; Herbert Aptheker, "Negro Casualties in the Civil War," *Journal of Negro History*, XXXII (January, 1947), 40–46.

7. George T. Downing to Charles Sumner, February 19, 1863, Sumner Papers, Houghton Library, Harvard University. On July 30, 1863, Lincoln issued an order stating that for every Union prisoner killed in violation of the laws of war, a rebel prisoner would be similarly executed. For every Union soldier enslaved or sold into slavery, a rebel soldier would be placed at hard labor on the public works. Except for the Fort Pillow Massacre and other scattered instances of murder after capture, the South did not treat Negro prisoners barbarously. But the Confederacy did refuse to exchange Negro prisoners, contributing to the prisoner-exchange breakdown which

caused overcrowding in both Union and Confederate prisons. See Cornish, *The Sable Arm*, Chap. 9.

8. Henry Greenleaf Pearson, *The Life of John A. Andrew* (2 vols., Boston, 1904), II, 71–74.

9. Purvis to J. M. McKim, February 18, 1863, McKim Papers, Cornell University Library.

10. *Christian Recorder*, February 7, 1863.

11. Quoted in *Douglass' Monthly*, V (March, 1863), 802.

12. Douglass to Gerrit Smith, March 6, 1863, Smith Papers, Syracuse University Library.

13. *Douglass' Monthly*, V (March, 1863), 802.

14. *Pacific Appeal*, April 25, 1863.

15. *Liberator*, May 22, 1863.

16. *Ibid.*, May 29, 1863.

17. Margaret Leech, *Reveille in Washington, 1860–1865* (New York, 1941), p. 253.

18. *Christian Recorder*, June 20, 1863.

19. *Liberator*, June 12, 1863.

20. *Christian Recorder*, June 20, 1863.

21. John Mercer Langston, *From the Virginia Plantation to the National Capital* (Hartford, 1894), pp. 205–17.

22. *Liberator*, September 4, 1863.

23. *Christian Recorder*, July 11, June 27, 1863.

24. *O.R.*, Ser. 3, Vol III, p. 1115.

25. *Liberator*, June 19, 1863.

CHAPTER XIII
NEGRO SOLDIERS PROVE THEMSELVES IN BATTLE, 1863

1. William Wells Brown, *The Negro in the American Rebellion* (Boston, 1867), pp. 167–71.

2. *O.R.*, Ser. 1, Vol. XXVI, Pt. i, p. 45.

3. Published in the *National Intelligencer*, August 24, 1863.

4. *New York Times*, June 11, 1863.

5. Published in the *Union* (New Orleans), July 14, 1863.

6. *O.R.*, Ser. 1, Vol. XXIV, Pt. ii, p. 467.

7. Charles Dana, *Recollections of the Civil War* (New York, 1899), p. 86.

8. Thomas' official report to the Secretary of War, October 5, 1865, in *O.R.*, Ser. 3, Vol. V, p. 119.

9. "Faith" to "Hope," June 11, 1863, in the Carter Woodson Collection, Library of Congress.

10. Elizabeth Botume, *First Days Amongst the Contrabands* (Boston, 1893), p. 152.

11. Quoted in Brown, *Negro in the Rebellion*, pp. 280–81.

12. George W. Williams, *A History of the Negro Troops in the War of the Rebellion* (New York, 1888), pp. 195–96.

13. Quoted in *ibid.*, pp. 196–97.

14. Lewis Douglass to Amelia Loguen, July 20, 1863, Woodson Collection, Library of Congress.

15. New York *Tribune*, September 8, 1865.

16. Mrs. Weld to Gerrit Smith, July 28, 1863, Smith Papers, Syracuse University Library.

17. Grant to Lincoln, August 23, 1863, Lincoln Papers, Library of Congress.

18. Roy P. Basler, ed., *The Collected Works of Abraham Lincoln* (9 vols., New Brunswick, 1955), VI, 408–10.

19. Christopher A. Fleetwood Papers, Library of Congress.

CHAPTER XIV
THE STRUGGLE FOR EQUAL PAY

1. *Anglo-African*, February 13, 1864.

2. "War Letters of C. P. Bowditch," *Massachusetts Historical Society Proceedings*, LVII (1923–24), 431, 434, 436, 444.

3. *O.R.*, Ser. 3, Vol. III, pp. 1126–27.

4. *Ibid.*, Ser. 3, Vol. IV, p. 431.

5. *House Exec. Docs.*, #83, 38 Cong., 2 Sess., p. 29.

6. *U.S. Statutes at Large*, XII, 269, 599; *O.R.*, Ser. 3, Vol. III, p. 252; Fred A. Shannon, *The Organization and Administration of the Union Army, 1861–1865* (2 vols., New York, 1928), I, 71–72.

7. Frederick Douglass, *Life and Times of Frederick Douglass* (Hartford, 1882), pp. 386–87.

8. Quoted in Luis Emilio, *History of the Fifty-Fourth Regiment of the Massachusetts Volunteer Infantry, 1863–1865* (Boston, 1894), pp. 136–37.

9. *Christian Recorder*, January 2, 1864.

10. *Ibid.*, March 5, 1864.

11. New York *World*, December 13, 1863.

12. Quoted in Emilio, *Fifty-Fourth Massachusetts*, p. 179.

13. *Christian Recorder*, April 23, 1864.

14. *Ibid.*, July 2, 1864.

15. "War Letters of C. P. Bowditch," *loc. cit.*, p. 469.

16. Charles B. Fox, *Record of the Service of the Fifty-Fifth Regiment of Massachusetts Volunteer Infantry* (Cambridge, Mass., 1868), pp. 27–29, 33; Emilio, *Fifty-Fourth Massachusetts*, p. 190; Herbert Aptheker, "Negro Casualties in the Civil War," *Journal of Negro History*, XXXII (January, 1947), 39.

17. *Christian Recorder*, March 19, 1864.

18. *Ibid.*, April 6, 1864.

19. *U.S. Statutes at Large*, XIII, 129–31. On March 3, 1865, Congress passed a measure granting full retroactive equal pay to all Negro regiments that had been promised equal pay when they were enrolled. By this law the freedmen in the South Carolina regiments and some ex-slaves in other regiments were also given equal pay retroactive to the time of their enlistment. *U.S. Statutes at Large*, XIII, 488.

20. Emilio, *Fifty-Fourth Massachusetts*, pp. 220–21.

21. Quoted in *ibid.*, pp. 227–28.

22. Ruffin to Josephine Ruffin, October 16, 1864, Ruffin Papers, Howard University Library.

CHAPTER XV
NEGRO SOLDIERS IN THE UNION ARMY, 1863–64

1. *The Colored Citizen*, November 7, 1863.

2. Elijah P. Marrs, *Life and History of the Rev. Elijah P. Marrs* (Louisville, 1885), pp. 17–20.

3. Published in the *Anglo-African*, September 24, 1864.

4. Poughkeepsie *Daily Eagle*, July 20, 1863.

5. John Jay, *The Union League Club of New York, Its Memories of the Past* (New York, 1868).

6. *Christian Recorder*, March 12, 1864.

7. *Ibid.*, May 28, 1864.

8. Turner to the editor of the *Christian Recorder*, February 4, 1865, in the *Christian Recorder*, February 25.

9. Frances P. Beecher, "Two Years with a Colored Regiment, A Woman's Experience," *New England Magazine*, XVII (January 1898), 536.

10. Robert Cowden, *A Brief Sketch of the Organization and Services of the Fifty-Ninth Regiment of United States Colored Infantry* (Dayton, Ohio, 1883), pp. 60–61.

11. Joseph T. Wilson, *The Black Phalanx* (Hartford, 1888), p. 504.

12. Quoted from the New York *Age* in Wilson, *Black Phalanx*, pp. 506–7.

13. Thomas Wentworth Higginson, Journal, entry of March 24, 1864, Higginson Papers, Houghton Library, Harvard University.

14. Social Science Institute, Fisk University, "Unwritten History of Slavery: Autobiographical Account of Negro Ex-Slaves," Social Science Source Documents, No. 1 (Nashville, 1945), p. 253.

15. *Ibid.*, pp. 150–51.

16. B. A. Botkin, ed., *Lay My Burden Down: A Folk History of Slavery* (Chicago, 1945), pp. 199–201.

17. Dudley T. Cornish, *The Sable Arm: Negro Troops in the Union Army, 1861–1865* (New York, 1956), pp. 173–75; Albert Castel, "The Fort Pillow

Massacre: A Fresh Examination of the Evidence," *Civil War History*, IV (March, 1958), 37–50.

18. *Reports of the Committee on the Conduct of the War*, "Fort Pillow Massacre" (House of Representatives, 38th Cong., 1 Sess., Report #65, Washington, 1864), pp. 17, 25–28.

19. *Christian Recorder*, April 23, 1864.

20. "R.H.C.," in *Christian Recorder*, April 30, 1864.

21. *O.R.*, Ser. 1, Vol. XXXII, Pt. i, p. 588.

22. *Liberator*, July 22, 1864.

23. Letter printed in the Philadelphia *Press*, July 12, 1864.

CHAPTER XVI
BLACK TROOPS IN THE FINAL YEAR OF WAR

1. *O.R.*, Ser. 3, Vol. IV, p. 789.

2. Dudley T. Cornish, *The Sable Arm: Negro Troops in the Union Army, 1861–1865* (New York, 1956), p. 266.

3. New York *Herald*, June 18, 1864.

4. Philadelphia *Press*, quoted in *Liberator*, July 22, 1864.

5. *O.R.*, Ser. 1, Vol. XLII, Pt. i, pp. 848–50.

6. Edward M. Main, *The Story of the Marches, Battles, and Incidents of the Third United States Colored Cavalry* (Louisville, 1908), pp. 118–23.

7. Thomas J. Morgan, "Reminiscences of Service with Colored Troops in the Army of the Cumberland, 1863–65," in *Personal Narratives of Events in the War of the Rebellion, being papers read before the Rhode Island Soldiers and Sailors Historical Society* (No. 13, 3rd Series, Providence, 1885), pp. 11–48.

8. *O.R.*, Ser. 1, Vol. XIV, Pt. i, p. 508.

9. *Ibid.*, Ser. 3, Vol. IV, p. 369.

10. Mrs. Child to Elisa Scudder, April 22, 1864, Child Papers, Cornell University Library.

11. Lincoln to Isaac Schermerhorn, September 12, 1864, in Roy B. Basler, ed., *The Collected Works of Abraham Lincoln* (9 vols., New Brunswick, 1955), VIII, 2.

12. Elijah P. Marrs, *Life and History of the Rev. Elijah P. Marrs* (Louisville, 1885), pp. 55–57.

13. Charles B. Fox, *Record of the Service of the Fifty-Fifth Regiment of Massachusetts Volunteer Infantry* (Cambridge, Mass., 1868), pp. 56–58.

14. Herbert Aptheker, "Negro Casualties in the Civil War," *Journal of Negro History*, XXXII (January, 1947), 12, 47–48; Cornish, *The Sable Arm*, p. 265; John W. Blassingame, "The Organization and Use of Negro Troops in the Union Army, 1863–65" (Master's Thesis, Howard University, 1961), pp. 113–14.

15. *Liberator*, August 5, 1864.

16. New Orleans *Tribune*, February 10, 1865.
17. Cornish, *The Sable Arm*, pp. 214–17.

CHAPTER XVII
THE CONFEDERATE DECISION
TO RAISE A NEGRO ARMY, 1864–65

1. *O.R.*, Ser. 1, Vol. III, Pt. ii, pp. 587–91.
2. *Ibid.*, Ser. 4, Vol. III, pp. 959–60.
3. *Ibid.*, Ser. 4, Vol. III, pp. 1009–10.
4. *Ibid.*, Ser. 4, Vol. VIII, pp. 1012–13.
5. Charles H. Wesley, *The Collapse of the Confederacy* (Washington, 1937), pp. 164–66.

CHAPTER XVIII
CIVIL RIGHTS AND DESEGREGATION IN THE NORTH

1. Leon Litwack, *North of Slavery* (Chicago, 1961); Carter Woodson, *The Education of the Negro Prior to 1861* (New York, 1915), pp. 276–78, 309–35; Henry W. Farnham, *Chapters in the History of Social Legislation in the United States to 1860* (Washington, 1938), pp. 216–20.
2. Edward Dicey, *Six Months in the Federal States* (2 vols., London, 1863), I, 70–73.
3. *Anglo-African*, January 7, 1860.
4. *Liberator*, August 15, 1862.
5. *Douglass' Monthly*, IV (November, 1861), 557.
6. Bates' decision was printed in Edward McPherson, *The Political History of the United States of America, during the Great Rebellion* (Washington, 1865), pp. 378–84.
7. Edward McPherson, *The Political History of the United States of America, during the Great Rebellion* (Washington, 1865), pp. 239–40, 242–43, 593; *U.S. Statutes at Large*, XII, 351, 407, XIII, 515.
8. *Pacific Appeal*, April 5, 1862.
9. *Ibid.*
10. *Ibid.*, May 3, 1862.
11. "C.P.S.," in *ibid.*, September 13, 1862.
12. *Ibid.*, July 5, August 2, September 6, 1862; Boston *Commonwealth*, April 17, 1863.
13. Arthur Cole, *The Era of the Civil War, 1848–1870, Centennial History of Illinois*, Vol. II (Springfield, 1919), pp. 225–26, 333–35.
14. *Anglo-African*, January 14, 1865.
15. Cole, *Era of the Civil War*, pp. 336–37.
16. *Students' Repository*, I (July, 1863), 5.

17. Emma Lou Thornbrough, *The Negro in Indiana* (Indianapolis, 1957), pp. 203, 233.

18. *Douglass' Monthly*, IV (February, 1862), 593–94.

19. Printed in William Still, *A Brief Narrative of the Struggle for the Rights of the Colored People of Philadelphia in the City Railroad Cars* (Philadelphia, 1867), p. 5.

20. *Thirtieth Annual Report of the Philadelphia Female Anti-Slavery Society* (1864), pp. 23–24.

21. Still, *Brief Narrative*, pp. 7–9.

22. Philadelphia *Press*, July 21, 1864.

23. *Christian Recorder*, July 30, 1864.

24. Philadelphia *Press*, August 31, 1864.

25. Letter from the Rev. Robert J. Parvin, published in the Philadelphia *Press*, March 22, 1865.

26. Still, *Brief Narrative*, pp. 11–13.

27. Ira V. Brown, "Pennsylvania and the Rights of the Negro, 1865–1887," *Pennsylvania History*, XXVIII (January, 1961), 48–49.

28. Augusta to Capt. C. W. Clippington, February 1, 1864, printed in *Congressional Globe*, 38 Cong., 1 Sess., p. 554.

29. *Ibid.*, pp. 553–55; *U.S. Statutes at Large*, XIII, 537.

30. Olive Gilbert, *Narrative of Sojourner Truth* (Battle Creek, Mich., 1884), pp. 184–87.

31. *Anglo-African*, January 4, 1862.

32. Margaret Leech, *Reveille in Washington, 1860–1865* (New York, 1941), p. 239; Benjamin Quarles, *Lincoln and the Negro* (New York, 1962), pp. 233–34.

33. Douglass' article in Allen Thorndike Rice, ed., *Reminiscences of Abraham Lincoln by Distinguished Men of His Time* (New York, 1888), pp. 191–93.

34. The ceremony was described in the New York *Tribune*, February 9, 1865.

35. *Pacific Appeal*, September 27, 1862.

36. *Ibid.*, June 20, 1863.

37. Irving H. Bartlett, *From Slave to Citizen: The Story of the Negro in Rhode Island* (Providence, 1954), pp. 52–58.

38. A copy of this petition is in the John Hay Library, Brown University.

39. Bartlett, *From Slave to Citizen*, p. 59; *Special Report of the Committee of Education on the Condition and Improvement of Public Schools in the District of Columbia . . .* (Washington, 1871), pp. 328, 334–35.

40. *Special Report, Committee of Education*, p. 343.

41. New Orleans *Tribune*, February 17, 22, 1865.

42. Milton R. Konvitz and Theodore Leskes, *A Century of Civil Rights, with a Study of State Law Against Discrimination* (New York, 1961); Carter

Woodson, *The Education of the Negro Prior to 1861* (New York, 1915), pp. 309–35.

CHAPTER XIX
WARTIME DISCUSSIONS OF RECONSTRUCTION
AND NEGRO SUFFRAGE

1. *Proceedings of the American Anti-Slavery Society, at its Third Decade Anniversary, Dec. 3d and 4th, 1863* (New York, 1864), pp. 114–15, 118.

2. *Anglo-African*, April 21, 28, May 5, 19, June 30, 1860; *Douglass' Monthly*, III (October, 1860), 345.

3. Published in the *Principia*, October 20, 1860.

4. Leo H. Hirsch, Jr., "The Negro and New York, 1783 to 1865," *Journal of Negro History*, XVI (1931), 423.

5. Published in the *Christian Recorder*, December 19, 1863.

6. Published in the *Anglo-African*, May 14, 1864.

7. *L'Union*, September 27, 1862. Translated by Roger Des Forges.

8. *Ibid.*, December 30, 1862. Translated by Roger Des Forges.

9. *Ibid.*, December 1, 1863.

10. Roy P. Basler, ed., *The Collected Works of Abraham Lincoln* (9 vols., New Brunswick, 1955), VII, 53–56.

11. Fred H. Harrington, *Fighting Politician: Major General N. P. Banks* (Philadelphia, 1948), pp. 140–44.

12. Published in *Liberator*, April 1, 1864.

13. Basler, *Collected Works of Lincoln*, VII, 243.

14. *Liberator*, April 15, 1864.

15. *L'Union*, May 17, 1864. Translated by Roger Des Forges.

16. *Ibid.*, June 21, 28, 1864. Translated by Roger Des Forges.

17. *Ibid.*, May 26, 1864. Translated by Roger Des Forges.

18. *La Tribune de la Nouvelle Orléans*, November 10, 12, 1864. Translated by Roger Des Forges.

19. New Orleans *Tribune*, December 6, 1864.

20. *Ibid.*, November 18, 1864.

21. Quoted in *ibid.*, January 19, 1865.

22. *Proceedings of the National Convention of Colored Citizens, Held in the City of Syracuse, N.Y., Oct. 4–7, 1864* (New York, 1864), pp. 57–60.

23. *Liberator*, December 23, 1864.

24. *Anglo-African*, December 17, 1864, April 15, 1865; *Liberator*, January 27, March 3, 1865.

25. *Liberator*, March 3, 1865.

26. Quoted in the New Orleans *Tribune*, January 7, 1865.

27. *Proceedings of a Convention of the Colored Men of Ohio, held in*

Xenia, on the 10th, 11th, and 12th days of January, 1865, with the Constitution of the Ohio Equal Rights League (Cincinnati, 1865), p. 17.

28. New Orleans *Tribune*, January 15, 1865.

29. Henry Highland Garnet, *A Memorial Discourse Delivered in the Hall of the House of Representatives, Washington, D.C., on Sabbath, February 12, 1865* (Philadelphia, 1865), pp. 85–89.

30. *Christian Recorder*, March 25, 1865.

31. *La Tribune de la Nouvelle Orléans*, January 24, 1865. Translated by Roger Des Forges.

CHAPTER XX
LAND FOR THE LANDLESS

1. *Anglo-African*, November 23, 1861.

2. *Liberator*, August 15, 1862.

3. Letter from George N. Williams, printed in the *Christian Recorder*, June 20, 1863.

4. Quoted by Thomas Wentworth Higginson in his Journal, entry of November 21, 1863, Higginson Papers, Houghton Library, Harvard University.

5. Foster to William Goodell, January 14, 1864, published in the *Principia*, January 28, 1864.

6. New Orleans *Tribune*, September 10, November 29, 1864.

7. See James M. McPherson, *The Struggle for Equality* (Princeton, 1964), pp. 248, 256.

8. *Ibid.*, pp. 249–55.

9. Don Carlos Butler (written down by Laura Towne) to Abraham Lincoln, May 29, 1864, Lincoln Papers, Library of Congress.

10. Published in the Philadelphia *Press*, May 31, 1864.

11. The minutes of this conference were published in the *Liberator*, February 24, 1865.

12. McPherson, *Struggle for Equality*, pp. 257, 408–9.

13. Part of a speech by Douglass at Elmira, New York, on August 1, 1880, manuscript copy in the Frederick Douglass Papers, Frederick Douglass Memorial Home, Anacostia Heights, Washington, D.C.

CHAPTER XXI
THE NEGRO'S ATTITUDE TOWARD LINCOLN, 1864–65

1. *Christian Recorder*, September 12, 1863.

2. *Pacific Appeal*, January 9, 1864.

3. New Orleans *Tribune*, August 25, 1864.

4. Douglass to Edward Gilbert, May 23, 1864, published in the *New York Times*, May 27, 1864.

5. *Liberator*, May 20, 1864.

6. *Ibid.*, July 22, 1864.

7. Washington *Chronicle*, September 8, 1864.

8. Published in the *Liberator*, September 23, 1864.

9. Douglass to Tilton, October 15, 1864, Tilton Papers, Buffalo Public Library.

10. *Anglo-African*, September 24, 1864.

11. James Ruffin to Josephine Ruffin, October 16, 1864, Ruffin Papers, Howard University Library.

12. New Orleans *Tribune*, November 29, 1864.

13. Quoted in Elizabeth Botume, *First Days Amongst the Contrabands* (Boston, 1893), p. 178.

14. Published in *Liberator*, May 5, 1865.

15. New Orleans *Tribune*, April 20, 1865.

16. Edgar Dinsmore to Carrie Drayton, May (?) 29, 1865, George Washington Flowers Memorial Collection, Duke University Library.

CHAPTER XXII
THE NEGRO FACES THE FUTURE

1. *Pacific Appeal*, August 2, 1862.

2. *Liberator*, May 22, 1863.

3. *Christian Recorder*, July 16, 1864.

4. *Ibid.*, February 11, 1865. This editorial was reprinted in the New Orleans *Tribune*, March 9, 1865.

5. Susie King Taylor, *Reminiscences of My Life in Camp* (Boston, 1902), pp. 50–52, 61–67.

A NOTE ON SOURCES

The number of sources, both primary and secondary, touching upon the story of the Negro in the Civil War is immense, and it is impossible here to include a complete or comprehensive bibliography of this material. The paragraphs that follow will delineate only the major sources for this documentary. Many of the pamphlets, articles, memoirs, and reminiscences consulted in the preparation of this book are cited in the notes, and the student wishing a more thorough guide to the sources for an understanding of the Negro's role in the Civil War should check the notes.

The first attempt to chronicle the record of the black man in the war was made by William Wells Brown, *The Negro in the American Rebellion* (Boston, 1867). Brown relied on newspaper articles, interviews, and his own memory of the war to compile his account, which was readable but rather partisan and anecdotal in nature. More thorough, but badly organized and repetitive, are George Washington Williams, *A History of Negro Troops in the War of the Rebellion* (New York, 1888), and Joseph T. Wilson, *Black Phalanx* (Hartford, 1888). Both Williams and Wilson were Negroes, and both had served in the Union Army. Another disconnected and anecdotal work is James M. Guthrie, *Camp-Fires of the Afro-American* (Philadelphia, 1889), by a white man who had served as a chaplain in a Negro regiment.

Modern studies have added a great deal to our knowledge of the Negro in the Civil War. These studies include Herbert Aptheker, *The Negro in the Civil War* (New York, 1938), a brief and militantly pro-Negro account; Bell Irvin Wiley, *Southern Negroes, 1861–1865* (New Haven, 1938), written from the point of view of the Southern white man; Benjamin Quarles, *The Negro in the Civil War* (Boston, 1953), a very readable and fairly comprehensive account; Dudley T. Cornish, *The Sable Arm: Negro Troops in the Union Army, 1861–*

1865 (New York, 1956), which is an excellent study of its subject; and Benjamin Quarles, *Lincoln and the Negro* (New York, 1962), an enlightening and enjoyable book.

Some articles that shed light on various aspects of the Negro's part in the Civil War are Herbert Aptheker, "Negro Casualties in the Civil War," *Journal of Negro History*, XXXII (January, 1947), 10–80; Herbert Aptheker, "The Negro in the Union Navy," *Journal of Negro History*, XXXII (April, 1947), 169–200; Williston H. Lofton, "Northern Labor and the Negro During the Civil War," *Journal of Negro History*, XXXIV (July, 1949), 251–73; Bernard H. Nelson, "Legislative Control of the Southern Free Negro, 1861–1865," *Catholic Historical Review*, XXXII (April, 1946), 28–46; and Charles H. Wesley, "The Employment of Negroes as Soldiers in the Confederate Army," *Journal of Negro History*, IV (1919), 239–53.

Some of the Negro participants in the Civil War later wrote memoirs that contained accounts of their role in the conflict. Some of the more interesting of these reminiscences are Frederick Douglass, *Life and Times of Frederick Douglass* (Hartford, 1882; paperback edition, with introduction by Rayford W. Logan, Collier Books, New York, 1962); Elizabeth Keckley, *Behind the Scenes* (New York, 1868), an account of life in the White House during the war written by (and possibly ghost-written for) Mrs. Lincoln's black seamstress and confidante; John Mercer Langston, *From the Virginia Plantation to the National Capital* (Hartford, 1894), by an Ohio Negro lawyer who later became Virginia's first and only Negro Congressman; and Susie King Taylor, *Reminiscences of My Life in Camp* (Boston, 1902), by the escaped slave who became a laundress and teacher in a South Carolina Negro regiment. Ray Allen Billington, ed., *The Journal of Charlotte L. Forten* (paperback edition, Collier Books, New York, 1961), contains some fascinating material on Miss Forten's experiences as a teacher of the freedmen on the South Carolina Sea Islands.

Biographical information on prominent Negroes has been obtained from many sources, the most accessible of which are Richard Bardolph, *The Negro Vanguard* (Vintage Books, New York, 1961); William Wells Brown, *The Black Man: His Antecedents, His Genius and His Achievements* (Boston, 1863); Vernon Loggins, *The Negro Author* (New York, 1931), and William J. Simmons, *Men of Mark* (Cleveland, 1887).

The number of pamphlets, broadsides, semi-official and official reports during the Civil War dealing with some aspect of the Negro question is legion. A few of the more important and interesting items are the *Proceedings of the National Convention of Colored Citizens, Held in the City of Syracuse, N.Y., Oct. 4–7, 1864, with a Bill of Wrongs and Rights; and the Address to the American People* (New York, 1864); the *Proceedings of a Convention of the Colored Men of Ohio, held in Xenia, on the 10th, 11th, and 12th days of January, 1865; with the Constitution of the Ohio Equal Rights League* (Cincinnati, 1865); *Second Annual Report of the Freed-*

*men and Soldiers' Relief Association (Late Contraband Relief Association),
Organized, August 12, 1862* (Washington, 1864); Henry Highland Garnet,
A Memorial Discourse Delivered in the Hall of the House of Representatives, Washington, D.C., on Sabbath, February 12, 1865, with an Introduction by Dr. James McCune Smith (Philadelphia, 1865); and William Still,
*A Brief Narrative of the Struggle for the Rights of the Colored People of
Philadelphia in the City Railroad Cars* (Philadelphia, 1867). The most important of the many government publications relating to the freedmen is
*War of the Rebellion: A Compilation of Official Records of the Union and
Confederate Armies* (Washington, 1880–1901), which contains a great deal
of material on the Negro as a soldier, a laborer, and a freedman scattered
through its 128 volumes.

By far the most important sources for this book were the Negro and
abolitionist newspapers. Of the newspapers edited by white men, the *Liberator* was the most significant, for it contained a great deal of material on
the activities of Negroes in New England. The *National Anti-Slavery Standard*, official organ of the American Anti-Slavery Society, also furnished
some items on the role of the black man in the war. The *Pine and Palm*,
started in May 1861 by James Redpath as a spokesman for Negro emigration, included many articles and editorials relating to the colonization issue. The *Pine and Palm* was suspended in October 1862, when Redpath
dissolved his Haytian Bureau of Emigration.

Of the weekly newspapers published and edited entirely by Negroes,
the New York *Anglo-African* was probably the most important at the time
of the Civil War. Founded in July 1859 by Thomas Hamilton, the *Anglo-African* carried the motto "Man must be Free!—if not through the Law,
why then above the Law." The paper was suspended for lack of funds in
May 1861, and re-established in August of the same year by Robert Hamilton (Thomas Hamilton, Robert's brother, meanwhile had died). The *Anglo-African* continued weekly publication except for a temporary suspension
after the New York Draft Riots of July 1863 until it was permanently discontinued in the fall of 1865. Unfortunately, a complete file of the paper
is unavailable today. Most of the issues from April 1862 through the end
of the war are not extant, so a potentially rich source has been rendered
less valuable because of the nonsurvival of a majority of its issues.

A complete file of the *Christian Recorder* for the Civil War years *is*
extant, however, and the *Recorder* constituted one of the most important
sources for this book. The only available file of the *Recorder* for the war
years is housed in the Mother Bethel A.M.E. Church in Philadelphia, and
has never before been used by scholars. The *Christian Recorder* was
founded about 1856 as the official organ of the A.M.E. Church, and was
published weekly in Philadelphia, the central headquarters of the denomination. It was suspended in 1859 or 1860, and re-established in 1861. The
Recorder contained a great deal of secular as well as religious news, and

served as a spokesman for Philadelphia Negroes as well as for the A.M.E. Church. It was edited by the Rev. Elisha Weaver.

Another weekly Negro newspaper, moderately useful for this book, was the *Pacific Appeal*, published in San Francisco from April 1862 to March 1864 by George Anderson and edited by Philip Bell. Since San Francisco was rather far away from the centers of war, the *Appeal* concerned itself mostly with local affairs, but it nevertheless contained a significant amount of material relevant to this documentary.

Douglass' Monthly was a monthly newspaper in magazine format that served as Frederick Douglass' personal organ and also as a journalistic spokesman for all Northern Negroes. The *Monthly* was probably the only Negro newspaper in the North that attracted any sizable number of white readers. Douglass discontinued his *Monthly* in August 1863, mainly in order to free himself for more time on the lecture platform.

The prosperous and intelligent free Negro community in New Orleans supported two newspapers (nonsimultaneously) during the Civil War. The first was *L'Union* (the *Union*), which was published triweekly from September 1862 until July 1864. *L'Union* was a four-page paper in tabloid format, with two pages printed in English, and two pages in French. The file is incomplete, with most of the English pages missing, but a substantial percentage of the French pages have survived, and they formed an important and fascinating source for this book. Even more important was the bilingual New Orleans *Tribune (La Tribune de la Nouvelle Orléans)*, which was published from July 1864 to October 1864 as a triweekly, and thereafter until 1869 as a daily paper. The file of the *Tribune* in both languages is complete. These two Negro newspapers served as spokesmen not only for the free Negroes of New Orleans, but for the freedmen of Louisiana, and in a broader sense, for all Negroes in the South. The *Tribune* was read not only by Negroes but also by a sizable number of white radicals in New Orleans.

Three other Negro newspapers were of limited value for this book. The *Colored Citizen* was a weekly Negro paper published in Cincinnati from late 1863 until after the war, but unfortunately only the issue of November 7, 1863, is extant today. In Baltimore, a few young black men put out several issues of a weekly newspaper called the *Lyceum Observer* in the summer of 1863, but only the issue of June 5, 1863, has survived. And in Spartanburg, Indiana, Samuel H. Smothers, principal of the Union Literary Institute, a private academy for Negroes, edited a quarterly magazine called the *Students' Repository* from July 1863 through October 1864. Most of the articles in the *Repository* were essays by students on abstract subjects, so the journal has limited value as a source on the Negro in the Civil War.

Several collections of personal letters contained material of value for this documentary. The large collection of Frederick Douglass Papers at the Douglass Memorial Home in Anacostia Heights, Washington, D.C., includes a disappointingly small number of letters from the Civil War period. Of more value, perhaps, were the Christian A. Fleetwood Papers, in the Library of Congress. Fleetwood was a young free Negro from Baltimore who joined the Army in 1863, rose to the rank of sergeant, and received a Congressional Medal of Honor. His papers include several interesting letters plus a diary that Fleetwood kept before and during his military service. There are a few letters of interest in the George L. Ruffin Papers at Howard University, and a larger number of letters in the Jacob C. White Papers at Howard. White was a prominent Philadelphia Negro, and the collection contains several interesting letters from Northern Negroes to his son, Jacob C. White, Jr., a schoolteacher in Philadelphia who later became a leader in the Pennsylvania Equal Rights League. The Carter G. Woodson Collection of Negro letters in the Library of Congress also includes several letters from the Civil War era.

AN AFTERWORD ON BIBLIOGRAPHY

The explosion of scholarship in black history since 1965 has amplified and refined our understanding of many issues treated in *The Negro's Civil War*. The main thrust of this scholarship, however, has been to confirm the central thesis of *The Negro's Civil War*: that blacks played an active, crucial role in the war and in the consequent abolition of slavery. The historical literature on the activities of Southern blacks in the war is ably summarized by Clarence L. Mohr, "Southern Blacks in the Civil War: A Century of Historiography," *Journal of Negro History*, 69 (1974), 177–95. A useful reference work is Charles H. Wesley and Patricia Romero, *Negro Americans in the Civil War: From Slavery to Citizenship* (2nd ed., rev. 1969).

The process of emancipation as experienced by the slaves has received a great deal of attention, stimulated in part by the publication of the interviews with ex-slaves done in the 1930s by the Works Progress Administration: see George P. Rawick, ed., *The American Slave: A Composite Autobiography*, 18 vols. (1972) and a 12-volume supplement (1977); and Charles L. Perdue, Jr., and Robert K. Phillips, eds., *Weevils in the Wheat: Interviews with Virginia Ex-Slaves* (1976). These aged former slaves recalled with sometimes startling clarity the events of the war and the coming of freedom, making the interviews a rich source for the re-creation of that central experience in the history of black Americans. The Pulitzer Prize–winning study by Leon F. Litwack, *Been in the Storm So Long: The Aftermath of Slavery* (1979), uses these interviews as well as a wide variety of other sources to paint a rich portrait of the process and meaning of emancipation. A doctoral dissertation that studies the area where most slaves were emancipated during the war itself is Armstead L. Robinson, "Day of Jubilee: Civil War and the Demise of Slavery in the Mississippi Valley, 1861–1865," Ph.D. dissertation, University of Rochester, 1976. Several studies of the experiences of slaves in the transition to freedom during the war have greatly expanded our understanding of that process: Victor B. Howard, *Black Liberation in Kentucky: Emancipation and Freedom, 1862–1884* (1983); Barbara J. Fields, *Slavery and Freedom on the Middle Ground: Maryland During the Nineteenth Century* (1985); John Cimprich, *Slavery's End in Tennessee, 1861–1865* (1985); and Clarence L. Mohr, *On the Threshold of Freedom: Masters and Slaves in Civil War Georgia* (1986). A wealth of documents accompanied by explanatory and interpretive material can be found in Ira Berlin, Barbara J. Fields, Thavolia Glymph, Joseph P. Reidy, and Leslie L. Rowland, eds., *The Destruction of Slavery*, Series I, Volume I of *Freedom: A Documentary History of Emancipation* (1985) and *The Wartime Genesis of Free Labor: The Lower South*, Series I, Volume 3 of the same project (1990). These studies help to remedy the largest gap in our knowledge of blacks in the Civil War at the time *The Negro's Civil War* was first published—the experiences of the three million slaves who stayed on the farms and plantations within Confederate territory as well as the one million or so who came within Union control during the war. Another study, James H. Brewer, *The Confederate Negro: Virginia's Craftsmen and Military Laborers, 1861–1865* (1969), portrays the important role that slaves and free blacks played in the Confederate economy. An outstanding collection of documents, interwoven with the author's narrative and analysis on the model of *The Negro's Civil War*, tells the story of the Confederate debate over emancipating and arming the slaves to fight for the South: Robert F. Durden, ed., *The Gray and the Black: The Confederate Debate on Emancipation* (1972).

The economic consequences of emancipation and the postwar evolution of sharecropping are analyzed by Roger L. Ransom and Richard Sutch, *One Kind of Freedom: The Economic Consequences of Emancipation* (1977). The outpouring of scholarship on slavery during the 1970s included a number of studies that paid considerable attention to the collapse of the institution and utilized evidence from the Civil War years to provide insights on the experiences of both slavery and emancipation: see especially Herbert G. Gutman, *The Black Family in Slavery and Freedom, 1750–1925* (1976); Eugene D. Genovese, *Roll, Jordan, Roll: The World the Slaves Made* (1974); Paul D. Escott, *Slavery Remembered: A Record of Twentieth-Century Slave Narratives* (1979); and several of the essays in Willie Lee Rose, *Slavery and Freedom* (1982).

Several recent studies have evaluated the wartime and postwar efforts of Northern freedmen's education societies and the Freedmen's Bureau to establish schools for the freedmen. Two monographs that tend to be critical of the paternalism of white educators are Ronald E. Butchart, *Northern Schools, Southern Blacks, and Reconstruction: Freedmen's Education, 1862–1875* (1980), and Robert C. Morris, *Reading, 'Riting, and Reconstruction: The Education of Freedmen in the South, 1861–1870* (1981). More balanced and sympathetic toward the complex motives and the problems faced by freedmen's teachers both black and white is Jacqueline Jones, *Soldiers of Light and Love: Northern Teachers and Georgia Blacks, 1865–1873* (1980), which contains material on the wartime background and context of postwar education; James M. McPherson, *The Abolitionist Legacy: From Reconstruction to the NAACP* (1975), Part II; and Joe M. Richardson, *Christian Reconstruction: The American Missionary Association and Southern Blacks, 1861–1890* (1986). All of these books discuss the way in which the freed people themselves responded to, participated in, and sometimes transformed the purpose of education in their attempts to build a new community of freedom; this is the central theme of Robert Francis Engs' fine study, *Freedom's First Generation: Black Hampton, Virginia, 1861–1890* (1979). The letters of two Northern teachers who worked in the vicinity of Hampton are Henry Lee Swint, ed., *Dear Ones at Home: Letters from Contraband Camps* (1966). For the missionary and educational activities of the most vigorous black religious denomination, see Clarence E. Walker, *A Rock in a Weary Land: A History of the African Methodist Episcopal Church during the Civil War and Reconstruction* (1981). For the Union army's role in education, see John W. Blassingame, "The Union Army as an Educational Institution for Negroes, 1862–1865," *Journal of Negro Education*, 34 (Spring, 1965), 152–59.

Because of its focus on the perceptions and actions of blacks as recorded in their own words, *The Negro's Civil War* discussed only briefly the evolution of the Union government's wartime policies toward freedmen's affairs. This question, however, became a major focus of several monographs published during the 1970s and 1980s which measured the Northern government of the 1860s by the standards of civil rights activism a century later. Not surprisingly, these studies concluded that the freedmen's policies of the government and the occupation army were halting, halfway, marred by racist assumptions, lacking in commitment to genuine racial change, and that these policies laid the groundwork for the postwar status of the freedmen as a landless, dependent people. The principal study reflecting this viewpoint is Louis Gerteis, *From Contraband to Freedman: Federal Policy toward Southern Blacks, 1861–1865* (1973). Because the Union army occupied much of the lower Mississippi valley during most of the war, the largest number of freedmen came under Union control in this region and most of the recent historical literature has focused on it: see especially C. Peter Ripley, *Slaves and Freedmen in Civil War Louisiana* (1976); William F. Messner, *Freedmen and the Ideology of Free Labor: Louisiana 1862–1865 (1978); Thomas F. May*, "Continuity and Change in the Labor Program of the Union Army and the Freedmen's Bureau," *Civil War History*, 17 (1971), 245–54; James T. Currie, *Enclave: Vicksburg and Her Plantations, 1863–1870* (1979); Ronald L. F. Davis, *Good and Faithful Labor: From Slavery to Sharecropping in the Natchez District, 1860–1890* (1982); and Michael Wayne, *The Reshaping of Plantation Society: The Natchez District,*

1860–1880 (1983). A fascinating case study of blacks on the Davis Bend
plantations of Jefferson Davis and his brother Joseph is Janet Sharp Her-
mann, *The Pursuit of a Dream* (1981). A book that devotes most of its
attention to the postwar years but includes an account of Northern wartime policies with respect to land and labor that set the pattern for postwar
developments is Lawrence N. Powell, *New Masters: Northern Planters during the Civil War and Reconstruction* (1980). The critical perspective of
nearly all these studies tends to justify those black leaders and white abolitionists, quoted in *The Negro's Civil War*, who denounced the government's conservative policy toward land and labor in the occupied South.
At the same time, however, the thesis of some of these books, as expressed
by Louis Gerteis, that the government's policies precluded any "fundamental changes" in the "antebellum forms of economic and social organization in the South," goes much too far. Contemporary black observers of
and participants in these events certainly believed that the war accomplished "fundamental changes" in their status, even if some of them
advocated more radical change.

Several of the books cited in the previous paragraph include brief discussion of another issue that is treated in *The Negro's Civil War*, the issue
of wartime political reconstruction and Negro suffrage. This issue is a
prominent topic in Peyton McCrary's excellent book, *Abraham Lincoln and
Reconstruction: The Louisiana Experiment* (1978), which includes a detailed analysis of the political role of New Orleans' free black community.
Like the leaders of that community, whose writings are liberally quoted in
The Negro's Civil War, McCrary is critical of Lincoln's moderate course on
Reconstruction. For a somewhat different perspective on New Orleans'
"free coloreds," which sees them as more interested in protecting their
privileged position than in promoting radical change and equal rights for
the freed slaves, see David C. Rankin, "The Impact of the Civil War on the
Free Colored Community of New Orleans," *Perspectives in American History*, 11 (1977–78), 349–418. A fascinating autobiography that sheds light
on the black community in New Orleans and the New Orleans *Tribune is
Jean-Charles Houzeau, My Passage at the New Orleans "Tribune": A Mem-
oir of the Civil War Era*, ed. with an Introduction by David C. Rankin,
tranlsated by Gerard F. Denault (1984). A fine monograph is John W. Blassingame, *Black New Orleans, 1860–1880* (1973). For the rest of Union-
occupied Louisiana as well as New Orleans, the first section of Ted Tunnell,
War, Radicalism and Race in Louisiana 1862–1877 (1984) is invaluable.
The story of Nashville and of middle Tennessee under federal occupation
is told in Peter Maslowski, *Treason Must Be Made Odious: Military Occupation and Wartime Reconstruction in Nashville, Tennessee, 1862–1865*
(1978) and Steven V. Ash, *Middle Tennessee Transformed, 1860–1870: War
and Peace in the Upper South* (1989).

Reconstruction in Tennessee and especially in Louisiana became the focal points for wartime controversies within the Republican party, controversies that revolved around the role that freed slaves would play in the new governments to emerge from the war. Two books by Herman Belz analyze these controversies and the movement toward an equal rights consensus within the Republican party: *A New Birth of Freedom: The Republican Party and Freedmen's Rights, 1861–1866* (1976) and *Emancipation and Equal Rights: Politics and Constitutionalism in the Civil War Era* (1978).

Abraham Lincoln, of course, was the central figure in these developments. Just as Lincoln towered over all other contemporaries in the consciousness of blacks during the Civil War, so have his views and policies toward blacks been the subject of continuing scholarly scrutiny since the initial publication of *The Negro's Civil War*. A number of black writers have noted and criticized Lincoln's expressions of white supremacy, his support for colonization as a solution of the race problem, and his caution on the issues of emancipation and equal rights: see especially Lerone Bennett, Jr., "Was Abe Lincoln A White Supremacist?" *Ebony*, 23 (1968), 35–38, 40, 42; George Sinkler, *The Racial Attitudes of American Presidents from Abraham Lincoln to Theodore Roosevelt* (1971); and Nathan Irvin Huggins, *Slave and Citizen: The Life of Frederick Douglass* (1980). Plenty of evidence to sustain such criticisms can be found in Lincoln's writings on race, which have been conveniently brought together in Arthur Zilversmit, ed., *Lincoln on Black and White* (1971). More balanced evaluations of Lincoln's racial views can be found in Robert F. Durden, "A. Lincoln: Honkie or Equalitarian?" *South Atlantic Quarterly*, 71 (1971), 280–91; Don E. Fehrenbacher, "Only His Stepchildren: Lincoln and the Negro," *Civil War History*, 20 (1974), 293–310; and George M. Fredrickson, "A Man but Not a Brother: Abraham Lincoln and Racial Equality," *Journal of Southern History*, 41 (1975), 39–58, which emphasize that Lincoln's racial attitudes were flexible and capable of change, that they were more humane than those of most white Americans of his time, and that the President moved toward more liberal views and policies in response to the exigencies of war and emancipation and especially in response to the contribution of black soldiers to Union victory. The step-by-step progress of Lincoln's views toward emancipation is chronicled by Hans Trefousse, ed., *Lincoln's Decision for Emancipation* (1975). The fullest, subtlest, and most persuasive argument for the essential liberalism of Lincoln's racial attitudes in the context of his time, and for the firmness and wisdom of his leadership on the issues of emancipation and civil rights, is LaWanda Cox, *Lincoln and Black Freedom: A Study in Presidential Leadership* (1981). Several of the essays in James M. McPherson, *Abraham Lincoln and the Second American Revolution* (1991) elucidate Lincoln's attitudes and policies concerning slavery, emancipation, and the concept of liberty.

The racism of large segments of the Northern population, who found a home principally in the Democratic party, is thoroughly described by V. Jacque Voegeli, *Free but Not Equal: The Midwest and the Negro during the Civil War* (1967), and Forrest G. Wood, *Black Scare: The Racist Response to Emancipation and Reconstruction* (1968). Wartime anti-black violence culminating in the New York draft riots is described in James M. McPherson, ed., *Anti-Negro Riots in the North, 1863* (1969), and Adrian Cook, *The Armies of the Streets: The New York City Draft Riots of 1863* (1974). This climate of hostility toward emancipation and black people was one important factor in the gradualism of Lincoln's and the Republican party's approach to the issues of emancipation and civil rights during the war. A fascinating and provocative study of the nation's principal black crusader for freedom and against racism is David L. Blight, *Frederick Douglass' Civil War* (1989).

More than a quarter of *The Negro's Civil War* concerns the record of black soldiers and sailors in the Union army and navy. Since its publication, a considerable amount of new work has appeared on this question. Mary Frances Berry's brief monograph, *Military Necessity and Civil Rights Policy: Black Citizenship and the Constitution, 1861–1868* (1977), argues that the need for black military assistance in the Civil War was the principal factor leading to emancipation and to the beginning of an equal rights policy, a beginning cut short when black military manpower was no longer needed. David L. Valuska, "The Negro in the Union Navy, 1861–1865," Ph.D. dissertation, Lehigh University, 1973, is the best study of this subject, and reduces the estimated number of blacks who served in the navy from the 29,000 mentioned on p. 160 of *The Negro's Civil War* (an estimate derived from Herbert Aptheker's earlier work) to fewer than 10,000. Walter L. Williams, "Again in Chains: Black Soldiers Suffering in Captivity," *Civil War Times Illustrated*, 20 (May, 1981), 36–43, is an excellent account of the fate of black prisoners of war. A superb compilation of documents with penetrating headnotes and contextual essays is Ira Berlin, Joseph P. Reidy, and Leslie Rowland, eds., *The Black Military Experience*, Series II of *Freedom: A Documentary History of Emancipation* (1982). An excellent study of black soldiers and their white officers is Joseph T. Glatthaar, *Forged in Battle: The Civil War Alliance of Black Soldiers and White Officers* (1990).

JAMES M. MCPHERSON
PRINCETON, NEW JERSEY
DECEMBER 1990

INDEX

Adams, Charles Francis, 152
Africa, American Negroes
    vindicate civilization of, 109–
    12
African Civilization Society, 137;
    establishes Negro schools in
    Washington, 141
Alston, William J., 262–3
American Anti-Slavery Society,
    12, 91, 99, 275, 313
Andrew, Gov. John A., 22;
    recruits Negro regiments, 175–
    6,192; and issue of equal pay
    for black troops, 201
Anglo-African, Negro newspaper,
    11, 81, 110, 145, 197, 347;
    criticizes political parties in
    1860, 4; on outbreak of war,
    17–18; advises Negroes to
    form military companies, 30–
    1; urges emancipation as war
    measure, 37; denounces
    Lincoln's revocation of
    Fremont's emancipation edict,
    41–2; praises Lincoln's
    proposal of gradual
    emancipation, 43–4; on
    emancipation in District of
    Columbia, 45; on race

prejudice in North, 69; on
    anti-Negro mob in Brooklyn,
    70; denounces Lincoln's
    colonization proposal, 92; on
    environmental causes of Negro
    inferiority, 104; urges Negroes
    to join army, 177–8; on
    motives of Negro soldiers,
    181–2; urges confiscation and
    redistribution of Southern
    land, 297–8; advocates Lincoln
    re-election, 310–11
Augusta, Maj. A. T., 265–6

Banks, Gen. N. P., 242;
    establishes freedmen's labor
    system in La., 130; system
    denounced by Negroes, 130–2;
    ednucational program praised
    by Negroes, 132–3; recruits
    Negro regiments in La., 171–2;
    and Negro soldiers at battle of
    Port Hudson, 187, 189; and
    reconstruction in La., 281–2,
    283, 306
Barton, Clara, 142
Bates, Edward, 253–4
Beecher, Frances, 215
Beecher, Col. James, 215

INDEX

364

New Orleans (continued)
Orléans), Negro newspaper,
280, 348; denounced Banks's
freedmen's labor system, 131–
2; praises Banks's education
provision, 132–3; urges
desegregation of all walks of
life, 273–4; opposes political
distinction between quadroons
and full-blooded Negroes,
287–8; opposes special literacy
qualification for Negro
suffrage, 288–9; on formation
of La. Equal Rights League,
293; urges agrarian reform in
South, 299; opposes Lincoln
re-election, 306–7; laments
Lincoln assassination, 312
"New York City and County
Suffrage Committee of
Colored Citizens," 276
New York Times, 165–6, 189
New York *Tribune*, 80; on
purpose of war, 22; on exploit
of William Tillman, 156; on
success of Negro soldiers, 170–
1; on Northern attitude
toward Negro troops, 187; on
courage of black troops at
Fort Wagner, 195
New York *World*, 203
Nordhoff, Charles, 123
Ohio Equal Rights League, works
for racial justice, 292–3

Pacific Appeal, Negro
newspaper, 313, 348; criticizes
Lincoln's revocation of
Hunter's emancipation edict,
46; on environmental causes
of Negro inferiority, 104–5;
maintains equality of Negro
race, 112; urges repeal of
"black laws" in California,

254–5; advocates Lincoln's re-
election, 305–6
Parham, William H., on formation
of Negro military companies,
34–5; changes mind about
emigrating to Haiti, 90; on
reluctance of Negroes to join
army, 175–6
Parker, John, escapes to the
North, 25–8
Peake, Mary, 141
Pennington, J. W. C., writes
petition for abolition of
slavery, 40–1; on New York
draft riot, 75–7
Pennsylvania Equal Rights
League, appeals for racial
justice, 291–2
Philadelphia, racial segregation in,
259; campaign to abolish
streetcar segregation in, 259–65
Philadelphia *Press*, 59–60, 67,
260, 262
Philbrick, Edward S., 58, 122–3
Phillips, Wendell, 140
Pine and Palm, emigrationist
newspaper, 35, 81, 89, 347;
suspended, 91
Pinkerton, Allan, 149–51
Pomeroy, Samuel C., 97–8
Port Hudson, battle of, and
bravery of black troops, 181–
2, 187–9
Powell, Aaron M., 91
Powell, William P., 40, 73–4
Purvis, Robert, welcomes
disunion, 12; denounces
colonization proposals, 97–8;
on significance of innate
inferiority argument, 101–2;
denounces denial of officers'
commissions to Negro soldiers,
176–7; optimisitc about
Negro's future, 313–15

racial discrimination, *see*
segregation
Radical Abolition party, 8–9
Raymond, J. Anderson, 112
Redpath, James, and Haitian
emigration movement, 80–91,
347
Remond, Charles L., 175
Republican party, Negroes
chastise for antislavery shortcomings in 1860, 3–9; some
Negroes support in 1860, 9–
10. *See also* Lincoln, Abraham
Rhode Island, school
desegregation in, 271–3
Rivers, Prince, 298
Rock, John, criticizes Republican
party in 1860, 4–5; on
Lincoln's slowness to act
against slavery, 47–8; opposes
emigration to Haiti, 83;
opposes Lincoln's colonization
proposals, 92–3; denies innate
inferiority of Negro, 102–3; on
racial discrimination in
Boston, 252–3; accredited as
Supreme Court lawyer, 269;
urges agrarian reform in
South, 298
Roudanez, Jean Baptiste, 282–84
Rue, Rev. Mr., 52
Ruffin, James, 207, 311
Russell, William H., 16, 55–6

Saxton, Gen. Rufus, 167, 304
Scobell, John, Negro spy for
Union Army, 149–51
secession, many Northern
Negroes welcome, 11–13
segregation, and racial
discrimination, widespread in
North before Civil War, 249–
53; progress made in abolition
of during war, 253–74

Seward, William H., 48, 98, 152
Seymour, Horatio, 212
Shaw, Col. Robert G., 192–3
Shepley, Gen. G. F., 281, 283
Sherman, Gen. William T., 67,
303–4
Simms, Abram C., 204
Smalls, Robert, captor of the
Planter, 156–60
Smith, A. P., 94–5
Smith, Gerrit, 8–9, 48, 325
Smith, J. B., 81
Smith, James McCune, opposes
emigration to Haiti, 85–6;
urges Negro suffrage in New
York, 276–7
Smith, Gen. William F., 227–8
Smothers, Samuel H., 10, 348
Springfield *Republican*, 22
Stanton, Edwin M., and
enlistment of Negro soldiers,
169, 172; initial opposition to
Negro army officers, 176; and
issue of equal pay for Negro
soldiers, 200–1, 203; praises
fighting of Negro troops in
Va., 227–8; and issue of land
for freedmen, 303
Stearns, George L., 175, 232
Steedman, Gen. J. B., 236, 237
Stevens, Thaddeus, 203, 304
Still, William, leads fight against
Philadelphia street-car
segregation, 259–61
Strong, Gen. George C., 193
Students' Repository, Negro
newspaper, 348; urges repeal
of Indiana "black laws," 258
Sumner, Charles, 44; spearheads
drive to abolish discrimination
in Washington, 254, 265–6;
presents John Rock as
Supreme Court lawyer, 269;
presents petition for Negro